AMERICAN FICTIONS

Elizabeth Hardwick

American Fictions

THE MODERN LIBRARY

NEW YORK

To Joy de Menil, with my gratitude

Preface

Writers often complain about critics and criticism and yet they also complain when no criticism of their work appears in the press. Of course, the very act of offering a book, a musical composition, a group of paintings will always arouse thought about it, bring to mind comparisons, placings, the dare of exegisis. This is a natural activity, natural to the artist as well as to the interpreters. All imaginative creation is partly a revelation of the artist's critical intelligence: the question of an appropriate style, the disposition of the materials at hand, the framing and, in literature, the plot. About plot, the brilliant, dauntingly original English novelist Ivy Compton-Burnett wrote or said: "As regards plots I find real life no help at all. Real life seems to have no plots. And as I think plot desirable and almost necessary, I have this extra grudge against life." That's one artist's answer to the critic's sigh that a certain fiction is not "true to life."

At work, the fiction writer performs a personal critical judging of the pages before him in the effort to realize a vision, and thus the word *revision*. What to further explain, what to expand or to delete, what might be expressed differently: all of this a bow to the complexities of literature. In my life I have come across some strange, good-natured, energetic persons who have written novel after novel, each of considerable length. Somehow they do not have the habit or the wish or the inclination for revision and off the work goes and another starts, quite cheerfully, even if none has managed publication.

On this matter, consider the wonderful, productive Anthony Trollope. In his *Autobiography,* he declared that it was his invariable habit "to write with my watch before me, and to require from myself two hundred and fifty words every quarter of an hour." If one novel was completed before the daily stint had expired, he began another. In an old notebook I have copied, without attribution, someone's comment that Trollope's telling of his literary economy "extinguished the author's good name for a quarter of a century."

The essays printed here concern novelists and short story writers. In addition, I have included essays on other American writers who are not primarily in their creative lives drawn to the fictional form but to poetry, drama, and non-fiction prose. Hart Crane, Edna Millay, Sylvia Plath, Margaret Fuller, John Reed and Eugene O'Neill are figures in American literature of striking personal flair. Their biographies are stories of a kind, made vivid by suicide, early death or interesting self-dramatization. A certain flamboyance of reputation or fate gives them the aspect of something imagined, and so perhaps in an angular way we can think of them as fictions, creatures of national myth.

The present volume contains most of my last collection, *Sight-Readings,* and selected articles from previous books: *Seduction and Betrayal, Bartleby in Manhattan* and *A View of My Own.* The publication of a current novel or a biography about a living or dead author usually prompted my decision to comment. Some are introductions to a single book, and the essay "Seduction and Betrayal" grew out of the theme of the title. *An American Tragedy* and *The Scarlet Letter* are two American contemplations of this ancient, eternal human plot; in my essay they combine with the obvious examples from standard English and European literature and even with the opera *Don Giovanni.*

Elizabeth Hardwick

Contents

FICTIONS OF AMERICA

LIVES

LOCATIONS:

AN INTRODUCTION

The landscapes of fiction: houses and the things therein, nation-states and States of the Union, oceans, backland; winter nights and the old horse pulling the sledge through a driving snow, summer heat and the arrival of smothering love affairs. For the human drama, the surrounding landscape is not only field and sky but inhabits character and hangs its shadows over destiny. *Wuthering Heights is the name of Mr. Heathcliff's dwelling:* one of the most striking placements in fiction. The foretelling resonance of Wuthering and Heathcliff, the solemn musicality of the word *dwelling* could hardly be surpassed as mere sound. Neither name of place nor family name is consoling: a hard, dull wind, a wasteland, a slope of rock. The dramatically opposed names, Thrushcross Grange and Mr. Linton, are useful designations of a more pleasing pastoral world and might belong to anyone in the countryside.

In most fictions, the interiors of a household are the defining landscape of pride, lack, hope, negligence, pretension—to leave aside the powerful moral and personal shape of rural life with horses, cows and the drama of the seasons setting the scene.

"A rusty wooden house, with seven acutely peaked gables, facing towards various points of the compass, and a huge, clustered chimney in the midst." Hawthorne built his house and furnished it with all the things of the past and of the present, the time of the fiction. It is a crowded jumble of artifacts and ancestral treasures under a layer of dust: *The House of the Seven Gables.* The house begins and ends the novel and dominates the scene with historical curses of such malignant power that the original builder, Colonel Pyncheon, lies dead in an upstairs bed even as the town arrives for the housewarming celebration. It's a feudal castle placed on Main Street, where such important statements of display like to be. Inside, old mirrors, maps, a dark antique canopy bed with "ponderous festoons of a stuff which had been rich, and even magnificent, in its time"; a harpsichord which "looked more like a coffin than anything else." Infinite solicitude by the author for every nook and cranny and, as fortunes decline over the years, a notions shop, socially regressive, faces the street at the front. A feeble commerce it is to be, but everything on the shelves is noted: buttons, a pickle jar "filled with fragments of Gibraltar Rock"; a gingerbread concoction that is a little black boy going by the name of Jim Crow, a handful of marbles; on and on it goes. A curious accounting of domestic detail, rather wifely, to furnish the fictional world of old Salem. *The House* is a popular story, not quite one of Hawthorne's finest inspirations, but there he is in the midst of it. In the economy of an artist's life, furniture, spools of thread, barrels of flour, gingersnaps may not serve as moral or social clues but as—just stuff, the bits and pieces of imagined life.

Poverty and riches, good taste and the tinsel ornamentation of bad taste are contraries that battle on the page, stamping their marks in an indelible coloration. In the sentimental fiction of bygone days there is often a union of poverty with moral purity. You enter a modest cottage and if on a plain pine table there has been placed a snow-white cloth, the whiteness is not accidental. Someone is making a statement of values or of respectable habit in dismaying circumstances. The snow-white cloth tells of washtubs, the scrub board, a sunny clothesline and labor with a flat iron: the spare household of the neat and worthy poor. The simple evening meal, potatoes on the coals, a loaf of bread or something bought with the last pennies anxiously laid out on the grocer's counter. In the lamplight or the firelight when darkness falls a good wife or the faithful young daughter or granddaughter is mending or knitting.

I confess to an affection for these pictorial effects of which Dickens is a master, the poet of the starving child—"more porridge!"—and since there is to be a plot, he is also the great portraitist of the hideous villains, overfed always, maniacally stingy horrors who prey with a preternatural cunning on the bereft and needy. The vicious dwarf Mr. Quilp and little Nell, the hardworking Cratchits and Mr. Scrooge before his holiday reformation, and dozens more.

In our own literature, *Uncle Tom's Cabin* is a fiction of the good and the evil. Tom's cabin in Kentucky is only one of the plantation landscapes he will be transported to, in chains, after the practical negotiations of landowners, some of whom must sell slaves to pay debts incurred in high-living or respectable household accommodations. The cabin graces the title perhaps because it is in the past and is thus a memory, the homestead of youth that plays its role in fictions of all sorts. The cabin, showing the moral worth of the slave inhabitants, Uncle Tom and his wife, Aunt Chloe:

> In front it had a neat garden-patch, where, every summer, strawberries, raspberries, and a variety of fruits and vegetables, flourished under careful tending. The whole front of it was covered by a large scarlet bignonia and a native multiflora rose.... Here, also, in summer, various brilliant annuals, such as marigolds, petunias, four-o'clocks, found an indulgent corner.

In the kitchen, Aunt Chloe, Tom's wife, is preparing her incomparable batter-cakes and her "whole plump countenance beams with satisfaction and contentment from under her well-starched checked turban." Busy, clean and well starched: emblems of virtue. Uncle Tom is deeply pious, strong in the faith with Mrs. Stowe. Her last words to him and to the world are: "Think of your freedom, every time you see *Uncle Tom's Cabin;* and let it be a memorial to put you all in mind to follow in his steps, and be as honest and faithful and Christian as he was." (We may note that Mrs. Stowe in her union of domestic virtue and moral life will make the evil Simon Legree's plantation a dismal contrast to the glowing garden of Uncle Tom. Legree's place is mildewed jessamine, raggedy honeysuckle and weeds.)

The good poor do not have a noticeable position in contemporary fiction; perhaps the poor of Victorian times are as hard to come upon as the good seen without the qualifying eye that finds motive in the saint as easily as in the crook. Many contemporary characters seem identified by "relative deprivation" rather than outright poverty. They are eating too many fried foods in packages; they have old cars sitting on the lawn with the flat tire sinking into the grass; the television set is on day and night even if still in the woeful black-and-white. Their children are somehow dressed in the same manner as the car dealer's sons, and if there may have been some sleight of hand necessary to acquire the sneakers, that is not exactly criminal.

The bad rich remain in good literary standing, especially the *nouveau riche,* who are in command of funds that put old money, trust fund fortunes, into a sort of withering shade. Edith Wharton in *The Custom of the Country* and William Dean Howells in *The Hazard of New Fortunes* shaped bitter comedies about the pretension, the riveting, loud, almost revolutionary arrival in New York of money made in natural gas and hairwaving lotions and spending itself in grotesque acquisitions of showy household appointments. All those dollars of such curious provenance appear to be a historical threat to the nation, something like the contamination of the ozone by motor cars. The wonderful squandering hicks in Ring Lardner's stories of the "big town" have, on the other hand, a genuine, foolish pathos. Mrs. Gullible longing to meet the famous social queen Mrs. Potter Palmer, and when the collision is accomplished in the halls of a hotel, Mrs. Palmer asks her to bring the towels.

New York City, urbanism, is often spoken of as "electric." The Russian poet Mayakovsky: "After I learned about electricity, I lost interest in nature. Not up-to-date enough." Manhattan is not altogether felicitous for fiction. It is not a city of memory, not a family city, not the capital of America so much as the iconic capital of this century. It is grand and grandiose with its two rivers acting as a border to contain the restless. Its skyscrapers and bleak, rotting tenements are a gift for photographic consumption, but for the fictional imagination the city's inchoate density is a special challenge. Those who engage this "culture of congestion" today need a sort of athletic suppleness, such as we find in Tom Wolfe's *The Bonfire of the Vanities* and E. L. Doctorow's *Ragtime.*

Among the best of the older New York novels are two melancholy landscapes of defeat. Edith Wharton in *The House of Mirth* was free of superiority to the invading hordes from dumbbell towns in the hinterland and thus wrote a stinging portrait of "society" at the turn of the century. The mood is not elegiac or protective and is instead a picture of the remorseless struggle of a handsome, well-connected young woman to keep up in the rich world she was born to. It is a fiction about money, a genuine creation dramatically staged in Manhattan.

F. Scott Fitzgerald's *The Great Gatsby* is a supreme work of the imagination. It has a tonal purity of style, an unwavering accent of lamentation for those caught in a plot of tragic finality. In Jay Gatsby, Fitzgerald has created an American as unforgettable as Captain Ahab. A good deal of the action takes place on Long Island, but it is a New York City novel, Long Island being a weekend road out of and back to Manhattan. At Gatsby's house, "a factual imitation of some Hôtel de Ville in Normandy," every Friday "five crates of oranges and lemons arrived from a fruiterer in New York."

Jay Gatsby is an impostor, a man deeply interesting as a complex model of the imitative as a force in the creation of character, or if not character at least personality as a series of gestures. Gatsby has devised a name for himself, imagined an eloquent background of situations and accomplishments. The money he has made is also unreal and subject to disappearance, like a ghost vanishing at dawn. And yet he has his "greatness" as a dreamer who created his imaginary self in pursuit of an overwhelming love. So real is this unreal man, Gatsby, that you feel he might still be somewhere in New York today, perhaps on Park Avenue, a signifying address, or like Dreiser's Hurstwood fallen into hell, dying on the Bowery, yet another indicative address in the city.

Hurstwood in *Sister Carrie* is a provincial form of Gatsby, a doomed man of a lower order of desire who manages a New York saloon. His need for Carrie, an old love risen as a sort of star on the stage, leads him to the theft of the night's receipts he was to have deposited in a vault. Both of these men in pursuit of the loved one, the green light as Fitzgerald calls it, know only one kind of ambition. It is money, money in a hurry, not the weekly paycheck of a patient, plodding clerk, clocking in of a morning and out at dusk. They come to utter ruin, to death for Gatsby, but of the two only one, Gatsby, could truly be called great, in the author's conception. Hurstwood, in the majestic *Sister Carrie*, was imagined in the complex spirit of American realism.

Interiors: purchases that represent a hope for expression of private style even if dominated by the most autocratic arbiter of taste, the amount of money at hand, oddly known as disposable income. The spare and elegant, each selection *just so* and fitting together; modern wares if sought with scholarly precision can make claim to being the most expensive, outpacing the search for the cherry hutch or the Victorian claw-foot chair. Instead for knowing characters, citified couples, it will be bits and pieces such as a leather chair, an Eames copy in molded plywood, an architect's name on a coffeepot or a cocktail shaker. Mary McCarthy in her memoir celebrates a 1940s cocktail shaker by Russel Wright.

In most fictions, a change of interior is a move upward to a better house, a better address. In Philip Roth's *American Pastoral,* acute attention is given to the alterations of prosperity. The old family, father a dealer in hides, makes its way up to "finished basements, their screened-in porches, their flagstone front steps." Their children are in a more drastic, dreaming mode: "a barn, a millpond, a millstream . . . a fireplace large enough for roasting an ox, fitted with an oven door and a crane to swing an iron kettle on." Up and back to a colonial farmer's domestic landscape, all peacefully lying in history, with two cars in the garage.

In Richard Ford's *Independence Day,* the narrator is a real estate broker, an occupation that will be a gladiatorial combat with buyers in a blinding, paralyzing calculation of cost, street, neighborhood. Images of themselves encased in the mausoleum of their choice, fittings of small and large preference, turn out to be disorienting rather than defining. One troublesome couple wants to forsake its once-loved place in Vermont with "its cantilevered cathedral ceilings and a hand-laid hearth and chimney using stones off the place" for something else in New Jersey. But what?

Aesthetic models torment the greatly, famously rich in a violently expansive way. Bellevue Avenue in Newport, Rhode Island, which Henry James remembered as a pleasant summer escape to long walks, sea breezes and the town library, had when he visited it in 1904 become the nation's most notable exercise in monumentality. He found castles of Rhenish and French inspiration. White elephants, he calls them, "peculiarly awkward vengeances of affronted proportion and discretion."

The sad, history-heavy countryside, the pain of the Confederacy, the khaki-colored earth, the dusty, immemorial, drowsy streets, the cunning, secretive faces of the Snopes family, the fatal running of Joe Christmas and Miss Rosa Coldfield and Quentin Compson in the "empty hall echoing with sonorous, defeated names." William Faulkner, the grandest fictional talent our country has produced, land-obsessed and with an imagination of staggering fertility and scope, found in Mississippi an epic vision. Shrewd swamp-bred families, disinherited gentlefolk, immense plots that go back and forth in time and yet seem immovably still there, alive.

The landscapes of fiction, the houses and things, are a shell for the creation of human dramas, the place for the seven deadly sins to do battle with probity and reality or outrageous demand and vanity. The shells, the habitations of America are volatile, inventive, unexpected, imponderable, but there they are, everywhere. In recent American fictions, short stories and novels, you will find people cooking dinner inside or shaking the mop outside a trailer. This humble abode that does not weather but shows its age in a bit of rust or chipped paint is becoming more and more the primary "affordable housing" for citizens who cannot qualify for the expense of conventional home ownership and may not even prefer it.

People, large numbers of them, settle in their "park" on the outskirts of town, hook up the gas, electric and sewer lines, root utilities. Inside all is likely to be a place of old-time memory: rag rugs, a patchwork quilt, a ship's clock, hand-knit nylon pan-grippers providing a sort of Americana coziness. Trailer park, on the page or in speech, will mean hard up, and sometimes on the evening news it projects a sort of unsteadiness as when a relative, friend or ex-husband invades the hospitality to hide out until the police car, top light whirling and flashing, catches up.

In this world too there are wide separations of type and possibility to be found, degrees of identity. The very large, expensive homes rest down in Florida for the winter but take to the road for a summer change in Maine. These deluxe motor palaces may travel in groups for socializing. Up goes the plastic awning over the door; if the weather is agreeable, out comes a folding table and place mats, and on the lawn, as it were, the flat parking spaces for the spacious machines, there will be arrangements for tea or cocktails. In a photograph of an interesting early motor home, all was plain, handsomely utilitarian. Custom-made for Anne and Charles Lindbergh: puritans.

There's a leveling homogeneity in America today created by television. Each day it passes over the vast land mass, over the states nudging each other like the sovereignties of the Balkans, creating a unifying cloud of aesthetic properties and experience. East and West,

North and South are wrapped in a sort of over-soul of images, facts, happenings, celebrities. This debris is as sacred to our current fiction as gossip about the new vicar was to Trollope. And there it is on the page, informing the domestically restless households, father off somewhere, mother chagrined. Sons and daughters writing the books.

OLD NEW YORK

BARTLEBY IN MANHATTAN

While preparing some lectures on the subject of New York City, that is, the present landscape in which an astonishing number of people still live, sustaining as they do the numerical sensationalism that qualifies New York as *one* of the great cities of the world, if not the *greatest*, the orotund *greatest* being reserved with an almost Biblical authority for our country as a whole; and also on "old New York," with its intimidating claim to vanished manners and social dominion, its hereditary furnishings of aggressive simplicity and shy opulence which would prove an unsteady bulwark against the flooding of the *nouveau riche*—during this reading I thought to look again at Melville's story "Bartleby, the Scrivener," because it carried the subtitle "A Story of Wall Street."

There did not appear to be much of Wall Street in this troubling composition of 1853 about a peculiar "copyist" who is hired by a "snug" little legal firm in the Wall Street district. No, nothing of the daunting, hungry "Manhattanism" of Whitman: "O an intense life, full to repletion and varied! / The life of the theatre, bar-room, huge hotel, for me!" Nothing of railroad schemes, cornering the gold market, or of that tense exclusion to be brought about by mistakes and follies in the private life which were to be the drama of "old New York" in Edith Wharton's novels. Bartleby seemed to me to be not its subtitle, but most of all an example of the superior uses of dialogue in fiction, here a strange, bone-thin dialogue that nevertheless serves to reveal a pro-foundly moving tragedy.

(Melville's brothers were lawyers, with offices at 10 Wall Street; a close friend was employed in a law office and seems to have been worn down by "incessant writing." About the story itself, some critics have thought of "Bartleby" as a masterly presentation of schizophrenic deterioration; others have seen the story as coming out of the rejection of Melville by the reading public and his own inability to be a popular "copyist." Some have found in the story the life of Wall Street, "walling in" the creative American spirit. All of these ideas are convincing and important. "Bartleby" may be one or all of these. My own reading is largely concerned with the nature of Bartleby's short sentences.)

Out of some sixteen thousand words, Bartleby, the cadaverous and yet blazing center of all our attention, speaks only thirty-seven short lines, more than a third of which are a repetition of a single line, the celebrated, the "famous," I think one might call it, retort: *I would prefer not to.* No, "retort" will not do, representing as it does too great a degree of active mutuality for Bartleby—*reply* perhaps.

Bartleby's reduction of language is of an expressiveness literally limitless. Few characters in fiction, if indeed any exist, have been able to say all they wish in so striking, so nearly speechless a manner. The work is, of course, a sort of fable of inanition, and returning to it, as I did, mindful of the old stone historical downtown and the new, insatiable necropolis of steel and glass, lying on the vegetation of the participial *declining* this and that, I found it possible to wish that "Bartleby, the Scrivener" was just itself, a masterpiece without the challenge of its setting, Wall Street. Still, the setting does not flee the mind, even if it does not quite bind itself either, the way unloaded furniture seems immediately bound to its doors and floors.

Melville has written his story in a cheerful, confident, rather optimistic, Dickensian manner. Or at least that is the manner in which it begins. In the law office, for instance, the copyists and errand-boy are introduced with their Dickensian *tics* and their tic-names: Nippers, Turkey, and Ginger Nut. An atmosphere of comedy, of small, amusing, busy particulars, surrounds Bartleby and his large, unofficial (not suited to an office) articulations, which are nevertheless clerkly and even, perhaps, clerical.

The narrator, a mild man of the law with a mild Wall Street business, is a "rather elderly man," as he says of himself at the time of putting down his remembrances of Bartleby. On the edge of retirement, the lawyer begins to think about that "singular set of men," the law-copyists or scriveners he has known in his thirty years of practice. He notes that he has seen nothing of these men in print and, were it not for the dominating memory of Bartleby, he might have told lighthearted professional anecdotes, something perhaps like the anecdotes of servants come and gone, such as we find in the letters of Jane Carlyle, girls from the country who are not always unlike the Turkeys, Nippers, and Ginger Nuts.

The lawyer understands that no biography of Bartleby is possible because "no materials exist," and indeed the work is not a character sketch and not a section of a "life," even though it ends in death. Yet the device of memory is not quite the way it works out, because each of Bartleby's thirty-seven lines, with their riveting variations, so slight as to be almost painful to the mind taking note of them, must be produced at the right pace and accompanied by the requests that occasion them. At a certain point, Bartleby must "gently disappear behind the screen," which, in a way, is a present rather than a past. In the end, Melville's structure is magical because the lawyer creates Bartleby by *allowing* him to be, a decision of nicely unprofessional impracticality. The competent, but scarcely strenuous, office allows Bartleby, although truly the allowance arises out of the fact that the lawyer is a far better man than he knows himself to be. And he is taken by surprise to learn of his tireless curiosity about the incurious ghost, Bartleby.

The lawyer has a "snug business among rich men's bonds and mortgages and title deeds," rather than the more dramatic actions before juries (a choice that would not be defining today). He has his public sinecures and when they are officially abolished he feels a bit of chagrin, but no vehemence. He recognizes the little vanities he has accumulated along the way, one of which is that he has done business with John Jacob Astor. And he likes to utter the name "for it hath a rounded and orbicular sound to it and rings like unto bullion." These are the thoughts of a man touched by the comic spirit, the one who will be touched for the first time in his life, and by way of his dealings with Bartleby, by "overpowering, stinging melancholy . . . a fraternal melancholy."

A flurry of copying demand had led the lawyer to run an advertise-

ment which brought to his door a young man, Bartleby, a person se-
date, "pallidly neat, pitiably respectable." Bartleby is taken on and
placed at a desk which "originally had afforded a lateral view of certain grimy backyards and bricks, but which owing to subsequent erec-
tions, commanded at present no view at all." This is a suitable place for
Bartleby, who does not require views of the outside world and who has
no "views" of the other kind, that is, no opinions beyond his adamantine assertion of his own feelings, if feelings they are; he has, as soon
becomes clear, his hard pebbles of response with their sumptuous, tac-
iturn resonance.

Bartleby begins to copy without pause, as if "long famishing for
something to copy." This is observed by the lawyer, who also observes
that he himself feels no pleasure in it since it is done "silently, palely,
mechanically." On the third day of employment, Bartleby appears, the
genuine Bartleby, the one who gives utterance. His first utterance is
like the soul escaping from the body, as in medieval drawings.

The tedious proofreading of the clerk's copy is for accuracy done in
collaboration with another person, and it is the lawyer himself who
calls out to Bartleby for assistance in the task. The laconic, implacable
signature is at hand, the mysterious signature that cannot be inter-
preted and cannot be misunderstood. Bartley replies, *I would prefer
not to.*

The pretense of disbelief provides the occasion for *I would prefer not
to* soon to be repeated three times and "with no uneasiness, anger, impatience or impertinence." By the singularity of refusal, the absence of
"because" or of the opening up of some possibly alternating circumstance, this negative domination seizes the story like a sudden ambush
in the streets.

Bartleby's "I" is of such a completeness that it does not require support. He possesses his "I" as if it were a visible part of the body, the way
ordinary men possess a thumb. In his sentence he encloses his past,
present, and future, himself, all there is. His statement is positive indeed and the *not* is less important than the "I," because the "not" refers
to the presence of others, to the world, inevitably making suggestions
the "I" does not encompass.

Bartleby would prefer not to read proof with his employer; a little
later he would prefer not to examine his own quadruplicate copyings
with the help of the other clerks; he would prefer not to answer or to

consider that this communal proofreading is labor-saving and customary. About his "mulish vagary"—no answer.

As we read the story we are certain that, insofar as Bartleby himself is concerned, there is nothing to be thought of as "interesting" in his statement. There is no coquetry; it is merely candid, final, inflexible. Above all it is not "personal"; that is, his objection is not to the collaborators themselves and not to the activity of proofreading, indeed no more repetitive than daylong copying. The reply is not personal and it is not invested with "personality." And this the kind and now violently curious and enduring lawyer cannot believe. He will struggle throughout the tale to fill up the hole, to wonder greatly, to prod as he can, in search of "personality." And the hole, the chasm, or better the "cistern," one of the lawyer's words for the view outside Bartleby's desk, will not be filled.

What began as a comedy, a bit of genre actually, ends as tragedy. But like Bartleby himself it is difficult for the reader to supply adjectives. Is Bartleby mysterious; is his nature dark, angular, subterranean? You are deterred by Bartleby's mastery from competing with him by your command of the adjective. He is overwhelmingly affecting to the emotions of the lawyer and the reader, but there is no hint that he is occupied with lack, disuse, failure, inadequacy. If one tries to imagine Bartleby alone, without the office, what is to be imagined? True, he is always alone, in an utter loneliness that pierces the lawyer's heart when he soon finds that Bartleby has no home at all but is living in the office at night.

No home, living in the office day and night. Here, having exempted this story from my study of Manhattanism because of its inspired occupation with an ultimate condition and its stepping aside from the garbage and shards of Manhattan history, I was stopped by this turn in the exposition. Yes, the undomesticity of a great city like New York, undomestic in the ways other cities are not—then, and still now. Bartleby, the extreme, the icon of the extreme, is not exactly living in the office. Instead he just does not leave it at the end of the day. But it is very easy to imagine from history where the clerks, Nippers and Turkey, are of an evening. They are living in lodging houses, where half of New York's population lived as late as 1841: newlyweds, families, single persons. Whitman did a lot of "boarding round," as he called it, and observed, without rebuke, or mostly without rebuke, that the boarding house led the unfamilied men to rush out after dinner to the saloon or brothel, away from the unprivate private, to the streets which are the spirit of the city, which are the lively blackmail that makes city citizens abide.

Lodgings then, and later the "divided space" of the apartment house, both expressing Manhattanism as a life lived in transition. And lived in a space that is not biography, but is to be fluent and change-able, an escape from the hometown and the homestead, an escape from the given. The rotting tenements of today are only metaphysical apart-ments and in deterioration take on the burdensome aspect of "homes" because they remind, in the absence of purchased maintenance, that something "homelike" may be asked of oneself and at the same time denied by the devastations coming from above, below, and next door. Manhattan, the release from the home, which is the leaking roof, the flooded basement, the garbage, and most of all the grounds, that is, sur-rounding nature. "After I learned about electricity I lost interest in na-ture. Not up-to-date enough." Mayakovsky, the poet of urbanism.

So Bartleby is found to be living in the office day and night. But Bartleby is not a true creature of Manhattan because he shuns the streets and is unmoved by the moral, religious, acute, obsessive, beau-tiful ideal of Consumption. Consumption is what one leaves one's "di-vided space" to honor, as the Muslim stops in his standing and moving to say his prayers five times a day, or is it six? But Bartleby eats only ginger-nuts and is starving himself to death. In that way he passes across one's mind like a feather, calling forth the vague Hinduism of Thoreau and the outer-world meditations of Emerson. (Thoreau, who disliked the city, any city, thought deeply about it, so deeply that in *Walden* he composed the city's most startling consummations, one of which is: "Of a life of luxury, the fruit is luxury.")

To return, what is Bartleby "thinking" about when he is alone? It is part of the perfect completeness of his presentation of himself, al-though he does not present himself, that one would be foolhardy to give him thoughts. They would dishonor him. So, Bartleby is not "thinking" or experiencing or longing or remembering. All one can say is that he is a master of language, of perfect expressiveness. He is style. This is shown when the lawyer tries to revise him.

On an occasion, the lawyer asks Bartleby to go on an errand to the post office. Bartleby replies that he would prefer not to. The lawyer, seeing a possibility for an entropic, involuntary movement in this mastery of meaning, proposes an italicized emendation. He is answered with an italicized insistence.

"You *will* not?"

"I *prefer* not."

What is the difference between *will not* and *prefer* not? There is no difference insofar as Bartleby's actions will be altered, but he seems to be pointing out by the italics that his preference is not under the rule of the conditional or the future tense. He does not mean to say that he prefers not, but will if he must, or if it is wished. His "I" that prefers not, will not. I do not think he has chosen the verb "prefer" in some emblematic way. That is his language and his language is what he is.

Prefer has its power, however. The nipping clerks who have been muttering that they would like to "black his eyes" or "kick him out of the office" begin, without sarcasm or mimicry, involuntarily, as it were, to say to the lawyer, "If you would prefer, Sir," and so on.

Bartleby's language reveals the all of him, but what is revealed? Character? Bartleby is not a character in the manner of the usual, imaginative, fictional construction. And he is not a character as we know them in life, with their bundling bustle of details, their suits and ties and felt hats, their love affairs surreptitious or binding, family albums, psychological justifications dragging like a little wagon along the highway of experience. We might say he is a destiny, without interruptions, revisions, second chances. But what is a destiny that is not endured by a "character"? Bartleby has no plot in his present existence, and we would not wish to imagine subplots for his already lived years. He is indeed only words, wonderful words, and very few of them. One might for a moment sink into the abyss and imagine that instead of *prefer not* he had said, "I don't want to" or "I don't feel like it." No, it is unthinkable, a vulgarization, adding truculence, idleness, foolishness, adding indeed "character" and altering a sublimity of definition.

Bartleby, the scrivener, "standing at the dead-wall window" announces that he will do no more copying. *No more.* The lawyer, marooned in the law of cause and effect, notices the appearance of eyestrain and that there is a possibility Bartleby is going blind. This is never clearly established—Melville's genius would not want at any part of the story to enter the region of sure reasons and causality.

In the midst of these peculiar colloquies, the lawyer asks Bartleby if he cannot indeed be a little reasonable here and there.

" 'At present I would prefer not to be a little reasonable,' was his mildly cadaverous reply."

There is no imagining what the sudden intrusion of "at present" may signify and it seems to be just an appendage to the "I," without calling up the nonpresent, the future. From the moment of first refusal it had passed through the lawyer's mind that he might calmly and without resentment dismiss Bartleby, but he cannot, not even after "no more copying." He thinks: "I should have as soon thought of turning my pale, plaster-of-paris bust of Cicero out of doors." Ah. The "wondrous ascendancy" perhaps begins at that point, with the notion that Bartleby is a representation of life, a visage, but not the life itself.

The lawyer, overcome by pity, by troubling thoughts of human diversity, by self-analysis, goes so far as to take down from the shelf certain theological works which give him the idea that he is predestined to "have Bartleby." But as a cheerful, merely social visitor to Trinity Church, this idea does not last and indeed is too abstract because the lawyer has slowly been moving into a therapeutic role, a role in which he persists in the notion of "personality" that may be modified by patience, by suggestion, by reason.

Still, at last, it is clear that Bartleby must go, must be offered a generous bonus, every sort of accommodation and good wish. This done, the lawyer leaves in a pleasant agitation of mind, thinking of the laws of chance represented by his overhearing some betting going on in the street. Will Bartleby be there in the morning or will he at last be gone? Of course, he has remained and the offered money has not been picked up.

"Will you not quit me?"

"I would prefer *not* to quit you."

The "quitting" is to be accomplished by the lawyer's decision to "quit" himself, that is, to quit his offices for larger quarters. A new tenant is found, the boxes are packed and sent off, and Bartleby is bid good-bye. But no, the new tenants, who are not therapists, rush around to complain that he is still there and that he is not a part of their lease. They turn him out of the offices.

The lawyer goes back to the building and finds Bartleby still present, that is, sitting on the banister of the stairway in the entrance hallway.

"What are you doing here, Bartleby?"

"Sitting upon the banister."

The lawyer had meant to ask what will you do with your life, where will you go, and not, where is your body at this moment. But with Bartleby body and statement are one. Indeed the bewitching qualities, the concentrated seriousness, the genius of Bartleby's "dialogue" had long ago affected the style of the lawyer, but in the opposite direction, that is, to metaphor, arrived at by feeling. His head is full of images about the clerk and he thinks of him as "the last column of some ruined temple" and "a bit of wreck in the mid-Atlantic." And from these metaphors there can be no severance.

There with Bartleby sitting on the banister for life, as it were, the lawyer soars into the kindest of deliriums. The therapeutic wish, the beating of the wings of angels above the heads of the harassed and affectionate, unhinge his sense of the possible, the suitable, the imaginable. He begins to think of new occupations for Bartleby and it is so like the frenzied and loving moments in family life: would the pudgy, homely daughter like to comb her hair, neaten up a bit, and apply for a position as a model?—and why not, others have, and so on and so on.

The angel wings tremble and the lawyer says: "Would you like a clerkship in a dry-goods store?"

Bartleby, the unimaginable promoter of goods for sale, replies with his rapid deliberation. Slow deliberation is not necessary for one who knows the interior of his mind, as if that mind were the interior of a small, square box containing a single pair of cuff links.

To the idea of clerking in a store Bartleby at last appends a reason, one indeed of great opacity.

"There is too much confinement about that. No, I would not like a clerkship; but I am not particular."

Agitated rebuttal of "too much confinement" for one who keeps himself "confined all the time"!

Now, in gentle, coaxing hysteria, the lawyer wonders if the bartender's business would suit Bartleby and adds that "there is no trying of the eye-sight in that."

No, Bartleby would not like that at all, even though he repeats that he is not particular.

Would Bartleby like to go about collecting bills for merchants? It would take him outdoors and be good for his health. The answer: "No, I would prefer to be doing something else."

Doing something else? That is, sitting on the banister, rather than selling dry goods, bartending, and bill collecting.

Here the lawyer seems to experience a sudden blindness, the blindness of a bright light from an oncoming car on a dark road. The bright light is the terrible clarity of Bartleby.

So, in a blind panic: "How then would be going as a companion to Europe, to entertain some young gentleman with your conversation— how would that suit you?"

"Not at all. It does not strike me that there is anything definite about that. I like to be stationary. But I am not particular."

Definite? Conversation is not definite owing to its details of style, opinion, observation, humor, pause, and resumption; and it would not be at all pleasing to Bartleby's mathematical candor. Bartleby is *definite*; conversation is not. He has said it all.

But I am not particular? This slight addition has entered Bartleby at the moment the lawyer opens his fantastical employment agency. The phrase wishes to extend the lawyer's knowledge of his client, Bartleby, and to keep him from the tedium of error. Bartleby himself is particular, in that he is indeed a thing distinguished from another. But he is not particular in being fastidious, choosey. He would like the lawyer to understand that he is not concerned with the congenial. It is not suitability he pursues; it is essence, essence beyond detail.

The new tenants have Bartleby arrested as a vagrant and sent to the Tombs. The same idea had previously occurred to the lawyer in a moment of despair, but he could not see that the immobile, unbegging Bartleby could logically be declared a vagrant. "What! He a vagrant, a wanderer that refuses to budge?"

No matter, the lawyer cannot surrender this "case," this recalcitrant object of social service, this demand made upon his heart to provide benefit, this being now in an institution, the Tombs, but not yet locked away from the salvaging sentiments of one who remembers. A prison visit is made and in his ineffable therapeutic endurance the lawyer insists there is no reason to despair, the charge is not a disgrace, and even in prison one may sometimes see the sky and a patch of green.

Bartleby, with the final sigh of one who would instruct the uninstructable, says: *I know where I am.*

In a last urging, on his knees as it were, the lawyer desires to purchase extra food to add to the prison fare.

Bartleby: "I would prefer not to dine today. It would disagree with me; I am unused to dinners." And thus he dies.

Not quite the end for the lawyer with his compassion, his need to unearth some scrap of buried "personality," or private history. We have the beautiful coda Melville has written, a marvelous moment of composition, but perhaps too symbolical, too poetically signifying to be the epitaph of Bartleby. Yet he must be run down, if only to honor the graceful curiosity and the insatiable charity of the lawyer. He reports a rumor:

> The report was this: that Bartleby had been a subordinate clerk in the Dead Letter Office at Washington, from which he had been suddenly removed by a change in administration. . . . Dead letters! Does it not sound like dead men? Conceive a man by nature and misfortune prone to a pallid hopelessness, can any business seem more fitted to heighten it than that of continually handling these dead letters, and assorting them for the flames? . . . On errands of life, these letters sped to death. . . . Ah, Bartleby! Ah, humanity!

Bartleby in a sense is the underside of Billy Budd, but they are not opposites. Billy, the Handsome Sailor, the "Apollo with a portmanteau," the angel, "our beauty," the sunny day, and the unaccountable goodness, which is with him a sort of beautiful "innate disorder," such as the "innate, incurable disorder" represented by Bartleby. Neither of these curious creations knows resentment or grievance; they know nothing of pride, envy, or greed. There is a transcendent harmony in Billy Budd, and a terrifying, pure harmony in the tides of negation that define Bartleby. Billy, the lovely product of nature and, of course, not a perfection of ongoing citizen life, has a "vocal defect," the tendency to stutter at times of stress. By way of this defect, he goes to his death by hanging. Bartleby in no way has a vocal defect; indeed the claim this remarkable creation of American literature makes on our feelings lies entirely in his incomparable self-expression.

So, this bit of old New York, the sepia, horsecar Manhattan, Wall Street. Bartleby and the god-blessed lawyer. They were created by Melville before the Civil War and were coeval with John Jacob Astor's old age and the prime of Cornelius Vanderbilt. And yet here they are, strange apparitions in the metonymic Wall Street district where the exertions, as described by Mark Twain, were, "A year ago I didn't have a penny, and now I owe you a million dollars."

Looking down, or looking up, today at the sulky twin towers of the World Trade Center, "all shaft," the architects say, thinking of those towers as great sightless Brahmins brooding upon the absolute and the all-embracing spirit, it seemed to me that down below there is something of Manhattan in Bartleby and especially in his resistance to amelioration. His being stirs the water of pity, and we can imagine that the little boats that row about him throwing out ropes of personal charity or bureaucratic provision for his "case" may grow weary and move back to the shore in a mood of frustration and, finally, forgetfulness.

There is Manhattanism in the bafflement Bartleby represents to the alive and steady conscience of the lawyer who keeps going on and on in his old democratic, consecrated endurance—going on, even down to the Tombs, and at last to the tomb. If Bartleby is unsaveable, at least the lawyer's soul may be said to have been saved by the freeze of "fraternal melancholy" that swept over him from the fate he had placed at the desk beside him in a little corner of Wall Street. It is not thought that many "downtown" today would wish to profit from, oh, such a chill.

(1981)

Mrs. Wharton in New York

1.

Edith Wharton was born in New York City in 1862 as Edith Newbold Jones. Her mother was a Rhinelander, one of the poor ones, or more accurately not quite one of the rich ones. Her paternal grandmother was a Schermerhorn. Thus the "Knickerbocker element" survived in her pedigree. They were the remnants of the old Dutch patroons who were themselves early overwhelmed by immigrants from the British Isles and by British military force. It was early indeed, since Peter Stuyvesant surrendered and New Netherland or New Amsterdam became New York in 1664. From the beginning, the old society was beleaguered; had it not been, there would be no Manhattan, this world city as porous as cheesecloth. Traders from New England came down from Maine through Connecticut and were not at first as roundly welcomed as we might imagine today. And, needless to note, worse was to follow the little band of old New Yorkers; unappetizing hordes of foreigners collecting like flies and gnats around the carriage horses.

Into this enclave, old New York society, Edith Wharton was born. She took her positioning seriously, and the old stock with its thumb in the dike of Manhattan was one of her themes as a novelist. It might be said of this theme what Henry James wrote of Nathaniel Hawthorne: "It is only in a country where newness and change and brevity of tenure are the common substance of life, that the fact of one's ancestors having lived for a hundred and seventy years in a single spot would become an element of one's morality."

Being from New York, rather than from Salem, Massachusetts, Edith Wharton was not a Yankee and not a lingering Puritan conscience inhabited by ghosts and provincial scruples. She grew up a cosmopolitan from the first, early traveling abroad with her parents; she married after the usual biographical unsteadiness in the matter of broken engagements and again traveled abroad, then settled on Park Avenue and in Newport and, much later, built herself a grand house in Lenox, Massachusetts, kept traveling, finally sold the house, divorced her husband, Edward Wharton—"cerebrally compromised Teddy," as Henry James called him, summing up this wild manic-depressive who gave her a lot of trouble. Along the way, she had a three-year affair with the romantically overextended seducer Morton Fullerton. And then in 1913, after the divorce, she settled permanently in France. Yet there was more to it than that.

Edith Wharton was twenty-nine when her first short story was published and thirty-seven when her first collection appeared in 1899. Two years before, *The Decoration of Houses,* written with the architect Ogden Codman, had been published. Even though starting late, Edith Wharton quickly became a professional writer in the best sense of the phrase. She wrote steadily, novel after novel, made money, and spent money with a forthright and standard-bearing loyalty to those twins of domestic economy, taste and comfort.

She liked expensive motorcars and once told Henry James that the last of these had been purchased with the proceeds from *The Valley of Decision,* a two-volume mistake about eighteenth-century Italy with characters named Odo and the Duke of Monte Alloro that showed Italy can be as dangerous for certain English-language novelists as the vapors from the undrained marshes. (To the point: Hawthorne's *The Marble Faun,* a weary and unsuitable surrender to the moist murk a gloomy eye might discover in the beautiful country. Hawthorne himself did not make the common surrender to Italy and complained of "discomfort and miseries," found the Roman winter an unadvertised blast of chills, and could not countenance nudity in sculptures.)

Henry James, looking at Mrs. Wharton's motorcar purchased by the assault on Italy, and referring to *The Wings of the Dove,* is reported to have said, "With the proceeds of my last novel, I purchased a small go-cart, or wheel-barrow, on which my guests' luggage is wheeled from the station to my house. It needs a coat of paint. With the proceeds of my next novel I shall have it painted."

There is a tradesman's shrewdness in Edith Wharton's work. She knows how to order the stock and dispose the goods in the window. She was a popular author, or, to be more just, her books were popular, not always the same thing. (Even in her day there were writers, many of them women susceptible to sentiment, who trafficked in novels in the present-day manner—more soybeans on the commodities market.) Edith Wharton is free of lush sentiments and moralizing tears. In *The House of Mirth*, her triumph, she is not always clear what the moral might be and thereby creates a stunning tragedy in which the best and the richest society of New York reveals an inner coarseness like pimps cruising in Cadillacs.

Nevertheless, she is often caught up in contrivance as a furtherance of product. And she likes the ruffled cuff and transcontinental glamour, interesting enough in itself but speeding to pointlessness. The novel is viewed as a frank transaction between elements, elements to be laid out and pasted down like tiles in a frame. A "situation" is of course the necessity of fiction. Yet what of the cracks, the anxiety we sense in greater novelists about the very intention of the careful arabesques so purposefully designed and all of a sudden baked hard as rock?

In a story by Chekhov called "Terror," a young man has been flirting with the wife of his good friend, and she has been sighing in the Russian manner for him. Somehow, he at last takes her to his room, which the husband enters to get his cap left there earlier, set up, we would say, by the dramatist's art. At the end, the young man wonders: "Why has it turned out like this and not differently? To whom and for what was it necessary that she should love me in earnest and that he should come to my room to fetch his cap? What had the cap to do with it?"

Neatness of plotting; balancing of the elements by a handy coincidence beyond necessity: That is the way it often goes with this prodigious worker, busy at the morning's pages. She tends to lay hold with some of the gregarious insistence she displayed as the sort of hostess who organizes trips after lunch. Too many caps to be retrieved at the bedside of indiscretion, too much of a gloss. It's the last slap of the polishing cloth and then forge ahead in a majorful fashion.

The Reef, for instance: The young man is hoping to marry the recently widowed woman he has long loved. She puts him off with family affairs in her mother-in-law's château in France and with problems relating to her young child and to her stepson. All are Americans, but the château somehow appears as naturally as if it were a deed to a woodlot. In a fit of chagrin, the young man has an affair in a cheap Paris railroad hotel with a penniless American girl trying her hand at this and that abroad. This manifestation of impatience over and done with, the widow and the young man recombine, so to speak. And soon the girl from the railroad hotel turns up and will become engaged to the stepson, heir to the château and all the rest. The plot is suspenseful and executed with considerable gallantry and many Jamesian pauses in articulation—questions that are not quite asked, answers that hang in the air, the cues in the matter of a dialogue to a moral dilemma. The convenience of the young girl's turning up to be promptly fallen in love with by the heir is too brilliant, too tidy.

The Mother's Recompense: A mother has abandoned her husband and daughter, and New York society has erased the blot of her existence as if she were a smudge to be washed off a window. She lives abroad rather shabbily unanchored but has for a time the pleasant anguish of an affair with a younger man, who proves to be the great love of her life. When the old members of the New York family die, the daughter brings her mother back. It's a lottery ticket for the bolter: everything forgiven, luxury, and social reestablishment. Soon, the young man drops down on the scene; the daughter falls in love and means to marry him. You turn a corner, or rather a page, and there he is, or there she is. Moments of social comedy set out as deftly as the knives and forks; dramatic encounters in the splendid old arks of the Hudson Valley or in the mansions moving upward on Fifth Avenue.

Edith Wharton is a challenging figure just now. In her finesse and talent, her glamour and worldliness, she shares in some of the renewed affection for the threatened New York City architecture of the Beaux Arts period. Even her snobbishness and spendthrift ways are not remote from the activities of the haute couture ladies that daily fill the pages of the city's newspapers. With Edith Wharton, it was always an "approach up a red carpet," as the English man of letters Percy Lubbock says in his courteous but sly memoir of their friendship. She was, in most of her writing life, not one to loiter with curiosity about the crude crunch of New York, and she cannot even be claimed as an old-stock patriot since she fled the frontier and the American presence with its "vainglory, crassness and total ignorance."

In line with the contemporary appetite for tawdry revelation, the grande dame received a boost in her literary ratings thanks to R.W.B. Lewis's biography and the publication of a very knowing fragment of pornography found among her papers. She composed, yes, a father-daughter scene, a frankly hot exercise in appreciative specification not unlike Auden's "The Platonic Blow":

> Letting herself downward along the divan till her head was in a line with his middle she flung herself upon the swelling member, and began to caress it insinuatingly with her tongue. It was the first time she had ever seen it actually exposed to her eyes, and her heart swelled excit-edly: to have her touch confirmed by sight enriched the sensation that was communicating itself through her ardent twisting tongue. With panting breath she wound her caress deeper and deeper into the thick firm folds, till at length the member, thrusting her lips open, held her gasping, as if at its mercy.

The House of Mirth was written while Edith Wharton was still living in New York in 1905—or partly living in New York on Park Avenue when not at the new house in Lenox or in Newport or abroad. The tragic force of this ambitious early novel—early in her career at least—has to do with the broadness of conception, the immediacy of the strokes and scenes, rather than, as was so often later the case, a concentration upon details of manners, such as divorce for a woman. (It is interesting that in this novel one woman who seems to be invited everywhere has been divorced twice.)

It is a society novel of city mansions and great country houses, expensive bridge games, Paris clothes, and lavish weddings. Into this, the author has placed a perfect center, Lily Bart, a spectacularly resonant creation, trying to keep afloat after a very realistic collapse of the foundation of the part she was designed to play. Lily is spoiled, pleasure-loving, and has one of those society mothers who are as improvident as a tornado. The father comes home one day from "downtown," and while Lily is chattering about the need every day for fresh flowers in the house at twelve dollars a dozen, the weary man replies: "Oh, certainly my dear—give him an order for twelve hundred." There is a sardonic stress to his reply, and the father is asked if he is ill. "Ill—No, I'm ruined," he says.

Quite soon both parents are dead and Lily is sent to live with an aunt, an old goose in good society and well-heeled but dull and stingy in everything except an allowance for clothes. At the opening Lily is twenty-nine, beautiful, clever, an adornment for dinners and weekends that demand expenditures, at the bridge table for one, which she cannot afford and for which she is secretly in debt. It is clearly time for her to marry, after having foolishly turned down respectable offers. Marriage to a rich man is her aim, and early in the book she has her chance with a plodding, timid young heir, but certain acts of impetuosity and the news of her gambling debts frighten him away.

That is the way it goes. Every move Lily makes, whether innocent or calculating, leads to disaster and compromise. Her efforts go on very much in the manner of a continental farce. Although she is chaste, she tends again and again to be discovered in a sort of rumpled state. Men, married and otherwise, pursue her and, when rejected, blackmail her. Each scene is interesting, and if observers are always on hand to find her walking in the park when she'd rather not be seen or coming out of a house at the wrong hour, no unfortunate arrangement of circumstances is altogether without credibility.

The brilliance of the characterization lies in Lily's self-knowledge. She is never unaware of her own motives, and when her manipulations fail she does not impugn the self-interest of others working against her own. As one who has been on the town too long and who is poorer than anyone knows, Lily quite understands self-interest. She loses every gamble, and each opportunity snaps back like a trap. Her acquaintance with luxury is a fatal habituation. "Of luxury, the fruit is luxury," as Thoreau phrased it. At last, disinherited by her aunt because of "gossip," she sinks into irreversible poverty, an urban slide something like that of a luckless courtesan, although Lily Bart is only a New York society girl without means and without connections except of the kind that issue invitations. In the end, she takes an overdose of sleeping medicine.

Surrounding this personal debacle is a large society, not a representation of the city so much as a society that twists and turns upon itself, within the list, the mostly rich and sometimes dull and overfed. The predatory sexuality, the heartlessness, and the coarseness are quite startling when viewed against the more mildly rebuked, nostalgic renderings of the old guard in the later works.

For instance, Gus Trenor, whose credentials we cannot doubt since "with all his faults, Trenor had the safeguard of his traditions, and was less likely to overstep them because they were so purely instinctive." Of course, the "instinctive" graces are often out to lunch when life, here and elsewhere, scratches with its small and large irritations. Still, the rather glum and fumbling needs of poor Gus bring to mind instincts of the old urgency.

His wife is Lily's best friend, with all the relevant modifications of both words, and gives parties and weekends on Long Island, or is it up the Hudson? Mr. Trenor has appeared harmless enough but is insufficiently attended to. On one of the occasions, social, at Bellomont, his estate, he hears of Lily's desperate situation and offers to invest her last thousand dollars. Not long after, he presents her with ten thousand dollars, supposedly profit from a tip. Having gone to this trouble, Trenor turns as ornery as a ward boss. He gossips about the money and insinuates that there was no market tip; there was only his generosity, for which he wants womanly attentions of the usual concreteness. He sends her a telegram in his wife's name, summoning her late in the evening to his mansion on Fifth Avenue. Of course, the telegram is a trick of the most benighted asininity and Trenor is alone. He makes a clumsy effort to seduce Lily, but clumsy or not the intention is altogether realistic. Edith Wharton is bold about sex, even something of a nudging procuress when the plot allows. "Hang it, the man who pays for the dinner is generally allowed a seat at the table," the overheated man growls when he is rebuffed. (Lily's last act before committing suicide is to return, in the manner of Socrates before the hemlock, the profit from Trenor's "investment" on her behalf.) But where are the gentle manners, the agreeable repressions attendant upon civility learned at the tables set with the "du Lac Sèvres" and the "van der Luyden Lowestoft" and the "Dagonet Crown Derby"?

The House of Mirth in its flashlighting around New York casts its beam upon a Mr. Sim Rosedale. In the practice of the period, Rosedale is referred to as a "little Jew" and weighted down, as if by an overcoat in summer, with a thickness of objectionable moral and physical attributes—each readily at hand for the confident satirist. The fellow has made a lot of money downtown, and thus his path crosses that of the more or less well-bred Wall Street New Yorkers, who find him useful since their own capacities, with the help of spendthrift wives, are thinning like the hair on their heads.

Rosedale is ferociously set upon entering the society described in the novel; he has the money and is determined to have the dance. It must be said he comes upon the scene as free of family, traditions, religious or otherwise, as bereft of community as a scout on the plains. Rosedale is no slithering continental sybarite like August Belmont, but instead a shrewd, if uncouth, trader, and from history it might be doubted that he would be so quick to wish this particular dilution of himself and his fortune. The author understands it is fate and probity that lead the dull, rich Mr. Gryce to pass over Lily Bart and to unite his pile with that of the dull, rich Evie Van Osburgh. Edith Wharton would not, however, have known of Rosedale's possible familiar life, and so his muscular push into smart society must be taken as, well, natural.

In any case, the advancing Sim Rosedale is an important figure in this plot of threatening circumstances. Since Lily is beautiful, unmarried, and as fashionable as satin, Rosedale has settled upon her as the mate to show his accumulations to advantage. She refuses him, with "repugnance." But as her opportunities wither and her desperation augments, she decides to take the florid Rosedale and his millions after all. In a powerfully executed scene, Lily faces up and says, "I am ready to marry you whenever you wish." The crafty usurper turns her down. Her rotten luck, those scandal-mongering observers of her trek here and there on the stairs of a bachelor-filled apartment house and on a yacht in the Mediterranean and the compromising reportage they have engendered, are a fund of disadvantage. She is no longer a good investment.

Lily Bart is a flawed, self-absorbed, and, oh, yet decent beauty of the kind that tests the novelist's art. Sympathy is aroused by the honesty of her impulses, and she has an emotional clarity that makes even an occasional charity believable. Emotional clarity—honesty, in fact—is less efficient in society than garrulous self-justification. With Lily, this clarity is like a pinch of arthritis in her manipulating hand.

Her helplessness in poverty may be laid to society's withholding from the clotheshorse beauty the proper training for independence as a woman, independence being knowing how to work and forgo the dressmaker. There is a suggestion of the sadness of laboring incapacity in the exposition Edith Wharton has supplied. Certainly, Lily Bart is not a pioneering candidate for Radcliffe College; indeed, she cannot trim a hat, one of the occupations girls fallen from prosperity attempt in this as in other novels. Yet the author knows the lamentable inadequacy of "the modelling of her little ear, the crisp upward wave of her hair" as a preparation for a paycheck. And, above all, what she stresses is the blight of a conditioning for luxury without the means.

Lily Bart knows what she knows, coquetry for the most part, and to have been prepared otherwise would have been another novel. At one point, Lily explains that people think one can live *on* the rich, when the fact is that it takes money to live *with* the rich. To be without sufficient money is like diving into the concrete of a drained swimming pool. This novel is Edith Wharton's finest achievement because money is the subject, of greater significance than the crippling, if amusing and charming details of convention in a small, historically perhaps attractive but insignificant stockade. That at least was true of Manhattan even when it was "old."

2.

New York: No novelist in his or her volumes has set out to be the social historian of the actual city, this restless monster of possibility and liability. It is not easy to imagine a voraciousness to consume the remarkable, shapeless scope or, even in a practical condensation, to imagine a Zola tramping through the warehouses of meat at dawn or trailing the garment workers home to some godforsaken borough in the evening. The city itself has never been a whole as the other great cities were until recently, when New York's peculiar instability and visionary tribalism became a worldwide condition: Turks in Berlin, Arabs in Paris, colonials in London. New York literature is the literature of the precinct, whether it be the Mafia, Hell's Kitchen in Crane's *Maggie: A Girl of the Streets,* or Salinger's Glass family on Central Park West. A great claim is usually made for Edith Wharton as a social historian, although how that can be confirmed by so intensely hermetic an imagination is a puzzle.

The gorgeous innuendo of Henry James's New York pages in *The*

American Scene, the lilting metaphors of distress and dispossession: It was 1904 when the chagrined pedestrian made his way through the fatally designed "streets intersecting with a pettifogging consistency." He spent some hours on Ellis Island, the utopian gateway, and cautioned the unwary against doing the same. To witness the "inconceivable alien" in their herded numbers was to have "eaten of the tree of knowledge and the taste will be forever in his mouth." But the effulgent language of James's wounded curiosity can be said to redeem the space of his withdrawal, to honor the gross elaboration and "untempered monotony" of the Waldorf Astoria and to fix in a glance the very topography of the city lying in its rivers and "looking at the sky in the manner of some gigantic hair-comb turned upward."

New York, with its statistical sensationalism, is a shallow vessel for memory since it lives in a continuous present, making it difficult to recall the shape of the loss deplored, whether it be the gray tin of the newsstand or the narrow closet for the neighborhood's dry cleaning, there and gone over a vacation. As for people, the rapid obsolescence of deities makes its point each season; or, if surviving the gleeful erasure of fame, the penalties pursuing society's accommodation can be severe, or so it is often asserted by the fatigued famous.

In my time, the preservationists say, men got up when a woman entered the room. When poor Blanche DuBois, passing the louts at the poker table, says, "Don't get up, I'm only passing through," how is that to be understood without "tradition"? There's a bit of that in Edith Wharton.

The Custom of the Country (1913) was for the most part written in France. It is a curiosity of a hybrid kind. Here we have a fierce scold not of the alien from Odessa or Sicily but of the natives undertaking an interior migration from Apex City to Manhattan. Their landing, ready for absorption, is a twofold pain: Their pockets are lined with cash, and they don't know when to get up and when to sit down. The mode of the composition is split in the middle: one half a description of the invaders in a satiric accent, the other a whirlwind of folly and destruction on an international scale.

So we open to the Spragg family from Apex. Spragg, wanting to transpose itself to Sprague or something, but efficient, perhaps in suggesting many backcountry impediments and wonders of maladaptation not unlike those of Ring Lardner's hicks in *The Big Town,* or his

Mrs. Gullible finally achieving her wish to meet Mrs. Potter Palmer, doing so in a hotel corridor, and being asked to bring more towels.

Mr. and Mrs. Spragg are woebegone pilgrims, and the old father with his "lymphatic patience" brightened only by the Masonic emblem on his waistcoat is as unlikely a trader on Wall Street as the man behind the pickle barrel in the corner grocery. But he has made money in some way and the hajj to Mecca is, you might say, made on the roller skates of his daughter, Undine, who for a good while has been dreaming about Fifth Avenue in her Apex backyard. The choice of this family to bear the history of new money in the metropolis carries more of the tone of parody than of a serious imaginative decision.

William Dean Howells created similar migratory birds in *A Hazard of New Fortunes*. His Dryfoos tribe hits town with a fortune made from natural gas in Northern Ohio and Indiana. Natural gas would seem to be a very happy source for American finance, but the boomtown alteration of fortune does not decorate the newly rich man's psyche. In New York, old Dryfoos wails, "I ain't got any horses, I ain't got any cows. I ain't got any chickens, I ain't got anything to do from sun-up to sun-down." Dryfoos and his strike have, like the Spraggs, been transported by ravening daughters who want to bust into New York society.

It is no doubt prudent to have daughters if one would display in fiction the barbarities of social climbing and portray in all its anxious athleticism a passion for shopping. Of course, consumption and insatiability are the overhanging atmosphere of the city itself, gathering all classes, top to bottom, in its dreamy, poetic smother.

Undine Spragg arrives on the scene with youth, natural, and beauty, extraordinary, and every moral and practical liability a golden girl from the heart of the country can fold in her trunks. She is an infection, a glassy, little, germ-filled protagonist. We meet her set up with her family in the Hotel Stentorian, in rooms that go by the name of the Looey Suite, to be furnished with a good deal of oversized mahogany and gilt and laughable hangings on wall and window. Undine gets "round" right off and meets, without giving him notice, a young man, Ralph Marvell. Soon, she receives from his sister an invitation, which she throws in a basket, but which is rescued by a Mrs. Heeney, masseuse and manicurist, who cries out, Marvell! His mother is a *Dagonet*, and they live with old Urban Dagonet down on Washington Square!

Mrs. Spragg chews on this: "Why do they live with somebody else? Haven't they got the means to have a home of their own?" Undine, per-plexed and suspicious, questions why a sister should have written and why the invitation should ask the mother's permission when it is Un-dine who is asked to dine and why dine instead of have dinner and why write the note on plain white paper when pigeon-blood red is all the rage?—that kind of thing. *Go steady, Undine,* Mrs. Heeney advises.

Not long after, Undine is married to Ralph Marvell, and the plot ad-vances to the lamentable results of this—for him. The Marvells are old New York, impeccable in birth and manners, not rich, living in their comfortably shabby houses on Washington Square, three generations within. Ralph is bookish and perhaps will himself write books; he is quiet, charming, has been to Harvard and Oxford, tried law but didn't have a flair for it, and now does nothing apart from reading and living according to his nature.

The European wedding journey is the first foreign experience for Undine, and it proves to be an experience foreign to Ralph Marvell's previous life. Undine despises Siena, altogether too slow and too hot. When asked if the summer wasn't hot in Apex, she replies that she didn't marry to go back to Apex. In Paris, the Comédie is "stuffy," and the husband attends alone while she is busy and, surreptitiously, hav-ing the family rings reset and buying a lot of clothes without the money. In fact, the couple doesn't have money for the passage home, and there are turns of plot attendant upon that. Undine is piling up the wreckage, flooding the banks of the river, and leaving the Marvell her-itage and finances tumbled down in the mud.

Ralph Marvell is a creation of the novelist's art, and his attractive-ness is evident on the page. His marriage to Undine is, however, a sort of haystack of implausibility stuck in the middle of urban life. She is given only one quality and that is great beauty. Beauty will always be an assertion the reader is compelled to accept but cannot keep his mind fixed upon. The hair—was it red?—and the "glow" when some diversion pleases the beauty are not exactly traits to be probed so much as color floating and drifting without a trace.

Undine, the character, is a witch of ignorance, insensitivity, vanity, and manipulation. She is mean to her parents, indifferent to the child she finally bears, and impossible to imagine as anything other than te-dious. Whatever negotiable assets she has are practical only to certain vulgar sensualists, of which there are quite a few on the scene. She divorces Ralph Marvell without asking his permission and imagines after making herself fully available that she will cause Van Degen, a rich and decadent member of the Marvell set, also to get a divorce and to marry her. But the canny Van Degen thinks better of it and does not come forth.

Along the way, a most fantastical marriage for Undine does come about. She unites with the Comte Raymond de Chelles, a handsome young nobleman with ancient credentials, a house in the Faubourg, a château in Burgundy, little money to combine with Undine's less, since old Spragg has not prospered on Wall Street for all the reasons sufficient from the beginning.

Why must Edith Wharton and, in a different manner, Henry James decorate their pages with ancient titles to confound the romantic history of their Americans? Undine inflicts appalling indignities upon the poor Comte, but she is strangely imagined to be fidgeting about in the cold halls of a turreted castle. What is so interesting about Gilbert Osmond, the fortune hunter in *The Portrait of a Lady,* is that he acts like a prince of the realm but is indeed quite recognizable as an insufferable American expatriate, long resident in Florence. Prince Amerigo, in *The Golden Bowl,* fortunately does not flourish the papal title, and he is mostly seen maneuvering about London offering his fate to Americans, too many of them as it turns out.

But how peculiar it is to have the delightful, candid Christopher Newman in *The American* set off in pursuit of the daughter of the noble De Bellegarde family. The ancient Europeans will be cut from the cloth, stamped out one after another without distinguishing shapes, a bit like the weird American manufactures from which Newman made his finally unsuitable millions. The titled Europeans represent mystery, inflexible pride, hidden motive, inscrutable manners, melodrama, and unreality: trappings, fuss, and feathers that must stand in the place of the author's having real knowledge or observed experience of the character and intimate life of Europeans so high.

Howells in *A Hazard of New Fortunes* has one of the odious Dryfoos shopping, primping daughters make a similar leap into the European bog. Christine Dryfoos meets her fate in the person of a French nobleman "full of present debts and of duels in the past." It is added that the father and his natural-gas dollars can manage the debts, but the duelist had better watch out for Christine, "unless he's practised with a panther."

The international novels are in fact novels of traveling Americans meeting each other abroad with a few natives thrown in. In *The Golden Bowl,* the Ververs cast their immense fortune at the foot of a prince, but the prince is a passenger, and the motors of the action are in the hands of the Ververs and the American, Charlotte Stant. Mme. Merle, so mysterious, is finally just another American, like the radical-chic Princess Casamassima, another visitor like the Touchetts, whose gifts will buy for Isabel Archer a fantasy of native blood, Gilbert Osmond, decorated with impecunious winters abroad, a little collection of things, and the hauteur of his meaningless displacement.

Undine at last finds a perch on Fifth Avenue as the wife of Elmer Moffat of Apex, an old pal to whom she had been briefly married as a girl. The discovery of her concealment of this fact is a contingent reason for Ralph Marvell's suicide. So Undine will travel from the picket fence to Fifth Avenue on the back of Apex Elmer, loud and red-faced as a fire truck. Elmer is now a railroad magnate, like—can it be?— Commodore Vanderbilt. The much-used bride is to be largely rewarded, and when the dispenser is Edith Wharton the loot will be lavish and banal. Undine is to have "a necklace and tiara of pigeon-blood rubies belonging to Queen Marie Antoinette, a million dollar cheque . . . a new home, 5009 Fifth Avenue, which is an exact copy of the Pitti Palace, Florence."

As a social historian, Edith Wharton does not pause to get it just right, on the dot. She proceeds from a very generalized memory and an often commonplace fund of attitudes. *The Custom of the Country* has placed its points at extremities that undermine the evolutionary rush of the actual city. The invading Visigoths with their rude instruments of fortune, like Spragg's marketing of a hair-waver from which comes Undine's name and his later having a worthless parcel of land upon which Apex was to build its water system, are not the usual transfers to Manhattan. The middle-sized towns of the Middle West would be more likely to claim the powers of Spragg and to contain the gossip-column ambitions of dressing-up Undine. The old Spraggs' rustic souls are fashioned out of impermeable materials, and the city casts its stones of enlightenment their way without making a dent.

New York City is a frame in these novels, not a landscape: 5009 Fifth

Avenue? Even less well foretold is the failure to understand the magical progression of taste, so hasty, in the newly rich of the city. For what is easier than the acquisition of acceptable responses? Culture, as society finds it, is not saturation but an acquaintance with the labels of things valued, be it the Parthenon or white walls. The culture of consumption is infinitely accommodating, and the terms of cultural dissemblance are an available cosmetic, another pot of rouge. Very few Undines would scorn Siena or the Comédie Française, scorn out loud. Quickly, the proper patience appears, no matter how deep the stab of boredom in an actual confrontation.

The Marvell house on Washington Square, the seat of the genteel opposition, is one thing, but in New York "divided space" is preeminent, and the hotel and apartment living the hick Spraggs embrace cannot be thought of as retrograde. Was there in old New York an aristocratic style, an intimate weave of obscure inherited practice and value? Perhaps, but the style as it has come down to us was always drowning in the city's hyperbolic congestion of effects, the glare of the futuristic, the fantastical democratizing compulsion of Manhattan's eternal newness.

When Henry James set up his house in *Washington Square,* he did not force the historical inappropriateness of the terms found in the novels of Edith Wharton. He placed in his house, a memory dear to him from his youth, a member of the professional upper classes, with no worrisome tics about who might be a Dagonet, who a Van der Luyden. Dr. Sloper is an intelligent, hard-nosed, serious practitioner in a useful arena of knowledge, a possible New Yorker. True, the doctor is said to have married into one of the "best" families, but this has no dizzying command over the rather surgical common sense with which he approaches family affairs. What has its woeful effect upon him is that his wife has died and left him an improbable daughter. This chagrin is not unreasonable, or unthinkable perhaps, for a metropolitan gentleman. Catherine is dear, awkward, unfashionable, and indeed would seem to have many qualities of a Boston girl transplanted carelessly to New York. In Boston, among the Yankees, Catherine's modesty and the plainness and wish to please would not be impediments in a girl of good family.

In New York, Catherine is a perturbation. When the selfish, false idler, Morris Townsend, begins to court her, the doctor's intervention is cruel and practical. He is shrewd about Townsend and with his oily, ironic efficiency is not mindful of the fruits of his shrewdness in the broken heart of his daughter. The novel is a perfectly faceted diamond, clear in its icy progression. The drama sits on its corner downtown as confidently as the house Dr. Sloper built for himself. Social habits, conventions, prohibitions of the group have no part in the dilemma. Dr. Sloper knows his objections to Townsend as frankly as if the young man had come begging with a tin cup. Townsend does not care for Catherine, wishes only to marry her money, and while the sophisticated doctor can no doubt understand both, he sees that the conditions promise to be baneful down the road.

Wharton's *The Age of Innocence* has great appeal because of the charm of the two figures, Ellen Olenska and Newland Archer. If it has a definition, an engine, it is divorce as a social stigma, a disability not to be incurred by a woman. She must, no matter what provocation, hang on legally, even if at a distance. She must not for a mere wish to be free of it all act on her own behalf. Ellen Olenska, a Mingott connection, has married a titled swine of a Pole. She has left him and returned to New York; he will take her back, but there is no thought of his swaying from whatever disgusts have been his pleasure. If she divorces, there will be scandal, and she will lose her money brought to the marriage and what is spoken of as "everything else."

The scandal of the intriguing Countess, with her irregular escape from her husband, combined with the powerful Mingott clan's displaying her in the family opera box, bring forth the beginning gasps of curiosity and social dismay. It is not a very weighty casualty, and yet Edith Wharton must find something to give reality to the deputed social standards. Good manners and the family plate are not sufficient for drama. Hindrance and exclusion are needed to give the old dominion coherence, to act as a sort of velvet rope in a museum protecting the plunder. Of course, there is great provincialism afoot here, since we know from Proust that a great French aristocrat can drop his Croix de Guerre on the floor of a male brothel without diminishing his prestige.

A good deal of the plot is concerned with who will come to a dinner in honor of the Countess, who will visit her, and so on. The loyalties of the old families are tested, and the best, the oldest, the most valued come forth bravely to smile over the canvasback ducks and to shame the timid, the complacent, and the insecure.

Ellen Olenska is glamorous and in tribute to her cosmopolitan life a bit exotic, a bit of a bohemian in her "little house" on an unfashionable New York street. She reads Paul Bourget, Huysmans, and the Goncourt Brothers. Newland Archer, conventionally reared by doting, placid women, a cousin to everyone who is anyone, has just married an unimaginative, nice young woman of his own set. Archer and Ellen Olenska fall in love, and it is a flaming passion that almost sends the lovers to a hotel room. The consummation is withheld, the Countess Olenska, divorced, returns to Europe, and Archer grows into a husband and father with bittersweet memories, recorded in one of those codas that span the years and might well have been forgone.

Edith Wharton suffered throughout her marriage to the Boston bon vivant, Teddy, as he was called. Teddy was worldly, liked the pleasures of dog and stream and wine cellar. He had no interest in scholarship, high or low, but took over a good deal of the management of houses and practical affairs and that went well, until it didn't. The two seem to have been a poor sexual match. Edith had her three-year affair with Fullerton, her strong affections for Henry James and others, especially for Walter Berry—a New York Van Rensselaer, an expert in international law and widely considered a snob, in her own vein. She was buried by his side, in Versailles.

Morton Fullerton, Harvard, son of a minister in Waltham, Massachusetts, became a political and cultural journalist, at one time the correspondent from France for the London *Times*. Fullerton seems to have been an attractive, perhaps we could say a lovable, young man. In his love life, he is something like a telephone, always engaged, and even then with several on hold. Whether he wished so many rings on his line is hard to tell; perhaps he was one of those who would always, always answer. In any case, among his callers were, in youth, Ronald Gower, a homosexual and friend of Oscar Wilde; Margaret Brooke, the Ranee of Sarawak; his cousin, Katherine Fullerton Gerould; Victoria Chambert, whom he married and with whom he had a child while living with a Mme. Mirecourt—and Edith Wharton.

When you have decided that Fuller likes older women—the Ranee and Mme. Mirecourt—he takes up with those younger, his cousin and Victoria Chambert. At the time of his affair with Mrs. Wharton there was a balance with no special signification: she was forty-five and he was forty-two. The Fullerton women tracked down thus far by academic prurience seem to have been of a forgiving nature and remained friendly to him throughout the years. Mme. Mirecourt clung like a burr and, as an expression of her enduring affection, was quite troublesome.

Teddy Wharton fell into the care of psychiatrists and into mood-swing follies, even going so far as to set himself up with a girl in a Boston apartment. He ran through his wife's money, and his increasing instability led to divorce. Twenty-eight years they had together, and, insofar as one can know, most of them were useful if not "satisfying" in the current sense. But then how satisfying could the dear love of the ambivalent Walter Berry have been? Edith Wharton appears to have been a type found in abundance on the contemporary scene: surprisingly sexy when the availabilities allowed, but owing to a dominant attraction to stylish amusements, happily surrounded by homosexuals, always, of course, of the right sort.

Once the deed was done, the divorce signed, she seemed to settle with a forward-looking fortitude. Even in her day, divorce was common in the best society, and it might be thought she held on to the prohibition mostly as a literary device to serve as a dramatic expression of the old manners—a necessary addition to the appointments of the house and the seating at the table. She used divorce again and again in her fiction, even sometimes seeming to entertain a certain moral nostalgia for its rigors. There is no doubt it was a handy circumstance for exile and for "cutting." The bald fact was that there were not many other stands to be taken in her created world, where the virtues were birth, the grand style, if suitable, with the rich Van der Luydens; good taste and modesty of pretension, the old bourgeois style, with the Marvells.

Edith Wharton had never been "modern" as a writer and had few theoretical questionings about the shape of the novel. "I certainly don't think Edith often read," Percy Lubbock wrote. Visiting her, he sometimes felt "a book had a scared look as she carried it off, as though it knew what it was in for." Yet she was a celebrated novelist, bore many honors, and experienced the threat of displacement in the clamorous, avant-garde elation of the 1920s. *The Waste Land* did not receive her favor, and *Ulysses* was to be named "school boy drivel." Living in upholstered exile, in the manner of Mrs. Wharton and Bernard Berenson, may have the gloomy effect of attaching one to intransigence in the arts, against the uprooted impertinence of modernism.

Mrs. Wharton had her turf, that almost forgotten sepia New York, to be turned over and over again, like setting the plow to the family farm every spring. A group of four short novels, under the title *Old New York* and boxed together, appeared in 1924. At the time of writing them, she was living in her final grand house, Pavillon Colombe, in Saint Brie, France, not far from Paris.

False Dawn, subtitled *The 'Forties,* proposes the adventures of a young man sent out on the civilizing Grand Tour and deputed to bring back works of art for his father's collection: Guido Reni, Carlo Dolci, and the like. Instead, spurred on by the development of a friendship with a young Englishman, who, we are asked to believe, is John Ruskin, he purchases Carpaccio, Fra Angelico, Giotto, and Piero della Francesca. The choices lead to his being disinherited by his father and scorned by old New York. Complacency and backward taste appear to be the indictment. "Carpatcher, you say this fellow's called. . . . Something to do with those new European steam-cars, I suppose, eh?" the outraged father cries out. Satiric dialogue, engaging enough in conversation, is a crash of dissonance on the Wharton page. And she likes to preen a little, to glide up on Ruskin and sneak up on the unlikely Piero purchase as if they were two cups of tea at Doney's.

In *The Spark,* a crusty old New Yorker claims to have learned human wisdom from a talkative fellow while being nursed in a Washington hospital after Bull Run. It is the dear bard Whitman himself. *The Old Maid,* another of the novellas, is a skillful melodrama set in the 1850s and telling of the sadness of an unwed mother's having to pretend to be a devoted aunt as she watches her child grow up, a condition as common in the villages as in the city.

The *Old New York* volumes are anecdotal fictions. There is not much air in them. Throughout Edith Wharton's work the society is small and its themes repetitive. The reader will become a sort of cousin of the blood as the defining names appear again and again. Memory has been emptied out by the long years abroad, and a certain perfunctoriness and staleness hang over the scene. Christine Nilsson will be singing *Faust* at the Academy of Music; the carriage will give way to the coupé. Characters go to balls and dinners and stop by to drink tea. They scarcely set foot on more than a few predictable blocks and on the way do not pass restaurants or saloons or thieves or workmen going home. Manhattan is a "set" but with no sense of crowds.

An early story, "Bunner Sisters," was rejected by an editor and put aside for many years before being offered in a collection. It is one of the author's most interesting works and an extraordinary wandering from the enclave. The sisters make trimmings and sew on ribbons in their dismal tenement; they meet a dreary opium addict, a wreck of a German who fixes clocks and who devastates their miserable struggle. The details of existence are vivid; the author knew at one time that people took streetcars, bought a few pennies worth of food with fierce concentration upon the cost, made pitiful journeys to the wastes of New Jersey. Gradually, the feel and the spell of the city were lost and only interiors remained, the stuffs of definition.

Ethan Frome is a village tragedy, and the tale is cut to the measure of rural New England as a strong popular image. The village is named Starkfield; Ethan is a melancholy, silent, and longing country man, ruined by the slow agony of life with his complaining, "sickly" wife, the kind whose neurosis is colored by a run on patent medicines. His hope for redemptive love by way of the young servant girl, Mattie, is thwarted, and their attempt to commit suicide by sledding down a dangerous hill on a splendid snowy night produces not death but a crippled, altered Mattie to be taken in by the now triumphant wife, and the three to be left to their eternal rural isolation and misery. There is less experience of life in this story than in "Bunner Sisters." Short as *Ethan Frome* is, it is heavily designed and shows the difficulties encountered in the telling, the structure. It is operatic, *opera verismo,* with the power to retain its grip on the memory, as the long popularity of the work indicates.

Dreiser's *Sister Carrie* was written in 1900, five years before *The House of Mirth* and twenty years before *The Age of Innocence.* Dreiser, from the Middle West, went over the city on foot, as it were, striking out from the first ring of the city's chimes, the trainman's call of "Grand Central Station!" The first flat is on Seventy-eighth and Amsterdam, and soon Nassau Street is mentioned. The horns of the ferryboats sound in the fog; there is Broadway to give its lessons, and the glaring celebrity of Delmonico's, and Sherry's, too; serge skirts at Lord and Taylor, lights on Plaza Square, and dinner for $1.50, rooms set apart for poker, casinos, barbershops, advertisement billboards, Wooster Street, a half pound of liver and bacon for fifteen cents, chorus girls, soldiers on the street, a strike, significant in the plot. And, of course, the Bowery and Potter's Field for Hurstwood. Carrie at the end will rock in her chair in the Waldorf, the golden monument of the period, and try to read *Père Goriot,* urged upon her by an ever-upward Ralph Marvell sort.

The plebeian "tinsel and shine" of Carrie's destiny and the bankrupt disaster of Hurstwood are not Edith Wharton's world, nor must it have been so. Still, she works with her own tinsel and is a recorder of dreams much less true to the city, as history, than those of Sister Carrie. Density of experience is lacking and not, we gather, lamented. In her novels, Manhattan is nameless, bare as a field, stripped of its byways, its fanciful, fabricated, overwhelming reality, its hugely imposing and unalterable alienation from the rest of the country—the glitter of its beginning and enduring modernity as a world city.

(1988)

Henry James:

On Washington Square

The James family came from New York State, the father having been born in Albany. Whether they are New Yorkers in the sense of the city is not altogether certain since they fled it early and did not like it much when they came back from time to time. Still the city, its streets, its fluid, inconstant, nerve-wrung landscape, had a claim upon Henry's imagination, even if the neglectful civic powers did not properly return the claim.

In any case, Henry James was born in New York City in 1843, in a house on 21 Washington Place, a street adjacent to Washington Square, itself a small park announcing the end of lower Fifth Avenue and adorned by an ambitious bit of architecture that James would describe as "the lamentable little Arch of Triumph which bestrides these beginnings of Washington-Square—lamentable because of its poor and lonely and unsupported and unaffiliated state." That was in 1904, when the sixty-one-year-old author returned from abroad to write *The American Scene,* his prodigious impressions of his homeland from New England to Palm Beach, impressions fresh, he hoped, as those of a curious stranger but still "as acute as an initiated native."

He would, of course, return to Fifth Avenue and to Washington Place. There, he found what he called a "snub." The birthplace of 21 Washington Place had been "ruthlessly suppressed" in one of those early convulsive seizures of destruction New York City to this day does not see as a defect in the municipal nervous system so much as an explosive, rather pagan, celebration of the gods of engineering and speculation. James, viewing the "amputation" of the birthplace, is led to confess that he had somehow imagined on Washington Place "a commemorative mural tablet—one of those frontal records of birth, sojourn, or death, under a celebrated name." This is an affecting aside of family and personal pride, a controlled twitch of chagrin, from which he retreats by observing the supreme invisibility of a plaque, acknowledging some long-gone worthy, placed on an apartment door in a fifty-story building, one of the "divided spaces" that were to be the principal habitations in the city.

—

The novel *Washington Square*, published in 1880, when James was thirty-seven years old, is an early work, at least early in style and in the untroubled presentation of its strong and thoroughly lucid plot. The novel is not strikingly under the domination of its place-name, but we note that the author allows himself a moment of autobiographical diversion, an insertion more or less of his private relation to the title:

> I know not whether it is owing to the tenderness of early association, but this portion of New York appears to many persons the most delectable. It has a kind of established repose which is not of frequent occurrence in other quarters of the long, shrill city; it has a riper, richer, more honorable look . . . the look of having had something of a social history . . . It was here that your grandmother lived, in venerable solitude . . . It was here that you took your first walks abroad, following the nursery-maid with unequal step and sniffing up the strange odour of the ailantus-tree which at that time formed the principal umbrage of the square.

In the opening pages of the novel, Dr. Sloper has set himself up in a new house on Washington Square. The doctor is a credible, highly interesting man of the professional class who has achieved the status accruing to the serious practice of medicine. He is busy, successful, intelligent, witty—an engaging figure on the city scene, and while learned in the medical arts he is not "uncomfortable," by which it is meant that Dr. Sloper is one of those popular physicians whose personal attractiveness will somehow soothe the tortures of treatment. He has a well-to-do clientele and is passed by referral from one "good family" to another in the way that was usual before the age of intense specialization.

The doctor has moved to Washington Square from a house near City Hall, a part of the city being turned into offices and other structures of business. In moving uptown, he is following the direction of residential preference in the early 1880s—one of the details of metropolitan dynamics that interested "old New Yorkers" such as James and Edith Wharton. With a rather vagrant historicism, these authors like to follow, in a mood of amusement, the displacements of fashion as they try to place their characters on the city map. Thus, we are told that the doctor's dead wife had been "one of the pretty girls of the small but promising capital which clustered around the Battery and overlooked the Bay, and of which the uppermost boundary was indicated by the grassy waysides of Canal Street." The doctor has now made his own move uptown, but his drama is not residential; it is familial, an intense battle, almost military, of strategy, retreat, and attack, fought with his daughter, Catherine Sloper.

The doctor is in his fifties, and, while not a man to offer futile protests against the devastations of fate, he has endured two painful wounds, or perhaps we should say three. He lost a treasured son at the age of three and then lost a much-loved wife—a beautiful woman with a fortune, social standing, and every domestic charm—lost her at the birth of a second child, "an infant of a sex which rendered the poor child, to the doctor's sense, an inadequate substitute for his lamented first-born, of whom he had promised himself to make an admirable man."

His was a genuine grief, with the added gall of a professional frustration in having been unable to ensure the survival of his family. But there is the surviving daughter, Catherine, now grown into a robust, rosily—rather too rosily—healthy young woman. Facing this last, lone Sloper, the doctor can assure himself that "such as she was, he at least need have no fear of losing her." The "such as she was" is the plot of *Washington Square:* the destiny of the daughter and the father's tone in his relations with her.

The beginning pages are written in a comedy-of-manners style, and each turn is amusing, calmly and confidently expert. Such a style will command, with its measured cadences and fine tuning, a bit of benign condescension toward the cast and toward the friendly modesty of the New York social landscape in the first half of the nineteenth century. Thus, it is said of the doctor, "He was what you call a scholarly doctor, and yet there was nothing abstract in his remedies—he always ordered you to take something."

Washington Square was written after James made his literary and social "Conquest of London," as Leon Edel phrases it in the title of the second volume of his James biography. The author had breakfasted with Turgenev, met Tennyson, Browning and Gladstone, visited the great country houses, and indeed, as a cosmopolitan, wrote most of *Washington Square* in Paris. It is a perfect novel of immense refinement and interest, and one feels the execution gave James little trouble— that is, if one keeps in mind the breathless deliberations of the fictions that were to follow. Of course, the moral and psychological insinuations of this early work are not finally so self-evident as they appear to be on the lucid pages.

At the time James was devoting himself to the portrait of Catherine Sloper leading her life in her father's "modern, wide-fronted" house on lower Fifth Avenue, he was already thinking of the more challenging American girl, Isabel Archer, and the complex duplicities of *The Portrait of a Lady,* published soon after. In any case, when he was gathering the New York edition of his novels, which began to appear in 1907, he unaccountably excluded *Washington Square.* Perhaps it seemed to him a small, provincial tale after he had sent heiresses to Europe to test themselves and their American dollars on the ferocious competitions of the international scene. The American girls in the "large" novels are weighted with nuance and with the fictional responsibility to live up to their rather inchoate but grand attributions. Catherine, housebound in New York and incurious about the great world beyond, may have appeared a sort of vacation, one that allowed James a wonderfully relaxed compositional tone when compared with that of *The Wings of the Dove* or *The Golden Bowl.*

Catherine Sloper is an heiress but not a beguiling "heiress of the ages"; she is heir only to money. Indeed, the early descriptions of Catherine are composed with such a boldly discounting eye, such intrepid divestment, that the reader feels a wince of discomfort. Catherine is large and homely, but, at the beginning, a contented, virtuous girl of her class. She is guileless, affectionate, docile, and obedient. She has a "plain, dull, gentle countenance," and, although drastically without coquetry, she wishes to please, most of all to please her father. "She was not quick with her book, nor, indeed, with anything else." Along the way of depiction, James himself seems to draw back from the distance imposed by the manner of composition. If he does not quite retreat, we can say he takes a short little step to the side before persevering to write, "though it is an awkward confession to make about one's heroine, I must add that she was something of a glutton."

And there are woeful brush strokes ahead: Catherine's clothes, her "lively taste for dress." This "taste" causes her father to "fairly grimace, in private, to think that a child of his should be both ugly and overdressed." There is to be the merciless comedy of the "red satin gown trimmed with gold fringe" into which Catherine will more or less pour herself for an evening party at which her cousin's engagement is to be announced. There, in the awful red dress she will meet her fate, the fortune hunter Morris Townsend, meet that fate in the company of her other fate, her adored, "ironical" father.

So Catherine will meet Morris Townsend—extraordinarily handsome, "beautiful," she calls him—a New Yorker who has been knocking about the world rather than staying at home to sell bonds or to enter the law. In his knocking, he has spent his small inheritance and seems to have spent his friends and made himself unwelcome. Back in his native city, he claims to be looking about for something to do; meanwhile, he is staying with his sister—in fact living on his sister, who is in very reduced circumstances as a widow with five children. A sordid record with a few travel stickers from European hotels. Townsend is a distant connection of the young man Catherine's cousin is to marry. At the party, he goes for Catherine's attention with the watchful concentration of a sportsman waiting for the game to fly in the range of the gun.

Catherine, surprised by joy, as it were, is overwhelmed, hard hit with the rustic fluster of her inexperience. She will be joined by the tirelessly articulating duenna, Mrs. Penniman, Dr. Sloper's widowed sister, who lives in the motherless house and acts as a sort of chaperone and companion for the girl. Mrs. Penniman completes the quartet of the action, her addition to the stage being a fluff-filled swoon of sentimentality and a very intrusive meddling. In the support of Townsend's dubious campaign, Aunt Penniman will show herself as insistent, canny, and devious, as if she were awaiting a broker's fee.

With the unexpected courtship of Catherine, the tone changes; we are not, after all, to witness a deft seduction in the Restoration mode but a tangle of coldness, calculation, and conflicting motive, all at Catherine's expense. If the result is not quite a tragedy, it is a conclusion of most serious and lasting heartbreak. Perhaps in terms of fictional art, James was wise to give Catherine the works: her dismaying vital statistics, her dumpiness, and her baffled maneuvering will set her up like one of those dolls at the country fair, ready to be idly knocked down for a prize. Still, she, all unstylish blushes and innocent gratitude, will profoundly solicit the sympathy of the reader as a heroine from real life, one not so remote from readers of both sexes, each of whom will have some defects in the lottery of romance. (I would not go as far as Leon Edel and claim that Catherine is "the image of himself [James] as victim of his brother's—and America's—failure to understand his feelings." The sibling rivalry Edel greatly favors as the psychological burden and ultimate creative spur of Henry's triumphant life—the wound and the bow—will even find William James lurking in the shadow of Dr. Sloper.)

Dr. Sloper, the most interesting and complicated character in the novel, is perhaps villainous in his genial, confident presence in the family and his also genial, confident intrusions into the love affair. He is a father who will ask when Catherine appears in the disastrous red satin dress, "Is it possible that this magnificent person is my child?" Told of Townsend's pursuit, he will puff on a cigar and reply, "He is in love with this regal creature, then?" Because the doctor is smart and observant himself, we are not surprised to learn that he thinks Catherine "as intelligent as a bundle of shawls." The "ironical" accent in the doctor's intercourse with his daughter is flamboyant, if lightly tossed about. One feels he enjoys the exercise of this established mode of communication; by it, he has turned a flaw of character, the absence of paternal propriety, into a manner, or a mannerism.

The plot of *Washington Square* is simple in its framing. Time is running out for Morris Townsend, and he must find someplace to land. Before meeting Catherine, he has obviously known of her inheritance from her mother, some ten thousand a year, and can figure out for himself her expectations upon the death of her father. So he makes his way to the side of the pleasant, wallflowerish Catherine. And, doing so, he picks up the admiration, if merely as an exciting diversion, of Aunt Penniman. The widowed chaperone's conspiracy on his behalf is immediate, like the burglar charming the housemaid over the fence and coming away with the key to the kitchen door. Visits to the house on Washington Square take place, and Catherine quickly falls into a kind of alarmed love.

Townsend means to marry Catherine, but he is quick to sense the impediment of Dr. Sloper, whom he is not foolish enough to imagine an easy conquest. And Sloper is, as feared, not in the least attracted to Townsend. The doctor says, "He is not what I call a gentleman. He has not the soul of one. He is extremely insinuating; but it's a vulgar nature. I saw through it in a minute. He is altogether too familiar—I hate familiarity."

Townsend will naturally decide that the doctor finds him unsuitable only on the ground of his poverty. He understands the doctor's power but not the fact that this particular father is the last person to imagine an adventurer like Townsend captivated by the unqualified Catherine. Shallowness, idleness, and insincerity, not poverty, are the grounds of Dr. Sloper's contempt:

> The fact that Morris Townsend was poor—was not of necessity against him; the doctor had never made up his mind that his daughter should marry a rich man. The fortune she would inherit struck him as a very sufficient provision for two reasonable persons, and if a penniless swain who could give a good account of himself should enter the lists, he should be judged quite upon his personal merits.

The doctor wishes Catherine to be loved for her moral worth—he gives her that virtue, if not much else.

Dr. Sloper's caustic, teasing banter with his daughter offends but does not amount to inattention; after Catherine has announced her engagement, he can be said to be very much on the case. He will make his way over to Second Avenue to call upon Mrs. Montgomery, the sister with whom the suitor is living. This, the most brilliant scene in the novel, provides a formal advancement of the plot and an advancement of the subtleties in the disposition of James's New York City physician. He has married a rich woman, and we gather he himself is of a respectable if not glittering family, but he is self-created and not a snob.

He goes downtown on Second Avenue, a swerve to the east, an unpromising direction at that time. Basil Ransom in *The Bostonians* lived as an impecunious young lawyer from the defeated South on that outré avenue, lived in close acquaintance with the "fantastic skeleton of the Elevated Railway, overhanging the transverse longitudinal street, which it darkened and smothered with the immeasurable spinal column and myriad clutching paws of an antediluvian monster." Excursions into the slushy, unreclaimed portions of Manhattan had for James the fearful, if beckoning, aspect of an assignation. In the New York City sections of *The American Scene,* we experience alarm for his palpitating heart as he goes—portly, sensitive, alert gentleman with a walking stick—into the immigrant's New Jerusalem, into Little Italy, and visits the portentous hordes with their bundles pouring forth from Ellis Island. In *Washington Square,* Mrs. Penniman, heavily veiled, embarks upon a perilous journey to an "oyster saloon in the Seventh Avenue, kept by a negro," in order to consummate another of her fatuous, capriciously encouraging interviews with Morris Townsend. But then that lady has had some experience of the outside of things, since we have been told that she accepted her brother's invitation to live in Washington Square with "the alacrity of a woman who had spent ten years of her married life in the town of Poughkeepsie."

So the doctor will venture downtown to Second Avenue, where he will observe with approval Mrs. Montgomery's neat little house of red brick and, inside, the tidy, if pitiable, efforts at decoration—"desultory foliage of tissue paper, with clusters of glass drops," and so on. He notes the cast-iron stove "smelling strongly of varnish" and finds the widowed lady to be "a brave little person," to whom he gave "his esteem as soon as he had looked at her."

The visit is crucial in every sense. The doctor states, without qualification, that Catherine will have her ten thousand a year, but if she marries Townsend, "I shall leave every penny of my own fortune, earned in the laborious exercise of my profession, to public institutions." The visit, in a guarded way, also reveals that Mrs. Montgomery has been giving money, of which she has little, to her brother, who takes it since he has none. In the end, the poor sister, having in the conversation formed an idea of the good nature and vulnerability of Catherine, says, "Don't let her marry him!"

Catherine, incurably smitten, would marry without her father's consent, painful as the possibility might be. This immovable passion and defiance are most interesting to the doctor. " 'By Jove,' he said to himself, 'I believe she will stick—I believe she will stick!' " And so she does, even after a year abroad, the old family deprogramming hope, a year of misery and intellectual waste since she "failed to gather animation from the mountains of Switzerland or the mountains of Italy." She does not relent, and Townsend is waiting, having, with the hospitality of Mrs. Penniman, made himself at home in the house on Washington Square, smoking the doctor's cigars, sitting by the fire, and listening to the aunt's prediction that Catherine will in the end get her father's fortune.

When she returns, Townsend is still idly trying to discount the possibility of disinheritance; thus, a remarkable dialogue between the two young people takes place, beginning with Catherine:

> "We must ask no favours of him—we must ask nothing more. He won't relent, and nothing good will come of it. I know it now—I have a very good reason."
> "And pray what is your reason?"
> She hesitated to bring it out, but at last it came.
> "He is not very fond of me!"
> "Oh, bother!" cried Morris, angrily.

Townsend ungraciously, surreptitiously, takes his leave, and that is the story.

The plot, among the novels of James, is an open one of a simple heart ruthlessly manipulated, of trust and goodwill dishonored. The central drama is between Catherine and her father, a drama of serious moral questions beyond the struggle of their opposing wills. There is not much questioning to be done on behalf of Morris Townsend, a young man of every conceivable vanity, a natural squanderer of money, friendships, family, anything at hand.

One of the footnotes James has placed in the seduction of Catherine's money is that Townsend, although destitute, puts a remarkably high value upon himself. When Catherine announces she will defy her father and is ready to flee the house with her "lover," she can rightly wonder why her ten thousand should not be sufficient. The repudiation of this income because it will not be augmented at her father's death is an insult of the most severe kind—and another folly committed by the conceited squanderer who imagines he can do better, whether by some vague plans for business or by way of a woman with a greater fortune.

Money in exchange for love is the dilemma of many of the heroines in James's novels. And a most curious way he has with it. Isabel Archer in *The Portrait of a Lady* is, by a tangled and not altogether credible route, willed seventy thousand pounds. She is given the money so that she can be free, so that she can achieve her best self, which, as it turns out, is to make her the object of fortune hunters, just as the rich Milly Theale in *The Wings of the Dove* will be. Love, or the appearance of it, is to be paid for by American money, paid in cash in a transcontinental intrigue that is dark and vastly complicated.

Catherine has been denied beauty, gaiety, all the romantic mystery and glamour of the heiresses abroad. James took the dare of the negative. Catherine is as alone as an animal in a field. No Lord Warburton is seeking her hand as she decides to choose another; no lively young female friend attends her wandering; and if her response is reckless, as it is, the recklessness comes not from her own gift for desperate decision but from credulity and isolation.

The troubling aspect of the doctor's destruction of Catherine's romance lies in the fact that he intrigues with more brio than we can countenance. On the other hand, does the reader wish Catherine to succeed in marrying Townsend? The best that can be said for the match is that the contract of life should guarantee the right to make one's own mistakes. James had thought deeply about the need to "experience," to take the dare, to live, and to him, sedentary as a monument, to live meant personal experience, to risk love. Catherine does "stick," as her father discovers with astonishment.

She meets "The Beast in the Jungle":

> To have to meet, to face, to see suddenly break out in my life; possibly destroying all further consciousness, possibly annihilating me; ... striking at the root of all my world and leaving me to the consequences, however they shape themselves.

We are not sure how greatly Catherine understands consequence at the time of her defiance, but she comes to understand humiliation and heartbreak. When a shabby, shopworn Townsend returns years later to ask for friendship, her answer is no. "You treated me too badly. I felt it very much; I felt it for years."

Washington Square is a perfectly balanced novel, narrow in its focus, rather claustrophobic, yet moving along with a speed suitable to the importunate demands of Morris Townsend in the matter of "settling" himself. In *The Notebooks,* James records the novel's origin in a story he heard from his friend the actress Mrs. Fanny Kemble. She told of her own handsome, penniless, selfish brother's pursuit of a "dull, plain, common-place girl, only daughter of the Master of King's Coll., Cambridge, who had a handsome private fortune (£4000 a year)." She was of that "slow, sober, dutiful nature that an impression once made upon her, was made for life." Her father disapproved of the engagement and vowed she would not get a penny of his money if she married. The young man, like Townsend, for a time thought the father could be brought around, but when it was clear there was to be no remission of the disinheritance, the suitor made a rapid retreat, leaving the girl desolated and never to marry. We note that here, too, there is a Mrs. Montgomery in the wings and that, when asked for advice by the unfortunately enamored young woman, she "advised the young girl by *no means* to marry her brother."

It was all there, the structure, the actors to be set down in New York on Washington Square. But James, assembling the bricks and mortar of the action, gradually found Catherine Sloper deeply entrenched on the inside, rather than the witty outside, of his imagination. Magically, he paces through each pause in her articulation, each artless question, each accumulation of baffled emotion, and thus Catherine comes to attract, profoundly. Her painful yet original dimensions come through to us slowly, as if in a haze, in contrast, for instance, to Isabel Archer's claims, rich and brilliant as they are, which begin by assertion: "You wished a while ago to see my idea of an interesting woman. There it is!"

Catherine is just raw feeling itself and literalness. Humbly, she tries to make her way through a crushing thicket of casual remarks, hoping to discover a literalness equal to her own and important to her understanding of her situation. "Did *he* say that?" she will ask Mrs. Penniman, who is busily reporting some putative exchange with Townsend. And, "Did *he* tell you to say these things to me?" By the force of her singular concentration in the midst of the offhand and careless, she achieves a sort of personal, moral independence and certainly the dignity of the stubbornness and fidelity of her feelings.

And James was to take the father, merely a presence, an instrument, in the anecdote from which the plot derived, and create Dr. Sloper, a grand perplexity, a puzzle of disappointment and self-assurance. He is accustomed to control and boldly exercises it, but he dashes against a daunting sheet of rock: Catherine's feelings. The doctor is perhaps finally to be seen as Catherine's personal protector against certain disaster, but he is a protector of such provoking lapses and gaps that we cannot wish him victory. In the end, his victory, if that is what it is, does not rescue Catherine. Only Morris Townsend's abandonment can accomplish her salvation, if that is what is accomplished.

In any case, Catherine has lived, has known the assault of love. And when she says of her father, "He is not very fond of me," she has bitten of the fruit of knowledge, experienced the classical recognition moment and the power of enlightenment. Perhaps we can say that Catherine will become as clever as her father and can inflict upon him the fiercest vexation, which will amount to his genuine and lasting distress. Long after the romance with Townsend has been devastated beyond renewal, her father will still wish her to promise that she will not, at his death, marry the young man. Her answer: "I cannot promise that, Father."

The matter of the promise beyond the grave reveals Dr. Sloper's utter failure to understand where his daughter has been and where she is. As a final stroke of perverse underestimation, he reduces her portion in his will and writes: "She is amply provided for from her mother's side; . . . her fortune is already more than sufficient to attract those unscrupulous adventurers whom she has given me reason to believe that she persists in regarding as an interesting class." Catherine's comment about the punitive last testament is: "I like it very much. Only I wish it had been expressed a little differently." A proper burial for the interesting, ironical New York City physician.

(1990)

Americans Abroad

THE GENIUS OF MARGARET FULLER

So passed away the loftiest, bravest soul that has yet irradiated the form of an American woman: Thus wrote the editor Horace Greeley. Yet before this noble soul, Margaret Fuller, passed away, many would have forgone *irradiated* in preference for *irritated*. She was brave and lofty, and she did irradiate and also irritate, irritate herself especially with strained nerves, fantastical exertions, discomforts large and small.

Margaret Fuller, a New England creation, commemorated in Mount Auburn Cemetery in Cambridge in impressive blocks of stone, was born in the wrong place, the place thought to be the only right one for an American intellectual in the nineteenth century. That is, she was born in Cambridgeport, Massachusetts, around Harvard, Boston, Concord, and all the rest. She sprang out of the head of all the Zeuses about: her father Timothy Fuller, Emerson, Goethe. The head being the protesting organ it is, she suffered life-long from migraine headaches, and even as a young girl left on the scene more than a bit of the fatigue and sense of pounding insistence thought to be the dispensation of a learned woman. There were many enlightened and cultivated women about, but she was the only seriously learned one in her circle, perhaps in the country.

As a life, a biography, hers is the most dramatic, the most adventuring of all the "flowerings." Her life was strikingly split into two parts by experience and ended by tragedy. Staying at home in Concord and Boston, she might have ended as comedy.

She was born into an incestuous air, this world that provided as a wife the sister of one's best friend, as a husband, the son of a family connection. Hawthorne married Sophia Peabody; Emerson married Ellen Tucker; Henry Adams married Marian Hooper, the daughter of Dr. Hooper and a Sturgis on the maternal side. This sexual handiness, as it were, the prudent over-the-fence alliances, narrowed experience in Margaret Fuller's circle but seemed to produce around Boston and Concord a domestic placidity that encouraged the high notes of Transcendentalism, a local philosophical blending, an indefinable idealism of the divinity within humanity, union with nature, the "eternal One." Henry Adams, thinking of Emerson and pondering his own non-Boston experience of the nation as a whole, thought all this *naïf.*

(It is almost elevating to learn from a discreet footnote here and there that Clarence King, the distinguished geologist and Adams's great friend in *The Education of Henry Adams,* was the common-law husband of a New York black woman and the father of a son by her. King himself was from Newport, Rhode Island, and a graduate of Yale rather than Harvard; perhaps this climate slightly to the south had an effect upon this far-flinging, if that is what it was. Allowing for the condescension of "common-law," King apparently wished to do right and to honor the union. Upon his death, Mrs. King brought a lawsuit to secure for her son the trust fund assured her in King's letters. She lost, defeated by the WASPs and their mastery of *per stirpes.*)

Margaret Fuller did not attract the passion for neighborly unions. Indeed, one might say her only true American lover was Professor Perry Miller of Harvard, born more than a century later. Margaret Fuller herself was born in 1810 and was thus seven years younger than Emerson. She was the daughter of Timothy Fuller, a scholarly man, graduate of Harvard, representative in Congress from Massachusetts, and later a practicing lawyer. His education of his daughter began early. Like John Stuart Mill, she was put in the stocks, and one of her finest pieces of writing has to do with the memory of her father's wish to make her "heir to all he knew."

Thus I had tasks given me, as many and various as the hours would allow, and on subjects beyond my age; with the disadvantage of reciting to him in the evening, after he returned from his office. . . . I was often kept up till very late; and as he was a severe teacher, both from his habits of mind and his ambition for me, my feelings were kept on the stretch till the recitations were over. Thus frequently, I was sent to bed several hours too late, with nerves unnaturally stimulated. The consequence was a premature development of the brain, that made me a "youthful prodigy" by day, and by night a victim of spectral illusions, nightmare and somnambulism, which at the time prevented the harmonious development of my bodily powers and checked my growth, while, later, they induced continual headaches, weakness, and nervous affections, of all kinds. As these again reacted on the brain, giving undue force to every thought and every feeling, there was finally produced a state of being both too active and too intense, which wasted my constitution, and will bring me,—even although I have learned to understand and regulate my now morbid temperament,—to a premature grave.

Overwork, as she names it. Hysteria and the nightmares, whatever torments remembered, the result was a storehouse of knowledge and certainly an identity, even a vanity. Long after her father subsided as a tutor, she spent her youth in frantic application, reading, as Emerson wrote, "at a rate like Gibbon's." Thomas Wentworth Higginson's biography has her, at the age of fifteen, up at five, with the hours laid out: one for the piano, one for Sismondi's *European Literature* in French; then Brown's philosophy, then a lesson in Greek; in the evening, two hours reading in Italian, a bit of walking, more piano, and retiring at eleven to write in her diary.

Thus, we have the forced bud continually self-forced, nerve-wrung, eccentric, and, as we might expect, proud of her learning, aggressive in conversation, tremendously eager for friends, given to crushes, and yet with it all a devoted daughter. Timothy Fuller died suddenly, leaving the family in a bad way. At this moment, Margaret had planned to accompany the Farrar family to Europe. But she gave it up and remained at home to help in the support of her brothers and sisters. This meant teaching. First, a spell at the Temple School, Bronson Alcott's leafy squirrel house of learning; and then a real position for two years in Providence, whence in a letter to Emerson she made one of her many confident pronouncements that were to be long remembered and to decorate her memory in the manner of a bit of local scandal: "I see no divine person; I myself am more divine than any I see—I think that is enough to say about them." After two years, she returned to Boston to make her way as a writer, beginning with a translation of Eckermann's *Conversations with Goethe*.

From the first, she was a figure, a star, a somewhat blinding one, constantly talked about as a sight to be taken in, like Bronson Alcott's unworldliness and Thoreau's recalcitrance. Conversation was her love and even if some were fearful in approach because of the intrepid "truthfulness" of her social exchanges ("Stand from under!" Emerson cautioned himself), she had the trait of all conversationalists: an immense availability. She liked to visit and sometimes stayed too long. One of the saddest periods of her youth came after her father's decision to retire from the Boston scene and to take his family to the smaller village of Groton, thus removing his daughter from the company of the young men and professors around Harvard with their spiritual and intellectual interests.*

Her mission was self-culture, as one memorialist phrased it. And always the wish to uplift others, friends, anyone. She practiced a kind of hot Transcendentalism alongside Emerson's cooler sort. She could be found holding an arm, gazing into eyes, insisting upon inspiration, sublimity, and *grow, grow, grow*.

She was very noticeable to the men around Harvard, some of whom she had known earlier at a private academy where she, although a female, was allowed at fifteen to go for special study in Greek recitation. There was her mind to startle and also her appearance, her black cloak, and many odd features of the head, not always easy to describe.

The Transcendentalist Frederic Hedge, her friend from his Harvard days: "No pretension to beauty then or at any time, her face was one that attracted, that awakened a lively interest."

Emerson: "nothing prepossessing. Her extreme plainness—a trick of incessantly opening and shutting her eyelids—the nasal tone of her voice—all repelled; and I said to myself, we shall never get far."

---

* It was from Bell Gale Chevigny's book, *Margaret Fuller: The Woman and the Myth*, with its masterly organization of many then-unpublished letters, along with the comments of contemporaries, that I came first to understand the complexity of Margaret Fuller and her situation.

Poe worried about her upper lip, which, "as if impelled by the action of involuntary muscles, habitually uplifts itself, conveying the impression of a sneer."

William Henry Channing on the matter of her neck found its curve "swan-like when she was sweet and thoughtful, but when she was scornful or indignant it contracted, and made swift turns, like a bird of prey."

J. R. Lowell: "a pythoness."

Oliver Wendell Holmes: "ophidian."

The concentration upon appearance is somewhat overwrought among those who took beauty if it arrived on the doorstep and did without if a fine and useful character prevailed. Emerson's first wife, Ellen Tucker, has been described as a "remarkable beauty"; Ellen Fuller, Margaret's younger sister, was a romantic charmer who married the romantic, quite unsteady, charmer Ellery Channing. Henry Adams, writing about his engagement to "Clover" Hooper, said, "She is certainly not handsome; nor would she be quite called plain, I think."

So, Margaret Fuller was homely, even distracting in mannerisms, but she charmed by an overwhelming responsiveness and curiosity and had many women friends from whom she received confidences and to whom she gladly gave advice. Emerson, in his essay after her death, wrote that she wore her friends "like a necklace of diamonds around her neck" and that "her friendships, as a girl with girls, as a woman with women, were not unmingled with passion, and had passages of romantic sacrifice and ecstatic fusion."

Be that as it may, it was her habit throughout her years in America to presume on male friendships, pushing them to intentions that were not forthcoming, with a result very distressing to her spirits. She is so often not quite in touch, confused perhaps by the dramas of friendship, a sort of insufficiency in nuance, missing signals. Soul mates appeared—or so it seemed—but her "soul" was too soon declarative and consuming.

First, her cousin George Davis is said to have "thwarted her." Then a true falling in love with a member of her circle and a close friend, Samuel Ward: "No, I do not distrust you, so lately have you spoken the words of friendship. You would not be so irreverent as to dare to tamper with a nature like mine, you could not treat so generous a person with levity . . . if you love me as I deserve to be loved, you cannot dispense with seeing me . . . J'attendrai." Still, the nestlike scene, and it turned out that Samuel Ward, a close friend, was going to marry another close friend of his and also a close friend of Margaret Fuller's— Anna Barker. Later in New York she was to experience the painful debacle of her "romantic" connection with a man named James Nathan.

Emerson and Margaret Fuller formed a complicated alliance and one of the most interesting friendships between a man and a woman in American literature. Before their meeting and while Emerson was still a clergyman, she was somewhat doubtful of fame in the pulpit. "It is so easy for a cultivated mind to excite itself with that tone." On the other hand, she was eager to show him her translation of Goethe's drama *Tasso.* They met in 1835, and she first visited Emerson in Concord in 1836. "His influence has been more beneficial to me than that of any American, and from him I first learned what is meant by an inward light."

Emerson found her, at the age of twenty-six, well read in French, Italian, and German literature but needy in the matter of English literature. He pressed upon her the works of Chaucer, Ben Jonson, Herbert, Sir Thomas Browne, and others. The absence of English fiction represents Emerson's indifference to the form as perhaps too much shackled to event and casual life. Of Dickens he wrote: "London tracts . . . local and temporary in his tints and style, and local in his aims."

Margaret Fuller "adored" Mme. de Staël and was often called the "American Corinne" because of her dramatic and romantic presentation of herself. She came to forgive George Sand for the laxness of her life and greatly admired her and her work. But what would she have thought of the refined obscenities of *Clarissa?* Of *Tom Jones* or *Tristram Shandy?* The mixed and complex English fictional tradition cannot be what Emerson meant when, in "The American Scholar," he called for "the meal in the firkin; the milk in the pan; the ballad in the street; the news of the boat; the glance of the eye; the form and gait of the body," but where was one to find the expression of "the common and the low" if not in English fiction? It is the development of Margaret Fuller's style—not to be laid at the door of Emerson—that suffered from an absence of dogs and cats and rude particulars and the humorous. She did not have Emerson's wit, his rapid concentration of an image, a quick short sentence. She told him that he used too many aphorisms, and he said that if he used too many, she used too few.

Her letters are a heat of energy, warmth of friendship, family love, and family duty, a blazing need to communicate, no matter the aching head and midnight coming on. In the New England period, there is also a wrenching struggle with nature, the woods, sunsets, moonlights. "The incommunicable trees begin to persuade us to live with them, and quit our life of solemn trifles." Emerson: "What is a farm but a mute gospel?"

The sweetness of the Massachusetts countryside, the little villages, the fields and woods and streams. This is what they had—literary genius in a sort of retirement; rustication, snowy nights and early flowers. The great writer Thoreau redeemed the nature-writing workshop in Concord with his daunting struggle in letters and notebooks to catch the kiss of a moonbeam and honor the hoot of a barn owl. It was Thoreau's genius to carry landscape and weather as far as they could go.

Hawthorne in his notebooks fought with the whortleberry bush and the gleam from the lighthouse at Marblehead. "And its light looked very singularly, mingling with the growing daylight. It was not light, the moonshine, brightening as the evening twilight deepens; for now it threw its radiance over the landscape, the green and other tints of which were displayed by daylight, whereas at evening all those tints are obscured." And so on, with here and there a hit: the neighbor's ox who looked very much like Daniel Webster.

Margaret Fuller attempted, early, a composition on the passion-flower and would sometimes advise one to see a certain sunset at *exactly a quarter to six*. A great deal of moonlight occupies her pen. Emerson, in his memoir, is rather contemptuous of her naturing, even though he himself may be said to have led the charge for these confrontations.

> Margaret's love of beauty made her, of course, a votary of nature, but rather for pleasurable excitement than with a deep poetic feeling. Her imperfect vision and her bad health were serious impediments to intimacy with woods and rivers. She never paid—and it is a little remarkable—any attention to natural sciences. She neither botanized, nor geologized, nor dissected.

What was not known then, and certainly not known to herself, was that her nature was profoundly urban and her talent, in the end, was for sightseeing, meeting people, for issues; her gifts as a writer were for a superior journalism. Everything that happened, in her head, in her reading, in her travels, was there to be used. In 1843, she made a journey to the western part of the country, and the next year her first original book was published, *Summer on the Lakes.* She sees a lot, thinks about the Indians, the settlers, Chicago, immigrants, and forswears a descriptive account of Niagara Falls. "Yet I, like others, have little to say, where the spectacle is for once great enough to fill the whole life and supersede thought, giving us only its presence. . . . We have been here eight days, and I am quite willing to depart. So great a sight soon satisfies, making us content with itself, and with what is less than itself."

In Concord, visiting the Emerson house, the second Mrs. Emerson— not a beauty like Ellen, who died young of tuberculosis—experiences the discomforts arising from the presence of a husband-adorer and disciple in the house, waiting for him to be free to inspire, to read his poems aloud, to take a nature walk. Hurt feelings, tears; Mrs. E. asks Margaret to take a walk with her one evening and M. answers that she cannot because she is going to walk with Mr. E. That sort of thing.

And the inevitable "friendship" discussions with Emerson, heavy with feeling on Margaret Fuller's side. She wants some sort of exclusiveness, recognition: "I am like some poor traveller of the desert, who saw, at early morning, a distant palm, and toiled all day to reach it"— followed by a transparent Persian fable, which Emerson pretends not to understand. And, another letter,

I have felt the impossibility of meeting far more than you; so much, that if you ever know me well, you will feel that the fact of my abiding by you thus far, affords a strong proof that we are to be much to one another. . . . How often have I left you despairing and forlorn. This light will never understand my fire.

Emerson in his memoir does not avoid analysis of this disconcerting appeal for more, more.

Our moods were very different; and I remember, that, at the very time when I, slow and cold, had come fully to admire her genius, and was congratulating myself on the solid good understanding that subsisted between us, I was surprised at hearing it taxed by her with superficial-ity and halfness. She stigmatised our friendship as commercial. It seems her magnanimity was not met.

Together they began *The Dial* in 1840, with Margaret Fuller as the editor for two years. It was a Transcendentalist forum, "to lift men to a higher platform." Criticism, it was felt, would be most useful to the soul of the country, and, not to be forgotten, criticism is what the group was able to compose and thus to celebrate Genius and the Transcendental calling.

Fuller offered an essay on Goethe, the supreme genius, a defense against accusations of immortality and egotism. Her essay is intense and rather more parochial than it need be, except for being addressed to an audience alarmed and distrustful. "Pardon him, World, that he was too worldly. Do not wonder, Heart, that he was so heartless. Believe, Soul, that one so true, as far as he went, must yet be initiated into the deeper mysteries of Soul."

Emerson thought the Goethe essay her best, and Professor Perry Miller views it as a moment in history. Here Margaret brashly defends *Werther* against the prevailing American opinion that it was a foul corrupter of youth; and she praises *The Elective Affinities,* which American men regarded as the nadir of sensual depravity. Viewed in this perspective, Margaret's essay is a basic document in the history of intellectual freedom in the United States.

The work on *The Dial* exhausted her, and Emerson assumed the editing for the next two of the magazine's four years. "I remember, after she had been compelled to relinquish the journal into my hands, my grateful wonder at the facility with which she assumed the preparation of laborious articles that might have daunted the most practised scribe."

———

Conversations. The famous gatherings in Boston in which Margaret Fuller led and instructed a number of well-bred women began in the rooms of Miss Elizabeth Peabody on West Street. The object was "to pass in review the departments of thought and knowledge, and endeavor to place them in due relation to one another in our mind." Since eloquence was the leader's gift, she had to do a good deal of orating to pinch the minds of her fellow explorers into speech. The account of one conversation that survives is a comedy, and perhaps that is why it survives. The topic was "What Is Life?" Pushed and prodded, a Miss C. replied, "It is to laugh, or cry, according to our organization."

"Good," said Fuller, "but not grave enough."

Another reply by Mrs. E., perhaps the second Mrs. Emerson, who was an attendant, " 'We live by the will of God, and the object of life is to submit,' and went on into Calvinism."

When pressed to give her own idea of what life is, M.F. began with "God as Spirit, Life, so full as to create and love eternally, and yet capable of pause."

The conversations were said to spread her fame about town. She dressed for them and assumed a sibylline manner quite extraordinary. Some thought she got the idea from Bronson Alcott's everlasting questioning and his Orphic Sayings. But what seems more likely is that the conversations were a sort of reduced, miniature, and homebound wish for a platform, and a platform such as Emerson had in his lectures in this hall and that, in little towns and cities. She, too, could speak on the great subjects, but Miss Peabody's parlor, excitable as it was in the hour before noon, with the wives of the great men, Mrs. Bancroft, Mrs. Child, Mrs. Parker, and various Misses looking on, was the only lyceum available.

The second part of Margaret Fuller's life was to last only six years, from 1844 until her death in 1850. Act 2 was overcrowded with incident after the pastoral, repetitive Act 1, which was book after book, the same friends, much talk, letters, reviews, and the management of *The Dial*. In spirit, it was a sort of treadmill of enthusiasms for Goethe, Beethoven, Michelangelo, Raphael, Mythology, the Classics, French socialism—all written down, somewhere. "Her pen was a nonconductor" merely signified her flat failure as a poet, which of course she had struggled with also. Emerson continued to think of her as a talker, a parlor orator, or even as a monologist "who seldom admitted others upon an equal ground with herself." She could also gossip, which frightened him. "The crackling of thorns under the pot."

In *The Dial*, she published "The Great Lawsuit—Man versus Men; Woman versus Women." The article was much expanded and elaborated into *Woman in the Nineteenth Century*, published in 1845. And then she left Boston for New York, thought at the time to be an outpost in the intellectual life. "The high priestess of Transcendentalism cut her ties with the provincial homeland," Perry Miller wrote.

"Let them [women] be sea-captains if they like." This offhand swat to seafaring Massachusetts, the China trade, the widow's walk at the top of the house, the codfish cake for breakfast, remains the best-known statement in Margaret Fuller's long, prolix defense of women. The work was completed in less than two months, during a vacation in a Hudson River town, and probably written without a library, except for the one in her head. It is a compendium of custom relating to women, ancient and modern opinion buried in poetry, literary allusion, and common observation. The index lists Elizabeth Barrett Browning, Dante, Desdemona, Petrarch, Plato, Spinoza, Swedenborg, Xenophon, and many others. The author herself appears in the disguise of a certain Miranda, well educated, taught honorable self-reliance from the cradle, privileged in learning and preparation for independence of thought; and not hindered by beauty from the development of talents and sense of self. "She was fortunate in a total absence of those charms which might have drawn to her bewildering flatteries, and in a strong electric nature, which repelled those who did not belong to her, and attracted those who did."

It is a bookish book, a fundamental document in the history of feminist thought. An intense, pleading tone, elevated, careful not to give offense, but determined. The strong and dignified women of literature and history—Iphigenia, Antigone, Britomart, the French Revolution's Madame Roland ("O Liberty, what crimes have been committed in thy name!")—appeal to her more than the powerful, devious Queen Elizabeth, "without magnanimity of any kind."

Margaret Fuller certainly knew Mary Wollstonecraft's *Vindication of the Rights of Women*. Here, she makes an unaccountable mistake, seeing Mary Wollstonecraft's marriage to the prodigious nitwit William Godwin as her best claim upon our attention: "a woman whose existence better proved the need for some new interpretation of woman's rights, than anything she wrote."

Mary Wollstonecraft's work is much more homely and practical, less rhetorical and less respectful—and more cynical about the world. She despises women brought together in boarding schools; too much giggling and lounging about in dirty undergarments. "Parental affection is, perhaps, the blindest modification of perverse self-love," and she asserts that the habit of overlooking the faults of one's parents inclines the child to overlook his own. "The two sexes mutually corrupt and improve each other."

Mary Wollstonecraft's worldliness may have offended Margaret

Fuller. She does not mention the *Vindication,* but points instead to Godwin's book in support of his wife. The omission indicates a distaste, just as distaste, conscious or not, might explain why Emerson in his cramped and complicated essay on Fuller, thought by some to be patronizing but in fact the most alive and brilliant words written about her, never mentions *Woman in the Nineteenth Century,* the work that established her fame in America and abroad.

In Fuller's book, we notice again and again the belief in the "electrical" and "magnetic" element in women's nature. "Women who combine this organization with genius are very commonly unhappy at the present time." What makes *Woman in the Nineteenth Century* affecting beyond its arguments for education, independence, and so on, is the pathos of autobiography lurking in the text. Even the often lamented diversions into higher learning and allusion show the will to transcendence. She herself, in the wide sweep of her being, is the best American woman the nineteenth century had to offer; and she is, for all that, merely a phenomenon, an abandoned orphan. That is part of what the book means to say.

Emerson on Margaret Fuller: "A complacency that seemed the most assured since the days of Scaliger." Also, "the presence of a rather mountainous ME." Who can doubt it? But what the whole span of her life shows is that she got it all from being around Boston at the transfiguring moment and would have lost it all had she not escaped. She was a sort of stepchild, formed and deformed by Concord, by the universalism and the provincialism. Emerson notes this so-willing adaptation to the best of the intellectual landscape, as well as its gradual unsuitability, not only to the fact that she was a woman who had to earn her living, but to her nature. Among other things, she was not a solitary, not a gardener.

> I think most of her friends will remember to have felt, at one time or another, some uneasiness, as if this athletic soul craved a larger atmosphere than it found; as if she were ill-timed and mis-mated, and felt in herself a tide of life, which compared with the slow circulation of others as a torrent with a rill.

She was altogether too familiar in the minds of New Englanders. They loved her—the word is not too strong even for Emerson's feelings.

Noble, truthful, faithful, brave, honest: The words appear again and again in what was written and said about her. Yet it is the fate of an eccentric to be repetitive in the hometown. There is no intermission. Each appears in his hat and coat and tics day after day. The first thing to be noticed as she moves to New York and then to Europe is that she is no longer quite so noticeable, so fixed and peculiar, perhaps because being one of many, even if Poe, a New York acquaintance, divided the world into men, women, and Margaret Fuller. Above all, Transcendentalism—"going to heaven in a swing" as one mocker put it—nearly turned her into a fool.

She moved to New York in December 1844, invited by Horace Greeley to be a professional book reviewer for the *New York Tribune* and also to contribute general articles; and invited by Mrs. Greeley to stay with them in their house in the Turtle Bay section of the city. For the paper she wrote reviews and "pieces" on just about everything: the theater, concerts, prisons, asylums, poor women, institutions. Her reviews were, for the most part, short and quickly written. She gives too much space to the novels of Charles Brockden Brown and too little to James Fenimore Cooper and the stories of Hawthorne, although she is generally favoring in her glances. She made a striking attack on Longfellow as "artificial and imitative." As a critic, she does not have the mind for the details of a work but rather for its general effect, and so there is a sameness in the language and a tendency, strong, to moral description of literature. "The atmosphere of his verse refreshes," and again, "a lively though almost sensuous delight in the beautiful," "the richness and freshness of his materials," and so on. She has little notion of the power of William Prescott's *Conquest of Mexico*.

The most interesting of the critical pieces in the *Tribune* is a cool and sly rebuke to Emerson's *Essays: Second Series*. A maddening part of the review is taken up with a description of a populace too busy and too shallow to grasp the fineness in its midst. This is followed by an interesting, but again generalized and exhorting, picture of Emerson on the platform. "One who could see man in his original grandeur ... raising to the heavens the brow and the eyes of a poet." Yes, Emerson is a father of the country. But then in an indirection, as if some disembodied critic and not herself were speaking: "The essays have also been obnoxious to many charges. ... The human heart complains of inadequacy, either in the nature or experience of the writer, to represent its full vocation and its deeper needs. . . . These essays, it has been justly said, tire like a string of mosaics or a house built of medals." A string of mosaics or a house built of medals—one of her best prose moments. At the expense of the master and still a friend to whom she wrote letters up to the end.

Then the entrance in 1845 of James Nathan, when they were both about thirty-five years old, he being six months or so younger, both unmarried, but he certainly more *experienced*. Nathan was born in Holstein, Germany, came to New York as a young man, worked in the "commission business," but, in common with many another, liked to wonder if he had not sold the soul of a poet for, well, what?— "commissions" perhaps. He had blue eyes, played the guitar, and after a meeting at the Greeleys', took her to see a plaster model of the city of Jerusalem.

Alas, she is quite soon set off, on the road again. A large group of letters begins, because the Greeleys didn't much like Nathan and the two had to meet here and there, missing each other at planned meetings; and as a writer, she has the natural inclination, highly developed, to put every turn of feeling on paper.

When they went to see the model of Jerusalem, she learned that Nathan was a Jew, and although at times Fuller had shown the inclination of the period to Jewish stereotyping, she takes a quick leap. "I have long had a presentiment, that I should meet—nearly—one of your race, who would show me how the sun of today shines on the ancient Temple—but I did not expect so gentle and civilized an apparition and with blue eyes!"

A lot is to be discovered. Nathan was in the process of rehabilitating a "maiden" and when the maiden turns out to be his mistress, so far as we can tell from M.F.'s letters, his explanation, too, has to be taken in. "I only wished to be satisfied, and when you told me how you viewed the incident I really was so. Do not think of it ever again."

Then Nathan makes an "assault upon her person," as it was spoken of at the time. She rebuffs him, but here it is possible to think of more complication of feeling, during and after, than most commentators might find evident. She writes to him, of course, and quickly about this "sadder day than I had in all my life." She had been exposed to "what was to every worthy and womanly feeling so humiliating." And,

I know you could not help it. But why had fate drawn me so near you? . . . You have said that there is in yourself both a lower and a higher being than I was aware of. Since you said this, I suppose I have seen the lower! . . . Will you not come with me before God and promise me severe truth, and patient tenderness, that will never, if it can be avoided, misinterpret the impulses of my soul?

Nathan sends her a little dog, a burdensome gift for one moving here and there in the city and working day and night and writing to him day and night. The letters become quite frenzied with that pitiful wonder of the injured person of what she might have done wrong. Nathan is given to confessions of weakness that interest her, being new, no doubt. "Your hand removes at last the veil from my eyes. It is indeed myself who have caused all ill." What is unbalancing in this episode is that she is still writing in the transcendental mode of friendship and beauty and perfect trust in which the "assault"—unthinkable in Boston among familiars—was confusing but quite a new circumstance to think about.

But the weighty letters, the difficulty of reading them to say nothing of responding, this made its mark, and Nathan took flight to Europe, with the "maiden" along and promising to return. She wrote and received no answer. Did the letter arrive? Had his letter gone astray? When he does write, it is to ask for a favor, and then months pass without a word.

In 1846, she left the *Tribune* and sailed at last for Europe, where she still hoped to unite once more with Nathan. In Edinburgh, he wrote that he was being married, but he refused to return her letters, refused even a second request, saying, "I shall do nothing with them but what is right, manly, and honorable." He promised to destroy the letters but did not do so. His son tried to sell them. In the end, Nathan left a stipulation in his will that they should be published. And published they were, in 1903, a half century after Margaret Fuller's death, as *The Love Letters of Margaret Fuller*, with a fatuous, unnecessary introduction by Julia Ward Howe and a swinish "reminiscence" by Nathan, written in 1873 and apparently left with the letters for posterity.

I cannot suffer their [the letters'] exquisite naturalness and sweetness to sink into the grave. . . . I can wreathe no fresher laurels around the cherished memory of Margaret than by showing, through these letters, that great and gifted as she was as a writer, she was no less so in the soft and tender emotions of a true woman's heart.

"Had I only come ten years earlier! Now my life must be a failure, so much strength has been wasted on abstractions, which only came because I grew not in the right soil," Margaret Fuller wrote to Emerson, from Italy. She went first to England and Scotland, with letters from Emerson to Carlyle and others; useful, but she was herself known. *Woman* had been published in England, *The Dial* was admired, and her reviews in the *Tribune*—along with the fact that she was, in the same journal, to support herself abroad by interviews with "personalities" and descriptions of the scene—did not hinder any more then than now.

She met everyone, even the aged Wordsworth at Grasmere and De Quincey, and picked up gossip. "It seems the cause of Coleridge's separation from his family was wholly with himself; because his opium and his indolence prevented his making any exertions to support them."

The most important meetings of her later life were with two vivid, spectacular, radical intellectuals: Giuseppe Mazzini, fabulous throughout Europe, and Adam Mickiewicz, the great Polish poet and patriot. And another meeting with a young Italian, the Marchese Giovanni Angelo Ossoli, by whom she had, at the age of thirty-eight, a son out of wedlock and whom she later married or did not marry.

Most of the admiring commentaries on Margaret Fuller are eager for her to "find herself as a woman" and also to become a radical in social reform. It is not possible to know if she found herself as a woman, but she did love and was loved by Ossoli, although she was careful not to claim apotheosis.

She became a radical by way of her passionate response to the European unheavals of 1848. (Emerson was in Europe in 1848, and she wrote him from Rome: "Why did you not try to be in Paris at the opening of the Assembly? There were elements worth scanning.") There was social reform and then some around Concord, but as an aesthete she was bored by Brook Farm, and the Boston Abolitionists were "so tedious, often so narrow, always so rabid and exaggerated in their tone." Her thoughts about political agitation changed when she began to connect the antislavery movement with the liberation of Italy, for which she hoped in her *Tribune* dispatches to arouse American sympathies.

It was at the Carlyles' that she met Mazzini.[*] He was in exile, raising money for Italian refugees, planning a campaign of return, writing in all the leading English journals not only on politics but on art and literature, and charming almost everyone in the nation with his great personal beauty and the purity of his idealism and self-sacrifice. "The most beautiful man I ever saw," was the comment of men and women alike. The cause of Italian liberation and the character of Mazzini, and later that of Garibaldi, electrified the English literary imagination and found its way into countless poems, novels, and plays. In 1879, almost thirty years after Margaret Fuller's death, there appeared an imaginary conversation in verse, written by the radical journalist W. J. Linton. The title was "Mazzini and the Countess Ossoli." At the end of this curious bit of versifying, Mazzini has left the stage and "the Countess, alone, prays for him."[†]

The friendship with Mazzini was genuine in England and grew even closer in Rome. They held many important things in common, Mazzini wrote to his mother, whom Margaret Fuller visited when her boat landed in Genoa. Before leaving England for Paris, there had been a plan to smuggle Mazzini into Italy in disguise and with a false American passport. More than one thing went wrong and just as well.

In Paris, Fuller met Mickiewicz at George Sand's apartment. Their encounter, he said, was one which "consoles and fortifies." She was "a true person" and "the only woman to whom it has been given to touch what is decisive in the present world and to have a presentiment of the world of the future."

Mickiewicz was a bohemian, more forthright and intimately observing than the spiritual Mazzini. To Fuller, he suggested, and apparently without any wishes of his own, that the first step in her deliverance "is to know whether you are permitted to remain a virgin."

When Mickiewicz came to Rome to recruit among the Poles living in exile, he stayed in her lodgings, and when she was suffering from illness brought on by her pregnancy, he was the first to be told the secret.

---

[*] I am indebted for much about the European period of Margaret Fuller's life to Joseph J. Deiss, *The Roman Years of Margaret Fuller.*

[†] Harry Rudman, *Italian Nationalism and English Letters,* p. 167.

"You are frightened at a very natural, very common ailment, and you exaggerate it in an extravagant manner," he told her. Mickiewicz was to be the child's godfather, but he was not about when Ossoli, determined upon the baptism both for his Catholicism and to legitimate the child, proceeded with the certification.

Fuller and Ossoli met in Saint Peter's Church, after an Easter service. Somehow, Fuller became separated from her companions, and while wandering about the church was asked by a young Italian if he could be of help. They walked back across the Tiber to the Corso. So, Mickiewicz said when he was told, it was at last to be, "*un petit Italien, dans l'église.*"

Ossoli was twenty-seven, ten years younger. His mother died when he was a boy, and he lived in the family palazzo with his older brothers and sisters and their ailing father, whom he was taking care of. Later, much about Ossoli was obscured or questioned, either by malice, the secrecy of his connection with Margaret Fuller, or by his reserve and scant English. What seems to be true is that he was from an old family long attached to the Papacy, not rich, and certainly conventional in thought. His father and one older brother were high papal functionaries; two other brothers were in the Pope's Guardia Nobile. It seems, although it is disputed, that he had Republican sympathies before meeting Margaret Fuller, rather than that she swayed him in that direction. In any case, he joined the Civil Guard, put himself in much danger, and with the fall of the Republic would have had to flee Rome in any case.

The marriage, or the "underplot," as Henry James called it: Soon after their first meeting he proposed marriage, not necessarily legal. Margaret Fuller drew back. "The connection seemed so every way unfit." Instead, she went off to Florence and Venice as planned, but after a few months she changed her mind and returned to Rome, with almost nothing to live on.

Were they ever actually married? There is confusion here and no sure date or place. The impediments to marriage were many, among them the difficulty of getting a dispensation to marry a Protestant and the confusion of bureaucratic documentation in the city's chaos. Also, Ossoli did not wish to be disinherited of the little property that was to come to him on his father's death. (His unfriendly brothers, owing to his Republicanism, managed to disinherit him in any case.) Then there is the question of whether Margaret Fuller cared about marriage vows. William Henry Channing argued that marriage was against her principles. Emerson thought otherwise: "When it came to be a practical question to herself, she would feel that this was a tie that ought to have the solemnist sanction; that against the theorist was a vast public opinion, too vast to brave." Some evidence can be made to support an actual marriage between the two, but uncertainty remains.

During 1849, Margaret witnessed the flight of the Pope, the announcement of the Constituent Assembly, the declaration of the Republic, and Mazzini's triumphant entrance into Rome. The happiness did not last long; French troops intervened, and the slaughter of the siege of Rome set in. She herself nursed the wounded, along with one of Europe's most celebrated beauties, the romantic, radical Princess Belgioiso. Margaret Fuller's conquest of the "radical chic" figures in Italy—and even of her conservative friend, the important, rich Marchesa Arconati Visconti—seemed to have come about in a natural, unexceptional fashion. She was not seen to be too *exalté*, aggressive, and learned—after all, they knew their Tasso, Dante, and the divine Raphael also.

There had been a cooling off, a winding down, we imagine, achieved by the surrounding acceptance of herself, her learning, her rapturous zeal and gift for friendship. She was as she was, interesting, unique in many ways, and companionable. Only her writing still suffered from orphic diffusion, from a sentimental femininity of accent. "Hard was the heart, stony and seared the eye, that had no tear for that moment."

Her dispatches to the *Tribune*, covering all the great events, were written in the first person and were personal in every sense, filled with pleading, and descriptive passages a bit commonplace. There is also concern for the diplomatic and military tangle of alliances and events. Her Republican bias is candid, in a manner that would not be thought suitable today. Indeed, her reports of disillusionment with the waverings of Pope Pius IX outraged the Catholic diocese in New York. Complaints were made, but Greeley published the accounts uncensored.

Toward the end of her stay in Rome, her writing begins to show a greater control and becomes more graceful and useful, with fewer "effects" that stress her own emotions.

I entered the French ground, all hollowed and mapped like a honeycomb. A pair of skeleton legs protruded from the bank of one barricade; lower, a dog had scratched away its light covering from the body of a man, and discovered it lying face upward all dressed; the dog stood gazing on it with an air of stupid amazement.

By the end of June, the Republic had fallen to the French troops, and the losers were fleeing. The Ossoli family left for Florence and the following summer embarked for America. The last years of Margaret Fuller's life had been horrible: poverty, overwork, illness; her son nearly starved to death in the town of Rieti where she had left him with a wet nurse in order to return to Rome to make her living.

All the while, she had been preserving documents, taking notes, in addition to her dispatches, for a work to be called "History of the Italian Revolution." The loss of the book has been lamented. She had made inquiries about the possibility of publication in England, which were refused. Part of her reason for returning to America was that she thought it would help in making the arrangements for publication.

She asked Emerson's advice, and the answer shows that he was well aware of her "situation" with a husband, perhaps, and a little boy, certainly. Her family and various others had been informed. (Earlier, when she was awaiting the birth of the child, she received a letter from Emerson, in Paris at the time, quite sweetly urging her to come home with him, where he said he would find a pleasant little house for her.) But now the possibility of the return of the irregular family was not so agreeable to imagine. He advised that Italy was an important advantage to her work. "It is certainly an unexpected side for me to support—the advantage of your absenteeism."

However, return she did, even if in a spirit of gloom about her reception, her devastating poverty, Ossoli's poor prospects, her ill health and exhaustion. They could not afford a steamer and took a merchant boat, a voyage of over two months. She packed all her documents, her notes, and the letters between herself and Ossoli, as well as others. The manuscript for the book was stored in another box.

The journey was a disaster from the start. The captain took sick of smallpox and died; the child contracted the disease but lived. The ship went on, reaching New Jersey for a landing in New York the following day. Trunks were brought from the hold, the child dressed in his best, America to be faced. A fierce storm came up in the night and the ship began to go down off Fire Island. It started to sink near enough to the shore for some of the passengers to make land by the use of a plank; some drowned in a like attempt. A steward tried to take the child to shore but was swamped by a wave. Margaret Fuller was last seen in a white nightgown, holding the broken mast. The body of the child was recovered and claimed by the Fuller family. The box of letters and other personal documents survived, but the manuscript box was lost. The bodies of Margaret Fuller and Ossoli were not recovered. Bell Chevigny came upon a note in the Harvard Library that indicated that the bodies were indeed found, put in coffins, and shipped to Greeley, who refused to take any kind of action. The captain of the boat in this account worried about his jurisdiction in the matter and buried the bodies at night on Coney Island.

"I have lost in her my audience," Emerson said. Thoreau, not the dearest of her friends, paid her the finest tribune—a journey to Fire Island to look for the remains. Margaret Fuller was forty years old when she died.

———

Epilogue: Perfidious Hawthorne. The background is rather sketchy, although Hawthorne's dislike is not surprising. An early entry in his journal: "I was invited to dine at Mr. Bancroft's yesterday with Miss Margaret Fuller; but Providence had given me some business to do, for which I was very grateful."

Two years later, a more pastoral entry:

After leaving the book at Mr. Emerson's I returned through the woods, and, entering Sleepy Hollow, I perceived a lady reclining near the path which bends along its verge. It was Margaret herself. She had been there the whole afternoon, meditating or reading. . . . She said that nobody had broken her solitude, and was just giving utterance to the theory that no inhabitant of Concord ever visited Sleepy Hollow, when we saw a group of people entering its sacred precincts.

Perhaps a bit of irony in the final clause.

Sophia Peabody Hawthorne, the placid, settled wife of the disturbed, settled Hawthorne, on "The Great Lawsuit":

What do you think of the speech Queen Margaret Fuller has made from the throne? It seems to me that if she were married truly, she would no longer be puzzled about the rights of women. This is the revelation of woman's true destiny and place, which can never be *imagined* by those who do not experience the relation.

No doubt Hawthorne would have expressed it differently, as men and women married to those not concerned with the refinements of writing have good reason to know.

Hawthorne's *The Blithedale Romance*, in which the principal character, Zenobia, is often identified with Margaret Fuller, appeared in 1852, two years after her death. The death was a profound shock to the New England countryside, with the grieving family and old friends caught up in the tragedy and faced with the sharp conundrum of the life. While Hawthorne was writing *The Blithedale Romance*, the *Memoirs of Margaret Fuller Ossoli*, with an account of the history of the family and personal essays by Emerson, James Freeman Clarke, and W. H. Channing, was being composed and arranged. Both books appeared in the same year.

The "striking" remarks by Emerson do not altogether reveal his own and the others' great swell of reverence for their departed friend. The memorial volume edited, omitted, and even destroyed with a free hand; it also wished to assure that the object of veneration was safely married at the time of the conception of the child. Later scholars have been quick to point out the moral scrubbing of documents and to see the volume as a reduction of the vitality of the subject. Still, *Memoirs*, containing many letters and reminiscences of encounters among the group, is extraordinarily interesting and moving; it is possible to view it as the true salvaging of Margaret Fuller's life and thought, which otherwise might have been greatly shadowed in American literary history.

The setting of *The Blithedale Romance* is, as Hawthorne said, "based on my experiences and observations at Brook Farm," the hopeful and not quite practical socialist community established in Roxbury, outside Boston. Hawthorne also insists that the characters are fictional. Nevertheless, Zenobia, "the high spirited Woman, bruising herself against the narrow limitations of her sex," was thought by contemporaries to be a reflection of Margaret Fuller.

There are elements that correspond, but Hawthorne knew as a novelist that he could not have as the central figure a heroine he saw as wholly unappetizing. Had he drawn Margaret Fuller as he saw her, the results are not pleasing to anticipate, but the novel would have been less foolish, as in many ways it is; it might have been a strange modern fiction.

Zenobia is a great and riveting beauty; she is rich, with a mysterious past. She is a performer and a sort of writer with a "magazine signature." She is a feminist who "scorns the petty restraints that take the life and color out of other women's conversations." Zenobia, pretentious, nevertheless has no real culture, "her mind is full of weeds," which Hawthorne may have believed about Margaret Fuller, even though her culture was greater than his and greater than he needed.

In the book, the narrator, close to Hawthorne himself, has a sudden intuition about Zenobia. He divines, by some special mannish knowledge: "Zenobia is a wife! Zenobia has lived and loved!" The revelations about Margaret Fuller were distressing not only to the morals but to the vanity of the Concord circle. She was an "adulteress" and, if married at all, the wife of a titled foreigner, all rather exotic and *superior*. *The Scarlet Letter* was begun the year of the death off Fire Island. No just connection can be made but in practical reality Margaret Fuller was the big A in the experience of the countryside. In *The Blithedale Romance*, it may be noted that Zenobia, in a gruesome description, drowns herself because of love for an unworthy man.

In 1858, Hawthorne made his own Italian journey, and one of the things he did was to run down, like a detective, the Margaret Fuller and Ossoli affair. Hawthorne left in his notebooks an account of a conversation with Joseph Mozier, an Ohio merchant who had gone to Florence to become a sculptor and who had known Fuller. These strange unearthings, violent and above all relishing in tone, are contradictory to the facts and to the moral and emotional remembrances of Margaret Fuller in Italy and at home.

Hawthorne is concerned to remove the title "Marchese" from Ossoli and, if he cannot quite do that, to reduce him to a boy picked up on the street, an idiot, and to see Margaret Fuller as a sort of desperate procuress. His recording of his conversations with Mozier reflects as much his own feeling as that of one who had known Margaret Fuller in Italy.

Mozier ... then passed to Margaret Fuller, whom he knew well. His developments about poor Margaret were very curious. He says that Ossoli's family, though technically noble, is of no rank whatever; his elder brother, with the title of Marquis, being at the time a working bricklayer, and the sisters walking the streets without bonnets—that is, being in the station of peasant girls. . . . Ossoli, himself, to the best of his [Mozier's] belief, was Margaret's servant, or had something to do with the care of her apartments. He was the handsomest man Mozier ever saw, but entirely ignorant even of his own language, scarcely able to read at all, destitute of manners; in short, half an idiot, and without any pretensions to be a gentleman. . . . As for her towards him, I do not understand what feeling there could have been, except it was purely sexual; as for him towards her, there could hardly have been even this, for she had not the charm of womanhood. . . . She had a strong and coarse nature, too, which she had done her utmost to refine with infinite pains, but which of course could only be superficially changed. . . . Margaret has not left in the minds of those who knew her any deep witness to her integrity and purity. She was a great humbug; of course with much talent, and much moral reality, or else she could not have been such a great humbug.

She had no manuscript, Hawthorne insists; it did not exist. And he concludes:

Thus there appears to have been a total collapse in poor Margaret, morally and intellectually, and tragic as her catastrophe was, Providence was, after all, kind in putting her, and her clownish husband, and their child, on board that fated ship ... a strange, heavy, unpliable, and in many respects, defective and evil nature ... she proved herself a woman after all and fell like the lowest of her sisters.

(1986)

A Bunch of Reds:
John Reed

Are you an *American* American? Lenin asked John Reed. The revolution would not be unmindful of the "human interest" attaching to the spirited and sunny Bolshevik from the United States. Clearly Reed was something apart from Lenin's Russian and European experience bitterly acquired in prison and exile and recorded in his florid, vitriolic disputes in the old *Iskra* and elsewhere. John Reed was not a Pole, not an Italian anarchist, not a Jew, not a Menshevik, not a socialist revolutionary. In truth he was what he appeared to be, a charming enthusiast of the revolution, a genuine American with no jarring memories of Zimmerwald debates, of Kautsky polemics, of Rosa Luxemburg.

Could he even be called a Marxist since he was not attracted to exegesis or to study in some American equivalent of the British Museum, or the libraries of Zurich? Nevertheless he was a revolutionary, not just a leftist, and certainly not an "infantile leftist" with their accusing utopianism. And, of course, like so many others, he was a world revolutionary, believing in the overthrow of capitalism, first here and then there, by way of strikes and insurrections. The gradualism of the Socialist Party was not agreeable to Reed's temperament and he was, after the victory in Russia, determined upon its replacement in America by some form of the Communist Party, recognized and unified, as it were, by the Comintern.

Reed is a curiosity and his political biography is held together by theatricalism and by his seizing upon, as a journalist, the dramatic moments of the class struggle; that is the moment when the stage is lit by a strike, by Pancho Villa and his horsemen in northern Mexico, and by the Bolshevik seizure of the government in November, 1917. Certainly these are natural landscapes for the reporter-participant, the brilliant, early master of radical "new journalism."

And circumstances made Reed what is called a legend. Even so striking a book as *Ten Days That Shook the World* could only make the author famous, celebrated, widely known, still one among others. It was early death that made him legendary, always bright and free of the ruins of time. At thirty-three he died in Soviet Russia of typhus and was buried in the Kremlin. So here is a radical American idealist, an activist with youthful, beguiling impetuosity; and all somehow illuminated, charmingly colored by his having been a treasured child of the American bourgeoisie, a westerner from Oregon, a graduate of Harvard, tall and good-looking in the old Greenwich Village gifted days.

Reed died in 1920, his book and his *persona* lived on, but there would inevitably be sixty years later some sketchiness in public memory. And now, in 1981, he has been revivified in Warren Beatty's film *Reds,* an expensive, ambitious, romantic celebration of American radicalism, a celebration of love, vitality, and bohemianism. "Who were they? Were they socialists?" Adela Rogers St. Johns asks about Reed and his wife, Louise Bryant. She does not remember them and yet she is, we must say, on the right track. Had the film been made in her earlier days Mrs. St. Johns, a Hearst reporter very knowledgeable about Hollywood, would indeed have remembered. Pictorial, synoptic, imagistic history, united with the extraordinary grip of the visage of screen actors on the memory, lasts a generation at least, and often longer.

Reds—the candid title, connected in the mind with "a bunch of"—sets the good-natured tone of this representation of a bloody, suffering, unbearably complex historical period, the period that ended for Reed with the Russian Revolution. For radical Americans in love like John Reed and Louise Bryant the catastrophic time of war and devastation of the past of Europe was washed in a silvery light, the light of "when we were young and believed in something."

Warren Beatty, in so far as the mind can concentrate a film personage, does not appear to be in reality a violation of the historical John Reed. Indeed they are both "making history" in accordance with the useful and possible media at hand, and the sixty years intervening are interestingly foreshortened by the persistence of type. It is no wonder Beatty took upon himself so many of the professional duties of the enterprise; it is as if he feared the intrusiveness of alien spirits born, as it were, under the wrong sign. A like sense of osmotic recognition perhaps directed his most successful invention, the inclusion of persons, some of whom had known Reed and some not, who were alive at the time of World War I and who in their stray, broken, lifelike remarks attest to the past in the present, to the fading but not yet extinct silvery world—the way we were.

The witnesses do not reveal so much about Reed as about the endurance of the mask and its meeting with opinion which are finally personality—the quintessential union achieved by John Reed in his youth, Henry "Fucking" Miller, working-man Heaton Vorse, the old swaggart Hamilton Fish, the refined, liberal Roger Baldwin, and above all the restless individuality of two distinguished English women, Dora Russell and Rebecca West: these persons act in the place of the conventional newsreel, banner, and headline to establish the mood of history and the claim of a certain root of factuality.

Trotsky at the end of *The History of the Russian Revolution* writes: "Parliamentarianism illumined only the surface of society, and even that with a rather artificial light. In comparison with monarchy and other heirlooms from the cannibals and cave-dwellers, democracy is of course a great conquest, but it leaves the blind play of forces in the social relations of men untouched. It was against this deeper sphere of the unconscious that the October Revolution was the first to lay its hand."

The "deeper sphere of the unconscious" laid its hand upon revolutionaries, on individuals, rather than upon the state, the embodiment, which had no relief from a conscious, wary, cunning, and unending struggle for power. As the Russian poet Alexander Blok wrote, in a revolution "everything is confused as in a tavern, a fog." But the enthusiast, whether of the right or of the left, is frightened of the fog and naturally sees it as an impediment to forward, march.

Reed, the enthusiast, seems to have discovered his political self when he met Big Bill Haywood in 1913. Haywood, the leader of the IWW, was at the time of the meeting leading a strike of 25,000 textile workers in Paterson, New Jersey. Haywood himself had outstanding courage and revolutionary political ideas; he also had a useful working-class charisma that riveted the attention—a "massive, rugged face, seamed and scarred like a mountain." In Paterson, where police and company brutality was extreme, Reed went to report on the plight of the mostly foreign-born workers who had been organized under the banner of the IWW. "Immediately Reed fell in love with these Italians, Lithuanians, Poles and Jews, small, dark, tough, boisterous men who cheered the IWW, incessantly sang union songs and fearlessly denounced their jailors."*

He was arrested for some minor interference and jailed for four days in the same cell with the noted Italian radical, Carlo Tresca. (Tresca was assassinated—some said by the Comintern, some by the "mob," acting for fascists—in front of his office on lower Fifth Avenue in the 1940s, and one of my own New York memories is of the twilight gathering of a small group, always including Norman Thomas and Dorothy Kenyon, on the spot of his death for an anniversary memorial service.) From the IWW and the experience at Paterson Reed received what appears to be his only cluster of political principles: syndicalism. This lasted throughout his life, even after he and a good many of the Wobblies were consumed by the Communist Party after 1917.

The principles were One Big Union and open war against the excluding craft unions of the conservative AF of L under Samuel Gompers; direct action by way of strikes and boycotts for the overthrow of capitalism; opposition to mediation, parliamentarianism, running for office as a minority political party; antimilitarism and opposition to America's entrance in World War I, the war of "profits." These principles dominated Reed's distaste for the Socialist Party, even though as early as 1912 Debs had received 900,000 votes as a candidate for President and was to receive 914,000 when he ran from his jail cell in 1920. And most importantly the principles and his experience of them in America informed what seems to have been Reed's only serious dis-

---

* Much of the information about John Reed in this article comes from *Romantic Revolutionary*, by Robert A. Rosenstone (New York: Alfred A. Knopf, 1975; Vintage, 1981). Rosenstone's research in articles, manuscripts, foreign sources, and Reed bibliography is exhaustive. His biography is an exemplary source of interest and fact for anyone who wishes to reflect upon Reed's career.

pute with the direction taken by the Bolsheviks after the victory of 1917: that is the decision that the radical American workers, whom Reed emotionally and ideologically saw himself to represent, should "bore from within" the more powerful AF of L, which Reed detested. By these alliances they were to achieve a mass following.

Also at Paterson what might be called the popularity of Reed's personality, the *noblesse* of it, was immediately manifest. He was *noticeable,* vivid, under a sort of enchantment with his princely dash and large sympathies. Perhaps because he held whatever political ideas he had in a haphazard and personalized manner, Reed was not attracted to the urge for organizational power, an almost inevitable handmaiden to the theorist in action. In political activity, what are abstractions good for except to be imposed upon groups, opponents, the flow of events? Or to provide substance to the *critique,* a mental activity, souring enthusiasm, and uncongenial to the expressive sans-culottism of Reed's nature.

His moment as a radical journalist is the *showdown,* the possibility of a reversal of power and the appearance out of the darkness of the forest of powerful men, with the object always of redeeming, reversing the sufferings of the powerless. Reed enters the showdown with a happy receptivity, always, even at Paterson, under the star of his own *engagé* foreignness. He is a striker at Paterson, one of *los hombres* with Pancho Villa in Chihuahua, and an instant Bolshevik in Russia. He is trusted because he is not disputatious and indeed he has brought with him to the scene only the wish that the revolt, the insurrection might succeed. He is the troubadour of the main event and it would be withholding to stifle the spirit with too great a pause for "details" that trouble. The *torrent révolutionnaire,* the mob, *les malheureux* in the streets, at the barricades, ragged armies, strong leaders—for these his gift is ready. Reed does not seem to know much about past history and the only historical reference in *Ten Days* is to Carlyle, very briefly.

When he meets Pancho Villa he is impressed with "the most natural human being I ever saw—natural in the sense of being a wild animal." In turn Villa is impressed and soon Reed is riding with *la tropa,* sleeping with the *compañeros,* and writing: "I made good with these wild fighting men and with myself." There is banditry, expropriation, revolutionary justice by execution; and there is Justice, the turnover, the awakened peasantry, the blaze of a new dawn. Reed's account of the

Mexican Revolution is brilliantly alive and moving. Walter Lippmann wrote about it: "The variety of his impressions, the resources and color of his language seemed inexhaustible ... throngs of moving people in a gorgeous panorama of earth and sky."

Because Reed wrote in a powerful, rhythmical, descriptive style he is again and again spoken of as a poet, "the poet of the revolution," and so on. When he goes about the country agitating against conscription and about the Russian Revolution, he is reminded by his friends that he is, essentially, "a poet" and he thinks of himself as such—at times. The truth is that his uniqueness was precisely fulfilled in his prose and he is in no sense genuine otherwise. His love poems are conventional and quite expendable, along with, except for information, such of his letters as appear in books devoted to his life. His efforts to command the inclusive Whitman style are boasting and predictable in language.

> I have shot craps with gangsters in the Gas-House district....
> I can tell you where to hire a gunman to croak a squealer,
> And where young girls are bought
> and sold, and how to get coke
> on 125th Street....

The generalized experience offers little to this writer who needs the landscape of heroic action in what he sees as a just cause. To describe, feel, and experience is his gift; to heighten observation by a free and lovely fluency of language at a moment when all is given, accepted, beyond reflection. World War I, which he covered in a desultory manner, was not a source for his literary inspiration. The long, slogging, murderous destruction of men and history was lamentable, but, for his talent, it was not dramatic, being too dense and blurred.

The narrative power of *Ten Days* is astonishing when one considers the amount of information needed for Reed's audience—not to mention the need of the author himself when he gets down to the page—and the effort to organize the documentation, the decrees, shifting alliances, committee meetings, newspaper accounts, without which the book would be only a dazzle. The *esprit* is unflagging; the rush through history and chaos is the rush to victory. The pace of the book is the pace of the victorious tide. It is all youthful, high-spirited, with none of the disfiguring vehemence of the polemicist because Reed is a mind too newly born for moral carping. And he is a comrade without memories. In truth Reed doesn't really know a soul there in the "vastness"; he hasn't a single Russian friend and is not humanly acquainted with a foot of the earth.

For the others it was not so fresh and always blooming. When Angelica Balabanoff, the daughter of a wealthy land-owning Russian family and a revolutionary since her youth, is sent by the Party to work in Odessa, "the mention of Odessa made me shudder." Her relatives, from whom she was long estranged for political differences, had gone to Odessa in order to be able if necessary to escape to Turkey. (Her mother escaped to Turkey and died of starvation there.) Madame Balabanoff dutifully goes to Odessa and while outside her office she can hear the shouts of Long Live Comrade Balabanoff, her anti-Bolshevik sister is ushered in, a sister dressed like a beggar and so miserably altered she is hardly recognizable.

It is no diminishment of his stunning reportage to say that for Reed the October Revolution is pageantry from a moonscape. "In Smolny Institute the Military Revolutionary Committee flashed baleful fire, pounding like an overloaded dynamo." And, "Vast Russia was in a state of dissolution. . . . Old Russia was no more; human society flowed molten in primal heat, and from the tossing sea of flames was emerging the class struggle, stark and pitiless—and the fragile, slowly cooling crust of new planets." Power, vastness, newness, throbbing, rushing, rising, unrolling are the signifiers of the grand purpose, the necessity, the destiny of history. Petrograd falls, and then the bombardment of the "holy" Kremlin itself, and then the pause for the funeral of the Martyrs of the Beginning of World Revolution, and then: "I suddenly realized that the devout Russian people no longer needed priests to pray them into heaven. On earth they were building a kingdom more bright than any heaven had to offer and for which it was a glory to die. . . ."

There is revolution and then there is also love. With the leaders in Russia, love stories are not often in the advance guard of experience. Lenin's mistress, Issa Armand, is not even mentioned in Trotsky's biography of Lenin or in his history of the Russian Revolution. Trotsky must have known of her death from cholera in 1920 and of Lenin's stony grief, mentioned by other memorists, when she is taken to be buried in the Kremlin, near to the grave of John Reed. As for Lenin's wife and comrade, Krupskaia, she lived on, a survivor sometimes troublesome enough to lead Stalin to say that if she didn't watch out, he would find someone else to be Lenin's widow.

Rosa Luxemburg's biographer spoke of her love for her husband, Leo Jogiches, as one of the "great and tragic love stories of socialism." And certainly Emma Goldman was a lover. Her account of her life soon after she arrived in America as a young woman is detailed by short headlines at the top of the page. They read in breathless succession: Sasha Makes Love to Me; I Respond to Fedya; and Most [Johann] Confesses Love for Me. Most was an anarchist-terrorist—"propaganda of the deed"—whose criticism of Sasha (Alexander Berkman) after he had shot Henry Clay Frick led to the next Emma Goldman autobiographical headline: I Horsewhip Most. As she did on the stage of one of Most's lectures, ending the scene in a majorful manner by breaking the whip in two.

In *Reds*, the love of John Reed and Louise Bryant is not one of the great stories of socialism. Its landscape for the most part is the America of Oregon, Greenwich Village, Croton-on-Hudson outside New York. Much of it is out of classic film romantic comedy—fighting and making up, husband sent to the sofa, husband in the blazing kitchen, and in this case the historically permissible "free love" infidelities of Louise Bryant.

Louise Bryant met Reed when he was on a visit to his family in Portland. The meeting was brief and thoroughly *fateful*. She left her husband, went to New York, and married Reed not long after. Louise Bryant is interesting as an American woman who was not so much complicated as murky and given to the improvisations of survival.*

She came from the working class and while this might be a picturesque idea to some of the Greenwich Village intelligentsia, Louise Bryant knew it to be a soot-flecked reality. Her father was born in the mining region of Pennsylvania, worked in the mines, and by self-education became a school teacher and a reporter, finally working on newspapers in San Francisco, where the daughter was born, before he vanished completely from the family scene. The destruction of records in the San Francisco fire was a release to the imagination and

---

* *So Short a Time*, by Barbara Gelb (New York: W. W. Norton, 1973; Berkley 1981), is the only biography of Louise Bryant and it is a necessary source for her life.

in Granville Hicks's biography of Reed, Louise gave out the information that she had been "brought up by her grandfather, the younger son of an Anglo-Irish lord." Instead she was brought up by her mother and stepfather, a railroad conductor, in Wadsworth, Nevada, and made her way *out*, to the University of Nevada and the University of Oregon. When she married her first husband in Oregon she was twenty-two, but preferred to be thought nineteen. In New York with Reed she was twenty-nine, but chose to be twenty-five.

Louise Bryant's life is like a traditional realistic novel of which she is the heroine under the domination of an ordained curve of fortune. Unpromising beginnings, sloughed off gradually by charm and by a fierce feminist determination for a worthy self-identification; romantic dishonesties, either profitless or gratuitous, but meant to ensure against something; the upward swing of many successes and no more relative than usual in "success"; and a truly terrible ending, without necessity, without preparation as it seems, except in a Hardy-like fate.

The triangle, supremely interesting in real life and so often the very blood of literature, was a natural mode for this driven coquette from the provinces and at almost every important point in her life with Reed the inclination, with its more or less forgivable deceptions, goes along like a handbag. Her affair with Eugene O'Neill began when the three of them were in Provincetown, continued "heavily" when she invited O'Neill to the house in Croton while Reed was in a hospital in Baltimore for the removal of a diseased kidney. When she returned, two months ahead of Reed, from the first trip to Russia, her immediate action was to get in touch with O'Neill. The way of the world had intervened; O'Neill had taken up with someone else and the affair was not resumed. In *Reds*, Louise Bryant's character is given a greater degree of common sense than one can document. Also in certain fluent declamations and in the hintings of moments of "concerned" silence, she is made to appear the possessor of political wisdom, a sort of intuitive feminine guardian against the follies of radical enthusiasm.

In the group of artists and writers in the Village, more was necessary for a woman than attractiveness and compatibility of views, views about love, women's suffrage, and so on, which Louise had come to before she met Reed. Still it was necessary to be something, if only rich like Mabel Dodge. So, without spectacular talent but with a steady energy she became a political journalist. In Petrograd with Reed she found her subject and *Six Red Months in Russia,* her book of dispatches based on her *four* months in Russia, came out in 1918, a year before *Ten Days,* published in 1919.

The stories, as she calls them in an introduction, "gathered together on the edge of Asia, in that mystic land of white nights in summer and long black days in winter...," are naive and written in the style of light feature-journalism, with many exclamation points that serve sometimes as irony or as a clue to excited emotion. "Kerensky again in the limelight! Kerensky visiting the world's capitals and hobnobbing with the world's potentates!" An effort is made to sort out the unnerving complexity of the political parties, to explain the Democratic Congress and to "explain away" the dissolution of the Constituent Assembly, but it is a rendering finally of the author's own ignorance and nervous incapacity as a historian. "I was present at the opening of the Constituent; it was a terrific performance from beginning to end. About eight o'clock the delegates assembled and the air fairly crackled with excitement." In an interview at the recruiting office of the Women's Battalion, where patriotic women from all classes had enlisted to fight the Germans, she was told that some of them were in the Winter Palace when it fell and were rumored to have been raped. Here Louise Bryant is more sympathetic and her conversational, quick-impression style is more suitable.

Interviews with Breshkovskaya and Spirodonova, two great women of the revolutionary period, are sketches of vivid personalities who, somewhat unfortunately for Louise Bryant, have political ideas outside her comprehension. Breshkovskaya, the Grandmother of the Revolution as she is called, was heroic and dramatic and old. She was also a right-wing socialist revolutionary and unwelcome after the fall of the Provisional Government. Louise Bryant writes: "History almost invariably proves that those who give wholly of themselves in their youth to some large idea cannot in their old age comprehend the very revolutionary spirit with which they themselves began; they are not only unsympathetic to it, but usually they offer real opposition. . . . It is a question of age."

The handsome, learned Spirodonova had in her youth killed the sadistic Lupjenovsky, governor of Tambov. For this act she spent an appalling, eleven brutalizing years in prison in Siberia until she was released when the February Revolution broke out. "Spirodonova as a member of the Left Socialist Revolutionist Party is surrounded by a number of the finest young idealists in Russia. Hers is the only party that in a crisis rises above party for the benefit of the nation. It will have more and more to say as the revolution settles down."

The folly of this prediction is scarcely credible. When John Reed returned to Russia in 1919 to get recognition for the Communist Labor Party of America, Spirodonova, who opposed what she saw as the Bolshevik betrayal of the peasants, was again a "martyr," in and out of Soviet prisons. Because of her revolutionary fame she was perhaps the first to be incarcerated under the "nervous breakdown" euphemism. Emma Goldman tells of talking to Reed about the case and hearing his claim that the imprisonment was due to acute neurasthenia and hysteria. On this matter Emma Goldman's comment was brief and dismissing: "As to Reed, unfamiliar with the language and completely under the sway of the new faith, he took too much for granted."

Six Red Months in Russia sold fairly well and the author went about the country lecturing to large audiences. "Miss Bryant appears a demure and pretty girl, with a large hat, a stylish suit, and gray stockings. . . . In a burst of applause, the demure little speaker sits down." Thus was achieved the professional identity she very naturally wanted.

Her return to Russia to "rescue" Reed is not entirely the epical samaritanism of the film. She did not pass over the icy tundra, nor did she go to the prison in Finland where Reed had been held after his second Russian journey. She went to Russia by way of Murmansk and for various reasons, one of which was to be reunited with Reed, even though she was not fully aware, because of the difficulty of communication, of the suffering he had endured in solitary confinement. When she took off she was "bursting with guilt" over an affair she had been having with Andrew Dasburg, formerly Mabel Dodge's lover. She told Dasburg she wanted to continue her career as a journalist of the revolution, and also to dissuade Reed from coming home lest he go to prison on the indictments handed down for criminal anarchy and other charges during the Palmer Raids.

Her letter to Dasburg is interesting because of the remarkable persistence of her triadic confusions. "If J comes he will only go to prison and that will be horrible. Always to know he is there—more dependent than ever—it would destroy us, you can see that. It would destroy all three." *All three* is full of future intention to be worked out *somehow*. And "more dependent than ever" points to those midnight, untrammeled characterizations of the absent one, very much in tune with her telling Eugene O'Neill that Reed was impotent, which he was not. Reed's affairs, after he met Louise, are, at least in history, nameless phrases: "Jack romping around the house with a naked female" and "a desultory passion for a young Russian girl kept Jack too busy for sustained writing."

Three years after Reed's death, Louise Bryant had a sensational affair with William Bullitt, the rich Philadelphia diplomat who was later ambassador to Russia. He divorced his wife, married Louise, and they had a daughter. Bullitt was thirty-one and Louise was thirty-five, although keeping a bit ahead by being a bit behind she admitted only to being thirty. What seemed to the world a splendid social coup led to, or coincided with, one of those unpredictable, unaccountable swervings of human character. She began to drink heavily, spent time in sanitariums, and drove Bullitt to shame and fury. After seven years he sued for divorce and was awarded custody of the child. She returned to the Village, took up with a slippery younger man, brought him to court for stealing a valuable antique comb, and, oh the old chestnuts, the old songs, giving it to the famous Village restaurant owner, Romany Marie.

She left the Village for Paris and lived there a miserable life of drink and drugs. Janet Flanner's description: "When she came back to Paris she was in the lowest stage of degradation. One of the last times I saw her was on a rainy night when I was walking along Rue Vavin in Montparnasse. Literally out of the gutter rose a terrifying creature. Her face so warped I didn't recognize her."

The sudden meeting, the rainy night, the gutter—how like those endings in French novels of the sweet little tart or music hall singer, done in. Louise Bryant died in 1936 at the age of forty-nine, and if she ended in the manner of Balzac or Zola, she was in life, I think, more like Sister Carrie. Even her journalism might remind one of the theatrical success of Carrie, some aspect of performance that is not art and yet a public definition.

Reed called *Ten Days* "intensive history," and perhaps he meant history intensified by his feeling. Bolshevism came to be thought of as a magical phenomenon which not only consumed radical parties but embraced and erased all other radical political ideas. Power was a great part of this mystical inclusiveness and the mere fact of embodiment was an overwhelming, if irrational, magnification of value. The messianic mode and profound inexperience separated Reed from those who made the revolution, those whom Hannah Arendt in *On Revolution* called professional revolutionists who arrive on the scene from the "jail, the coffee house or the library."

But no matter what his "innocence" he is led as if he were merely another seeker of power into the simplications of propaganda. The intellectuals of the Menshevik Party, he asserts, by virtue of their education "instinctively reacted to their training, and took the side of the propertied classes." And "the only reason for Bolshevik success lay in their accomplishing the vast and simple desires of the most profound strata of the people." It is unthinkable that he could feel or write after a stirring speech by Trotsky anything close to what was written by the great diarist of the period, Sukhanov: "With an unusual feeling of oppression I looked on at this really magnificent show."

The revolution, the scene, drew Reed slowly into a degree of participation unusual for a foreign journalist, even for a radical one. Waiting for his transit visas at the end of the first trip, Reed attended the meeting of the Constituent Assembly and easily accepted the Bolsheviks' decision on dissolution after they failed to win a majority. The Constituent Assembly, providing for elected, representational government, was a sacred item on the agenda of the future and the Bolsheviks had bitterly condemned the Provisional Government set up after the overthrow of the Tsar for failing to honor this hope. The Bolsheviks in electoral defeat decided the Assembly was a bit of "bourgeois counter-revolution," and Reed, according to Rosenstone's research, was "not disturbed."

In addition he spoke at the Congress of the Soviets to great applause and joined the Red Guards in patrolling the streets and worked for the Bureau of International Propaganda. In his efforts to get back to America with his notes intact, Reed thought of having himself appointed a Soviet courier and for a time Trotsky actually proposed that Reed be appointed Soviet consul to the United States. Fortunately that did not happen and he returned to write *Ten Days*, to become famous, and to enter radical political life as an *exalté* representative of his ideas, or rather of his experience *there*, at the very moment. A new vocabulary, pulled out of the sludge of militarism, would now need to direct his actions: tactics, strategy, maneuver.

He joined the Socialist Party in bad faith and participated with Louis Fraina in a left-wing split whose aim was to Bolshevize the party.* There was a further split between Reed and Fraina and both went to Moscow in 1919 for the meeting of the Comintern, with Reed representing the Communist Labor Party and Fraina the Communist Party, composed mainly of many foreign-language radical groups. Reed's return seems to have rested upon his acknowledging himself as the American most known to the Soviet leaders and most likely to achieve recognition for his branch of the party. When he arrived the revolution had hardened like a footprint in cement and there was no way to avoid knowledge of the evident suppression of political opposition, the rule of the Communist Party bureaucracy, the consolidation of the power of the secret police, the Cheka. The knowledge could not be avoided, but there was—as always—interpretation.

Reed traveled about the demoralized, starving country, seeing and partly seeing. He brought hyperbolic greetings from the American workers and was received with great enthusiasm which seemed to testify to the endurance of the heroic phase. According to Rosenstone's research, he was prepared to see the repressions as necessity and to find the opposition of the peasants rooted in their petty-bourgeois

---

*Louis Fraina: a life of one miserable opaque drama after another, all wonderfully told in Theodore Draper's *The Roots of American Communism.* Fraina cannot be summarized because his is a story of circular details, plots ever-returning to haunt as in nineteenth-century fiction. Under the shadow of a strange spy charge by a perjurer when he went to Russia with Reed, but exonerated after a "trial" by the Comintern, the Party felt he was, nevertheless, cloudy and chose Reed to be the member from America of the Executive Committee. Fraina was exiled to Mexico, given $50,000 for Party work, of which the sum of $4,200 would bring him into Party disrepute as an "embezzler." Returned to Europe, back once more in New York under the name of Charles Skala; went to work in a dry goods store for $12 a week, finally employed as a proofreader.

In his evenings he decided to write a review on corporate ownership which was published in *The New Republic,* under a new name which he gradually made distinguished, Lewis Corey. Corey wrote analytical books on capitalism, taking a Marxist view, became a professor of political economy at Antioch College even though he had never been to high school. His past, in and out of the graces of the Communist Party, caused him fantastical difficulties and, notwithstanding his anticommunist position, he was subjected to threats of deportation by the American government. As Draper writes, "The man who began as Louis C. Fraina and ended as Lewis Corey provided the complete symbol of the American radical in the first half of the twentieth century." (In the film Fraina speaks with an Italian accent, which perhaps serves a useful purpose for dramatic variety. The fact is that he came to the United States at the age of three.)

mentality. He welcomes the threat of the hated conscription for the peasants to bring them out of isolation, into education so that each peasant "will return to his village a revolutionist and propagandist." The Cheka was not alarming since it was only acting against traitors and the shooting in one short period of 6,000 men was justified since "this is war." Coarseness enters the mind of the enthusiast as quietly as a faint, hardly noticeable cerebral accident.

It is necessary, it is necessary. Even the church bells are imagined to be ringing out this terrible refrain at the end of Victor Serge's great, tragic novel about the betrayal of the revolution, *Conquered City*—his Petersburg where perhaps he brushed by Reed and Louise Bryant as they were rushing to the "great Smolny ablaze with light." And when Reed is going about the Russian countryside, the poet Tsvetaeva is writing about the soldiers:

> He was white and now he's red—
> The blood reddened him.
> He was red and now he's white—
> Death whitened him.

After the meetings with the executive committee of the Comintern the dispute about the American Party was settled by the decision to unite the factions and Reed was chosen for the committee. He prepares to leave for home, taking with him $14,000 in diamonds and $1,500 in currencies, "Moscow gold," to assist the Communist Party of the U.S. He was captured in White Finland, put in prison as a spy, where he stayed for almost three months in solitary confinement, before being returned to Petrograd and Moscow. In Moscow he waited for the summer meeting of the Comintern, made speeches, and was always a striking, admired, if singular, figure.

At this time he had the dispute with Zinoviev and Radek over the Party line about the AF of L. Reed felt strongly that the Soviets did not understand the labor situation in America and indeed it would be sticky for him, with his Wobbly history and convictions, to carry this autocratic, "united front" decision on his shoulders. He agitated, he resigned from the executive committee, and he gave in, withdrew his resignation, and the domination by the Soviets of the Communist Parties of the world became another necessity.

In the film, Zinoviev is the enemy, the symbol of autocratic rule and cynicism, and Reed is cast as a "dissident." In the role Jerzy Kosinski is in a sense an idealization of Zinoviev. His dramatic hawk nose, thin-lipped whine, and lemon-chewing precision are what Zinoviev might better have been for dramatic purposes, for style. In reality Zinoviev, who was executed in the first of the old Bolshevik purges of 1936, was a pudgy, jowly, irritating agitator, one of the original mesomorphs of the Politburo, a physiognomy of enduring replication.

At Baku, the mad gathering of Turks, Persians, Arabs, and others, to which Zinoviev took him, Reed was dismayed by the distorted transla-tion of his speech and by the use of Islamic "holy war" rhetoric from Moscow. From these last months before his death arises the question of Reed's final attitudes toward the Soviet Union. To find this attractive person sunk at the end in the airless Communist Party provokes the salvaging instinct on the part of some such as Max Eastman, now on the other side and unwilling to surrender the corpse of this glorious friend of his youth. Late conversations described by Angelica Bala-banoff indicate Reed's resentment of Zinoviev and a general sadness and depression about the Soviet scene. Louise Bryant gives testimony of a bitter disillusionment to Balabanoff and says that Reed died be-cause he had lost the will to live. However, just after his death she had written Eastman that "he would have died days before but for the fight he made." Her testimony is erratic in the extreme, moving from disil-lusionment to some auditors, complete denial to others, and her record even includes an accusation that Reed was a secret agent for the United States. Louise Bryant returned to Russia after Reed's death and wrote the dispatches that appear in *Mirrors of Moscow,* published in 1923. At this time she, who had never been content to be The Wife, was The Widow, legendary. Her book shows no diminution of her passion for the revolution, which had become her *spécialité.* The secret police "were back again protecting now a revolutionary government as ener-getically as they once protected the Tsar!"

Emma Goldman believed that Reed had maintained belief in the revolution until the end. Louis Fraina, who was at the death scene, wrote, "As one of the two or three Americans who saw him before his death, I can affirm that Jack Reed kept all his loyalty to the Soviet Union and communism." There is a sympathetic and very interesting account of Reed's life and his relation to Soviet communism in Theodore Draper's *The Roots of American Communism.* Draper, a brilliant, fair-minded historian, does not give up Reed's possible disillusionment easily and he feels in the end that "Reed was probably as disillusioned as it was possible to be and still remain in the movement." Rosenstone disagrees with this more or less on the grounds of Reed's nature and temperament and while he sees distress he does not find that it would be sufficient cause, for Reed, to be rightly considered disillusioned at the time of his death.

John Reed was a morally attractive man marked by generosity and openness and for the most part unacquainted with the torments of ambivalence. Still he is not deep enough or reflective enough to be a moral hero and his life at the end shows the damage of a too-eager receptiveness. The curious last lines of Granville Hicks's biography tell of the funeral and the speeches by Party leaders. "For Bukharin and Radek and the others the death of John Reed was only an incident in the struggle for world revolution. He would have approved." A peculiar epitaph for one who was only thirty-three and whatever he may have been was never content to be only an incident.

(1982)

Gertrude Stein

In the midst of her unflagging cheerfulness and confidence, Gertrude Stein can be a pitiless companion. Insomniac rhythms and melodious drummings: She likes to tell you what you know and to tell it again and sometimes to let up for a bit only to tell you once more: "To know all the kinds of ways then to make men and women one must know all the ways some are like others of them, are different from others of them, so then there come to be kinds of them."

Her writing, T. S. Eliot once said, "has a kinship with the saxophone." That could be one of her own throwaways, but she would not have used a word like *saxophone*. The saxophone is an object with a history, and she didn't care much for nouns with such unique significance.

What can Eliot mean? The saxophone, invented in 1846 by Adolphe Sax, has little standing in the hereditary precincts of the classical orchestra. So it must be that Gertrude Stein is a barbaric and illicit intrusion. Preceding the curiosity of the saxophone, Eliot said about her work: "It is not improving, it is not amusing, it is not interesting, it is not good for one's mind." No doubt, Eliot wasn't aware of the improvisations of the great American masters of the saxophone.

In any case, Gertrude Stein was born in 1874, nearly thirty years after the birth of the saxophone. Her family and its situation must have been the womb of her outlandish confidence, confidence of a degree amazing. She was, after all, determined to be, even if *in absentia,* or because of that exile, our country's historian. There is nothing hothouse in this peculiar American princess. For one thing, she is as sturdy as a turnip—the last resort of the starving, and native to the Old World, as the dictionary has it. A tough root of some sort; and yet she is mesmerized and isolated, castlebound, too, under the enchantments of her own devising.

Confidence is highly regarded by both citizen and nation; it is altogether warm and loving. Without confidence, fidelity to death, as it were, the work Gertrude Stein actually produced cannot easily be imagined. Other writings, perhaps, since possibility was everywhere in her; but not what we have, not what she did. In her life, confidence and its not-too-gradual ascent into egotism combined with a certain laziness and insolence. It was her genius to make the two work together like a machine, a wondrous contraption, something futuristic and patented for her use.

She wrote her Cambridge lecture at the height of her fame, while waiting for her car to be fixed. She sat down on the fender of another car and, waiting around, wrote "Composition as Explanation." Several hours it took her: "Everything is the same except composition and as the composition is different and always going to be different everything is not the same." So it was. And: "Now if we write, we write; and these things we know flow down our arm and come out on the page." Yes. So she told Thornton Wilder.

Many wires and pieces of string went into the contraption, the tinkering, and the one result was that she wrote at great length and used a vocabulary very, very small. It was her original idea to make this vocabulary sufficient for immensities of conception, America, Americans, being perhaps her favorite challenge. When she is not tinkering, we can see her like a peasant assaulting the chicken for Sunday dinner. She would wring the neck of her words. And wring the neck of sentences, also.

Miss Stein lived until 1946, through two world wars and much else. Perhaps she never seemed young, and everyone would certainly have wished for her to live on and on, since there is a Methuselah prodigiousness about her. Everything we know about her life contributes to her being.

When was she not a prodigy—and even without exerting herself to represent the exceptional in action? She went to Harvard and studied with William James. Anecdotes appeared on her doorstep, anecdotes quite enduring. No, she didn't want to take an examination because the day was too fine. William James understood and gave her the highest mark in the course, if we can trust the *Autobiography of Alice B. Toklas,* which we can and cannot.

Premedical studies at John Hopkins; that is part of her aura. Perhaps she's a scientist, so look, when the pages confuse, for the rigors of the laboratory. She abandoned the medical studies, and we must say that, too, added something to the whole. The willful simplification she practiced can make her, to some, appear to be a philosopher in the most difficult mode of our own period.

It will be said William James taught her that everything must be considered, nothing rejected. Simple enough and not quite a discovery. What you can say is that while she was not learning, actively not learning, other young women were going to finishing schools, primping, dancing, and having babies, and she was becoming Gertrude Stein. Every refusal was *interesting,* a word she liked very much.

Both of her parents were German Jews. Whether she thought of herself as Jewish is hard to say. Perhaps she didn't, or not quite. She didn't like to be defined and that helped her to stay on in Occupied France. Her brother Leo thought of himself as Jewish, even at Harvard—or (why not?) certainly at Harvard.

Her parents were, in terms appropriate for American history, early settlers. That she knew and took in seriously. If, as one can read, the definition of Old New York, of New York aristocracy, is to have made your money before the Civil War, the Steins were aristocrats. The Stein brothers, one of whom was her father, arrived in 1841; her mother's family had settled in Baltimore previously.

A Stein Brothers clothing store was set up in Baltimore with success, but Gertrude's father and the brother moved on to Allegheny, Pennsylvania, where she was born. Then quite soon the characteristic behavior of the family began to assert itself. They showed a desire to take off, for Europe. They are inclined to be Americans abroad.

The family finances are not easy to make out, at the beginning or at the end. But even when the Allegheny store was not quite flourishing, Amelia Stein took herself and the children to Vienna. There they lived with governesses and tutors, the lessons and practices of the upper class. The Steins early on must have realized that one could be almost rich in Europe at that time without being rich enough at home. And they liked to buy things, to go shopping. The mother and children went to Paris to buy clothes and trinkets and to have a good time. In a later period, while Gertrude and Leo remained abroad, the older brother, Michael and Sarah came back to stun California with their collection of modern paintings.

From Pennsylvania, the family settled in Oakland, California, and the father, Daniel Stein, went into the streetcar business—a good career move, it would be called nowadays, even if Daniel was not quite the master of it. He died when Gertrude Stein was seventeen, and she wrote about his disappearance: "Then our life without a father began a very pleasant one." But more of that later, about the pleasantness of not having family members and the strain when you have them.

The older brother, Michael, took over the family business and made good investments for the fine purpose of not having to work. He was able to set Gertrude and Leo up abroad: a princely situation. Michael and Sarah were connoisseurs of the new, not of the refectory table from an old monastery or the great decorated urns to put in the hall and fill with dead reeds. For a time, they lived just outside Paris in a house designed by Le Corbusier.

In this family, you are not concerned with provincials—never at any point in their history. Not one of them seemed afflicted with puritanical, thrifty scruples, with denial or failure of nerve. Works of art were, in the end, their most daring and prudent investment. The paintings and the great international celebrity of the creative one, Gertrude, and even the fading claims of Leo make of the Steins one of the truly glittering American families. They stand in history along with the Adams and James families—along with if not quite commensurate with. They were immensely important in the history of American taste, by way of their promotion of modern painting through their collections and in their influence on the many painters, writers, and intellectuals who came to the *salon* on the rue de Fleurus.

The Cone sisters of Baltimore, contemporaries of the Steins, were to merit a kind of immortality when they used their cottonmill fortune to buy Manets, Renoirs, Cézannes, and Matisses for the later glory of the Baltimore Museum. Acquisition has need of special conviction and taste, but neither of the Cone women could claim for themselves an art to rank with that of Cézanne and Picasso—a claim that Gertrude Stein did not hesitate to make.

Picasso, bewildered by the Stein entourage, coming and going in

Paris, said: "They are not women. They are not men. They are Americans."

The Stein family was to be The Making of Americans. "It has always seemed to me a rare privilege, this of being an American, a real American, one whose tradition it has taken scarcely sixty years to create." There is no doubt Gertrude knows how to look at it, this subject of being American—the sixty years names it just right. An amused chauvinism—that is her tone. And elsewhere she notes that America is the oldest country in the world because it's been in the twentieth century the longest, something like that.

Still, it must be said Gertrude Stein feels more sentiment for America than she does for her fellow Steins, except as a subject. The mother, the Baltimore bride, faded into illness and at last died when Gertrude was fourteen: "We had already had the habit of doing without her." Simon, older (Gertrude was the youngest), ate a lot and was slow. Bertha, well, she never cared for Bertha: "It is natural not to care for a sister, certainly not when she is four years older and grinds her teeth at night."

The alliance between Gertrude and Leo ended in bitter contempt on both sides. It was said that Gertrude gave Picasso's portrait of Leo to Etta Cone in order to get it off the wall. When Gertrude died, she and Leo were so greatly estranged he knew of her death only by reading about it in the papers. His comment was: "I can't say it touched me. I had lost not only all regard, but all respect for her." They were an odd lot, except for Michael, but then, as she put it herself: "It takes time to make queer people, and to have others who can know it, time and a certainty of means."

Three Lives was finished in 1906, published in 1909—in every way a work of resonating originality, even if no aspect of its striking manner will persist in the eccentric shape of the works that follow. The stories are composed in the manner of a tale. The characters are sketched by a trait or two, and they pace through their lives, as the pattern has ordained; and then each one dies.

Sometimes there is an echo of realistic fiction, the setting of a scene, the filling in of detail, but we are given almost everything by assertion, and thus there is an archaic quality to the tone. But, of course, the tone is new, partly because of this archaic picturing. No other writer would have composed these moving portraits as Gertrude Stein composed them. One, "Melanctha," is of a higher order than the other two, "The Good Anna" and "The Gentle Lena."

Nothing is sentimental. We are not asked to experience more emotion than the scene can render; the stories do not manipulate in excess of their own terms. A distance is maintained, a distance—perhaps it is objectivity—that provides a fresh, bare surface for the sketching of the lives of the two German women of what used to be called "the serving class" and the extraordinary daring of the picture of Negro life and character as she has imagined it.

"Melanctha" is the most challenging as a composition, and the character is the most challenging because she has an interior life. The presentation is for the most part in dialogue of a radical brilliance that lies on the page with a calm defiance. It is as stunning today as when it was first written.

Whether this dialogue is the natural rhythm of Negro speech is not altogether the point. Such a rhythm if discovered for transcription cannot be copyrighted; no author can own it for a certain number of pages. On the other hand, it is clear that the language of "Melanctha" is some kind of speech rhythm not written down before, some catching of accent and flow the reader recognizes without being able to name. Of course, it is a literary language, constructed of repetition, repeated emphasis, all with great musicality. There is a stilted openness to it; that is, it is both declamatory, unnatural, and yet somehow lifelike. It is a courteous dialogue and not condescending because it does not proceed from models, from a spurious idea, from the shelf of a secondhand store.

Inauthenticity is so often remarked when authors need to find a speech for those not from their own class or experience. Stephen Crane's powerful but badly written *Maggie: A Girl of the Streets* is an example of prefab ethnic or class speech. "Hully gee!" said he, "does mugs can't phase me. Dey knows I kin wipe up d'street wid any tree of dem"—Hell's Kitchen.

Gertrude Stein's way in "Melanctha" is so simple and arresting that her ear, in an offhand passage, does have a ghostly attuning. Note the distribution of the *yous* in a plain bit of dialogue spoken by Melanctha's father: "Why don't you see to that girl better you, you're her mother." Pure ear, quite different from the formal cadences of Dr. Jeff Campbell, the mellifluous suitor with his high-pitched arias to the "wandering" Melanctha: "It certainly does sound a little like I don't know very well what I do mean, when you put it like that to me, Miss Melanctha, but that's just because you don't understand enough about what I meant, by what I was just saying to you."

Hemingway learned from Gertrude Stein how to become Ernest Hemingway. Perhaps one could say that. He decided most of all to strip down his sentences. (It is curious to learn condensation from Stein, who stripped, reduced, and simplified only to add up without mercy, making her prose an intimidating heap of bare bones, among other things.) One can see it in 1921—before they had met, but not before he would have read *Three Lives.* Perhaps he learned more from the *yous* than from the more insistent rhythms in "Melanctha."

From "Up in Michigan":

Liz liked Jim very much. She liked it the way he walked over from the shop and often went to the kitchen door to watch for him to start down the road. She liked it about his mustache. . . . She liked it very much that he didn't look like a blacksmith. She liked it how much D. J. Smith and Mrs. Smith liked Jim. One day she found that she liked it the way the hair was black on his arms and how white they were above the tanned line when he washed up in the washbasin outside the house.

And then he ends the paragraph: "Liking that made her feel funny." Gertrude Stein would not have written the last line. It is too girlish for her, and is a repudiation of the tone and rhythm that goes before.

Soon after *Three Lives, The Making of Americans* was resumed, since it had been started earlier. It was taken up—if that is not a contradiction of what it is, a dive into the deep waters of the Stein Sea. Down into the Stein Sea she went between 1906 and 1908, and the book was not actually published until 1925, for reasons not a mystery. It is very long. It swims about and about and farther and farther out with the murmurous monotony of untroubled waters.

The enormous ambition of the book is shown in the roundness of the title. It may be a sort of chronicle, imaginative history, of the Stein family, but that's the least of it. It is the making of Americans, just as she says. That is the intention.

In his introduction, Bernard Fay writes, not without leaning in the direction of her own style: "She likes too much the present; she is too fond of words; she has too strongly the love of life; she is too far from death, to be satisfied with anything but the whole of America."

Consider her idea of the bottom nature of human beings: "A man in his living has many things inside him, he has in him his way of beginning; this can come too from a mixture in him, from the bottom nature of him." So we live and so we die. "Any one has come to be a dead one. Any one has not come to be such a one to be a dead one. Many who were living have come to be a dead one." The cold, black suet-pudding of her style, said Wyndham Lewis.

The "continuous present" is another of her rhetorical discoveries, and it seems to be just a circling round and round, a not going back or forward. *Four in America:* It is not clear how much she knows about her four Americans, how much she wished to know about Ulysses Grant, Henry James, the Wright Brothers, and George Washington. Her meditations do not run to facts or dates, and her vanity would preclude a quotation or even an appropriation. Instead, she asks herself what the four would have done had they been other than what they were. Suppose Grant to be a saint, Henry James a general, the Wright Brothers painters, George Washington a novelist.

What is the difference between Shakespeare's plays and Shakespeare's sonnets? "Shakespeare's plays were written as they were written. Shakespeare's sonnets as they were going to be written." Sometimes an interesting bit comes upon one suddenly, like a handout on the street: "Henry James had no failure and no success." Everything is process. There is no need for revision since the work celebrates and represents process itself, like an endless stirring on the stove. One gift never boils away: She is a comedian.

Such was her gift, and she created a style to display the comedy by a deft repetition of word and phrase. To display the comedy of what? Of living, of thinking? The comedy of writing words down on the page, perhaps that most of all. She was not concerned with creating the structure of classical comedy, the examination of folly. What she understands is inadvertence and incongruity. Imperturbability is her mood, and in that she is herself a considerable comic actor, in the line of Buster Keaton.

Remarks are not literature, so she said. But the remark is her triumph. She lives by epigrams and bits of wit cut out of the stretches or repetition, as if by a knife, and mounted in our memory. Her rival in this mastery is Oscar Wilde, with whom she shared many modes of performance: the bold stare that faced down ridicule, a certain ostentation of type, the love of publicity and the iron to endure it.

I like a view but I like to sit with my back to it.

What is the point of being a little boy if you are going to grow up to be a man?

Before the flowers of friendship faded friendship faded.

I am I because my little dog knows me.

Ezra Pound is a village explainer, excellent if you were a village, but if not, not.

Oscar Wilde was an aesthete. Gertrude Stein thought up something more stylish and impressive. She came forth as an aesthetician: more severe and riddling, yet dandyish in her handsome wools and velvety in her sentences.

"Continuous present": Her most valuable continuous present or presence was the alliance with Alice B. Toklas. It appeared she could achieve herself, become Gertrude Stein, without Leo, and she found him expendable. He combined her vanity with a down-turning contentiousness and tedious pretension, all bereft of her revolutionary accent and brilliant dogmatism.

But still she ponders ones and twos and twos not being ones and then had the luck to turn a corner and find this small, neat person from California, one with the intelligence, competence, and devotion to complete the drama of the large, indolent, brooding, ambitious sibyl, herself.

They are a diptych: figures gazing straight ahead, with no hint of Cubist distortion. A museum aspect to their image—wooden, fixed, iconographic in the Byzantine style. They are serene and a bit sly in the direct gaze.

Everything works, above all the division of labor. Carl Van Vechten considered that Gertrude couldn't sew on a button, couldn't cook an egg or place a postage stamp of the correct denomination on an envelope. Alice's labors over the manuscripts, the copying and proofreading, with a numbing attention to the mysteries of the commas that are and the commas that are not, make of her a heroine of minute distinctions.

The *Autobiography of Alice B.* overwhelms by charm and the richness of the cast and the rosy dawn in Paris at the time. The tone and the wit of the composition stand in an almost perfect balance to the historical vividness of the moment. The book is valiant in self-promotion also, boldly forward in conceit, but that is what spurs the recollection. Otherwise it would not have been worth the effort, Gertrude Stein's effort.

She enjoyed the *Autobiography* a good deal more than some of the great personages on the scene. More than one felt himself or herself to be wrongly presented. Matisse was not amused; he charged she knew nothing about painting. Braque was dismayed by her account of the beginnings of Cubism. Tristan Tzara called her "a clinical case of megalomania."

"Testimony Against Gertrude Stein" appeared in *Transition.* Eugene Jolas, who edited the pamphlet, wrote: "There is a unanimity of opinion that she had no understanding of what really was happening about her, that the mutation of ideas beneath the surface of the more obvious contacts and clashes of personality during the period escaped her entirely."

No matter, she was now a bona-fide international celebrity and had an American public. Books, poems, lectures, plays appeared—and she appeared in person. She returned to America in 1934 for a lecture tour, and everyone knew she had said a rose is a rose is a rose. Newspapermen came to the ship, crowds were waiting at the dock. She and Alice were photogenic, and Gertrude was ready with a reply to every question. It is Oscar Wilde landing in America in the 1880s with nothing to declare but his genius.

She returned to Paris, and then there was World War II and the Occupation—tragic, complex events not suitable to her talent and disrupting to her comfort. Her removal from large events, the hypnotic immersion in the centrality of her own being, made it possible for this very noticeable couple to stay on in France, move here and there, get food, in a sense to brazen it out and be there when the Americans arrived. And wasn't she first and last an American, a true example of the invulnerability of the New World? To be imperturbable, root strong, can be a kind of personal V-day.

Wars I Have Seen, published in 1945, covers these ruminating years in the countryside. It reads like a diary, the recording of events of the day. Perhaps it was dictated to Alice in the evenings. The landscape of the Occupation provided splendid vignettes and an awesome and rich cud of complacency. She did not understand the war, and she did not like things to be troublesome, and so she is increasingly conservative. Both Pétain and Franco pleased her—comfort requires order, that she understood.

But, at last, she had to mull over the question of Jewishness:

The Jews have never been an economic power as anybody knows who knows and as everybody knows who knows. But the Europeans particularly the countries who like to delude their people do not want to know it, and the Jews do not want anybody to know it, although they know it perfectly well they must know it because it would make themselves to themselves feel less important and as they always as the chosen people have felt themselves to be important they do not want anybody to know it.

If it were not for the fact that the reader supplies his own vision of Gertrude and Alice hanging on with the fortitude of lambs hunting for the sheepfold, the whimsicality of *Wars* would offend. "Oh dear. It would all be so funny if it were not so terrifying and so sad."

She lived a long time with her wondrous contraption, the Model T of her style, and sometimes she could run on things with a turn of phrase, but sometimes not. So, she opines, "Soviet Russia will end in nothing so will the Roosevelt administration end in nothing because it is not stimulating it will end in nothing." From the sheepfold, she took up dangerous challenges and offered a work called "Reflections on the Atomic Bomb." She found that the bomb was not interesting.

Anyway, she, the first American, loved the GIs, and they loved her. But she didn't know anything about the young men, and *Brewsie and Willie* (1946) is the aesthetician's defeat. The dialogue is atrocious. She had forgotten that she must fabricate speech, not believe she has captured it at the train station. By now, she is speaking in her own voice, just like any other old person, and confident always, she addresses the nation: "Find out the reason why, look facts in the face, not just what they all say, the leaders, but every darn one of you so that a government by the people for the people shall not perish from the earth, it won't, somebody else will do it if we lie down on the job." And so on.

Finally she emerged as a strange figure, competitive and jealous and also unworldly in her self-isolation. She could not understand why *Ulysses*, radical and difficult—or so she had been told for perhaps she hadn't read it—should have been selling more than *The Making of Americans*. Joyce is difficult because he has more knowledge, more language, more rhythmical musicality than the reader can easily summon. With Gertrude Stein we are frequently urged to forgetfulness, to erasure of tonal memory, so that we may hear the hypnotic murmurings of what is a literature in basic English.

Gertrude Stein, all courage and will, is a soldier of minimalism. Her work, unlike the resonating silences in the art of Samuel Beckett, embodies in its loquacity and verbosity the curious paradox of the minimalist form. This art of the nuance in repetition and placement she shares with the orchestral compositions of Philip Glass.

(1987)

The Fate of the Gifted:
Djuna Barnes

Djuna Barnes died in 1982 at the age of ninety. For forty-one years, this avant-garde 1920s figure had been living in a small apartment in Greenwich Village, surviving on her meager royalties and a stipend from Peggy Guggenheim. This stipend itself was a sort of survival if one considers the embattled relationship she had with Miss Guggenheim and, almost unfailingly, with everyone else. The last years were proud and sad, frugal and lonely, and unproductive except for a verse play, *The Antiphon,* completed in 1954. I was present at the first reading of the play at Harvard in 1956, and the evening was dismaying. Djuna Barnes's long silence had ended in this play, which had about it all the anxious, self-destructive tones of an impossibility into which great effort and hope had been poured. T. S. Eliot, in support of his long friendship with her, was in the audience, and he was also perhaps recklessly present in *The Antiphon,* a vehement, overwrought *Family Reunion* of badly written, declamatory verse and intense, unanchored bitterness of feeling. That night, Djuna Barnes, a writer of wild and original gifts, reminded me in her person of one of those *mutilé de guerre* posters of the First World War. She was a wounded hostage of some kind and somehow abandoned, but just what the line of her fate had been was difficult to know.

To her name there is always to be attached the splendor of *Nightwood,* a lasting achievement of her great gifts and eccentricities—her passionate prose and, in this case, a genuineness of human passions. A love of literary pastiche and parody made her earlier works, *Ryder* and *Ladies Almanack,* an astonishment of wit, as well as a wearying fluency of capital letters, archaic turns of speech, mannerism, and general mischievousness and amused perversity.

A certain balkiness seems to have been part of her character, and her career showed little aptitude for the sturdy and inspired exploitation that turned the most improbable of her contemporaries, Gertrude Stein, into an institution. For Djuna Barnes, Joyce was the inspiration and grandeur of the period. In Paris, she formed a friendship with him which was strong enough for him to have given her the original manuscript, with his annotations, of *Ulysses.* With her usual rotten luck, she was forced to sell it before it commanded a price that might have saved her from the penury and dependence of so many years of her life.

Andrew Field's biography, *Djuna: The Formidable Miss Barnes,* is not a work of any special vivacity. It is under considerable strain in all its parts and can only chatter along desperately about one who was noted for her silences. The title is the first indication of a perplexity. *Formidable* and *Miss Barnes* cannot easily draw us into the riddle, and the primness of the words does not telegraph the creative and personal hardships of the life. He tells of only one meeting with her, in 1977, and from that we conclude that he did not succeed in getting much out of her. Field's book is best when it reads like notes for another book. The portrait of certain Greenwich Village characters such as Guido Bruno, apparently the model for Felix Volkbein in *Nightwood,* and a nuisance named Elsa Baroness von Freytag-Loringhoven are amusing period pieces from the old days. The American expatriates in Paris— Hemingway, Natalie Barney, and others—are sketched in once more from the well-known documentation. There is a struggle with the written work of Djuna Barnes, but Field finds it hard to stay the course for fifteen rounds, and so there is a good deal of sparring with the names of characters and the names in real life and the name of Jake Barnes in *The Sun Also Rises* and what, if anything, the correspondence might indicate.

Djuna Barnes was born in Cornwall-on-Hudson, New York, in 1892. Her father, whom she hated we are told and believe, was a pretentious ne'er-do-well bohemian with mistresses and not much else. Her mother was English, having been born in Rutland. The parents were divorced and the grandparents were divorced and there is a tangle of half brothers and sisters. Quite early, Djuna had to undertake the support of her mother and three brothers, and she did this with admirable energy and talent in the New York newspaper world. The newspaper style of the time was jazzy enough but rather primitive as a vehicle for her talents. Nevertheless, a recent selection from this work, *Smoke and Early Stories,* shows her early mastery of a Firbank-like dandyism and theatricality. From "Paprika Johnson":

> The boy from Stroud's was a tall blond wimpet who had put his hands into his mother's hair and shaken it free of gold; a lad who had painted his cheeks from the palette of the tenderloin, the pink that descends from one member of a family to the other, quicksilver running down life's pages.

In Greenwich Village, she knew Edmund Wilson, Edna Millay, and Eugene O'Neill. She wrote for *Smart Set, Vanity Fair,* and *The Little Review.* She went to Paris and knew all the interesting artists of the time. The wonderful photographs by Man Ray and Berenice Abbott show her to have been extraordinarily chic and good-looking. During this time, she wrote *Ryder, Ladies Almanack,* and *Nightwood,* and by 1940 she was back in New York, where she lived for four more decades.

The life of this remarkable American woman seemed to follow step-by-step the journey of the gifted of her time. Her experiences had a typicality about them: high literary ambitions, a lot of drinking, little money, London, Paris, Berlin and desperate encounters along the way. She was a lesbian in her life and in her work, although there were affairs with men, an abortion fairly late on. "I'm not a lesbian. I just loved Thelma," she said in Field's account. This is a remark. Field thinks of her as "basically heterosexual," whatever that might mean. In fact, "basically" appears to lean the other way, and there is little evidence that she anguished over the fact of lesbianism, even though the terrible Thelma Wood was an anguish indeed. Thelma is the Robin Vote of *Nightwood,* just as Djuna Barnes herself is, in the way of the transformations of literature, the Nora Flood.

Thelma Wood was an American who made sculptures with large feet rather like her own. In spite of that, she was a dashing beauty with a bit of money at times. She drove a red Bugatti, cruised the lesbian bars, drank enormously, lied, teased, was unfaithful, and gave Miss Barnes the miserable fate of wandering the streets at night looking for her. In *Nightwood,* she has the nature of a destructive, forgetful beast. Janet Flanner called her "the bitch of all times." So this love affair was a draining, spirit-crushing disaster, and at last it was broken off. After that, Miss Barnes stayed with Peggy Guggenheim in England, knew the lovers and friends collected there, was stormily friendly with Antonia White and rather more peacefully with Charles Henri Ford. But somehow her friendships did not work out much better than her love affairs. A difficult and unhappy nature she seems to have been— prickly, proud, and sarcastic.

Ryder is a daunting work, published in 1928 when the author was thirty-six. The dreadful father, here called Wendell Ryder, and his three women—mother, wife and mistress—are the center of this tale, as perhaps it can be called. There is an abundance of incident, some of it corresponding to known autobiographical details. Still, there cannot have been an intention to create the feeling of a genuine family chronicle, since events and persons are by style put at a distance of several centuries. In a chapter called "Wendell Discusses Himself with His Mother," the dialogue runs:

> Sometimes I am a whore in ruffled petticoat, playing madly at a pack of ruffians and getting thrippence for my pains; a smartly boxed ear, or a bottom-tingling clap a-hind . . . and once I was a bird who flew down my own throat, twangling at the heart cord, to get the pitch of my own mate-call.

Even the essential facts of narrative information are rendered in a mannered tone that often has the cadence of translation: "At the end of three weeks, his shadow was exceeding lean. On the coming of Saturday he was sacked. (His companions in clerking saying that it was due to his delivery of prussic acid to a weaning lady in Chiswick, in place of bismuth.)"

The pastiche, parody, and flow are accomplished with outstanding virtuosity of language, witty juxtapositions and reversals, and a wonderful ending line for the book and for Wendell: "And whom should he disappoint?" *Ryder* is a curiosity, showing its period, the 1920s, only in a sophisticated and conscious malice and in the studied, learned manipulation of styles. The zest and the jest are embraced perhaps too lovingly. The manner itself is the intention, and the ear is bookish and rather overwhelming.

The "Englishness" of Djuna Barnes's work, after her early apprenticeship, is perhaps to be laid at the door of her rejected American father. There is scarcely an American rhythm or cadence in her work, and even the description of Nora's American background in *Nightwood* has the generalizing aspect of something worked up rather than known from birth—for example, the atmosphere of Nora's house: "The Drummer Boy, Fort Sumter, Lincoln, Booth, all somehow came to mind; Whigs and Tories were in the air."

The famous Dr. O'Connor of *Nightwood* makes his first appearance in *Ryder*. And he is there as he will be—a monologist. Dr. O'Connor, an American going about Paris, talked and talked, both in life and in novels by Americans other than Djuna Barnes. Andrew Field runs the doctor down and finds that his performances received a mixed reception, with some remembering him as fantastical and amusing and others, of course, bored out of their skulls in his presence. In any case, his real name was Dan Mahoney, and he was a very noticeable queen around the Paris bars. He blued his eyelids and coated his eyelashes and covered his heavy beard with face powder. He claimed to have served in the navy and to be a medical doctor, but he was the sort whose name does not appear in the records of institutions. Aside from his fabrications, he spoke of himself, truthfully, as "poor Minnie Mahoney, the girl whom God forgot." Fashionable lesbians liked him, and he was cozy company.

"A slight satiric wigging," Djuna Barnes called *Ladies Almanack*, and it is just that. Many of the lesbian women in Paris appeared in this amiable calendar, which "featured" Dame Evangeline Musset (Natalie Barney), Lady Buck-and-Balk and Tilly-Tweed-in-Blood (Lady Una Trowbridge and Radclyffe Hall). The book was privately printed in Paris in 1929 and "hawked along the Left Bank by bold young women." It is a teasing and bold production and very much *written*, not tossed off, and again in the mock English Lit manner.

Now this be a Tale of as fine a Wench as ever wet Bed, she who was called Evangeline Musset and who was in her Heart one Grand Red Cross for the Pursuance, the Relief and the Distraction of such Girls as in their Hinder Parts, and their Fore Parts, and in whatsoever Parts did suffer them most, lament Cruelly, be it Itch of Palm, or Quarters most horribly burning.

It is possible to see in this book and in *Ryder* a crippling facility for inspired verbal cartooning. After the freedom, the parodying dash and dazzle with no necessity for the restraints of verisimilitude and narrative coherence, the small production of this large talent is a loss not altogether surprising.

Nightwood is a novel of intrepid originality. It appeared in 1936, published in England by Faber at the strong urging of T. S. Eliot. Eliot supplied an introduction, thereby giving his unique imprimatur to assist a daunting work of the imagination. Even this most important and promising lift to a career in literature was met with down-dragging decisions, some aesthetic and some practical. Djuna Barnes herself cut the manuscript to a third of its original length, and Eliot supplied the title. The expectation of loss caused the firm to publish without an advance and to claim 25 percent of the American rights.

The reviews in England, especially those by Edwin Muir, Dylan Thomas, and Graham Greene, were favorable. In America the reaction was largely negative, and the "Elizabethan tragedy" claims of Eliot's introduction were considered high-flown and dropped from the second American edition. Considerable impertinence attended this most sober and ambitious achievement in the work of Djuna Barnes.

Nightwood opens in the formal, instructing manner of a European novel, perhaps a German one. The beginning pages are laden with ancestral claims, old furniture detailed in wood and decoration, portraits on the wall, the lady in "great puffed and pearled sleeves," a gentleman on a charger. "The blue of an Italian sky lay between the saddle and the tightened rump of the rider." Thus the introduction of Felix Volkbein, a stiff-necked Jew, with the false title of Baron, a haughty, romantic obsequiousness and elaborate imitative leanings. "He kept a valet and a cook: the one because he looked like Louis the Fourteenth and the other because she resembled Queen Victoria." Some have questioned the more or less lengthy, in terms of this short book, intrusion of Volkbein at the beginning of a work to which he is not central. But he is attentive to structure and quite soon meets the human core of the novel—Dr. Matthews O'Connor, Robin Vote, and Nora Flood. Indeed, he rushes in and marries Robin, whom we first observe in a deathbed scene: "On a bed, surrounded by a confusion of potted plants, exotic palms and cut flowers, faintly over-sung by the note of unseen birds." Robin is not dead, she is only dead drunk.

Volkbein's elaborate aspirations for ancestral validation in no way prepare us for his marriage to the wayward Robin. Still, perhaps it is useful for a plot in which a hieratical and abstract conception of character almost precludes the usual conventions of psychological patterning. The characters are the subjects of a ruminating intelligence, and almost anything might be said about them by the author. Here, we do not have an accumulation of biography; instead, character is seen as a timeless intimation of universal buried life. Robin Vote: "Such a woman is the infected carrier of the past; before her the structure of our head and jaws aches—we feel that we could eat her, she who is eaten death returning, for only then do we put our face close to the blood on the lips of our forefathers."

Nightwood is a love story. Were it not, the high-pitched brilliance of the writing would offend by its disjunction from feeling. The love of Nora Flood for Robin Vote is a sort of sacramental agony, and for this affliction the devices of style, the demonism of the heavy night airs, have a ghastly appropriateness. Nora and Robin are American women who meet at a circus, under the gaze of a lioness with "her furious great head with its yellow eyes afire." Nora is said to be a Westerner, but there is no dust of Omaha or Sacramento about her. Like enchanted creatures, they immediately begin to travel to Munich, Vienna, Budapest, and Paris. The misery begins as each night Robin stands by the door, saying, "Don't wait up for me." Since Robin is the object of obsession, another American woman becomes obsessed and takes her off.

The nighttime misery of a desperate love holds the novel together and allows even the uncertain significations of Dr. O'Connor's monologues. He is a dog of the night, going from bar to bar, saying as he leaves a chance acquaintance, "The lady will pay." In the most powerful scene in the book, Nora seeks him out at home, or in the pitiful room that passes for the home of this person alive only in the presence of others. She finds him on a dirty bed in a woman's flannel nightgown:

The doctor's head, with its over-large black eyes, its full gun-metal cheeks and chin, was framed in the golden semi-circle of a wig with long pendent curls that touched his shoulders, and falling back against the pillow, turned up the shadowy interior of their cylinder.

Dr. O'Connor is asked to think about the night and about love. He is ready, fully prepared; he is precocious, ludicrous, pedantic, and a consolation. To Nora's "What am I to do?" he answers:

> Be as the Frenchman, who puts a *sou* in the poorbox at night that he may find a penny to spend in the morning—he can trace himself back to his sediment, vegetable and animal, and so find himself in the odour of wine in its two travels, in and out, packed down beneath an air that has not much changed its position during that strategy.

Or he answers something else, at length. Dr. O'Connor, as I read it, is to be taken seriously because he is seen as providing in all his appearances the consolations of language itself, of memory, of jumbled information, of metaphor. "Was it at night that Sodom became Gomorrah? It was at night, I swear!" On and on. He is a fruitful creation of loquacity just as the animalistic Robin is a devastation by silence. But Eliot was wise to see the mischief of this rhetorical Satan going to and fro. As we have the novel now, we could not usefully have more of Dr. O'Connor.

Eliot's introduction sees the powerfulness of Dr. O'Connor and that "such a character needs other real, if less conscious, people in order to realize his own reality." He wants to insist upon the naturalness of the work as fiction, to see it as having some of the practical experience of human existence: "Felix and his child are oppressively real." Some of this is the kindness of the wish to aid in the marketplace a seemingly unmarketable inspiration. He ends: "What I would leave the reader prepared to find is the great achievement of the style, the beauty of the phrasing, the brilliance of wit and characterization, and a quality of horror and doom very nearly related to that of Elizabethan tragedy."

There is the Black Mass ending of *Nightwood* in which Robin in front of a "contrived altar, before a Madonna," and with two burning candles, turns into a dog to fight with a true dog nearby, both biting and barking until they give up, "lying out, her hands beside her, her face turned and weeping; and the dog too gave up then, and lay down, his eyes bloodshot, his head flat along his knees." This is revenge indeed, and a minor Elizabethan bloody finale it is.

As a work of its own period, *Nightwood* is not minor, though it is decadent. The literature of decadence with its ornamental style, artificiality, its relishing horrific incident, is common today in America with Norman Mailer and others, and so perhaps the charge is not impugning. Now, *Nightwood* appears more acceptable to the sensibilities than it might have in 1936, during the reign of documentary portrayal of what the actual was thought to be. It is a work of the imagination, a recognizable and frightening love story, accomplished with a high, cool, and loyal belief in the possibilities of words in place and out of place, vocabulary stretched and strained, incident and arrangement without practical preparation—all, in this case, instruments of revelation.

Andrew Field has learned what he could about Djuna Barnes, and it is not to his discredit that there isn't much to tell. There is a sadness in the life. She seemed to fall aside after she had done her best work. Her nature is not easy to take hold of. There was little luck, and to that she added a bit of obstructive paranoia. Thus, she suffered.

(1983)

WIND FROM THE PRAIRIE

THE PRAIRIE POETS:
CARL SANDBURG, VACHEL LINDSAY,
AND EDGAR LEE MASTERS

Roll along, Prairie Moon,
Roll along, while I croon.

Around World War I, writers from the American Middle Western states began to appear on the literary scene. In fiction, there were Theodore Dreiser, Sinclair Lewis, and Sherwood Anderson, and also the three known as the Prairie Poets, Carl Sandburg, Vachel Lindsay, and Edgar Lee Masters.

Looking into the new biography of Carl Sandburg, a work of exhaustive, definitive coziness in the current American mode of entranced biographical research, I was reminded of having some years ago taken from the library stacks a curiosity, a biography of Lindsay written by Edgar Lee Masters. If Carl Sandburg can be said to have managed shrewdly the transactions of his declamatory, bardic career as a national treasure, born in Illinois on a corn-husk mattress, the other two rose and fell disastrously and literally. Vachel Lindsay committed suicide, and Masters died in want, having been found broke and sick in the Chelsea Hotel in New York and rescued to die in a nursing home.

The two men, Lindsay and Masters, are not quite soul mates. Their union is geographical, a territorial, circumstantial linkage to a mythographic Middle West, the putative spiritual grasslands of the vast native country. Lindsay was a naive, manic evangelist, preaching the Gospel of Beauty, and carrying with him on his incredible cross-country hikes the Christian fundamentalism and Anti-Saloon teachings of his youth—along with, of course, the prairie, the conviction of being the voice of some real America, *in situ,* that must be honored, as if under threat of extinction by a flood. As a versifier he had no more caution than a hobo hitching a ride, but somehow his voice prevailed for a time, even with some of the respected critics of the day. He appeared and appeared, willing to recite at a high-school reunion as well as in London, where, according to a later biographer, Eleanor Ruggles, "he and his mother met Robert Bridges, venerable laureate and defender of the tongue [*sic*], and John Masefield, always Vachel's admirer, came in from Boars Hill to pay his respects." Feverish days, but, toward the end, in Washington, D.C., an audience of two hundred walked out, puzzling the performer and Edgar Lee Masters but attributed in the Ruggles biography to a microphone failure of which the poet was unaware.

Edgar Lee Masters, for a good part of his life a successful lawyer in Chicago, was a lot smarter than Vachel Lindsay and certainly more worldly—but then everyone was more worldly than Lindsay. Masters was in religion a freethinker, set against the "hypocrisy" of the preachers, even more exasperated by the temperance movement, and along the way set against puritanical sexual inhibitions. He was a handsome man who, step by hesitating step, nevertheless made a rashly uncomfortable marriage to a fundamentalist, teetotaler young woman. He had children, stayed on, was unfaithful (listing in his autobiography nearly as many female loves as Goethe), finally divorced, and remarried a young woman—indeed, thirty years younger than he. Lindsay was one of those too friendly boosters with their often strange imperviousness and faltering sense of the appropriate. Masters was splenetic, the cemetery headstone his natural memorial, cranky in opinion, and, although very productive and for a time immensely successful, there was in his life a feeling of being undervalued, and even of seeing the whole country in an enormous displacement from virtue, pioneer and otherwise.

Of Lindsay, Masters said he was "impelled to write something about the poet who was native to Illinois, as I am in reality, and who knew the same people and the same culture that I do, and who practiced the art of poetry, as I have, in the same part of America, and under the same social and political conditions." In the end, as he reaches Lindsay's declining audience and death, he begins to see the life as a social rather than a personal tragedy, to view the native "singer" as a victim of the East, the money-grubbing, alienated world that preferred the poems of Robert Frost and E. A. Robinson, poets Masters finds essentially "English" in tone and landscape rather than American.

There's more to it than that from this strange man about his stranger fellow bard:

> The motley stocks and alien breeds which have taken America cannot be American until there is an America to mold them into Americans.... Lindsay might sing himself hoarse of the old courthouse America, the old horse and buggy America, the America of the Santa Fé Trail, of Johnny Appleseed.... Did the East, did these alien stocks want to be American? This is what Lindsay was up against. In this connection mention must be made of the Jews who are enormously numerous, powerful and influential. Jews are not Americans in the sense that the Jews are English or French, according to habitat.

Ezra Pound described Vachel Lindsay as a "plain man in gum overshoes with a touching belief in W. J. Bryan." Yes, there was "Bryan, Bryan, Bryan, Bryan," the poem celebrating the Free Silver populist, fundamentalist, and prohibitionist in his losing campaign against McKinley. Almost three hundred lines in which Bryan is seen as "the prairie avenger . . . smashing Plymouth Rock with his boulders from the West." His defeat was the "victory of Plymouth Rock and all those inbred landlord stocks" (perhaps it was) and also, in a wild extension, somehow the defeat of the "blue bells of the Rockies and the blue bonnets of old Texas."

Lindsay's life was one of intense, sentimental aggressiveness; and yet there is something unprotected about him. His unanchored enthusiasm has the dismaying aspect of being genuine and unforced, a sort of hysterical innocence, or so it seems. The cheerful, round-faced, fair-haired country boy was in fact town bred, born in Springfield, Illinois. Fate put his birthplace next to the house in which Lincoln had lived, and this—the nearness of the great, solemn son of the prairie, the hallowed walker of the streets of Springfield—had the effect of igniting the boy like a firecracker. Lincoln in Illinois had quite a contrary effect on Edgar Lee Masters, who wrote a long, scathing biography of the fallen president, composed with the racing eloquence of contempt for the man and for the "tyrannous plutocracy" that followed the Civil War.

Both Lindsay and Masters come from professional families. Masters's father was a self-made lawyer, a conscientious man of some influence in Illinois and given, at least in part, to liberal causes and worthy cases. The Lindsay family was an older combination of beliefs and habits. The father, as a young man in impecunious circumstances, worked his way through an Ohio medical school, set up practice in Illinois, and, after the death of his first wife, somehow saved enough for further study in Vienna. On the boat going to Europe, he met his future wife, a teacher of art and other subjects in Kentucky. Throughout their lives, with or without their children, the couple traveled quite a lot, going several times to Europe and even as far as Japan and China, but there were less cosmopolitan strains in the mother. She passed on to her son the ornamental, provincial "art-loving" claim of certain small-town American wives and also a good measure of the missionary qualities he displayed. Mrs. Lindsay was the organizer of church spectacles, liked to officiate in group meetings, attend conferences, and so on.

Her family was attached to the Campbellite Church, also known as the Christian Church. The church had been founded by Alexander Campbell and his son Thomas, originally Presbyterians and then, coming to believe in baptism by immersion, united with the Baptists, before finally breaking away—in one of those organizational disputes so peculiar to the Protestant denominations—to found their own Campbellite sect. From these roots, Vachel Lindsay got his fundamentalism and prohibitionism, the Gospel of Beauty, and a flair for expounding preacher-style. He was sent to the Art Institute of Chicago and later, in New York in 1905, studied with William Merritt Chase and Robert Henri but did not make notable progress as a painter or as a cartoonist.

All the time, Lindsay had been writing verses in his hymn-tune rhythms, reciting at the YMCA, and turning himself into a peddler. With his verses and drawings, the plain, open-faced, clean young man wandered the streets of New York, knocking on the doors of fish markets, Chinese laundries, and bakeries, stopping people to listen to his wares, canvassing, as it were, Hell's Kitchen. A curious, impervious nuisance, bringing to mind the intrepid appeals of the Jehovah's Witness bell ringers. And then he began his years of quite literally tramping across the country, pamphlets and verses for sale, doing missionary work for the Gospel of Beauty. He carried with him a character reference from the YMCA.

It was in California that Lindsay learned of the death of General William Booth, founder of the Salvation Army. And thus he came to write one of his first bizarre incantations, an unaccountable success for which the mind glancing back on our literary history is, well, dumbstruck.

GENERAL WILLIAM BOOTH
ENTERS INTO HEAVEN.
(To be sung to the tune of "The Blood of the Lamb"
with indicated instrument)

The works opens with bass-drum beats and:

> Booth led boldly with his big bass drum—
> (Are you washed in the blood of the Lamb?)
> The Saints smiled bravely and they said: "He's come."
> (Are you washed in the blood of the Lamb?)

The thing flows on apace and concludes:

> He saw King Jesus. They were face to face,
> And he knelt a-weeping in that holy place.
> Are you washed in the blood of the Lamb?

The submission appeared in an early issue of *Poetry* and Harriet Monroe in the annual prize giving of 1913 awarded it $100. A prize for $250 went to William Butler Yeats, the latter having been pushed for by Ezra Pound. Sometime later, when Yeats was in Chicago, Miss Monroe invited Lindsay to a dinner to which the various important writers on hand were invited. That evening Vachel Lindsay recited the whole of "The Congo" and was apparently "well-received" in spite of its being over two hundred fiercely resounding lines. This most extraordinary embarrassment in our cultural history achieved a personally orated dissemination scarcely to be credited. Anywhere and everywhere he went with it—the Chamber of Commerce, high schools, ladies' clubs, the Lincoln Day banquet in Springfield, the Players Club in New York, where Masters tells that its noise greatly irritated certain members.

"The Congo" is the supreme folly of Lindsay's foolhardy career. There is a sad, no doubt unconscious, complacency in its concussive hilarity, the compositional shove coming from

> an allusion in a sermon by my pastor, F. W. Burnham, to the heroic life and death of Ray Eldred. Eldred was a missionary of the Disciples of Christ who perished while swimming a treacherous branch of the Congo.

The work is subtitled "A Study of the Negro Race," and part one lies under the heading "Their Basic Savagery." The imagery, if such it can be called, is blackface American minstrel, except for a strophe about Leopold of Belgium in hell with his hands cut off.

With a "deep rolling bass," the prairie evangelist sets out on his crusade:

> Fat black bucks in a wine-barrel room,
> Barrel-house kings, with feet unstable . . .
> Beat an empty barrel with the handle of a broom . . .
> Boomlay, boomlay, boomlay, BOOM . . .
>
> THEN I SAW THE CONGO, CREEPING THROUGH
> THE BLACK,
> CUTTING THROUGH THE FOREST WITH A
> GOLDEN TRACK. . . .
>
> Tattooed cannibals danced in files;
> Then I heard the boom of the blood-lust song. . . .
> Boom, kill the Arabs,
> Boom, kill the white men,
> Hoo,Hoo,Hoo. . . .
> Mumbo-Jumbo will hoo-doo you.

The second section has the title "Their Irrepressible High Spirits." Here, on the Congo River, we run into a round of crapshooting, whoops and yells, witch-men dressed to kill, "cake-walk princes" in tall silk hats, coal-black maidens with pearls in their hair, and more Boom,

Boom, Boom. In the third section, "The Hope of Their Religion," the Apostles appear in coats of mail and, to the tune of "Hark, ten thousand harps and voices," ordain that "Mumbo-Jumbo will die in the jungle." The forests, the beasts, and the "savages" fade away, whispering, in a pianissimo, the dying strains of "Mumbo-Jumbo will hoo-doo you." The "bucks" are thus converted, all now down-home Campbellites.

What the far-flung audiences made of this infernal indiscretion is hard to imagine. There is always a market for "carrying on" in public, as we can confirm today. No doubt there was more condescension in the air than the reports would suggest. A performance organized in 1920 at Oxford University by Robert Graves can be read as an elaborate prank on the pretensions of the dons rather than as a tribute to the prairie poet—indeed, the sweating reiterations of the amateur elocutionist might recall Tom Thumb at Queen Victoria's court.

In any case, scholars can excavate in the old magazines many alarming commendations of this native genius, fresh voice, America's Homer, and so on. Harriet Monroe, a promoter of poetry and of the Middle West in tandem, wrote the introduction to the book publication of *The Congo and Other Poems.* The praise is short but unfortunately ranging in reference, like a kangaroo leaping over rich and spacious plains. Whistler and Whitman are called forth before a landing by Miss Monroe on the "old Greek precedent of the half-chanted lyric." The "Greek precedent" is one of those critical jokes like "the Jane Austen of the Upper West Side," but the claims of the Prairie Poets and subsequent idolators to the example of Whitman is an unending irritation.

"The Santa Fé Trail" is another noisy work, the theme seeming to be that the sound of the automobile—Crack, Crack, Crack—is trying without success to overwhelm the song "sweet, sweet, sweet" of a local Southwest bird known as Rachel-Jane. Then there is a salute to the firemen, "Clang, Clang, Clang," and an evocation of Jesus in "I Heard Immanuel Singing."

> He was ruddy like a shepherd.
> His bold young face how fair.
> Apollo of the silver bow
> Had not such flowing hair.

Tramping and reciting, forever in manic locomotion with notebook in hand to scribble whatever came into his head, head to be laid down at night on a YMCA pillow, leaving little time for romantic life. Actually, Lindsay comes across as more than a little girl-shy in spite of crushes here and there, one falling on the poet Sara Teasdale. But she married a rich shoe manufacturer and for a time was set up grandly in New York, until she too was mowed down by the drastic scythe of taste and died divorced, no longer rich, reclusive, and embittered. At last, Lindsay married a young woman from Spokane, a high-school teacher of English and Latin. She was twenty-three, and he was forty-six. They had two daughters and were always in financial distress, since his income came largely from recitations and a good portion went to agents and expenses. On the road, the listeners forever calling for "Congo" and "General Booth," Lindsay was to experience the pathos of repetition: exhaustion and insolvency.

Along the way, uphill and downhill, Lindsay wrote a most interesting book, fortunately in prose: *The Art of the Moving Picture,* first issued in 1915, revised in 1922, and later reprinted with an excellent appreciation of its worth in an introduction by Stanley Kauffmann. After the rant and carelessness of the verses, Lindsay concentrated his mind on the movies. Here it is, he must have decided as he rested his vocal cords in the darkness of the old cinemas—American, popular, infinite in variety, flung out to the folk with a prodigality very similar to his own production methods. He tries to organize what the films can do, sort out the types, explain the power of directors such as D. W. Griffith. For instance, "The Action Picture":

In the action picture there is no adequate means for the development of full-grown personal passion. The Action Pictures are falsely advertised as having heart-interest, or abounding in tragedy, but though the actors glower and wrestle and even if they are the most skillful labmasters in the profession, the audience gossips, and chews gum.

There are the Intimate Photoplays, the Splendor Pictures, which divide into Crowd Splendor, Patriotic Splendor, Religious Splendor, and so on. Concerning the intimate photoplay, he writes:

Though the intimate and friendly photoplay may be carried out of doors to a row of loafers in front of the country store, or the gossiping streets of the village, it takes its origin and theory from the snugness of the interior. The restless reader replies that he has seen photoplays that showed ballrooms that were grandiose, not the least cozy. These are to be classed as out-of-door scenery so far as theory goes, and are discussed under the head of Splendor Pictures. The intimate Motion Picture . . . is gossip *in extremis.*

The movies and their vagrant images for him, the lonely traveling man, had the seductive power of the saloon for others of his kind. He was seduced into a contemplation and wish for coherence absent from his verse making. Thus, he finds "noble views of the sea," common to early camera effects, allied to "the sea of humanity spectacles":

> the whirling of dancers in ballrooms, handkerchief-waving masses of people on balconies, the hat-waving political ratification meetings, ragged, glowering strikers, and gossiping, dickering people in the market-place. Only Griffith and his disciples can do these as well as almost any manager can reproduce the ocean. Yet the sea of humanity is dramatically blood-brother to the Pacific, the Atlantic, or Mediterranean. . . . So, in *The Birth of a Nation,* the Ku Klux Klan dashes down the road as powerfully as Niagara pours over the cliff.

A film version of Ibsen's *Ghosts* came to town, and Lindsay reports that it was not Ibsen and should have been advertised under the title "The Iniquities of the Fathers. An American Drama of Eugenics, in a Palatial Setting." The style of these reflections, offhand and colloquial, is usefully attuned to the subject and to his casual but transfixed attentions. Returning from the showing of Larry Trimble's *The Battle Hymn of the Republic,* he recorded that the girl at the piano played "Under the Shade of the Apple Tree" throughout. Among the virtues of the films are their usefulness, nonalcoholic, to the working classes, who, in the heat of summer, "under the wind of an electric fan, can witness everything from a burial at Westminster to the birthday parade of the ruler of the land of Swat."

Los Angeles is the Boston, the Florence of this great flowering, and the stars are national monuments. He pens a tribute to Mary Pickford, "doll divine," which will proceed to rhyme with "valentine." And Blanche Sweet: "Stately are her wiles / filling oafs with wisdom, / Saving souls with smiles." *The Art of the Moving Picture* is the prairie singer's finest, most lasting tribute to the American West, to Hollywood.

He was fifty-two years old when he committed suicide. It is not easy to be certain what was going on in his mind, but there seem to have been frightening mood swings, ups and downs, suspicions followed by remorse, in every way a sad collapse. Doctors were called in, but before a decision could be made for treatment, Lindsay drank Lysol, saying, "I got them before they got me—they can just try to explain this if they can."

Edgar Lee Masters was asked by Lindsay's wife to write a biography and given access to the papers—a very large fund of jottings, since Lindsay showed a self-preoccupation quite precocious, if that is the way to look at his keeping a daily diary almost from the time he first learned to write. Masters's work is rich in thorny attitudes, and that gives it a certain cross-grained interest, especially when compared to the ruthless coverage of the pertinent and impertinent, the sense of being on a long trip with the subject in the family car, that defines the research of Lindsay's other biographer, Eleanor Ruggles, as it does so many other conventional and academic biographies.

Lindsay's limitations are, if not stressed, at least acknowledged when Masters writes:

Lindsay dwelt forever in cuckoo cloudland. . . . He never grew up. The curled darling became a man of great emotional strength; but the memory of himself as the apple of his mother's eye, as the child wonder of grammar school. . . . a sort of Santa Claus grown up and made suitable for adult wonder and devotion.

On the other hand, we are asked to view the fantastical footnote, Lindsay, in conspiratorial terms:

Not being Eastern American he made only a slight impact upon it; and after the first excitement about his poetry subsided he was treated with supercilious indifference, and the field he had broken and harrowed and sowed was taken and reaped by pro-English artists. . . . They preferred the Arthurian legends to Johnny Appleseed and Andrew Jackson.

The accent of grievance, neatly correspondent to Masters's cast of mind, is not to the point in the matter of Vachel Lindsay, and in any case the shape of an individual career is mixed with so many contingencies it cannot easily support a translation to the general. But all that is nothing beside the fact that if Lindsay had some sort of talents, they were not for poetry. He did not write poetry, he wrote jingles and hymns and scenarios for his public appearances. The true melancholy of the life lies in the broad encouragement of his naïveté, the span of his performances, which would inevitably weary. His books were published, he was "famous," and yet somehow he remained a door-to-door peddler.

Edgar Lee Masters was born in 1869, and his major work, *Spoon River Anthology*, did not appear until 1915, although a few of the portraits in it had been published earlier under a pseudonym. He entered his father's profession of law and practiced in Chicago for almost thirty years. He was unhappily married and wrote in his autobiography: "Somehow little by little I got the feeling that my wife in spite of her almost meek compliance was enervating me and cutting off my hair and putting out my eyes." A bitter divorce finally came about, and Masters moved to New York with a new young bride and settled into the Chelsea Hotel, his wife going back and forth to teach in Pennsylvania.

In many ways a companionable man, friend of Mencken, Dreiser, and others who liked their cigars and schnapps, member of the Players Club, somehow Masters seemed to drift into reclusion. We may notice that although he was in partnership for almost eight years with Clarence Darrow in Chicago, the well-known lawyer does not appear in Masters's autobiography. Masters's son, by the first wife, in a memoir attributes this gap to the scandal of the divorce and the appearance on the scene of her replacement, some thirty years younger. Perhaps, he suggests, Darrow took at best a neutral attitude, and the estrangement followed. Also the son tells of visiting his father at the Chelsea. Ellen Masters, now his stepmother, did not seem to be on hand. Present, however, was another young woman, Alice Davis, who lived in the hotel and helped with manuscripts and whatever else she helped with.

In 1944, *The New York Times* printed a story telling that Masters had been taken to Bellevue Hospital suffering from pneumonia and malnutrition. The Authors League and the American Academy came to his rescue, the wife packed him off to a Pennsylvania nursing home, near to where she was teaching, and there he died six years later at the age of eighty-one. Not a happy roundup, even if there is a hint of self-willed recoil and collapse when one remembers the great industry Masters showed throughout his life in the production of works in many forms—verse, plays, novels, biography, and autobiography.

Spoon River Anthology (1915)—a book could scarcely be more of a success. Said to have sold more copies than any other previous work of American poetry, it was translated into all the European languages as well as into Arabic, Korean, and Chinese; it was also transformed for the stage and used as the libretto for an opera, performed at La Scala. The book is an "anthology" of the gravestones around Spoon River, an area near to Lewistown, Illinois, where Masters grew up. The dead come forth to speak the epitaphs of their lives, each one a short free-verse recollection, a sort of *conte,* very often remembering injuries or spoken with a surly ruefulness. The unquiet graves, some 214 of them—"all, all, are sleeping on the hill"—were thought to be some-what cynical and degrading to the quality of life lived in the Illinois villages of Masters's youth and from which he drew his ruminating characters.

The first one is "Hod Putt," who died by hanging for a robbery in his days of poverty after a life of toil. Seeing an opportunity for the last word, he notes with satisfaction that he lies next to a crook who prospered from clever uses of the possibilities of bankruptcy. "Now we who took the bankrupt law in our respective ways, / Sleep peacefully side by side." The verses today strike one not as acerbic so much as generally soulful, "filled with longing" poems; good, simple people seeking transcendence. "Of what use is it / To rid one's self of the world, / When no soul may ever escape the eternal destiny of life?"

The public appeal of the work must have been in the framing: first, the lachrymal country churchyard with the darkening granite of the tombstones lying in random placement as in village life; then, the brief, anecdotal summations, many of them reading like those civil-court cases that scrape the skins of the litigants into eternity. To this must be added the candid moral framing of the little stories, the accent on the scorned, the unlucky, the eccentric from whom the smothering "hypocrisy" of the village would exact its punishments.

The "valiant" departed one, "Jefferson Howard," is "Foe of the church with its charnel darkness, / Friend of the human torch of the tavern" and hounded by the "dominating forces"—Republicans,

Calvinists, merchants, bankers. In Spoon River, fate deals out repetitive cards, like the equalizing aspect of death itself. The aesthetic default of the work, pressing upon the mind as one name after another approaches its declaration, is that it could go on forever, the flat proseness of the language contributing, as the rocks in the sod are turned over again and again. There was indeed a second collection of Spoon River tales, a replication and consequent deflation of the original invention. (Another monologue-portrait was published during these years, "The Love Song of J. Alfred Prufrock.")

A biography, *Lincoln: The Man,* appeared in 1931. Hara-kiri, blood on the floor, Masters's as well as Lincoln's, an insult to the prairie, to Illinois, and perhaps to Carl Sandburg, or so Vachel Lindsay thought. The first part of Sandburg's Lincoln book, *The Prairie Years,* had been out for five years, and if its success embittered Masters, the emotion had its source in the picture of Lincoln rather than in the author's success in the market.

Masters's character is a puzzle, and it is hard to understand why this attractive and intelligent man, successful as a lawyer and a writer, should be such a sorehead. He is the village iconoclast, atheist, free lover, and more than a bit paranoid in the matter of local and national forces. He has *ideas* as some have freckles, and the book on Lincoln puts many of them on display with a good deal of eloquence, however alienating. The notion of the book is that the Civil War should not have been fought and that the aftermath—the domination of plutocrats, merchants, bankers, and the later imperial adventurism—was a disastrous drift. "Hebraic-Puritanism" is Masters's phrase for the moral insufficiency of the country. By this he does not appear to indicate anti-Semitism; instead, he felt a corrosive resentment of the Bible, Old Testament and New, and its power to shape the ethical climate of the nation. After the Civil War,

> as if in sublime malice, the choking weeds of Hebraic-Puritanism were sown; and thus the evils of empire and ancient privileges began to thrive, scarcely before the new wheat was started. Ages may be required for creative vision to stand externally in this field and its epos.

The overwhelming offense of the biographer was its picture of the character of Lincoln, who is seen as a creature of swamp-bred shrewdness, a sort of wary, calculating Snopes, retaining in the midst of certain superficial refinements the qualities of his father, Thomas Lincoln, who out of shiftlessness had sunk into the fetid habits of the "poor white" class. Masters stresses the fact that Nancy Hanks, Lincoln's mother, was illegitimate and in the enveloping mist of parental uncertainty had discovered or imagined her supposed father to be a well-bred Virginia planter. Lincoln claimed the presence of his more promising qualities to have come from the absent grandfather. "Lincoln was profoundly ashamed of the poverty of his youth, and of the sordid surroundings in which he grew up." Thus, his life was ruled by the determination to rise above his beginnings, "unlike the more honest Andrew Jackson and Walt Whitman."

The distinction and beauty of Lincoln's prose and of his platform style must be conceded—and also reduced. For Masters, this accomplishment and talent are suffused and diseased with the poison of the Bible: "Lincoln, whose only literacy was out of the Bible, and who developed an oratory from it, inspired by its artifice of emotional reiteration, and equipped with its sacred curses and its dreadful prophecies, its appeal to moralities where there was no thought, no real integrity." The Gettysburg Address is unfavorably compared to Pericles' funeral oration and subjected to a textual analysis on the matter of truth: "It was not true that our fathers in 1776 had brought forth a new nation; for in that year our fathers brought forth thirteen new nations, each of which was a sovereign state." Lincoln as a statesman and a thinker is accused of the "Hebraic-Puritan principle of assuming to act as one's brother's keeper, when the real motive was to become one's brother's jailer."

Out of indignation and obsession, Masters dug his own grave and sadly inscribed his own tombstone with the acid of the Spoon River meters. The resentment of the Civil War soldier, "Knowlt Hoheimer," killed in battle and lying up on the hill, might be his own epitaph:

> Rather a thousand times
> the county jail
> Than to lie under this marble
> figure with wings,
> And this granite pedestal
> Bearing the words, "Pro Patria."
> What do they mean, anyway?

Carl Sandburg lived to be eighty-nine years old, and he spent those years going here and yon, a hardy tumbleweed of a populist, blown by the wind across the plains. More than forty books to his credit and what for some would have been a burdensome accretion of honors, each one to be accepted and attended like the duties on the court calendar. Of course, he was sustained by the old pioneer energy, and as an early pop-art king his act—writing free-verse poems, collecting and performing *The American Songbag*—was inexhaustible. The six volumes on the life of Lincoln, "a folk biography" some critic was happy to describe it, spread over more than ten years, but of course he was on the hoof a good deal of that time.

These reflections come about from the strenuous busyness of Penelope Niven's new biography of Sandburg: over seven hundred pages, followed by another hundred of notes. This effort is a sort of rival to Sandburg's *Lincoln: Prairie Years, Chicago Years, National Hero Years*. Professor Niven says in her preface that her previous scholarship was of the sort to exclude the claims of this bygone figure, fallen from eminence, but "a decade after his death, I went to his Carolina mountain home," and then it appears that she fell into the corncrib, so to speak. That is, the vast Sandburg papers in libraries, in possession of the family, lying about in cartons. After this great haystack, the fodder of the book, was pulled apart, she began the Carl Sandburg Oral History Project of more than 150 interviews.

Having gone through the heap, settled into the poet and each member of the family, reliving their nights and days with an intrusive intimacy, the biographer wants to record each scrap. The index cards or data sheets come to have a claim of their own, and the affirmation, the yes, yes, of Sandburg's scurry through life is her own affirming journey. The book is tedious and sentimental and long, long, long. She likes participial descriptions such as "hearty and vigorous," or "erect and vigorous"—and who can doubt that's exactly what the wily old campaigner was, even though the biographer had never encountered him in life. The scholar of the papers, of *the life of,* knows, like some celestial Xerox machine, details that consciousness erases overnight.

One of the amusements of this biography is that it is a kind of informal history of the radio and television shows of the period, not unlike listening to the "golden oldies." Sandburg hit them all: the *George Jessel Show*, the *Milton Berle Show*, the *Dave Garroway Show*, the *Bell Tele-*

phone Hour. Ed Murrow comes in more than once, and with Norman Corwin, the prince of radio Americana, Sandburg had a "fruitful" relationship. At the Philharmonic Auditorium in Los Angeles, he was introduced by Edgar Bergen (sold out, standing ovation); the publication of the *Second American Songbag* had an introduction by Bing Crosby. Penelope Niven again and again calls Sandburg the "eternal hobo," but as his fame grows he is usually on his way to the studio or the auditorium.

For a number of years, or for a good part of them, the prairie poet was in Hollywood under contract. Two producers from MGM sought his services for an "epic film about the USA," an undertaking not designed to be a mere motion picture but a "great, ringing message to the people." Sandburg was to write a novel, following in shape a scenario written by Sidney Franklin. The novel would be published, then made into a film. For this he was given $100,000, and the project was a "challenge Sandburg could not resist." The end of it all, after story conferences, residence in the film colony, after years and years, was that the novel appeared under the name of *Remembrance Rock*, 1,067 pages of the American Dream, never made into a film, a critical failure, but in no way a money loss for the author. The second Hollywood adventure was a year and a half of work with George Stevens on *The Greatest Story Ever Told*. "He was not only a pioneer, but an adventurer and an explorer, in his own words a Seeker," Sandburg's biographer writes, her words ever echoing those of her subject.

Sandburg made a bold identification between his own career and the history of the great country itself. Roosevelt wanted him to run for Congress, we are told. He collected Harvard and Yale honorary degrees, among many others, Pulitzer Prizes for history and poetry, invitations to address a session of Congress—a lot of this adulation arising from assuming the mantle of Lincoln as a friend of the Family of Man, and so on. He missed out on a few things such as the Nobel Prize and felt a certain annoyance when President Kennedy, whom he had supported, invited Robert Frost to read a poem at his inaugural rather then himself.

Oscar Wilde called the prairies "blotting paper," and if they are so looked at Carl Sandburg can be said to have sucked up all the nutrients in the soil. His beginning voice in *Chicago Poems* (1916), celebrating the "City of the Big Shoulders," and lamenting the lot of the dispossessed, sustained him, it seems, into the Depression period and the years of the New Deal. As a child of Swedish immigrants, Sandburg was part of the Social Democratic movement in the Middle Western states, and that marked the rhythm of his life: the man, the striker, the dreamer, the immigrant toiler, friend of all mankind. His particular politics were New Deal and the Democratic Party. On and on he goes, each of his affirmations self-affirming.

The People, Yes is 179 pages long, with 107 sections—a statistical plenitude as typical of the Prairie Poets as of the wheat acreage of the region. In his notes, Sandburg writes of the work as coming out of "Piers Plowman, seven hundred years ago, a far better handbook and manual of democracy than either Dante or Donne"—a statement of such historical incongruity it raises questions of familiarity with the last two and maybe also the first of the antecedents named. No matter, the sprawl of the work is a "modern epic" and an "odyssey deep into the American Experience," in the reading by the biographer. In some ways, her spacious accommodations arouse sympathy since an attempt to analyze Sandburg's lines flowing down the pages would be profitless. His people, yes or no, are actually just indentured servants, and they did his work, sunup to sundown. The poet's acres and the house in the Carolinas are "open to the public as a National Park and National Historic Site." And that's it.

Spending time with the metered, or unmetered, minstrels of the Middle West is to invite a special melancholy, one not only aesthetic, although that defect predominates since they come into history as poets, not as preachers, philosophers, politicians, or entertainers. Birth or youth in Illinois marked them, a tattoo appropriate enough as experience, the turf of the imagination. Still, they were not ordinary citizens, state proud, but ones making a claim for what were, for the most part, hasty, repetitive, and formless verses, unlike, for instance, the inspirations of Hart Crane of Ohio.

Elitism, belief in the existence of exceptional talents, will here be scorned as a threat to the demotic voices of the prairie. Of course they, too, by publication, must make their entrance into the long tradition, an inescapable transition in the arts. As outlandishly successful as these poets were, the happy circumstance was, as usual, not sufficient, because of the wish for a higher validation that haunts the dreams of the popular.

All three had a proprietary feeling about the country, a longing to transform its restless genetic material into a *folk*, to fashion the inchoate strains into a hardy stock with the name "American" on it, like a packet of sunflower seeds. A futile parochialism for a nation that has ever been, to expropriate a phrase from Kafka, "a cage seeking a bird."

(1991)

ANDERSON, MILLAY, AND
CRANE IN THEIR LETTERS

Many people believe letters the most personal and revealing form of communication. In them we expect to find the charmer at his nap, slumped, open-mouthed, profoundly himself without thought for appearances. Yet, this is not quite true. Letters are above all useful as a means of expressing the ideal self; and no other method of communication is quite so good for this purpose. In conversation, those uneasy eyes upon you, those lips ready with an emendation before you have begun to speak, are a powerful deterrent to unreality, even to hope. In art it is not often possible to make direct use of your dreams of tomorrow and your excuses for yesterday.

In letters we can reform without practice, beg without humiliation, snip and shape embarrassing experiences to the measure of our own desires—this is a benevolent form. The ideal self expressed in letters is not a crudely sugary affair except in dreary personalities; in any case the ideal is very much a part of the character, having its twenty-four hours a day to get through, and being no less unique in its combinations than one's fingerprints.

In the letters of artists and public figures we may not find literary charm, but we do invariably get a good notion of how the person saw himself over the years. This vision does not always strike us as "acute"; we are often tempted to put some poor fellow wise on the subject of his own character, to explain that we are a lot more impressed by his dying on the gallows than by his last "God bless you" to his wife. It is difficult to think of a man except as the sum of his remarkable deeds, a statue surrounded by selected objects and symbols. Private letters are disturbing to this belief. What they most often show is that people do not live their biographies.

———

In the last year or so the correspondence of quite a number of our writers has been published—Pound, Sinclair Lewis, Hart Crane, Gertrude Stein, Sherwood Anderson, Edna Millay—and we have had memoirs on Willa Cather and others. The twenties, which only a few years ago felt so near, are gradually slipping back into that vault called American Literature, where the valuables are kept. The publication of letters is a compliment which suggests the writer is worth a kind of scrutiny not granted every author. As these writers begin to take on that faraway, mysterious, "historical" glaze, publications about them are of considerable importance; a certain ice of opinion, fact and fancy is already spreading over their images. And we cannot assume that eventually all letters, every scrap of interesting material will be published; what is more likely is that the selections, the biography, as we have them now will stand for a time.

It is, then, interesting that the first volume (who knows if there will be another?) of Sinclair Lewis' letters* should be entirely given over to communications he wrote and *received* from his publishers. Indeed, this correspondence is rather good fun, dealing as it does with the finagling, financing and advertising which, though uncommonly exposed to this extent, are in some way a part of literary history, as the billboard is a sort of cousin to the performance. We see Lewis composing a fan letter to be sent by his publishers to all the best writers of his day on the subject of that remarkable book *Main Street;* and wondering if perhaps something special isn't needed for the elegant eye and heart of Edith Wharton. This was all a part of the game, but we may doubt Lewis, much as he liked to appear in print, would have been delighted by this whole volume of business testimony.

Sherwood Anderson's letters† are unhappily selected for quite the opposite reason. They are often bleak and dull to read because they are

———

* *From Main Street to Stockholm.* Harcourt, Brace.
† *Letters of Sherwood Anderson.* Little, Brown.

chosen upon a principle of reckless high-mindedness, a remorseless tracking of Anderson the writer, the artist, the thinker, at the expense of biography. It is felt that Anderson the advertising man, Anderson before forty, was, though alive, a mute statistic; and even after he has been allowed existence at forty only his literary life is permitted. But with Anderson, "the man" is overwhelmingly important. He appears to have been splintered, repressed, uncertain in an exceptional way; in a very real sense his literary equipment began and ended with this painful state of being. Though he could sometimes grow mannered and arty, he is not particularly vivid if you isolate him as "an artist." It is as *a case* that he is unfailingly interesting, this peculiar rising and waning star, this man who brought to literature almost nothing except his own lacerated feelings. This latter circumstance, and not his Flaubertian dedication, is what makes us think of him sometimes as a typical American writer. With certain other authors an undeviating, purely literary selection would produce not only the most interesting but the truest portrait of the man: Ezra Pound's life seems to have been, almost literally, an *open book*.

Yet, even if one were to admit the validity of excluding all letters written before Anderson became an author, it seems a bit lofty to omit nearly everything that happened to him during the period of authorship. During these years Anderson divorced three wives and married a fourth; a much-married man without love letters gives us a jolt. There is no letter to Anderson's daughter, only two to his son Bob, who worked with him on the newspaper enterprise; a few more to his son, John, get under the wire because John too is an "artist," a painter, and letters relating to that calling are summoned. This selection makes Anderson seem distinctly hard and unreal; wives are divorced in a footnote or abandoned like unpromising manuscripts, grown children when addressed at all are usually given a lecture on art—and the author himself is as naked as can be, stripped to a man who is writing another book. Anderson's strange, restless soul, remarkable beyond all else for painful, shrinking feelings, is uneasy with his literary friends, Waldo Frank, Van Wyck Brooks, Paul Rosenfeld. Struggling to tell them what he is all about he is sometimes like a tenor with the stage all to himself: "I have been to Nebraska, where the big engines are tearing the hills to pieces; over the low hills runs the promise of corn. You wait, dear Brother! I shall bring God home to the sweaty men in the corn rows." Or again he is not so much complex as hidden and diffuse, singing in a voice not always recognizable from one day to the next. He is a man of the Middle West he tells us, close to the people, and yet all sorts of angels seem to be whispering in his ear, correcting his accent.

———

Edna Millay's letters*—after reading them you hesitate to know what you thought you knew about this poet. Can this be that sensational young woman of legend who burnt the candle, built the house on sand, kissed so many lips? More than once you find yourself thinking of quite another enduring American type, Jo in *Little Women,* the resourceful, sensitive, devoted girl, bobbing her hair, not to be a flapper, but to pay for Father's illness. These letters are very charming, although not in the sense one would care much to read them if they were not by Edna Millay, or at least by *someone,* for they haven't that sort of power which can be enjoyed apart from a beforehand interest in the writer. They show, for one thing, an intense, unmixed family devotion; not merely an affection for spruced-up memories of colorful relations, long dead ancestors from a region one no longer visits, not earnestness and the urgings of duty, but an immense love for the present, living, impinging kin. This world of nicknames, old jokes, little gifts flying through the mails is startlingly passionate. With friends too there is very often the same extraordinarily intimate style, the same devotion, fidelity, acceptance—and all the while we know Edna Millay was becoming more remote from everyone, enduring very early "a sort of nervous breakdown which interferes a bit with my keeping my promises," and later in hospitals with "an all but life-size nervous breakdown" and at last horribly alone in the country, cold, without even a telephone, dying miserably after a sleepless night. How is it possible with all this fraternal, familial feeling that the frantic, orphaned creature of the later years came into being? And how is it possible to begin with that this jolly, loving daughter and sister was in her most famous period in such violent revolt? Edna Millay seems to have had a wretched life, much more so than those persons whose earliest days were marked by a blighting, ambiguous relation to their families and later somewhat toward everyone. There is not anywhere a sadder story than this—the aching existence of this woman who loved and was

———

* *Letters of Edna St. Vincent Millay.* Harper.

loved by her family and friends, who, flaming youth and all, married only once and then, to all appearances, wisely. Even Emily Dickinson appears on happier ground in her upstairs bedroom.

It seems likely that Edna Millay's fame and success came too early; the racking strain of keeping up to this is suggested everywhere. And more important: I think Edmund Wilson in his fascinating and moving work on her undervalues the spectacular pain of the sort of success she had. She was a woman famous for her fascinating, unconventional personality, and for rather conventional poems. She was not in the deepest sense "famous" or much cared for by many of the really good poets of her own time. Hart Crane's opinion, written to a friend much stricken with Miss Millay, is interesting: "She really has genius in a limited sense, and is much better than Sara Teasdale, Marguerite Wilkinson, Lady Speyer, etc., to mention a few drops in the bucket of feminine lushness that forms a kind of milky way in the poetic firmament of the time (likewise all times);—indeed I think she is every bit as good as Elizabeth Browning . . . I can only say I do not greatly care for Mme. Browning. . . . With her equipment Edna Millay is bound to succeed to the appreciative applause of a fairly large audience. And for you, who I rather suppose have not gone into this branch of literature with as much enthusiasm as myself, she is a creditable heroine."

This was not an easy situation for Edna Millay to live with. You cannot give, as she did, your whole life to writing without caring horribly, even to the point of despair. And so in 1949 we find that she is planning a satire against T. S. Eliot. In this work she says there is to be, "nothing coarse, obscene, as there sometimes is in the work of Auden and Pound, and nothing so silly as the childish horsing around of Eliot, when he is trying to be funny. He has no sense of humor, and so he is not yet a true Englishman. There is, I think, in these poems of mine against Eliot nothing which could be considered abusive; they are merely murderous."

This is appalling. Edna Millay was not a stupid or even an excessively vain person. She knew, in spite of this wild cry, that the literary approval of Pound was to be valued more highly than that of Frank Crowninshield. (Critics are often wrong, but writers are hardly ever wrong, hide and deny it as they will, in knowing whose opinion really counts.) Her words are not those of a poet secure in her powers, and they are especially harsh for this writer, who was forever generous and warmhearted toward other poets, including nearly all of her feminine rivals. This hopeless, killing bitterness about her own place, as I believe the projected satire reveals, is the end of a whole life which one can at least imagine to have been thrown off its natural, impressive track by a series of seemingly fortunate fatalities. Perhaps she was not meant to go to Greenwich Village at all and certainly not to become famous in her youth. She was sensible, moral, steadfast, a kind of prodigy— among her circle hardly anyone except Edmund Wilson and John Peale Bishop even rose to the second-rate. Not nearly enough was asked of her and she had no time to prepare herself in solitude—until it was too late. It is a tribute, a terrible one, to her possibilities and hopes that she was unable to enjoy the comforts of a strong, public position and split in two. Very few critics can find in Edna Millay's poetry the power and greatness Wilson finds. Still there is something humanly delightful and pleasing in Wilson's obstinacy, like the great Ruskin putting Kate Greenaway among the finest living artists—as he did.

———

One cannot read even a few of Hart Crane's letters* without feeling the editor, Brom Weber, has made a tremendous contribution. (Of course the "contribution" is Crane's, but he could not have presented his own correspondence.) Fishing about in contemporary literature, Weber has dredged up a masterpiece, for these letters are marvelous, wonderful simply to read, important in what they add to our notion of Crane, and in an unruly, inadvertent fashion quite profound for the picture they give of America itself, and in particular the literary scene from 1916 to 1932, from Hart Crane at seventeen until his death at thirty-three. It is easy with this volume to be reminded of Keats's letters, and if Crane's are not quite so extraordinary as that the same must be said for most of English prose.

Poor Crane—a genius from Cleveland—with his little pair of parents, or his pair of little parents, so squeezing in their anxiety and egotism, so screeching in their divorce, the mother rather beached and given to a humble mysticism, the father, dazed and busy, a business success but not really. Crane's parents are curdling and outrageous by their very multiplicity in America, their typicality; they are as real and to be expected, this young couple, as Cleveland itself. Vast numbers of

———

* *The Letters of Hart Crane*, edited by Brom Weber. Hermitage House.

people under middle age now have parents like this and are these persons' only child. Hart Crane was merely a bit in the vanguard by getting there somewhat early. And the son himself, a poet, homosexual, drunkard, a suicide. One had not imagined much could be added to this macabre, but neat, biography. However, what the letters amazingly suggest is the disturbing possibility that Crane had a happy life.

Naturally, he was often much annoyed by his parents, but there is no doubt he was always much fascinated by them. He wrote this middling pair an extremely generous number of lively and often lengthy letters—a source of amazement when we consider Crane's bumming about, drinking, and the dizzy life he had made for himself away from home. In the end he was returning from Mexico, not to New York, but to Chagrin Falls, Ohio, planning fantastically to "be of some help" to his stepmother in the shrunken state of solid assets which became known at his father's death.

Contrary to the guilt feelings usually surmised, Crane seems to have "enjoyed"—no other word occurs to me—his homosexuality, taking about this the most healthy attitude possible under the circumstances. There is not the slightest suggestion in the letters that he worried about his inclinations or was trying to reform; if anything troubles him on this score it is continence, the lack of opportunity. For what it may be worth, we remark that his suicide came at a time when he was involved, and more than a little lukewarmly, with a woman. "You know you're welcome—more than that, my dear, to make this your future headquarters. I miss you *mucho, mucho, mucho*! But I don't think that either of us ought to urge the other into anything but the most spontaneous and mutually liberal arrangements."

Crane also "enjoyed" alcohol—his letters are heathenish in their failure to express intentions to liberate himself from this pleasure. He could, however, be remorseful over his drunken actions and there is no doubt he tried his friends' charity extravagantly. As the Russian proverb about drinking has it, "A man on foot is a poor companion for a man on horseback." Yet Crane somehow never seems to feel he is galloping to destruction. In this he is very different from Fitzgerald, who had in the midst of chaos the rather crosseyed power of gazing upon his deterioration as if he were not living it but somehow observing his soul and body as one would watch a drop of water slowly drying up in the sun. Crane, on the other hand, expresses over and over the greatest delight in alcohol; he sees himself as a true lover of the grape rather than a snuffling slave of the bottle and, though the results may be the same, the attitude alters the experience along the way. It is one thing to die in ecstasy and another to pass away, moaning, "I knew this stuff would get me in the end." (This is not suggested as the literal deathbed mood of either of these authors, but as a fundamental difference of attitude toward their "difficulties.")

Crane's letters are vivid in every respect—responsive, humorous, beautifully written, fresh—everything and more. The sheer power of mind they reveal is dazzling; his comments upon his reading, his contemporaries, his own work, even the landscape, are always interesting and usually brilliant. It is impossible to think of him, after this, as a natural who knows not what he doeth. What is so appealing about his mind is the utter absence of cant, artiness and fear—all those things Sherwood Anderson seemed to think were the "copy" a literary man was obliged to wring out of his skin. Even when Crane is wounded in his vanity—self-justifying and "true to human nature" as he will be in his explanation of lapses—there is always something solid and shrewd in the way he goes about reclaiming himself. One can see in him certainly a "neurotic need for affection" but there is also astonishing independence and balance. His melancholy is as short as his enjoyment of things is long. Very near the end, before he jumped into the sea, if he *did* jump, he is writing about the glorious Mexican Easter and the wonderful singers in the cafés ("has the old Hawaiian gurgling backed off the map") and detailing his incredibly funny difficulties with a drunken servant, Daniel. "I took the opportunity to talk to him about sobriety—meanwhile pouring him glass after glass of Tenampe. . . ."

Reading these letters it is hard to remember the withered and anesthetized tragedy we thought Crane had become. Yet you cannot easily account for the amount of joy in them and the joy you receive from getting close again to Crane's life. Perhaps it is his magical freedom from true *disgust* that makes you think this "doomed" poet was, after all, under the protection of a charm.

(1953)

VICTIMS AND VICTORS

SEDUCTION AND BETRAYAL

Seduction may be baneful, even tragic, but the seducer at his work is essentially comic. It is a question whether there is such a thing as seduction when the affections play a part; and yet this is a murky matter because of the way affections, even those of tenderness and concern, have a tendency to diminish and augment, to transform themselves under the influence of experience, satisfaction, or disappointment. The seducer as a type, or as an archetype, hardly touches upon any of our deep feelings unless there is some exaggeration in him, something complicated and tangled and mysteriously compelling about a nature that has come to define itself through the mere fact of sex. For the most part the word "seduction" indicates effort of a persevering, thoughtful sort. When it is successful we naturally look about for a lack of resolution and resistance in the object; guile and insistence are clever at uncovering pockets of complicity. A seduction is the very opposite of the abrupt, which is, of course, rape.

The most interesting seducers are actually rapists; for instance, Don Giovanni and Lovelace. Their whole character is trapped in the moil of domination and they drudge on, never satisfied, never resting, mythically hungry. The fact that the two characters mentioned are gentlemen gives a stinging complication to their obsessions. Ritual comes naturally to them and birth bestows rights and blurs cruelties. What we may feel is a misplaced elaboration of desire in a gentleman would be in a man of less imagination and of inferior social and personal decoration simply coarse or criminal. In the common man, excessive demand for sex is repulsive. Gentlemen merely run the risk of being ridiculous. To have in Ispagna alone, *mille e tre*, is a most exhausting dedication, and also quite funny.

The danger of ridicule must, in literature, be circumvented if the man is to retain force, magnetism, spirit. (Dignity is scarcely at stake, since it is the mark of a gentleman to look upon dignity as a quality given and once given the last to crumble.) When the Don in Mozart's opera is found in the first scene dragging Donna Anna about, rushing into her bedroom like a burglar, we know that he is a complete fool. ("How can I believe a nobleman guilty of such a crime?" Don Ottavio, another fool, asks.) It is only when the Don murders Donna Anna's father, the Commendatore, that he is redeemed as a character, a creation. He who was a fool has suddenly become sinister, evil, damned; the attention immediately shifts from the victim, the assaulted, sobbing woman, back to the great violator himself. The Don still does not have motive and we cannot understand his raging pursuits, yet we see how complete is his will, his defiance, how devastating his empty energy. The Don will ultimately have, in the opera, a cruel, useless courage in living out his nature to its very end.

In the waste of sensuality, boredom, compulsion, the Don never shows love or pity for the women. That we soon accept, aesthetically, as the frame of the plot of his existence; we are then free to go the next step with him. We accept that he is saved from being a fop by his equal lack of pity for himself. There is nothing self-protective in the Don. If he had called upon the favors of some higher nobility to intercede for him, he would be contemptible in every part of his nature. As it is, he is awful, trapped in his own being. His "extensive sentiments" and his "*tutte quante*" are a malignant growth which he, either by the charms of his character or the weakness of women, wishes to present as a caprice, a temperament, a disposition perfected by a fantast.

Donna Elvira's fascination with the Don makes her a more interesting person than Donna Anna, who is, after the murder and perhaps before, only interested in her father, a totemic figure well-dressed in stone. We do not know whether to call Donna Elvira's attraction under the name of love; perhaps, yes. She herself gives hints of some liking for exorbitance, and her love is scarcely put to the test of endurance because the Don gives her such a short tenure as his betrothed—three days in Burgos.

It is a lack in the Don that he doesn't understand the way Donna Elvira's passion for him makes him a more seductive and profound lover because she is interesting and complicated herself. It does not occur to him that she is an ornament his tawdry soul can well use. Instead he runs around in the shadows of her infatuation, inanely whispering, "*poverina, poverina*." But nothing indeed prepares us for his inexplicably ferocious jest in falsely reawakening Elvira's love only to pass his cloak to his lowly servant, Leporello, and command him to make love to her. The Don sinks here into the depths of coarse, personal dramaturgy. His invention has run out, his labors have exhausted his plotting imagination—and his own delight in the unworthy caper almost destroys him as a character. He would have returned to his condition of fool, if it were not that he is saved again by the indestructible romantic concentration of Donna Elvira. She is soon again pitying him, and by this eternal flaming of hers the Don is rescued from inane buffoonery and restored once more to his interestingly sinister shape.

The *illicit*, as R. P. Blackmur writes in his extraordinary essay on *Madame Bovary*, and its identification with the romantic, the beautiful, and the interesting, lies at the very center of the dramatic action in the novel form. "The more lawful the society, as we say the more *bourgeois* the society, the more universal is the temptation to the illicit *per se*, and the stronger the impulse to identify it if not with life itself at least with the beauty of life." For us now, the illicit has become a psychological rather than a moral drama. We ask ourselves how the delinquent ones *feel* about their seductions, adulteries, betrayals, and it is by the quality of their feelings that our moral judgments are formed. If they suffer and grieve and regret, they can be forgiven and even supported. If they boast or fall into an inner carelessness, what they are doing or have done can seem to be *wrong*. Love, even of the briefest span, is a powerful detergent, but "destructiveness" is a moral stain. In novelistic relations, where the pain inflicted is only upon the feelings of another person, everything is blurred. It is hard to know when rights have been exceeded or when obligations are adamantine.

In *The Scarlet Letter*, has Hester Prynne been *betrayed* by the Reverend Dimmesdale? If the matter lies only inside her own feelings, perhaps we would have to say that she is beyond betrayal. Betrayal is not what she herself feels, not the way her experience shapes itself in her mind and feelings. Love, the birth of Pearl, her illegitimate child, her prison term for adultery, her sentence to wear the letter A on her breast, the insufficient courage of her lover, Dimmesdale—what provocation, what abandonment. And yet these visitations, these punishments, are embraced by Hester like fate. They are the revelations out of which prophecy is made, and so they come to her, not as depressing clouds of consequence, but as opportunities for self-knowledge, for a strange and striking *stardom*.

Dimmesdale, on the other hand, is stunned by the illicit. It corrupts the air around him; he cannot breathe because of his sin. Thinness, pallor, trembling, wasting, heartsickness: such are the words that define his state. He feels his transgression more vividly than anything else in his life. He takes society's attitude toward his adultery with Hester and, thus outcast in his own being, he becomes the betrayed person, almost the *betrayed woman*. D. H. Lawrence's idea that the "greatest triumph an American woman can have is the triumph of seducing a man, especially if he is pure" is a Lawrence paradox arising out of his suspicious dislike of Hester Prynne. It is not true that she seduced Dimmesdale, but it is true in some deep sense that the sexes are reversed in the peculiar terms of his suffering, his sinking under it, the atmosphere around him of guilt, desperation, self-torture, and lonely remorse. The weak and the strong are clearly not where we would expect them to be. Moral courage is the dominating force in Hester Prynne, just as fearfulness, neurasthenic self-abasement are the fate of Dimmesdale.

Still, it would be outside history and a psychological falsification for us to look contemptuously upon poor Dimmesdale. He is occupied with God, truly; he has his mission on earth as a clergyman. His pastorate is serious, his integration in Puritan society is passionate. He is a man in time, living under the dispensation of his moment and his region, Boston, 1642. We cannot condemn his religious scruples, his Puritan dogmatism. We can understand his not wishing to remove himself, by the confession of adultery, from the possibility of bringing light and goodness to his world. It is actually Hester Prynne who is outside history. Her indifference to adultery, her staying on in Boston with her illegitimate daughter, Pearl, her defiance, the striking skepticism of her mind, the moral distance she sets between herself and the hysterias of the time—these qualities are the cause for wonder.

The heroine whose fate is defined by adulterous love is a central and enduring theme in fiction. Love and power are the landscape in which imagined destiny is lived. Power as a consequence of conventional love is suitable for comedies and for the intense dramas of the well-to-do classes and their daughters. Love destroys power in the great tragic heroines, in Greek drama, in Anna Karenina, in Cleopatra. It is infinitely more complicated and mixed in the bourgeois novel. What is asked of the heroine is not always a grand passion, but a sense of reality, a curious sort of independence and honor, an acceptance of consequence that puts courage to the most searing test.

In the novel, when the heroine's history turns about a sexual betrayal, it matters whether she is the central figure in the plot or a somewhat less powerfully and less fully considered "victim" on the periphery. If she is the central figure, psychological structure seems to demand a sort of purity and innocence. Not physical innocence, but a lack of mean calculations, of vindictiveness, of self-abasing weakness. Sexual transgression loses its overwhelming character as a wrong or as a mistake when the persons have virtues of a compelling sort, or spiritual goodness, or the grandeur of endurance. The inner life of the woman matters, what she feels and has felt, the degree of her understanding of the brutal cycles of life.

The problem of creating sympathy for the woman whose destiny must run the narrow road laid out after a disastrous surrender or seduction loomed larger in the minds of authors than it needed to loom. Fiction and drama have always been drawn magnetically to this plot, to this beginning of fated complication, and the situation inevitably partakes of the universal. The experience is common—richly, painfully known, easily imagined and felt. Lust—and then, for the women, stoicism. This is the highest choice. Yet, to be a heroine, to occupy the center of the stage as a sort of incarnation of love or sexual consequence, definite enrichments, heights, intricate particularities must set the woman apart. Her fall or her fate can only be truly serious if a natural or circumstantial refinement exists.

Again Hester Prynne is odd and we wonder how Hawthorne actually looked upon her indifference to society, her radical challenge, her sexual—what to call it?—valor. Of course, Hester is not very greatly under the spell of sensuality. Instead, she is an ideologue, making by way of her adulterous isolation a stand against Puritanism. In many respects, the characters in *The Scarlet Letter* are not characters at all, but large, fantastically painted playing cards. Symbolic action is Hester's role.

Prison, where the novel starts, is a natural school for radicals, especially for those of a theatrical disposition. And Hester Prynne is very much of that sort, a dramatic, theatrical radical. Another radical moralist of the time, Anne Hutchinson, is mentioned early in the book—a woman, banished, rejected, defiant. The two are united in their public characters: Anne Hutchinson begins where Hester ends, working on the minds of troubled women, nursing the sick. And indeed what is Hester's strength except a "covenant of Grace," and a "peculiar indwelling of the Holy Ghost" of the kind Anne Hutchinson laid claim to: both make the claim of personal experience above the social or doctrinal. "What we did had a consecration of its own," Hester says.

Hester is beautiful, dark-haired, dignified, a morally complicated woman who gradually takes on a "marble coldness." She seems dramatically uninterested in religion, just as she is strikingly free in her mind about adultery. "She assumed a freedom of speculation, then common enough on the other side of the Atlantic, but which our forefathers had they known it would have held a deadlier crime than that stigmatized by the scarlet letter." The essential decision of Hester's is "I will not speak," she will not implicate Dimmesdale. She refuses any of the self-saving possibilities—but why? Her "open ignominy" has a life of its own, growing out of the peculiar strength of *the heroine* as a general literary conception. Hester, actually, is in the classical mode: she has a fate rather than a character.

Henry James: "In spite of the relation between Hester Prynne and Arthur Dimmesdale no story of love was surely ever less of a 'love-story.' To Hawthorne's imagination the fact that these two persons had loved each other too well was of an interest comparatively vulgar; what appealed to him was the idea of their moral situation in the long years that were to follow." *The Scarlet Letter* is a drama of sin rather than of love. To Hester the idea that adultery is a crime is scarcely considered; she does not seem prepared to make a stand for "love" or for the purity of her feelings. She is not an apostle for sex. She is a "wild Indian" and, as Hawthorne says, with no reverence left for clerics, judges, gallows, fireside, or the church. It is not against her punishment that she flings herself—"the tendency of her fate and her fortune had been to set her free." She is a natural outcast of the superior sort: serious, somewhat vain of her dignified, sly endurance, attached to the symbolic and emblematic in the usual way of a radical wanting to signify ideas in an outward, concentrated way as he walks among the mass. It is true, as Lawrence says in fury, that she wears her damned A like a duchess's coronet. Everything about her is marvelously dramatic and challenging.

Of course, Hester cannot take the wickedness of adultery seriously because it has brought her little Pearl. Pearl is serious, living is serious, and from the natural pessimism of women with their "imprisonment" in consequence she draws a natural reprieve from the kind of moral lingering in the past that afflicts Dimmesdale. Pearl, her future, the far-flung, unknown life stretching out ahead of the sin: these mean nothing to Dimmesdale. He lingers back, preoccupied with the dead action, the fascination of transgression, the fearful power of it. He is truly in a state of lunacy, as Hester sees when they meet in the forest among the Indians.

Little Pearl, with her "hard, metallic lustre," is a true child of the Puritan inclination to worry the wound. She has no morals at all. She has very early leaped onto another level of possibility and will live it through without remorse or fearfulness. She becomes the glowing American girl abroad, sending home letters "with armorial seals upon them, though of bearings unknown to English heraldry." Out of this tale of repression and sorrow, of social isolation, spiritual torment, and historical hypocrisy, Hawthorne created two women with fanatical stamina, with an independence of mind and action that went beyond anything the world could rightly have asked of them in their time—or later. Mrs. Hawthorne said, when the book was read aloud to her, that she liked it but it gave her a headache.

Where does the strength come from? First of all it comes from the minds (the observations?) of men, since the novels were written by men and those by women draw largely upon the weight of these powerful conceptions and balance of relations. Women, wronged in one way or another, are given the overwhelming beauty of endurance, the capacity for high or lowly suffering, for violent feeling absorbed, finally tranquilized, for the radiance of humility, for silence, secrecy, impressive acceptance. Heroines are, then, heroic; but the heroism may turn into an accusation and is in some way feared as the strength of the weak.

The Wife of Bath, coarse, brilliant, greedy, and lecherous as any man, tells a tale of infinite psychological resonance. A young knight who is to be banished from the court for rape is saved by the intervention of the queen and her ladies. He is to regain his place in life by setting out upon a perilous journey to find the answer to the question: What is it women most desire? After the usual torments and trials, the winning answer is discovered: Women desire to have mastery over their husbands.

Novelists are often rather hard on those seduced and betrayed girls who are bereft of heroic quality. Without a transcendent purity of some degree to free them from rebuke and condescension, the girls choke in a tangle of weakness, sensuality, vanity, illusion, irresolution. Hetty Sorrel, in *Adam Bede*, is beautiful, ignorant, fond of clothes; she prefers handsome romantic men to good, kind ones. She dreams in the most provincial way of alliances far beyond her possibility as a poor farmer's niece. George Eliot lays the hand of doom on Hetty for her obtuse hope, her trembling eyelashes, her rushing surrender. She hasn't the quality to be tragic. Instead she is something smaller and lesser— she is miserable. But miserable in the most extreme way, because she is profoundly betrayed by her beauty, by the shallow and easy conscience of her lover, Arthur Donnithorne. Hetty becomes pregnant and sets out across the fields and roads to look for her absent lover; everything about her condition is marked by pain, confusion, helplessness. Love and abandonment have made her as deeply, hideously suffering as some starving, wounded animal. Her child is born and she kills it and is tried for murder.

One of the most brilliant moments in this book comes when we are allowed to enter the seducer's thoughts at just the moment when Hetty—far away—is being doomed. Arthur Donnithorne is daydreaming in his light-hearted, pleasantly self-loving way. He misses Hetty somewhat and yet he feels quite happy imagining that this girl, who has in life just been sentenced to death, must be what his will has ordained for her—agreeably settling down into her proper sphere with her appropriate husband, Adam Bede. Thank heaven it had turned out so well! he thinks.

George Eliot says about Hetty, "Hers was a luxurious and vain nature, not a passionate one." Hetty is susceptible and somewhat shallow. In fiction it is susceptibility that prompts the greatest anguish of betrayal. Women of a more complex character cannot be destroyed in the manner of Hetty Sorrel. Her beseeching glances are the key to an intolerable vulnerability, a lack of spiritual depth. Hetty is soon, as a consequence of seduction, utterly, pitifully desperate. There is everything moving in her bewildered flight to look for her lover, but it is moving in the way of a trapped creature. She has not learned much about herself or human nature; she knows only that she is desperate, miserable.

The author is ambivalent. She doesn't quite respect Hetty, and sympathy is mixed with the thread of exasperation. Hetty has been betrayed, and yet how hard it is to keep from blaming her just a little for her own hell. Sensuality is a burden and sometimes it is touching, but it is not grand, not heroic. Those who suffer from a mere consequence of love, pregnancy, are implicated in their own fall. The consequence is mechanical, universal, repetitive; it will not alone make a tragic heroine or a heroine of any kind. Secret sympathy for the man is everywhere in literature when the mere fact of this sexual cause and effect is the origin of the woman's appalling suffering. If she can be betrayed she is betrayable; we would not expect otherwise of him, the seducer. To accept consequence would ruin his life, be outside his plan, class, history—whatever his own plot may be.

Is it really expected that Arthur Donnithorne, a well-born young man of the gentry class, would marry Hetty, a penniless, beautiful, ignorant young farm girl? No. A reader coming forth with that simple solution would be drastically outside the spirit of the period and of the novel as it was written. Nothing appeared to be less simple than these matters of class in marriage. Fear of misalliances, complications of inheritance, played a grotesque role in the lives of the young, causing respectable girls to live under the shadow of chaperones whose dark ignorance and conventionality were like a withdrawing of the sun. The most elaborate manners, problems of introductions, of walks, of meetings, of parental tyranny, forced marriages, interrupted romances, make of the novels of Jane Austen a sort of social hieroglyph.

No, we accept Arthur Donnithorne's drifting away as we assume a harvest at the end of the summer. He himself comes to a pause in his love, a "natural" one that tells him romance is not static and fixed, but moving and changing in a fearful way. He would like to stop before misery falls, as if he were running from a thunderstorm. His way is a tenderly cruel letter, no doubt sharply and truly expressing his feelings as he understands them.

> I have spoken truly when I have said that I loved you and I shall never forget our love.... I cannot bear to think of my little Hetty shedding tears when I am not there to kiss them away.... And I feel it would be a great evil for you if your affections continued to be so fixed on me that you could think of no other man who might be able to make you happier by his love than I ever can.... And since I cannot marry you, we must part—we must try not to feel like lovers any more....

For Hetty the letter was "a horrible sensation" and her dull misery sets in. It is too late, for her; she is stabbed by the letter and stabbed by the consequence of "love"—her pregnancy, which Arthur does not know about. Yet she is not great enough for a transfiguration. George Eliot says that the letter "afflicted her pleasure-craving nature with an overpowering pain." In the use of "pleasure-craving" a judgment is made. We are directed to remember Hetty's thoughtless susceptibility, her lack of a proper cynicism, on the one hand, or a saving resignation, a revelation or premonition of danger on the other. But neither a moral nature nor a bright social intelligence instructs Hetty in the practical possibilities of her romance with Arthur Donnithorne.

She is a victim, of what? Her beauty and her love of trinkets, her insufficient analytical powers, her refusal of intuition, her sensuality, her coquetry, her social class and her lover's higher class. She is a victim of errors, impressions, imperfections. She is merely romantic in an ordinary way, an ordinary romance and longing are not "serious" attitudes for one in her position. Her expectations trivialize her feelings and later her pain, loneliness, and panic devastate her judgment so greatly that she covers her baby with leaves and abandons it in the woods. Hetty is pathetic, her fate is awful, we weep for her—but she is not a heroine. She is an instance, an example, a prisoner of cause and effect: flirtation, surrender, pregnancy, misery. This is the plot of existence.

The fact that Hetty Sorrel is only seventeen will not alter the plot or her downward spiral or our withholding from her, in the terms of the novel, the more deeply felt identifications. She suffers, yes, but we knew that was coming. Nothing surprises us about Hetty's misery. Her lack of foreknowledge is a pity, but it is not redeeming. This is the obdurate cycle. Hetty simply hasn't the right sort of nature, none of the heroine's patience or endurance of the conditions of life, none of those crafty, observant hesitations we would wish from the life of realistic country people. Everything is an illusion except her misery. Nor can she turn inward, for there is just a deadness there. She is like Emma Bovary at last trying to pray for relief from pain. Emma calls out to the Lord in the same words she had used for her lover. "It was to make faith come; but no delights descended from the heavens, and she arose with tired limbs and with a vague feeling of gigantic dupery."

Roberta, in Dreiser's *An American Tragedy,* is condemned to death for her ordinariness, her whining hopelessness, combined, of course, with pregnancy. Clyde Griffiths is scarcely more propitiously organized and endowed for life than Roberta and yet, in him, the vain, pleasure-loving sensuality that unhinges the fortunes of Hetty Sorrel has the character of social movement, economic hope. We can see that he and Roberta might have come together in loneliness and isolation, but we can also see that Clyde suddenly glimpsing the cars, "the gowns," the parties of Lycurgus will almost immediately find Roberta downward, depressing, beseeching, threatening, and therefore intolerable.

Clyde has the susceptibility of his ignorance. He too is in many ways a trusting, yearning *girl;* he wants to put his fate in the hands of women he feels are superior to him, who own things, who live—as he sees it—with assurance and glitter and possibility. Earlier he is "seduced" by the Green-Davidson Hotel in Kansas City. It is like Hetty with her trinkets. "The wraps, furs, and other belongings in which they appeared, or which were often carried by these other boys and himself across the great lobby and into the cars or the dining rooms or the several elevators. And they were always of such gorgeous textures, as Clyde saw them. Such grandeur."

And when Roberta is desperate, when she is most desolating to Clyde's wishes, it is just then that his shallow and passionate need for glamour, his hope for an easy sliding into prosperity, appear as a true possibility, a swooping stroke of luck. Of course, the reader knows more about Clyde than he can know; he is like Hetty—utterly, foolishly without reservations, without a saving reality. A more serious and thoughtful and genuine young man would have acknowledged the rebuffs, the petty snobbishness and corruption of the life he longed for. All Clyde can see in his pitifully longing dreams is that life seems to beckon, when it truly does not—and that Roberta is death, which she truly is. "For, as he now recalled, and with an enormous sense of depression, Roberta was thinking and at this very time, that soon now, and in the face of all Lycurgus had to offer him—Sondra—the coming spring and summer—the love and romance, gaiety, position, power—he was going to give all that up and go away with and marry her. Sneak away to some out-of-the-way place! Oh, how horrible! And with a child at his age!" Later in his reverie, he cries out, "The loss! The loss!"

The whole drive of the novel is to make us feel Clyde's loss, even though we know him born to be a loser. Still, Roberta is a heavy burden. He is young and his dream, if he is allowed to share in his uncle's prosperity, is to attain a corrupt, foolish, vain, and empty life. And yet the injustice is that he has no preparation even for that, no stamina or hardness; he has nothing except his own idle need for indulgence, fantasy, the trinkets of existence. What he needs he does not have: money, support of family, aggression, will. Nevertheless, Clyde is the center of feeling in the novel. We pity him and we pity Roberta and always we pity him more. By her death, Roberta is caught in the ultimate consequence of sex; but the electric chair for Clyde seems more horrible, a doom of many causes, the end of all the false promises of life. The deaths are not for love, but for sex—the annihilation at the end of the road when things go wrong and responsibility takes its toll.

For all Clyde's weakness and vanity, his impossible ignorance and unworthy folly, we agree that somehow Roberta is exacting too great a price. She asks his whole life, paltry and trashy as the life he wants may be. For her, what would have made it possible for us to accept her totally, not merely to pity her? Where does redemption for Roberta lie? In fortitude, austerity, silence, endurance. These acceptances for lowly girls are the only paths to moral dignity. The novel—deterministic, bourgeois in spirit for all of its questioning of the hard terms of life—always understands that the men must get on. Dimmesdale must preach and save souls; Clyde must get a job with his uncle and go with the crowd he ignobly admires; Arthur Donnithorne must take over his estates. To ask differently of them would violate the laws of social survival, would impose standards of revolutionary skepticism about the nature of all of society's arrangements.

The idea of sexual responsibility for the passions of youth cannot be understood as an ethical one. Clyde is twenty-one when he goes to the death chamber. Even allowing for the convention of outlandish youthfulness in the principal characters in literature we still cannot wish to decide fates because of fornication. Of course, it is not natural passion he is to pay for, but murder. Still, he was trapped by needs of the most ordinary sort, universal needs, universally satisfied without punishment.

Biology is destiny only for girls. Were everyone in the drama of biology more prudent and watchful of the social and financial outlines of his alliances these matters could be arranged, manipulated. But just as the illicit is the trembling attraction of the novel, so is the illicit between persons of different rank, different natures, a variation that stirs our sense of the dramatic instabilities and violations of love. We know that we are near our own time when a novel can concern itself, as *An American Tragedy* does, with two people, Clyde and Roberta, both deprived, stunted, pitiable. In spite of the equity of deprivation, it is Clyde's lack of resignation to a future darkened by Roberta's pregnancy that moves us, keeps our sense of the intolerable blackness of consequence alive. The mind protests for both of them. It is only that Roberta, trapped, miserable, imagines existence would be possible if only Clyde would take care of her, settle in for life. We cannot quite forgive her the simplicity.

———

The Kreutzer Sonata, by Tolstoy, is a work of great peculiarity. It is not of the first interest imaginatively, and there is a dense, frantic distortion in this pedagogic monologue on sex and the ills of marriage. It is a tract, inchoate, and yet noble, impractical, original. There are moments of dramatic genius: a wracking vision of marriage as jealousy nourished, hatred voluptuously fed, rage taken for breakfast. The whole of a man's sexual life comes under Tolstoy's agitated scrutiny— from the arrogant encounters of youth to the fevered tournaments of conventional unions. Tolstoy sees the line of "immorality" beginning in the young man's first relations with prostitutes and girls toward whom he feels no obligation; from there all of the later life of the sexes is either grossly or subtly poisoned. Life among men and women is a debauch the young are led to accept, even to expect, by custom, example, social convenience.

The actions the nineteenth century gathered together under the name of "debauchery" are never, in fiction, made entirely clear, but it seems very likely that many of them are understood in our time as healthy exertions of vital being. Debauchery, of course, still exists in our minds as a designation of brutal excess and deviation, even if it cannot stand as the name of the experiences of the man in *The Kreutzer Sonata*. "I did not understand," he says, "that debauchery does not consist simply in physical acts ... real debauchery consists in freedom from the moral bonds toward a woman with whom one enters into carnal relations. ..."

No doubt it is spiritual vanity and overreaching to hope to enchain the baffling, exciting, fleeting movements of the senses. Every moment of the present is rushing into its fate as the past. To give the past pre-eminence, sanctity, supreme right, is insupportable, a mad dislocation in the economy of personal experience. Nevertheless, the past is not a blur of memory, but a forest in which all of the trees are human beings, rooted, breathing, sustaining the ax, or withering. To think of the past as a series of agreements with others that make an everlasting claim on us is unreal, and yet it is one of the most interesting questions ever asked about the subject matter of so much art: youthful love. It is a radical questioning of the way society understands the flow of life, the rules it has made for the human collisions that are, finally, our biographies. It is a question that goes beyond an answer.

Resurrection is a much greater and more moving asking of the same question. The pure situation of this novel contains the essence of the theme of seduction and betrayal. Every balance is classical. A man, a nobleman, falls in love in youth with a serving girl on his aunt's estate. She is lovely and pure; he is generous, kind, better than most young men. The scene of their first coming together is tenderly ardent and promising. It is spiritually coherent, beautiful, merging like a mist with nature. When the night is over, a sweep of sadness causes the young nobleman to ask himself, "What is the meaning of it all? Is it a great joy or a great misfortune that has befallen me?" But then he remembers that everyone does it and he turns over and falls asleep.

Naturally the young man goes away, as he must, since all of his life is before him. It is a life at once free and fixed. Years and experience leave room for the accidental, the free flowing of existence; form and structure draw the prince inevitably into the anxious considerations of a man of his class. Shall he marry the shallow Princess Korchagina, whom he cannot even see without a feeling of impatience and weariness; shall he break off his affair with the wife of a friend; what to do about his estates?

For Maslova, the young girl, his first love, the seduction is a catastrophe. It is not a disillusion that will be washed away by time, but a tragic circumstance from which enormously varied lifelong sufferings begin to follow. She becomes pregnant, is turned out of the house; the child dies, and through poverty, ill-treatment, and despair Maslova finally becomes a prostitute and is accused of murdering an old client. The worst of her sense of abandonment comes when the prince does not even get off the train as it passes through the village some months after their affair, when she is already aware of her condition. Her horror is an intellectual crisis as much as a personal deprivation and pain. God and His laws are a deception. The prince who had treated her so heartlessly was the best person she knew; "all the rest were still worse." It came to her, as the train pulled away, that everyone lived for himself alone and she began to accept an existence encircled by melancholy, redeemed by a willed anesthesia toward the past, enriched only by the communal traditions of prostitution.

The novel's moral judgments lie upon the soul of the prince. Maslova has remained alive somewhere in his consciousness, a dormant germ of remembered feeling and guilt. They meet again when the prince is called to jury duty and Maslova is in the dock, her fate at the end of the trail that began long ago in a beautiful scene, a snowy midnight Mass in the village. The prince is overcome by a violent turmoil that shakes his whole being; he is seized with the wish for a grand restitution, a sacrifice, a determination to share Maslova's degradation and suffering as a prisoner in Siberia. This cannot merely be a flight of fancy. To face the dragon of responsibility would engage his whole life, his estates, his money, his friends, his career. All of the arrangements and assumptions of society went into his seduction and abandonment of the poor orphan on his aunt's estate. His expiation cannot be selective. In the end, Maslova refuses his sacrifice and will not marry him. It is too late for them.

Tolstoy was in his seventies when he wrote *Resurrection*. The indulgences of his youth thus presented themselves to his imagination as moral and social delinquencies, rather than as mere instances of man's inevitable practice. For this reason and despite the marvelous truthfulness of a great deal of the novel, it relies upon the silky transcendences of persons in the grip of a spiritual idea, characters who must go from flaw to virtue under the rule of justice and ethical revelation. However, it is certainly never Maslova's suffering and resignation we question. It is only Prince Nekhlyudov's profound sense of obligation, his heeding the affliction of memory, the bite of the past, that strike one as abstract, programmatic, untrue to life.

The title of the novel is accurate—drastic breaks with the customs ruling men and women are to be understood as a "resurrection," a surpassing. It is, after all, only an ideal, the dream of an old man in love with humility and longing to achieve a personal reformation upon which a reformation of society might begin. The novel was based on an incident that appeared in the press and stirred Tolstoy's thoughts and imagination. In spite of this, it is realistic only in the grand, elevated Russian novel sense, in that landscape where obsession and transfiguring guilt and expiation are real. No subsequent novel decided to gaze so directly into the abyss of sexual responsibility, to turn a limpid, childlike, old-man's eye upon the chaos of youth, to undertake a day of judgment account.

Richardson's *Clarissa* is openly, and at great, fascinating length, about seduction. Naturally, only a person who thought of himself as a moralist could sit down to write volume after volume of consummation threatened and delayed, assault planned and outwitted. Richardson thought, or told himself that he thought, of his brilliant creation as a sort of encyclopedia of male guile and treachery, an elaborate, defensive karate, by which the menaced girls of the eighteenth century could learn to protect their virtue. The detail is intricate, the postponements and escapes are frenzied, the characters extraordinarily well matched in their odd strengths. All of the action is accomplished under the strict baton of sexual suspense.

Clarissa is a disturbing mixture of wit and sentiment, of surface and disguise. A good deal of emotional anxiety accompanies the modern reader along the way here. The novel that caused all of England and Europe to cry—Rousseau yes, but Diderot!—and opened the seams of sensibility and romanticism, as if discovering new minerals in the soul, is harsh, ugly, and grotesque, concerned with a purely sexual conception of virtue and villainy, a conception heavily under our suspicion.

Insolence and courtesy, or at least an elaboration of manner passing for courtesy, are so closely interwoven in the style that they represent an aesthetic exhilaration. The wit, the speed, the expressive, fantastical elegance of the letters that tell, with the wonderful, lost slowness of past times, this violent story are the vehicle for an unmotivated need for sexual humiliation on the part of Lovelace and a need to encounter but avoid the violation on the part of Clarissa.

Clarissa is a bourgeois heroine, the defiant but deeply alert and prudent daughter of rich parents who have not reached the point of trusting the sentiments. (Clarissa's prudence is sexual; otherwise she makes every mistake possible to a clever, bossy, morally vain young girl.) The rich, handsome, brilliant rake Lovelace seeks to marry her, partly to unite her father's money with his own name and lands. Another suitor, whose property is close to that of the Harlowe family, is produced for Clarissa, but she does not love him. He is not lovable and she, asserting the dominance of feeling over calculation, refuses to marry him. She says she would rather remain single, and in many ways this threat appears to be, in fact, a condition Clarissa could have endured with a pleasure equal to fortitude. But the compulsion the stupid family puts her under is so great, the challenge to Lovelace is so sportingly exciting that he abducts her, and the intense, quivering drama of seduction and escape begins. Clarissa's virtue and Lovelace's determination: this is the balance of the longest novel in English.

The fact that the novel is written in letters is of the greatest importance. The depravity of the plot is in that way kept at a distance. And the use of letters modifies the inner life of the characters as we know them. A letter is not a dialogue or even an omniscient exposition. It is a fabric of surfaces, a mask, a form as well suited to affectations as to the affections. The letter is, by its natural shape, self-justifying; it is one's own evidence, deposition, a self-serving testimony. In a letter the writer holds all the cards, controls everything about himself and about those assertions he wishes to make concerning events or the worth of others. For completely self-centered characters, the letter form is a complex and rewarding activity. Both Clarissa and Lovelace are self-centered. They *must* tell their story, must objectify everything, even sexual assault. Reality lives in words.

Lovelace to his friend:

Her chamber door has not yet been opened. I must not expect she will breakfast with me. Nor dine with me, I doubt. A little silly soul, what troubles does she make to herself by her over-niceness! All I have done to her would have been looked upon as *frolic* only, a *romping-bout,* and laughed off by nine parts in ten of the sex accordingly. The more she makes of it, the more painful to herself, as well as to me.

The story moves back and forth in brilliant communications. It comes to a sordid end. Lovelace takes Clarissa to a mean, filthy brothel, finally puts her under the care of two revolting procuresses, has her drugged—and at last rapes her, since she will not have it otherwise. When she recovers, Lovelace wishes to marry her, but Clarissa refuses, wastes away, and dies. He is killed in a duel about the affair.

Lovelace is a monomaniac who seeks life through sex. He is somewhat like the sleepless seducers in Restoration comedy, but on a grander scale. His wildness, his nihilism, his brilliance, his boredom, his sexual pride, are altogether original and exceptional. There is, as in Don Giovanni, an absence of motive and an exorbitance of obsession. His fascination with Clarissa is usually spoken of as "love," and yet his determination is not to win her in marriage, although that is part of the plot, but simply to destroy her virtue. It nags him, exhausts him, bores him—but he will not leave off.

The plot moves on the unconscious curiosity Clarissa feels about Lovelace, her paralysis before the hypnotic appeal of his thoroughly deserved evil reputation. She says early in the book, "I like him better than I ever thought I should like him and, his faults considered, better than I ought to like him." What does she like in him? In every way she would wish the chance to reform him, to exercise her will to power in that fashion. A hopeless, ill-placed wish it is, but she is not easily deflected and is ever eager to find reasons for excusing his villainy. Should there be possible a means of interpreting the most dreadful behavior in Lovelace's favor she will find it, even though she never loses her hard-headed suspicion of him. "You may observe," Dr. Johnson said about Clarissa, "that there is always something she prefers to the truth."

Clarissa seems to entertain more hope for Lovelace than we do; at the same time she has none of our fascination with his mind, his cutting irony, his reckless skepticism. She knows little about all of this because she hasn't read his extraordinary letters—and we have. His driven energy, his interesting ruthlessness do not seem to be the springs of her attraction; she is compelled by his good looks and his bad reputation. It doesn't appear egregiously modern to speak of her hidden curiosity, her complicity in her own humiliation, her lingering about dangerous premises, the interest of the final drugged immobility which is the long delayed condition of her violation. Her dignity afterward is another thing—her saintly suffering, the apotheosis of degradation which truly ennobles her, like a salvation finally achieved. She is going to die and even that is plausible on the practical level in a world of early deaths, pneumonias, tuberculosis, decline.

Clarissa is not seduced, cannot be seduced, fraudulently led into adultery. She can be raped, just as anyone can be. This is the meaning of the violation in the book, that she is literally unseducible and if the man is bent upon consummation he will finally have to knock her out to have his way. Lovelace hates Clarissa's family for their bourgeois lack of excess and their hesitation about aristocratic indulgence. This is one of the reasons he grimly wishes to subdue the daughter. Even more he wishes to destroy Clarissa's will to power through virtue. As a rake, a clever man, he must have known a great deal about the need to dominate in a certain sort of aggressively pure woman. He is himself an independent, spoiled man and Clarissa's degree of overwhelming virtue enrages him and stabs at his sexual pride.

The frustrations imposed by virtue may annoy a man like Lovelace, but the destruction of them will not redeem him. He is redeemed by Clarissa's powerful attraction to him, her absolute need for him, her bewildering inability to withdraw from the game of seduction. There is a fire at the inn where they have taken rooms in the flight from her family. This occasion finds her in her bedroom, frightened, half-dressed, "exposed"—and indeed Lovelace sees the emergency as the opportunity to accomplish his wish. Screams, prayers, pleas, tears finally exhaust him, but not before he has behaved violently, heartlessly. What does Clarissa do? She puts him on a one-week probation.

Her experiences throughout the novel are extremely sordid. The inn and the prostitutes are quite startling in the authenticity of their squalor. "The vile house," Clarissa calls it. She lives in terror of Lovelace—the kind of "terror," domesticated, part of a risky tournament, a wife long married might speak of. "He terrified me with his looks, and with his violent emotions, as he gazed upon me. . . . Never saw I his abominable eyes look as they looked. . . . And yet his behavior was decent, for he snatched my hand two or three times, speaking words of tenderness through his shut teeth." Lovelace speaks of Clarissa as a "poor plotter" and we are bound to admit the accuracy of the observation, as she seeks the net she flees from.

Rage and vanity are Lovelace's traits. Virtue, love of power, and curiosity are the defining marks of Clarissa's nature. The novelist, Richardson, understands cruelty in his own angular, disguised way. It is only a few plunges downward to *Les Liaisons Dangereuses.* The two works are connected by their sexual and social brutality. The industriousness of *Clarissa,* the sense of an indefatigable, brilliant mind (Richardson's) behind it all, gives the work its outrageously fascinating character. But the power of the story lies in sex. Only on the surface is it a game of marriage and family. Clarissa is drugged and raped—this is the end of the line, a resolution. It may be a crime, but it is not exactly a betrayal of her expectations.

The intention of seduction is evident from the first meeting of Clarissa and Lovelace. Attraction, "love," is also at stake. If Clarissa is betrayed, she is betrayed in her determination to reform, and by her fussy capability all turned useless because of the undertow of fascination. Clarissa courts danger and then insists upon her safety. She is a middle-class girl, used to the love of her family, secure enough to defy, run away, and yet call upon the higher sensibilities of personal feeling as her judge. In that way she has none of the vulnerability of Tess, Hetty Sorrel, Jane Eyre, all of them poor and alone. After all, Clarissa lives in a social whirl of correspondents; she greets the morning mail as if it were a row of bodyguards. She replies, at length, in a frenzy, and is, thereby, the least isolated of threatened girls. Words are her protection. Her cries to heaven go out in the next post. Her powers are not perfect, but they reduce the insuperable Lovelace to rape, the most unworthy resource. Are they lovers, or opponents? They have furiously, curiously tested each other and the consummation is death.

———

Tess is the most perfectly conceived of the modern betrayed heroines. Peasant stoicism and a natural refinement of feeling are especially moving in her because of the hard soil they have grown upon. It is not pride that sustains her, that keeps despair from rotting the character. Pride would rest upon disappointed hopes in the matter of respect and consideration felt to be forthcoming, and it is just the absence of such expectation that distinguishes the afflicted heroine in the novel form. Hester Prynne does not have pride; she has endurance and intellectual principles. Maslova, in *Resurrection,* is supported by her world of the oppressed, accused, imprisoned, and in her earlier years by alcohol and depressed bouts of dissipation. It is part of the magic of Tolstoy's sympathy that allows her to be a drunken prostitute without losing the essential stoical, enduring heroine quality.

Pride is the way of the tragic Greek heroines—not the answer in the more practical, reduced world of the novel. Here the women must deal with betrayal as a fact of life. Through their experiences, the terms and promises of romantic love are brought into question in the deepest way. Sentimentality is false and shallow, and to rely on it is the mark of an inferior vision of life. Trust will not be honored, since it is difficult, in matters of love and sex, for human beings to hold to it. Life will not accommodate.

Hardy saw the necessity of rooting the beauty of Tess's character in plausible superiorities that would set her apart, without pretension, from her world. She comes late of the old noble line of d'Urbervilles and represents an impoverished thinning out of a dead ancient family. (It is interesting that the rest of her family, rather comically inclined to daydreaming and fecklessness, do not partake of any special qualities because of the thin thread of the bloodline.) Her seducer, Alec d'Urberville, does not have as true a claim to the name as Tess, but he is rich and, of course, all of his possibilities, the demands and blemishes of his character, are altered by the inward and outward results of riches.

Tess is also made a high school graduate so that she can be rescued from the benign ignorance of the other farm girls. But she is a farm girl, nevertheless, possessed of an extraordinary naturalness, fineness of nature, with everything rustic and simple and strong that a pure peasant culture could provide. The qualities of her nature, the way she is somewhat set apart, are necessary because she is to receive every blow and, as a heroine, must be worthy of her calamities—sex, love, pregnancy, abandonment, poverty, coarse work, ill luck, and finally execution for murder.

Tess's love affair with Alec d'Urberville is a sort of seduction, at least from the man's point of view. Seduction is his aim, and he works to accomplish it by flattery, pretense, and finally a rude, overwhelming insistence. It is not the usual seduction because Tess never really likes him. She is not swept off her feet by illusion and hope, and yields only with a hesitant acquiescence. It is life that acquiesces, not her nature or soul. She is much too real in her own feelings to put any trust in the intentions of Alec.

And yet it happens that the night with Alec d'Urberville ruins Tess's life, even finally takes her life. It is the beginning of the most painful, devastating series of entanglements and misfortunes. There is a child born after the seduction; she humbly takes the responsibility upon herself. The child dies and does not seem to have had great significance for her, perhaps because of her lack of love for the father. It is not the child that casts such a long shadow but the affair itself, her fall, her acquiescence. Through it she loses her real love, Angel Clare.

Angel is the son of a clergyman, and does not wish to go into the professions. He meets Tess when he comes to learn about farming at the dairy where she works. They fall in love, genuinely, truly. They marry. An unvoiced knowledge of human nature causes Tess to be silent about her earlier affair; hesitation is the measure of her hazy acknowledgment of Angel's limitations, of the narrowness of his break with the pieties of his class. On their wedding night, Angel himself confesses the dissipations of youth, and Tess, in a spirit of reciprocity, trust, and wish to unburden herself, confesses her own affair with Alec. Angel is horrified, leaves her, and goes off to Brazil. Like Dimmesdale he cannot ask fundamental questions about life. Any callousness is possible therefore, and his crushing rejection of Tess is one of the most cruel things in fiction. The dense brutality of it is felt bitterly because of Hardy's genius in revealing how great their love was and the miracle of their passing through the falseness of life to find this great and pure love. The deliberate destruction of miraculous love out of regard for—what? A vanity based on the dimmest flutterings of custom.

Dimmesdale's religion and Angel Clare's double standard are real enough, but it is not easy to give them an equal right to consideration. Religion was the whole of this life and after to Dimmesdale, and his last action is an "Election Day" sermon. For Angel, a skulking vanity and tribal narrowness caused him to abandon Tess. One feels at this point a certain attraction to the abstract in him; he would not have married Tess if he had not had a generalized, formal picture of her as a beautiful, virgin girl of the peasant classes he alone had discovered.

The truth of his real love for her is that he suffers almost as much as she from his abandonment and yet he cannot reverse the course of his pedantic decision. The end of the plot is that Tess kills d'Urberville and is executed for it. That is the last act of the drama that began on the night of her seduction.

Hardy sees Tess as a beautiful, warm soul run down by the dogs of fate, in her case the bloodhounds of sex and love, Alec d'Urberville and Angel Clare. Her acceptance, her endurance of the griefs of experience, are of the heroic kind; she meets suffering without losing her capacity for feeling. She is not surprised by loss and rejection and therefore never degraded by it. In Tess's life every adversity has its double. Her misery over the flight of Angel Clare goes hand in hand with a deepening poverty and a deadening solitude. Toward the end of the book her family is actually starving and it is for that reason she takes up with d'Urberville once more. She is defined by her work. The arch of her existence curves as much with work as with love.

Tess's early days on the green dairy farm are idyllic, and the fields and cows coincide with youth and love. In the end she is living in the dismal town of Flintcomb-Ash, working at a threshing machine rented by the day. The farm has become a factory and some critics think *Tess of the d'Urbervilles* is about the death of the English peasantry. The destruction of Tess's love is like some eternal winter, and the scene of her final despair is a bleak and barren epic:

> ... strange birds from behind the North Pole began to arrive silently on the upland of Flintcomb-Ash; gaunt spectral creatures with tragical eyes—eyes which had witnessed scenes of cataclysmal horror in inaccessible polar regions of a magnitude such as no human being had ever conceived, in curdling temperatures that no man could endure ...

In the end Tess kills d'Urberville because he ruined her life, even if her real ruin came from Angel Clare. Hardy has great pity for Tess and yet he has not made of her a theme but a whole person, one of the most original women in fiction because of her naturalness, which never exceeds the possible. He takes a view of the social forces working upon her in his subtitle, "A Pure Woman Faithfully Presented," and in chapter headings such as "The Woman Pays." She is nevertheless a paradox of the kind that seems to come unbidden into the minds of novelists when they face the plot of sex and its destructive force for women. She has, for all the truth that the Immortals are having their sport with her, for all the malign force of circumstance, suffered in a transcendent stoical way, accepting first her child and then the rejection by Angel Clare as a pattern of social destiny, deeply woven into the cloth of life.

The betrayed heroine, unlike the merely betrayed woman, is never under the illusion that love or sex confers rights upon human beings. She may, of course, begin with the hope, and romance would scarcely be possible otherwise; however, the truth hits her sharply, like vision or revelation when the time comes. Affections are not *things* and persons never can become possessions, matters of ownership. The desolate soul knows this immediately, and only the trivial pretend that it can be otherwise. When love goes wrong the survival of the spirit appears to stand upon endurance, independence, tolerance, solitary grief. These are tremendously moving qualities, and when they are called upon it is usual for the heroine to overshadow the man who is the origin of her torment. She is under the command of necessity, consequence, natural order, and a bending to these commands is the mark of a superior being. Or so it seems in the novel, a form not entirely commensurate with the heedlessness and rages of life.

The men do not really believe in consequence for themselves. Consequence proposes to them a worldly loss and diminishment they will not suffer. They will not marry the barmaid or the farm girl or the unvirginal. They will not confess to adultery when their success or their comfort hangs in the balance. They will not live with the mistakes of youth, or of any other period, if it is not practical to do so. Sex is a completed action, not a strange, fleeting coming together that mortgages the future. For this reason perhaps, the heroic woman had to be created in fiction. "Ah, she will not speak!" Dimmesdale cries out. When they take Tess away to be hanged and to bury her body under a black flag, she has nothing she can say except, "I am ready." Maslova, at the end of her story, turns to Prince Nekhlyudov and says, "Forgive me."

Sex is a universal temptation and activity and a great amnesty will naturally have to attend it throughout life. Scarcely anyone would wish it to define, enclose, imprison a man's being. Society has other things for him to do, being a soldier for instance—a group notoriously indifferent to sexual consequence. Obligation is so often improvident, against thrift. Still, the break with human love remains somewhere inside, and at times, under rain clouds, it aches like an amputation. But it is not *serious*. George Eliot said that she wrote novels out of a belief that a seed brings forth in time a crop of its own kind. How to the point is this metaphor for the plot of the illicit, the plot of love.

Now the old plot is dead, fallen into obsolescence. You cannot seduce anyone when innocence is not a value. Technology annihilates consequence. Heroism hurts and no one easily consents to be under its rule. The heroines in Henry James, rich and in every way luckily endowed by circumstance, are seduced and betrayed by surfaces, misled because life, under certain rules, is a language they haven't the key to. Feeling and desire hang on and thus misfortune (if not tragedy) in the emotional life is always ahead of us, waiting its turn. Stoicism, growing to meet the tyrannical demands of consequence, cannot be without its remaining uses in life and love; but if we read contemporary fiction we learn that improvisation is better, more economical, faster, more promising.

Sex can no longer be the germ, the seed of fiction. Sex is an episode, most properly conveyed in an episodic manner, quickly, often ironically. It is a bursting forth of only one of the cells in the body of the omnipotent "I," the one who hopes by concentration of tone and voice to utter the sound of reality. Process is not implacable; mutation is the expedient of the future, and its exhilaration too.

At the end of *Nana*, the beautiful, harassed courtesan's death mingles with the agitated beginning of the Franco-Prussian War. *"À Berlin! à Berlin! à Berlin!"* we hear outside. In her coffin, fouled by smallpox, passion and sensuality are reduced to a "bubbling purulence," a "reddish crust." It is more than that. It is the death of sex as a tragic, exalted theme. As Zola says, "Venus was rotting."

(1972)

Zelda

Zelda Fitzgerald's sad, wasted life seemed to have been buried beneath the ground, covered over by the desperate violets of Scott Fitzgerald's memories. It had gone by, we thought, interred in the mournful, expensive defeat of Fitzgerald's last years. "I left my capacity for hoping on the little roads that led to Zelda's sanitariums," he wrote. And why dig it up again? For it is a more than twice-told tale, capped by Ernest Hemingway's contemptuous epitaph in *A Moveable Feast*. There had always been about Zelda's collapse, even her death at last in a fire at a nursing home in North Carolina—"her body was identified by a charred slipper lying beneath it"—something of a reckoning, the price to be paid for recklessness beyond endurance, for drink and arrogance and carelessness with one's own life and that of those nearest. Or, perhaps, the reckoning, which was breakdown, insanity, was merely mysteriously there, compelling the earlier transgressions and excesses.

As persons, the Fitzgeralds were not, in my view, especially appealing. Their story has a sort of corruption clinging to it, the quality of a decadent fairy tale, some overgrown lushness and deformation. They seem, most of all, like incestuous brother and sister—brilliant, perverse, selfish—their handsome, self-loving faces melting into a mask. Sometimes they make one feel it is almost a deprivation to live without the correcting education of those common marital oppositions of temperament and taste.

In this couple defects were multiplied, as if by a dangerous doubling; weakness fed upon itself without a counterstrength and they were trapped; defaults, mutually committed, left holes everywhere in their lives. When you read their letters to each other it is often necessary to consult the signature in order to be sure which one has done the writing. Their tone about themselves, their mood, is the fatal one of nostalgia—a passive, consuming, repetitive poetry. Sometimes one feels even its most felicitous and melodious moments are fixed, rigid in expression, and that their feelings have gradually merged with their manner, fallen under the domination of style. Even in their suffering, so deep and beyond relief, their tonal memory controls the words, shaping them into the Fitzgerald tune, always so regretful, regressive, and touched with a careful felicity.

In nostalgia there is the pressure of ennui, and even the Fitzgerald youth, extraordinary, successful, special, so often seemed threatened by this backward-looking boredom and emptiness. This, along with evil circumstances and crippling vices, made the very existence of Fitzgerald's brilliant novels and stories a miracle. It was only at the end of his life, when he was composing the fascinating novel, *The Last Tycoon,* when he was tired and despondent but somehow, if only by time and fatigue and distance, free from the self-pity of his unproductive years, that he could subdue the half of himself that was Zelda. The mood of this last novel, not necessarily more interesting than the others by any means, was at least new and one felt a severing had been accomplished, an amputation, feared and longed for . . . But, as in a fairy tale, it was too late.

———

What then is the purpose of a biography of Zelda Fitzgerald (*Zelda,* by Nancy Milford) and a return to this thoroughly scrutinized marriage? Mrs. Milford is not very resolute as an analyst, nor is she a particularly interesting writer on her own. Still, setting out for the wife—the appendage, so to speak, the other side of the question—gives a peculiar vision, a different lighting to the stage. We cannot say that Zelda had ever been in the wings, in the dimness in any of the many Fitzgerald studies—this was scarcely possible for one so brightly noticeable. But Mrs. Milford has done something new. By concentration upon her subject, and even perhaps by inadvertence, she has brought troubling thoughts to our minds, shifted the balance of things, and made it possible for the reader to see in this unhappy woman—a fleeting paragon of the 1920s—an instance of unexpected moral complexity, an example of peculiar failure and the object of a kind of unnamable injustice—domestic, social, cultural?—and the victim of many miseries that were not always unavoidable. Of course, with Zelda it is well-known that many faults lay in herself and in her stars, but new to discover a frantic will to overcome them, a strong talent and intelligence struggling to live—and most surprising of all, incredible energy and longing for discipline. She appeared to experience the desperate creative urge that some have without even having an art. None of it was fully understood or valued by those around her, those in charge of her fate.

First, the vicious portrait of Zelda in Ernest Hemingway's *A Moveable Feast*. In these interesting chapters both of the Fitzgeralds are hit, like baby seals, by the hunter's club. Hemingway is smug and patronizing to Fitzgerald and urges upon us forgiveness by laying Fitzgerald's weaknesses and pains at the feet of his wife. Hemingway sees Zelda as a "hawk." She found him "bogus." In a memoir one would seem to be obliged to believe, to accept in the larger outlines, anecdotes recorded about distinguished contemporaries. Yet sometimes we cannot summon belief, since only the storyteller seems to be in his own skin. This is the case, in my view, with the demeaning anecdote in which Hemingway claims that Fitzgerald, humiliated, longing for reassurance, asked him to consider whether his "measurements"—Hemingway's title for this little memory is "A Matter of Measurements"—were adequate, since, he said, with great embarrassment and uncertainty, Zelda had told him he was not properly constructed to satisfy a woman. Hemingway took the poor questioner into the toilet, had an assessing look, gave a lordly verdict that all was as it should be, if looked at in profile as one gazes at statues in the Louvre, and that what was wrong was that Zelda, trying to put him "out of business."

It is very difficult for the mind to transport poor Fitzgerald, unzipped, to the WC—"*le water*," Hemingway calls it—but not at all hard to imagine Hemingway falling into his role of sexual surveyor, measuring and judging. Another reason for some skepticism about the details of the memoir is the fascinating passage about Zelda at the end.

> Zelda was very beautiful and was tanned.... Her hawk's eyes were clear and calm ... she leaned forward and said to me, telling me her great secret, "Ernest, don't you think Al Jolson is greater than Jesus?"

In Mrs. Milford's book this memorable high-camp remark is spoken to Gerald Murphy: "Gerald, don't you think Al Jolson is just like Christ?"

Before her first breakdown, Zelda provoked extreme distaste and disdain among her friends and in the mind of her husband by taking up, after casual lessons in her youth, the determination to become a ballet dancer. This is a matter of great interest, because as it emerges in Mrs. Milford's ordering of Zelda's letters and statements and hopes, this new activity becomes more or less a model of the way in which her ambitions were forever to be viewed. Her desire in ballet study was profoundly intense and strained; it meant, as her letters show, many different things to her—release ("sudden fame," it was ungraciously called) and escape from alcohol, idleness, emptiness, and dependency. She wanted to have something of her own, as she said over and over again. The enormous discipline required to study the ballet was not a deterrent, but rather something that appealed to her. The story has been told many times, as an example of insanity, of Zelda jumping out of a taxi in the middle of the street in Paris, for fear of being late for her lessons.

The ballet obsession came after a particularly bad time of quarreling and drinking. Fitzgerald's attraction to the young actress Lois Moran and his taunt that "at least the girl did something with herself" are thought to have played a part. Zelda began lessons with Catherine Littlefield in 1927 in Philadelphia, but the work became much more important to her a year or so later in Paris when she was studying with Madame Egorova. She went about her ferocious study with "grotesque intensity" and a driven, outrageous energy. Her husband was not relieved and freed for his work, as one might have imagined, but vexed and angered by her concentration and likely to see it as a vengeance against himself.

What Zelda admired, loved even, in Madame Egorova was "her poverty and dedication." The intensity, the practice, the determination, became so extreme Zelda was put in a hospital in Paris, where her great thoughts were grief for the loss of "her work," for the example of Madame Egorova who had, she said, "given her the greatest possible joy." Later on, her psychiatrists at the hospital were enlisted in the battle to destroy Zelda's concentration and passion. The reasons were always curious ones, no matter what she tried. It was felt that since she couldn't be "great" as a dancer, a painter, a writer, it was damaging to try; it was necessary to control her pleasure in these activities. About the dancing and the doctors' opposition to it she said, "The light in which the thing presented itself to me was: I had got to the end of my physical resources. . . . If I couldn't be great, it wasn't worth going on with, though I loved my work to the point of obsession. . . . It was all I had in the world at the time."

With a deep feeling of having been wronged, Fitzgerald wrote, "After having worked all day at home, I would want to go out at night . . . my wife, on the contrary, having been gone all day, wanted only to stay home and go to bed." One of the natural results of the long hours of ballet practice was the near ending of Zelda's need for alcohol. This gratuity was not greatly considered by anyone, apparently, nor was the sheer advantage of the discipline itself, the joy she took in it, the glaring clarity of the good it might do in providing her not fame as a great dancer, but a milieu in which to live and to find work and satisfactions of some related kind. Instead,

> Dr. Florel was absolutely certain that the way to Zelda's recovery did not lie in further dancing, and he too thought Scott should write to Egorova. But he suggested that Fitzgerald make clear to her their preference that in her answer she discourage Zelda, even if it was a gross deception.

(This was merely the first solicitation by husband and friends of a professional discouragement, sought for the victim's own good.)

They got their answer from Madame Egorova. It was far more positive than either of the men had wanted, but certainly less than Zelda would naturally have hoped for. It said what any observant, interested person could have seen for himself: she had started too late to become a first-class performer, but she had become by the sheer magnitude of perseverance and effort a good dancer and might have found professional work.

Zelda was diagnosed abroad by the distinguished Dr. Bleuler as a schizophrenic. She herself thought Dr. Bleuler "a great imbecile," but we have little reason to imagine other physicians would have been more moderate or hopeful in their predictions. Her mental confusion was sometimes alarming; she suffered, on occasion, disorientation, hallucinations, great fears and depressions, even to the point of a number of suicide attempts. But these low periods could not have been other than transitory because her letters throughout her illness are much too lucid, controlled, alive with feeling and painful awareness. She showed eccentricities, shifts of mood, odd smiles, nightmares, withdrawals, obsessive behavior—*at times.* At the same time, and much more to the point, is the lucidity, the almost unbearable suffering over her condition and her full recognition of it—and the most important and moving thing, an extraordinary zeal and strenuous effort to get well, be real, to function—above all *to work* at something. The latter desperate need is an astonishing desire and hope for one who had been a great beauty, who was the wife of a famous man, and who had lived a life of spectacular indulgence, along with *feminine* expectations of protection and love.

At her most ill an insight that was almost tragic persisted. She understood that something was wrong and that somehow she must pull out from under, by some strenuous effort of her own spirit. "I seem awfully queer to myself, but I know I used to have integrity even if it's gone now. . . . You've *got* to come and tell me how I was. Now I see odd things, people's arms too long or their faces as if they were stuffed and they look tiny and far away, or suddenly out of proportion." Almost worse than the mental suffering was a raging eczema that spread over her whole body, making it impossible to sleep. At times she was swathed in bandages from head to toe. These eruptions often followed a visit from her husband, and even periods of general improvement in her condition seemed, from the record, to coincide with his absence from her.

When they were still in France, Zelda was released from the hospital after a year and three months of treatment. Her case was summarized as "reaction to her feelings of inferiority (primarily toward her husband) . . ." She was stated to have had ambitions which were "self-deceptions" and which "caused difficulties between the couple." Fitzgerald, weary of his own guilt, was relieved to learn of a history of mental troubles on both sides of Zelda's family. When her brother committed suicide he said, "You see—it's not my fault—it's inherited."

His own drinking made him uncertain of his moral rightness. Zelda begged him to stop, but he resisted suggestions about this from such men as Dr. Adolph Meyer in Baltimore. He would fall back upon the complaint that Zelda was living on him, in every spiritual and material way. She was:

. . . under a greenhouse which is my money and my name and my love. . . . She is willing to use the greenhouse to protect her in every way, to nourish every sprout of talent and to exhibit it—and at the same time she feels no responsibility about the greenhouse and feels she can reach up and knock a piece of glass out of the roof any moment, yet she is shrewd enough to cringe when I open the door of the greenhouse and tell her to behave or go.

In Zelda's fight against insanity and dependency she turned, as many disturbed people turn—the educated ones at least—to the hope of release through the practice of art. This hope rests upon the canny observation, clear even to the deranged and sequestered, that artists do not require the confidence of society to the same degree as other workers. And Zelda had lived since her teens with self-indulgent, damaged, and successful artists. There was a strangeness, not altogether promising for her, in the number of things she could do well. After her interrupted work in the ballet she turned often to painting, even though her eyes were not very good. In 1934 thirteen paintings and fifteen drawings were exhibited in Cary Ross's studio and there had been an earlier showing in the lobby of the Algonquin Hotel. Perhaps this exhibition was a curiosity more than anything else. An article about it in *The New York Times* shows again her enduring, passionate wish for self-reliance and personal freedom from dependency on others.

From the sanatorium last week which she temporarily left against doctors' orders to see a show of Georgia O'Keefe's art, Zelda Fitzgerald was hoping her pictures would gratify her great ambition—to earn her own living.

The very center of this study of Zelda Fitzgerald has to do, in a peripheral but interesting way, with literature, with her relation to her husband's work and to her own writings. Unfortunately for her, the most pronounced of her gifts was indeed for writing. And here again she has the precious gift of fantastic energy—not energy of a frantic, chaotic, sick sort, but that of steady application, formed and sustained by a belief in the worth of work and the value of each solitary self. She does not seem to have received any special dividends from motherhood, and domestic life scarcely engaged her interest for a moment. Early in her marriage, a friend, Alec McKaig, wrote in his diary:

> Went to Fitzgeralds. Usual problem there. What shall Zelda do? I think she might do a little more housework—apartment looks like a pig sty.

Andrew Turnbull reports: "Once Fitzgerald told my mother that there was nothing to eat in the house except five hams."

Zelda's greatest gift to Fitzgerald as a writer was her own startling and reckless personality and his almost paralyzing love of it. From McKaig's diary: "Fitz made another true remark about himself . . . cannot depict how anyone thinks except himself and Zelda," and "Fitz confessed this evening at dinner that Zelda's ideas entirely responsible for 'Jelly Bean' & 'Ice Palace.' Her ideas largely in this new novel [*The Beautiful and Damned*]. . . ." Portions of her diary and her letters had been used in *This Side of Paradise*.

When Edmund Wilson was listing the influences on Fitzgerald's work (Midwest, Irishness, and liquor), the author said:

> . . . your catalogue is not complete . . . the most enormous influence on me in the four and a half years since I met her has been the complete, fine and full-hearted selfishness and chill-mindedness of Zelda.

John Peale Bishop's review of *The Beautiful and Damned* felt that the fictional heroine did not come up to Zelda as she was in life. Fitzgerald had not, he said, been able to get "the hard intelligence, that intricate emotional equipment of her prototype."

Articles and stories written by Zelda alone or by both of them were sometimes signed by Fitzgerald for commercial reasons. In 1924 Zelda had written pieces for *McCall's* and "during the remainder of 1927 she worked energetically on four articles, three of which were published the following year. The first, 'The Changing Beauty of Park Avenue,' was signed by both of them, even though in his Ledger Fitzgerald gave Zelda credit for the article. . . ." In 1928 she began writing short stories. "Each story was written in an astonishing but hazardous burst of energy. . . . Five of these stories were to be published by *College Humor*. . . . Nevertheless, without exception the stories were published under both Fitzgeralds' names." At this time began Fitzgerald's preoccupation with "material," his odd conception that there was such a thing for fiction, independent of its embodiment in style, character, and plot. He thought these stories of Zelda's had "been pretty strong draughts on Zelda's and my common store of material." He worried about certain characters in the stories, "both of whom I had in my notebook to use."

They had created themselves together, and they always saw themselves, their youth, their love, their lost youth and lost love, their failures and memories, as a sort of living fiction. It does not seem of much importance that the diaries and letters were appropriated, the stories wrongly attributed for an extra $500. Zelda herself did not seem greatly concerned about any of this. She wrote a mock review of *The Beautiful and Damned* in the *New York Tribune* and said, "I recognized a portion of an old diary of mine . . . and also scraps of letters. . . . Mr. Fitzgerald . . . seems to believe plagiarism begins at home."

The real reason for Fitzgerald's worry about "material" perhaps had to do with the narrow nature of their lives and interests. They had beauty and celebrity and they went everywhere, and yet they were outside history for the most part, seldom making any mention of anything beyond their own feelings. Life, then, even at its best was an airless cell, and personal existence, the knots and tangles, the store of anecdote really counted in the long run. If there is any culpability on Fitzgerald's part it may lie in his use of Zelda's torment to create the destructive, mad heiress, Nicole, in *Tender Is the Night*.

Then, in the midst of insanity and incarceration, an astonishing thing happened. Zelda quite suddenly produced a finished novel, *Save Me the Waltz*. The drama around this achievement is disheartening and discreditable to everyone except Zelda. She did not consult her husband, but sent it off to Max Perkins at Scribner's—and the horror of the ballet lessons began all over again. "On March 14th Scott wrote Dr. Squires in a fury. He had just received Zelda's manuscript. . . ." For four years, he went on in self-pity, he had been forced to work only intermittently on his own novel, "unable to proceed *because* of the necessity of keeping Zelda in sanitariums. . . ."

There was an outcry about "my material," and Zelda revised or deleted the offending passages. Again, one of those heartless letters went out, asking that Zelda be discouraged from hope. "Then he asked Perkins to keep whatever praise he wished to give Zelda '*on the staid side*'" and went on to say—not quite truthfully so far as the record shows—that the doctors at Phipps did not want Zelda to be made to feel too jubilant about "fame and money." It was decided that she was too unstable for superlatives.

Save Me the Waltz is a novel of usual length, quite well written, drawing on Zelda's own life, and is thus a mixture of sharply observed Southern scenes and a contrasting worldliness. It is an entirely creditable effort, one that any new writer might be proud of and that any publisher would be sensible to offer, even though it was not a success when it did appear. That it was composed, hurriedly, by a "hopeless schizophrenic" is scarcely to be believed if one looks at it today.

Institutions, asthma, eczema, guilt, loneliness: none of this had subdued Zelda's supernatural energy. She had always been able to call upon it, whether for swimming, dancing, or writing. Her routine at the hospital in North Carolina was a Spartan one of hiking, calisthenics, abstemious diet, and promotion of modesty and nunlike submission by the absence of mirrors and cosmetics. Zelda stayed in this odd place, endured it all, for years, always being reminded of her "limitations" and "permanent damage." She died there and left in addition to her "legend" another memorial to her unkillable energy—an unfinished novel she intended to call *Caesar's Things*.

What are we to make of all this? Zelda's letters from the hospital are clear and courageous and searing to read. Certain schizophrenics make a strong appeal by the way in which the very limitations of their character remind harassed, responsible, intricately coping people of what they have lost—dreaminess, narrowness of concentration, inwardness, withdrawal. Also these sick persons create guilt of a mysterious kind, whether by their own wish or merely by the peculiarities of their often luminous fixity. The will to blame, to hold them to account, soon appears futile to those closest. Instead the mad entwine their relations in an unresolved, lingering, chafing connection, where guilt, exasperation and grief for the mysteries of life continue to choke. Perhaps the nearest feeling is the immensely suffering and baffling connection between those living and those slowly dying.

Fitzgerald's assumption of responsibility was woefully burdensome to him—and to his wife—but we feel, thinking of them together, that the burden and his bearing of it were at the very center of his moral being. It was his plot, his story, his symbol, image, destiny, obsession. Very few lives are of a piece in the way the Fitzgeralds' were; with them youth and middle age are linked not so much in the chain of growth as in the noose of cause and effect. Middle age is a bill left by youth, and the idea of bankruptcy is a recurring one in their thoughts. But the responsibility, the bearing of a burden, are important for Fitzgerald's idea of himself, perhaps because of his shame for his many weaknesses. He is never entirely free of the need to examine his case once more, never quite able to leave off weighing the cost to his best self, and, for that matter, his worst self. He is unimaginable to us without the weight of money to be made for others, memories to be faced in the middle of the night, the teasings of regret and the pleasures of loss.

Still, in taking the responsibility, however grumblingly and at whatever sacrifice, he was, unlike Zelda, able to find in it an action, a self-definition. A burden accepted is both a hump on your back and a star in your crown. To have disappeared, quit, even to have diminished his immense involvement would have left Fitzgerald with an unendurable emptiness and a feeling of masculine failure. For he not only worked in Hollywood and wrote for the *Saturday Evening Post* to support his wife and daughter, but he kept, week after week, month after month, this relentlessly punishing involvement of letters, arrangements, advice, complaints, nostalgia, new hope, new despair. (Hemingway, for instance, seems to have put aside his wives like last year's tweed jacket. He is not even able to say why he left the beautiful Hadley and his charming son, Bumby. He speaks only, in that careless way he and the Fitzgerald generation share, of "new people" and in some way the never explained temptations to forgetfulness provided by "the rich.")

The picture of Zelda we get from her letters is a disturbing one. The marriage was a misfortune, for they were prodigal partners, like a business marked for collapse because of the ghostly, paralyzing similarities of their natures. They enjoyed their exaggerations and follies when life worked; otherwise their compatibility was a disaster. Each needed just what the other lacked. Zelda was, for all her beauty and daring, hiding a deep sense of personal ambition, a feeling that there was something unique and possible inside her if only she could get at it, use it. Her energy and discipline never came to much. There was nothing she had mastered at quite the right time in her life, and perhaps it was, in the end, her suffering and madness, her breakdowns that frightened her finally into seeking some sort of health through these frantic artistic efforts.

Naturally, the brilliance could not flower. The efforts to live, be reborn, to be free, were at war with her nature and the twisted love that burned out both of these lives. Zelda's talents were in no way comparable to Fitzgerald's. Does this make a difference? Is it to the point? Art was the religion of the 1920s, and thus there were many women married to the tempestuous gods of the period, women called to share the thunder and lightning. Zelda's case was special. She too was anarchic, inspired, brilliant, unsteady, very much in her own way like the gods of the arts, like the spoiled, gifted, and famous all around her. In her, alas, the madness was real rather than an indulgence.

It is sad that her wish to learn, to struggle up to a higher skill and seriousness only seemed a threat to others. Her ways of trying to get well were always strenuous and they seemed to others merely an additional illness, or a deeper falling. What other ways than writing, dancing, or painting were open to her? In any case, failure in these hopes is ordinary and no dishonor lies in the effort. If she had not been married to Fitzgerald her "ambition" would not have presented itself as a "competition." Perhaps the result would have been the same; it would have been looked at differently, however.

Living as a sort of twin, as husband and wife or brother and sister, is a way of survival. In the case of artists these intense relations are curiously ambivalent, undefined collaborations—the two share in perceptions, temperament, in the struggle for creation, for the powers descending downward from art, for reputation, achievement, stability, for their own uniqueness—that especially. Still, only one of the twins is real as an artist, as a person with a special claim upon the world, upon the indulgence of society. Many writers seem to long for these trembling, gifted, outstanding handmaidens, for they are aware that the prosaic, the withdrawn, the demanding, are terrible daily deterrents to art and that the presence of an intelligent, sympathetic, clever sensibility, always at hand, always bright and somehow creative, is a source, even a source of material. With Zelda the *collaboration* was frenetic, almost a matter of essential being, of sharing of vices, arrogance, indulgence, as well as a central conception of themselves and their beautiful destructiveness as the core of Fitzgerald's fictional idea. And, of course, Zelda was always an enormous problem to a man beset with problems.

In spite of the glaring differences, she can bring to mind the exalted twinness of Dorothy and William Wordsworth and the sadness that always stands there, threatening, at the end of a life lived so intensely and with such disturbing self-consciousness. Mrs. Milford's book about Zelda Fitzgerald has in it what one might speak of as considerable "woman interest." A few years back the interest lay in the tragic grandeur and glamour of her love story. Now I should think it rests entirely in the heroism of her efforts and the bitterness of her defeats. She was flawed and rich with liability, but we suddenly find ourselves discontent and more than a little resentful that this strange, valuable girl from Montgomery, Alabama, had to endure unnecessary rebuffs and discouragements—in a life where so much suffering was foreordained and beyond repair.

In the end we feel about Zelda Fitzgerald just what De Quincey felt for Dorothy Wordsworth: "respectful pity."

(1970)

SYLVIA PLATH

In Sylvia Plath's work and in her life the elements of pathology are so deeply rooted and so little resisted that one is disinclined to hope for general principles, sure origins, applications, or lessons. Her fate and her themes are hardly separate and both are singularly terrible. Her work is brutal, like the smash of a fist; and sometimes it is also mean in its feeling. Literary comparisons are possible, echoes vibrate occasionally, but to whom can she be compared in spirit, in content, in temperament?

Certain frames for her destructiveness have been suggested by critics. Perhaps being born a woman is part of the exceptional rasp of her nature, a woman whose stack of duties was laid over the ground of genius, ambition, and grave mental instability. Or is it the 1950s, when she was going to college, growing up—is there something of that here? Perhaps; but I feel in her a special lack of national and local roots, feel it particularly in her poetry, and this I would trace to her foreign ancestors on both sides. They were given and she accepted them as a burden, not as a gift; but there they were, somehow cutting her off from what they weren't. Her father died when she was eight years old and this was serious, central. Yet this most interesting part of her history is so scorched by resentment and bitterness that it is only the special high burn of the bitterness that allows us to imagine it as a cutoff love.

For all the drama of her biography, there is a peculiar remoteness about Sylvia Plath. A destiny of such violent self-definition does not always bring the real person nearer; it tends, rather, to invite iconography, to freeze our assumptions and responses. She is spoken of as a "legend" or a "myth"—but what does that mean? Sylvia Plath was a luminous talent, self-destroyed at the age of thirty, likely to remain, it seems, one of the most interesting poets in American literature. As an *event* she stands with Hart Crane, Scott Fitzgerald, and Poe rather than with Emily Dickinson, Marianne Moore, or Elizabeth Bishop.

The outlines of her nature are odd, especially in her defiant and extensive capabilities, her sense of mastery, the craft and preparation she almost humbly and certainly industriously acquired as the foundation for an overwhelming ambition. She was born in Winthrop, Massachusetts. Her mother's parents were Austrian; her father was a German, born in Poland. He was a professor of biology, a specialist, among other interests, in bee-raising. (The ambiguous danger and sweetness of the beehive—totemic, emblematic for the daughter.) Her father died and the family moved to Wellesley, Massachusetts, to live with their grandparents. The mother became a teacher and the daughter went to public schools and later to Smith College. Sylvia Plath was a thorough success as a student and apparently was driven to try to master everything life offered—study, cooking, horseback riding, writing, being a mother, housekeeping. There seemed to have been in her character no empty patch or seam left for the slump, the incapacity, the refusal.

An early dramatic death gives one, in a literary sense, a real life, a throbbing biography. People discovered they had known a vehement, disturbing genius in their school days; mere propinquity became a challenge, and the brief life has been the subject for memories of no special usefulness. Sylvia Plath does not come closer, shine more clearly. Poems have followed her poems, making their statements and to most of these her own harsh eloquence is the proper rebuke. We do not by any means have all of her letters, and the ones she must have written during the last year haunt the mind—that is, if she had the dependent, needy relationship that can make a letter an action, a true telling of feeling. The letters—at least the excerpts we have seen thus far—tend to be minimal, flat, suppressed, impersonal, rather more an instance of her lack of genuine closeness to the recipient than of any wish to reveal herself. A. Alvarez in *The Savage God* has done the greatest credit to the live person as he knew her. He is restrained, deeply knowledgeable about Sylvia Plath's poetry, and moved by the sufferings of her last days and the moment of suicide.

Sylvia Plath went on a Fulbright to Cambridge University. She met and later married the distinguished poet Ted Hughes, and after a year or so back in America they returned to live in England. Her first book of poems, *The Colossus,* was published in 1960, the same year her daughter Frieda was born. In 1962 her son Nicholas was born—and then life began to be hard and disturbing, except that she was able to write the poems later issued under the title *Crossing the Water.* She was separated from her husband, came back to London with two small children, tried to live and work and survive alone in a bare flat during one of the coldest years in over a century. *The Bell Jar* was published under a pseudonym just before she died, in February 1963.

In the last freezing months of her life she was visited, like some waiting stigmatist, by an almost hallucinating creativity—the astonishing poems in *Ariel* and in a later volume called *Winter Trees.*

The creative visitation was not from heaven, but from the hell of rage. Yet so powerful is the art that one feels an unsettling elation as one reads the lacerating lines. The poems are about death, rage, hatred, blood, wounds, cuts, deformities, suicide attempts, stings, fevers, operations—there is no question of coming to terms with them. There is no consolation in our experience of the poems but they are alive, filled with hurt, excitement; a grinding, grating joy in the perfection of the descriptive language overcomes hesitations of the spirit.

There are also poems about children, her own, who were intensely loved. And yet "child" and "baby" as mere words are often attached to images of pain and death. Many of the poems are *tirades,* voiced at such a pitch of eloquence and passion they take your breath away. She, the poet, is frighteningly there all the time. Orestes rages, but Aeschylus lives to be almost seventy. Sylvia Plath, however, is both heroine and author; when the curtain goes down, it is her own dead body there on the stage, sacrificed to her plot.

She has the rarity of being, in her work at least, never a "nice person." There is nothing of mystical and schizophrenic vagueness about her. No dreamy loss of connection, no manic slackness, impatience, and lack of poetic judgment. She is, instead, all strength, ego, drive, endurance—and yet madly concentrated somehow, perplexing. Disgust is very strong in her nature, but she faces things with a classical fierceness and never loses dignity. That is why her vision is more powerful and more pure than the loose abandon of other poets of her period.

She is capable of anything—that we know. Alvarez reminds us how typical of her nature is the scene in *The Bell Jar* in which she dashes down a ski slope without knowing how to ski; he remembers her reckless way with horses, and tells of a deliberate smashing of her own car in a suicidal burst before the final one.

It is not recklessness that makes Sylvia Plath so forbidding, but destructiveness toward herself and others. Her mother thought *The Bell Jar* represented "the basest ingratitude" and we can only wonder at her innocence in expecting anything else. For the girl in the novel, a true account of events so far as we know, the ego is disintegrating and the stifling self-enclosure is so extreme that only death—and after that fails, shock treatment—can bring any kind of relief. Persons suffering in this way simply do not have room in their heads for the anguish of others—and later many seem to survive their own torments only by an erasing detachment. But even in recollection—and *The Bell Jar* was written a decade after the happenings—Sylvia Plath does not ask the cost.

There is a taint of paranoia in her novel and also in her poetry. The person who comes through is merciless and threatening, locked in violent images. If she does not, as so many have noticed, seem to feel pity for herself, neither is she moved to self-criticism or even self-analysis. It is a sour world, a drifting, humid air of vengeance. *The Bell Jar* seems to be a realistic account of her suicide attempt during the summer before her senior year at Smith. But the novel is about madness as well, and that separates it from the poems. Death, in the poetry, is an action, a possibility, a gesture, complete in itself, unmotivated, unexamined.

The Bell Jar opens with the line, "It was a queer, sultry summer, the summer they electrocuted the Rosenbergs." The Rosenbergs are in no way a part of the story and their mention is the work of an intelligence, wondering if the sufferings of a solitary self can have general significance. Also with her uncanny recognition of connections of all kinds—sound, sensation—and her poetic ordering of material, the electrocution of the Rosenbergs and the shock treatment at the end of the book have a metaphorical if not a realistic kinship. In the end the Rosenbergs just mean death to Sylvia Plath. "I couldn't help wondering what it would be like, being burned alive, all along your nerves."

After a summer in New York, the girl goes back to Massachusetts and madness begins to close in on her. "I hadn't slept for twenty-one nights. I thought the most beautiful thing in the world must be shadow, the million moving shapes and cul de sacs of shadow. There was shadow in bureau drawers and closets and suitcases, and shadows under houses and trees and stones, and shadow at the back of people's eyes and smiles, and shadow, miles and miles of it, on the night side of the earth."

Committing suicide is desperation, demand for relief, but I don't see how we can ignore the way in which it is edged with pleasure and triumph in Sylvia Plath's work. In *The Bell Jar* she thinks of slashing her wrists in the tub and imagines the water "gaudy as poppies"—an image like those in her late poems. When she is unable to do the act, she still wants to "spill a little blood" for practice. "Then I felt a small, deep thrill, and a bright seam of red welled up at the lip of the slash. The blood gathered darkly, like fruit, and rolled down my ankle into the cup of my black patent leather shoe." These passages, and others much more brilliant in her poems, show a mind in a state of sensual distortion, seeking pain as much as death, contemplating with grisly lucidity the mutilation of the soul and the flesh. In "Daddy,"

> Every woman adores a Fascist,
> The boot in the face, the brute
> Brute heart of a brute like you.

With Sylvia Plath the submission to, the pursuit of pain are active, violent, *serious,* not at all in a Swinburnian mood of spankings and teasing degradation. Always, behind every mood, there is rage—for what reason we do not know, not even in the novel where the scene is open and explicit. In some poems the rage is directed blankly at her father, in others more obliquely, but with intensity, at her husband.

The actual suicide she attempted, and from which she was rescued only by great luck and accident, is very distressing in its details. The girl goes down into a cold, damp, cob-webbed corner of a cellar. There she hides herself behind an old log and takes fifty sleeping pills. The sense of downness, darkness, dankness, of unbearable rot and chill is savored for its ugliness and hurt. "They had to call and call / And pick the worms off me like sticky pearls" ("Lady Lazarus").

In real life there was a police search, newspaper headlines, empty pill bottle discovered; it was dramatic, unforgettable. Sylvia Plath was found, sent to the hospital, had shock treatment, and "the bell jar" in which she had been suffocating was finally lifted. The novel is not equal to the poems, but it is free of gross defects and embarrassments. The ultimate effort was not made, perhaps, but it is limited more in its intentions than in the rendering. The book has an interestingly cold, unfriendly humor. We sympathize with the heroine because of her drudging facing of it all and because of her suffering. The suffering is described more or less empirically, as if it were a natural thing, and the pity flows over you partly because she herself is so hard and glassy about her life.

This autobiographical work is written in a bare, rather collegiate 1950s style, and yet the attitude, the distance, and bitter carelessness are colored by a deep mood of affectlessness. The pleasures and sentiments of youth—wanting to be invited to the Yale prom, losing your virginity—are rather unreal in a scenario of disintegration, anger, and a perverse love of the horrible. The seduction of Esther Greenwood, as the heroine is called, is memorably grotesque and somehow bleakly suitable. The act leads to a dangerous, lengthy, very unusual hemorrhaging. The blood—an obsession with the author—flows so plentifully that the girl is forced to seek medical help. She rather grimly pursues the young man with demands that he pay the doctor's bill, as if in some measure to get revenge for an action she herself cooperated with in the interest of experience.

The atrocious themes, the self-enclosure, the pain, blood, fury, infatuation with the hideous—all of that is in *The Bell Jar*. But, in a sense, softly, hesitantly. The poems in *Ariel* are much more violent. Indeed, the celebrated poem "Daddy" is as mean a portrait as one can find in literature.

Suicides are frequent enough, but the love of death, the teasing joy of it are rarely felt. Hart Crane, Virginia Woolf, many others, committed suicide. Some believe even Sappho threw herself from a rock into the sea. We think of these self-destructive actions as more or less sudden or as the culmination of an unbearable depression, one that brings with it a feeling of unworthiness and hopelessness, a despair that cannot imagine recovery.

Some of the journals Virginia Woolf wrote during the days before her death have in them the glittering contempt of a Sylvia Plath poem such as "Lesbos."

> Viciousness in the kitchen!
> The potatoes hiss.
> It is all Hollywood, windowless.

It goes on:

> You have stuck her kittens outside your window
> In a sort of cement well
> Where they crap and puke and cry and she can't hear.

This poem was written in the last weeks of Sylvia Plath's life and I have no clue as to whether or not it was an actual scene. The excessive violence of the language, remarkable as it is, seems to come from a mind speeding along madly and yet commanding an uncanny control of language, sound, rhythm, and metaphor that is the very opposite of madness.

In the entry of Virginia Woolf's diary there is a similar impatience. "They were powdering and painting, these common little tarts... Then at Fuller's. A fat, smart woman in red hunting cap, pearls, check skirt, consuming rich cakes. Her shabby dependant also stuffing. ... Where does the money come from to feed these fat white slugs?"

Anger and contempt. And yet, when the day comes for Virginia Woolf, the pain of the illness bears down on her and she feels only apology, gratitude, and depression. Her letter to her husband reads, "Dearest, I feel certain that I am going mad again. I feel we can't go through another of those terrible times. ... I can't fight any longer. I know I am spoiling your life, that without me you could work." She weighted her skirts and managed to drown in the river.

With Sylvia Plath suicide is a performance. "Lady Lazarus" describes it with a raging, confident pride. There is no apology or fearfulness. Suicide is an assertion of power, of the strength—not the weakness—of the personality. She is no poor animal sneaking away, giving up; instead she is strong, threatening, dangerous.

I have done it again.
One year in every ten
I manage it—
      ("Lady Lazarus")

Sometimes the performance is a reposeful one, as in "Edge":

The woman is perfected.
Her dead
Body wears the smile of accomplishment,
The illusion of a Greek necessity

Occasionally, as in the ending of "Last Words," domesticity and annihilation are mixed together:

When the soles of my feet grow cold,
The blue eye of my turquoise will comfort me.
Let me have my copper cooking pots, let my rouge pots
Bloom about me like night flowers, with a good smell.
They will roll me up in bandages, they will store my heart
Under my feet in a neat parcel....

Sylvia Plath's preoccupation with the body at the moment of death
reminds me of Mishima, although her concern is not to be "fit" as his
apparently was, but simply to have the sensation of the corpse. With
both of these suicides the action is asserted as a value, a definition, a
pure leap. It is even sometimes thought of as beautiful, "pure and clean
as the cry of a baby."

The circumstances of her suicide in London, the expectation that a
girl would be coming in early to help with the children, the knowledge
that the man in the flat below awakened early, the note with the doctor's name and phone number: these facts lead Alvarez to speculate
that Sylvia Plath didn't *entirely* want to kill herself. She *risked* death—
and lost.

Suicide, in that view, is thought of as a cry for help, one that cannot
be uttered in the usual ways. The sheer fact of it was a tragic culmination, and yet it is not the death but the obsessions with it that are her
inexplicable subject matter. Torture, mutilation, destruction are offered as interesting in themselves, without any suggestions that they

are a "problem." Mishima tried to decorate his death with ideas of national policy which were, of course, ridiculous fantasies. Sylvia Plath always seems to be describing her self-destruction as an exhilarating act of contempt.

Perhaps it is important to remember that the poems are about suicide rather than about death as the waiting denouement of every life. The oddity of this is almost inexhaustible and the poems break with the universal theme of the passage of time, decay of the body, union with God, whatever death in the English poetic tradition has attached itself to. The idea of killing oneself, the sensuality of it, the drama of it, the prevision, based on other attempts, cannot fail to be a distortion, a decadence. The death wish, that limping, hanging-back companion to life, is, if it exists, an instinctual compliment to the vast and intricate efforts to survive. It is not one with a steady compulsion to jump, slit one's throat, swallow pills, turn on the gas.

The suicides are, then, a group apart, technicians, planners, plotters. Anne Sexton shares the wish, and her prose and poem about Sylvia Plath's death are strange, jaunty, casual and rather rapid, as if one were telling an anecdote in fear of interruption. She speaks of the two of them as "death-mongers," and tells with great excitement of the way they talked "their deaths in the Ritz Bar in Boston." Feel the air, imagine the scene, she says, "We talked about death with a burned-up intensity, both of us drawn to it like moths to an electric light bulb. Sucking on it!" The gaiety is profoundly saddening, the glittering eye frightens us. Anne Sexton tries, in a poem, to explain the peculiar concern for craft that dominates the suicide's imagination:

> *Like carpenters they want to know* which tools.
> *They never ask* why build.

Suicide is only one of the distressing themes in Sylvia Plath's work. There is fascination with hurt and damage and fury; she is a bluntly acute and rather heartless observer. There is a blind man at the table on a ship, feeling for his food. "His fingers had the noses of weasels. I couldn't stop looking." The bright reds of poppies and tulips become bloody and threatening. Gifts are not easily accepted. Slashing a finger in the kitchen is the occasion for "Cut," with its transfixed accuracy.

What a thrill—
My thumb instead of an onion.
The top quite gone
Except for a sort of hinge

Of skin,
A flap like a hat,
Dead white.
Then that red plush.

A bruise is, in like manner, painted in "Contusion."

Color floods to the spot, dull purple.
The rest of the body is all washed out.
The color of pearl.

Is the poem "Daddy" to be accepted as a kind of exorcism, a wild dramatic monologue of abuse screamed at a lost love?

You do not do, you do not do
Any more, black shoe
In which I have lived like a foot
For thirty years, poor and white,
Barely daring to breathe or Achoo.

Her father died of a long illness, but there is no pity for *his* lost life. Instead he is not the dead one; he is the murderer:

An engine, an engine
Chuffing me off like a Jew
A Jew to Dachau, Auschwitz, Belsen.
I began to talk like a Jew.
I think I may well be a Jew.

The association of her own pain with that of the Jews in Europe has been named very well by George Steiner, "a subtle larceny." The father did not kill anyone and "the fat black heart" is really her own. How is it possible to grieve for more than twenty years for one as evil and brutal as she asserts her father to have been? On the grounds of psychology every opposite can be made to fall neatly into place—that jagged, oddly shaped piece is truly part of a natural landscape if only you can find the spot where its cutting corners slip into the blue sky. The acrimonious family—yes, any contrary can turn up there, *logically* as it were. But even strangers, the town, are brought into the punishment of her father and this is somehow the most biting and ungenerous thought of all:

> There's a stake in your fat black heart
> And the villagers never liked you.
> They are dancing and stamping on you.
> They always knew it was you.
> Daddy, daddy, you bastard, I'm through.

She insists that she is the victim—poor and white, a Jew, with a pretty red heart. But she is a dangerous and vindictive casualty: "Herr God, Herr Lucifer / Beware / Beware." "Daddy," with its hypnotic rhythms, its shameful harshness, is one of Sylvia Plath's most popular and known works. You cannot read it without shivering. It is done, completed, perfected. All the hatred in our own hearts finds its evil unforgiving music there—the Queen of the Night.

Love for her children, what about that? Isn't it mitigating? There is warmth and even joy. The boy and girl are "two roses," a child's smile is "found money," children are "the one solid the spaces lean on," the baby is a "high-riser, my little loaf." But children also appear in the images of destruction. In "Edge" the woman who is perfected by death has her dead children with her.

> She has folded
>
> Them back into her body as petals
> Of a rose close when the garden
>
> Stiffens and odours bleed
> From the sweet, deep throats of the night flower.

A child's smile is a "hook." There is a poem about the deformities occasioned by thalidomide. In "Death & Co.":

> He tells me how sweet
> The babies look in their hospital
> Icebox, a simple
>
> Frill at the neck,
> Then the flutings of their Ionian
> Death gowns,
> Then two little feet.

What can we make of a poet so ambitious and vengeful, so brilliant and yet so willfully vulnerable? How can we judge such a sense of personal betrayal, such rage, and such deformed passions? Her work is overwhelming; it is quite literally irresistible. The daring, the skill, the severity. It shocks and thrills. She called—in a typically awful phrase—her last burst of poetry "the blood jet."

When the time came she had earned it by all those earlier poems, slowly, carefully written, by that long ambition, burning, waiting, learning, by her A's, her Phi Beta Kappa, her driven perfectionism, her arrogance, her madness controlled to just the right degree. The loneliness which Alvarez so compellingly preserves for us, the freezing flat—without curtains—the icy early mornings, furiously writing before the children cried and before the "glassy music" of the milkman, her husband off with someone else—there we have a "modern instance" if there ever was one.

It is not a question in these last weeks of the conflict in a woman's life between the claims of the feminine and the agonized work of art. Every artist is either a man or a woman and the struggle is pretty much the same for both. All art that is not communal is, so to speak, made at home. Sylvia Plath was furious. Alvarez writes:

> I suspect that finding herself alone again now, however temporarily and voluntarily, all the anguish she had experienced at her father's death was reactivated: despite herself, she felt abandoned, injured, enraged and bereaved as purely and defenselessly as she had as a child twenty years before.

The sense of betrayal, even of hatred, did not leave her weak and complaining so much as determined and ambitious. Ambitious rage is all over *Ariel* and in the poems written at the same time and published in *Winter Trees.* "The Applicant" is a very bitter poem about the woman's part in marriage. In "For a Fatherless Son" she speaks to the child about the absence of the father that will gradually grow in the child's consciousness like a tree:

> A death tree, color gone, an Australian gum tree—
> Balding, gelded by lightning—an illusion,
> And a sky like a pig's backside, an utter lack of attention.

And that is what her own life was like at the end—the husband and father's "utter lack of attention."

In the explosive energy of her last months I see a determination to "win." Indeed I feel, from the evidence of her work, that it is sentimental to keep insisting that the birth of her children unlocked her poetic powers. Why should that be? The birth of children opens up the energy for taking care of them and for loving them. The common observation that one must be prepared to put off other work for a few years is strongly founded. Of course, it is foolish to generalize and it is the work itself, its hard competitiveness that glare out at every turn. When she died she was alone, exhausted from writing, miserable—but triumphant too, achieved, defined and defiant.

The suicide of a young woman with the highest gifts is inevitably a circumstance of the most moving and dramatic sort. We cannot truly separate the work from the fascination and horror of the death. It is a fact that the poems in *Ariel* were read, while Sylvia Plath was alive, with full self-control and detachment by editors, who then rejected many that have since become important additions to our literature. In the end this does not strike me as more than an astonishment and it is certain the poems would have been published. Everything, everything is published, and no matter that the claim upon our attention is more often than not unfathomable. What is more teasing to the mind and the imagination is how the poems of a dramatic suicide would read to us if the poet had held on to life, given interviews, public readings, finished a second novel, more poems.

It is interesting to make the effort to read Sylvia Plath's poems as if she were still alive. They are just as brilliant, just as much creations of genius, but they are obscured and altered. Blood, reds, the threats do not impress themselves so painfully upon us. "Cold blanks approach us: / They move in a hurry." What is that? we wonder. Unhappiness, agitation, fear? "Edge" seems to be a Greek heroine, Medea perhaps, once more. "Last Words," a profoundly well-written poem:

> I do not want a plain box, I want a sarcophagus
> With tigery stripes, and a face on it
> Round as the moon, to stare up.

A beautiful poem in which, as the textbooks might say, the poet imagines her own death and is buried in a tomb, like an ancient Babylonian goddess of love. "The Detective," a prophetic poem about a death (or is it a murder?) that imagines us as we have become—detectives, putting the pieces together, working on the case. "Make notes," it says at the end.

Her poems have, read differently, the overcharged preoccupation with death and release found in religious poetry. For indeed she saw eternity the other night, also; she cries out "No end?" as Herbert does. But she was not religious; instead she is violently secular in her eternities, realistic about the life that slides from her side. Suicide was not a necessity to the passion and brilliance of the poems; nevertheless the act is a key, central to the overwhelming burst of achievement. She lived on her poetry during the last months of her life. Great she knew it to be; we feel that. It had to be *serious,* final. To imagine anyone's taking his life as a way of completing, fulfilling, explaining the highest work of that life may appear impudent, insulting to death. And yet is it more thoughtful to believe that love, debts, ill health, revenge are greater values to the human soul than creative, artistic powers? Artists have often been cruel to others for what they imagined to be advantages to their work. Cruelty to oneself, as the completion of creation, is far from unimaginable, especially to a spirit tempted throughout life to self-destruction.

If anything could have saved Sylvia Plath it would have been that she, in life, might have had the good fortune to know her own fulfillment, her hard, glittering achievement. In *The Review,* Douglas Dunn wrote about her: "Sylvia Plath was one of the most remarkable talents in any art of the decade, if not of the century." She has won the green cloth—no writer ever wanted it more. Or it would be more careful to say that she *earned* the green cloth and along with the first determination to be preeminent as a poet there came money and power, all by her own efforts. But it came too late, of course, and lesser spirits usurped the ground, began the sentimentalization of her own ungenerous nature and unrelenting anger.

Beyond the mesmerizing rhythms and sounds, the flow of brilliant, unforgettable images, the intensity—what does she say to her readers? Is it simple admiration for the daring, for going the whole way? To her fascination with death and pain she brings a sense of combat and brute force new in women writers. She is vulnerable, yes, to father and husband, but that is not the end of it at all. I myself do not think her work comes out of the cold war, the extermination camps, or the anxious doldrums of the Eisenhower years. If anything, she seems to have jumped ahead of her dates and to have more in common with the years we have just gone through. Her lack of conventional sentiment, her destructive contempt for her family, the failings in her marriage, the drifting, rootless rage, the peculiar homelessness, the fascination with sensation and the drug of death, the determination to try everything, knowing it would not really stop the suffering—no one went as far as she did in this.

There is nothing of the social revolutionary in her, but she is whirling about in the center of an overcharged, splitting air and she especially understands everything destructive and negative. What she did not share with the youth of the present is her intense and perfect artistry, her belief in it. That religion she seemed to have got from some old Prussian root memory of hard work, rigor, self-command. She is a stranger, an alien. In spite of her sea imagery—and it is not particularly local but rather psychological—she is hard to connect with Massachusetts and New England. There is nothing Yankee in her. So "crossing the water" was easy—she was as alien to nostalgia and sentiment as she was to the country itself. A basic and fundamental displacement played its part.

Sylvia Plath has extraordinary descriptive powers; it is a correctness and accuracy that combine the look of things with their fearsome powers of menace. It is not close to the magnifying-glass descriptions in Marianne Moore and Elizabeth Bishop, that sense these two writers have of undertaking a sort of decoding, startling in the newness of what is seen. When Elizabeth Bishop writes that the "donkey brays like a pump gone dry," this is a perfectly recognizable and immensely gratifying gift of the sort we often get also in Sylvia Plath. But the detail in Elizabeth Bishop's "The Fish" is of another kind:

> I looked into his eyes
> which were far larger than mine
> but shallower, and yellowed,
> the irises backed and packed
> with tarnished tinfoil
> seen through the lenses
> of old scratched isinglass.

Marianne Moore's abstruse, peering investigations, her shining, gleaming mirror reflect—more than anything else—words. For instance, "Smooth Gnarled Crepe Myrtle" and its flowing compounds:

> A brass-green bird with grass-
> green throat smooth as a nut springs from
> twig to twig askew, copying the
> Chinese flower piece—business-like atom
> in the stiff-leafed tree's blue-
> pink dregs—of wine pyramids
> of mathematic
> circularity; one of a
> pair.

In Marianne Moore and Elizabeth Bishop we are never far away from the comic spirit, from tolerance and wisdom—qualities alien to the angry illuminations of *Ariel*. But the tradition is also strong in Sylvia Plath—and taste, too, in the sense of craft utterly conquered and absorbed. Precision interests her, and she is immensely learned like the other two poets, never wishing to be a "natural" in any sense. She has also the power of the visual, part of the preference for precision over rhetoric. Perhaps this greed for particulars is the true mark of the poetry of women in our time. In the end, what is overwhelming, new, original, in Sylvia Plath is the burning singularity of temperament, the exigent spirit clothed but not calmed by the purest understanding of the English poetic tradition.

Long after I had been reading her work I came across the recording of some of her poems she made in England not long before she died. I have never before learned anything from a poetry reading, unless the clothes, the beard, the girls, the poor or good condition of the poet can be considered a kind of knowledge. But I was taken aback by Sylvia Plath's reading. It was not anything like I could have imagined. Not a trace of the modest, retreating, humorous Worcester, Massachusetts, of Elizabeth Bishop; nothing of the swallowed plain Pennsylvania of Marianne Moore. Instead these bitter poems—"Daddy," "Lady Lazarus," "The Applicant," "Fever 103"—were "beautifully" read, projected in full-throated, plump, diction-perfect, Englishy, mesmerizing cadences, all round and rapid, and paced and spaced. Poor recessive Massachusetts had been erased. "I have done it again!" Clearly, perfectly, staring you down. She seemed to be standing at a banquet like Timon, crying, "Uncover, dogs, and lap!"

It is a tragic story, completely original and unexpected in its scenes and its themes. Ted Hughes, her husband, has a poem about wives:

> Their brief
> Goes straight up to heaven and nothing more is heard of it.

That was not true of Sylvia Plath, and since we now have no choice perhaps there is no need to weigh and to wonder whether her awful black brief was worth it.

Eugene O'Neill: A Sketch

Eugene O'Neill is certainly a very disturbing American figure. Perhaps no one of such desperate agonies and continuing success can be thought of as anything except a very special case. And yet there are ways in which he seems to have stepped into the despairing, muddy tracks already made by the suffering and disappointments of Poe and Melville. O'Neill's story is nearly incredible. His was a singularly distressing life and temperament. Almost any one around had an easier time. His art, in its defects and its power, did not have the sureness of the tradition out of which Poe and Melville came—it is only the alienation, the sense of melancholy fate that he shares with the earlier writers. O'Neill seems to have produced his work in unusual pain, because of his lack of the ordinary verbal gifts most important writers take for granted. One turns away from reading the new books* that have followed upon the success of his posthumous plays much puzzled, feeling here is the old story of misery and creation, but lived out in a special anguish and wonder and mystery.

As a life, the O'Neill story unfolds like that most dismal and constricted of Russian family novels, *The Goloviev Family*. You feel the O'Neills are under a blight—or "curse," to use a more O'Neillish word.

---

* *O'Neill,* by Arthur and Barbara Gelb; *The Tempering of Eugene O'Neill,* by Doris Alexander; *O'Neill and His Plays,* edited by Oscar Cargill, N. Bryllion Fagin, William J. Fisher.

At every turn there is heartlessness and emotional deprivation and which is the cause, which the effect one cannot know. One tragedy after another—tragedies of excess, of self-destruction, of refusal and escape. And the foundation of all this, as we see it, was built upon the unusually successful talents of the father and the son.

Eugene O'Neill was the son of a popular actor, James O'Neill. *A Long Day's Journey into Night* gives the son's idea of his family, but, purely as biography, it is too much the chagrined son's view of his father and leaves out the cheerful, industrious and "lovable" side of the old actor as other people remembered him. Still, "other people" do not write the family story; it is always written from inside the prison, not from the street. The O'Neill children—Eugene and his brother, Jamie—were certainly exposed to the peculiar neglect that the very existence of a famous parent is so likely to create: the neglect, in this instance, left generations of devastation in its wake. The neglect will usually be coupled with a subtle and frightening expectation. The gifts of the parents must somehow be turned into a distinct and special advantage for the child. Eugene O'Neill's parents moved about in the way usual then among theatrical people. Mrs. O'Neill went along. The boy was put in boarding school at an early age. The successful, busy father and the weak, appealing mother—in Mrs. O'Neill's case, a drug addict. Eugene's brother, Jamie, became the most pathetic of alcoholics. He was a misbegotten creature, and died of drink at forty-five. Jamie had no gifts as an actor and yet, in as much as he worked at all, he worked on the stage, playing without distinction minor roles in productions in which his father was the star. Unlike Eugene, the other son did not have the talent or the sturdiness to withstand what seemed to have been unusual strains. Jamie was fond of his weak mother and pulled himself together briefly after James O'Neill died. But soon his mother died too, and Jamie, without any moral necessity left, quickly drank himself to death.

Eugene's youth and early theatrical career were spent under the shadow of his own intense alcoholism. Drink is a character in this tale, coming and going on the stage with fateful persistence. In his youth Eugene once attempted suicide and his drinking was always of the suicidal kind—oblivion sought in "Hell's Hole." The saving thing was his really extraordinary capacity for work. (Forty-five published plays are listed in the index made by Mr. and Mrs. Gelb.) O'Neill's character and his actions were very much of the 1920s; he was a typical artist of that time: radically removed, in one sense or another, from comfortable society, irresponsible, and yet wholly dedicated to art, persisting in work in spite of disastrous personal relations. There are fashions in lives as in works.

———

When Eugene O'Neill himself became a father, the tragedies of his own family were not only repeated but redoubled. He was strangely vindictive, monumentally neglectful. His first son, Eugene, Jr., was not a son at all in the early years of his life. O'Neill's first marriage had come about in the most careless, unromantic way, after the girl, Kathleen, became pregnant. (O'Neill's father wondered why she would want to marry a "drunken bum"—his son.) The divorce came quickly after the marriage. Kathleen later married again and O'Neill's son took his stepfather's name until, at the age of eleven, he learned his true identity, that he was Eugene O'Neill, Jr., the son of the famous dramatist. It is interesting to learn that Eugene, Jr., was doing rather badly until he discovered his real father. He reacted to this news by reform, trying to become worthy. He succeeded brilliantly for many years and then he, too, this most promising person, was compelled to destroy himself, first by drink, and then, literally, by suicide. In spite of his gifts and his hard work, the young O'Neill could not break the ice of his father's appalling self-concentration, his withholding of himself, his really strange indifference. As it was, Eugene, Jr., came closer to his father than the two children by a second wife. Shane and Oona O'Neill seem to have been actually disliked by their father. Shane was weak and sensitive and deteriorated under the indifference. In his will, Eugene O'Neill cut off his children and their descendants from any share in his considerable property. He left it all to his third wife, Carlotta, and after her death to whatever heir she might want to choose.

O'Neill seems to have felt the claims of his parents and his brother more strongly than those of his children. He could feel sorrow for his mother's drug addiction, but seemed without pity for the addiction of his son. He could be sentimentally involved in the deterioration of Jamie; he lived in his own past, "a son and a brother." The Gelbs say, "O'Neill, father of three children, had no interest in the world his progeny would inhabit. He was occupied exclusively with the world that had shaped his forebears and himself. In his view the O'Neills ended with him." Perhaps his own successful creative life had made him harsh about weakness. O'Neill was shy, insecure and difficult; his steady effort to create significant dramatic works took everything out of him. He was restless and for the last decade of his life—for that at least—really ill. His third wife, Carlotta, seems, from these books, to have felt a possessive fidelity not without its own agonies for the self-consuming O'Neill. "Born in a hotel room and died in a hotel room," he is reported to have said of himself.

———

And the plays. They are nearly always singular and impressive and nearly always, in some detail or another, not quite realized. The editors of *O'Neill and His Plays* come down rather hard on the dissatisfied critics. "O'Neill's plays are particularly vulnerable to the newer critical methodology . . . There is an implication in Ferguson's discussion of Cummings' *him* that its inability to command an audience is somehow to its credit, and that, by contrast, O'Neill's ability to attract audiences to his plays is to his discredit."

One's doubts about O'Neill create a sense of guilt and unworthiness. A titan, an American! Awkward giants belittle us all. But there is no doubt that nearly every work of O'Neill's has blemishes—"lack of humor, sententiousness, sentimentality," Rosamund Gilder says in a friendly review of *The Iceman Cometh.* Lionel Trilling's very interesting and early essay on the "genius" of O'Neill puts his case very well when he speaks of "the power of genius itself, quite apart from its conclusions . . . In O'Neill, despite the many failures of his art and thought, this force is inescapable." George Jean Nathan thought the author of *Mourning Becomes Electra* "the most courageous, the most independently exploratory, the most ambitious and resourceful dramatist in the present day Anglo-American theatre." On the doubtful side consider: Eric Bentley's brilliant "Trying to Like O'Neill," Mary McCarthy on *The Iceman Cometh,* Edmund Wilson's description of the early plays as "rather second-rate naturalistic pieces that owe their eminence, not to their intrinsic greatness, but as Marx said of John Stuart Mill, 'to the flatness of the surrounding country.' " Wilson feels, however, that O'Neill is a sure artist when he creates characters from the lower classes, or the sea, those who speak in the vernacular.

Was it O'Neill or the European drama of Ibsen, Strindberg and Chekhov that freed American theater from falseness and gentility?

Now, re-reading O'Neill's plays of forty years ago, the early ones, such as "*The Hairy Ape*," *All God's Chillun Got Wings,* one learns with surprise how persistent, how intrinsic perhaps, the strength and the weaknesses of O'Neill are in the American drama as a whole. Force, much true observation, a serious determination to turn the ugly material of American life into drama—these are the really moving particulars in O'Neill's struggle. And he is successful over and over as these plays, for the most part thrilling and true, step around those blocks of wood—the impossibly badly drawn characters, like the two women in "*The Hairy Ape*"—as if they were hurdles in a race. The very least one can say about *All God's Chillun* is that it is the best play about the drama of the Negro and the white race. (How tame *Deep Are the Roots* and other works written for the stage seem by comparison.) And *The Emperor Jones,* for all its "Who Dat?" dialogue, is a very successful masque, a pure bit of avant-garde theatre, not yet surpassed in this country. Yank, the pride-wounded stoker in "*The Hairy Ape*," is truly a symbolic creation; his descendants, in all their variations, have populated the American stage ever since and there is little chance they will die out soon.

The writing in the plays was thought by Hofmannsthal, an early admirer of O'Neill's, to fall short of the dialogue in Strindberg and Ibsen. Hofmannsthal wrote, ". . . the characters in O'Neill's plays seem to me a little too direct; they utter the precise words demanded of them by the logic of the situation . . . they are not sufficiently drenched in the atmosphere of their own individual past." Perhaps that is it—for in the end the defects of really strong work are as hard to define as the strengths. A certain humility is necessary about the lowly, badly hammered nails if the poor house, completed, moves you to tears. If the dialogue is so cumbersome how can the drama, projected through the dialogue, make its way into our senses?

The answer seems to lie in O'Neill's sincerity, his profound involvement in these plays. He went on and on and somehow he triumphed. The success of *Strange Interlude* is something like the success of Dreiser's *American Tragedy.* Sometimes literature is not made with words. It was a good instinct that told O'Neill to write long plays—the last thing one would ordinarily recommend for the unfelicitous, repetitious writer. *Strange Interlude* has some very bad writing. Nina speaks of "Giving her cool, clean body to men with hot hands and greedy eyes which they called love! Ugh!" (A shiver runs over her body.) The very title of the play comes in the dialogue at the end: "Strange interlude! Yes, our lives are merely strange dark interludes in the electrical display of God the Father!" And yet *Strange Interlude* is a convincing drama. The length is justified because the characters do change in a dramatic and life-like manner as they grow older, act after act. The young Sam Evans becomes, in a later act, the middle-aged, smug, wealthy Evans; Nina goes from hysteria to a period of domestic contentment and back to hysteria.

One thing is certain: in American drama O'Neill is preeminent. The extraordinary effect of *A Long Day's Journey*—the tale at last told of James O'Neill, the drug addict mother, the drunkard Jamie, and the difficult Eugene himself—was a fitting requiem for this peculiar, heroic career. T. S. Eliot thought it, "one of the most moving plays I have ever seen."

(1962)

SNAPSHOTS

MARY McCARTHY

Mary McCarthy! "*The Man in the Brooks Brothers Shirt*! That's my Bible!"
I once heard a young woman exclaim. No doubt the famous short story
is rightly understood as a sort of parable representing many a young
girl's transgressions, even if it does not concern itself with the steps in
the sinner's rehabilitation. It would be hard to think of any writer in
America more interesting and unusual than Mary McCarthy. Obviously she wants to be noticed, indeed to be spectacular; and she works
toward that end with what one can only call a sort of trance-like seriousness. There is something puritanical and perplexing in her lack of
relaxation, her utter refusal to give an inch of the ground of her own
opinion. She *cannot conform*, cannot often like what even her peers like.
She is a very odd woman, and perhaps oddest of all in this stirring
sense of the importance of her own intellectual formulations. Very few
women writers can resist the temptation of feminine sensibility; it is
there to be used, as a crutch, and the reliance upon it is expected and
generally admired. Mary McCarthy's work, from the first brilliant *The
Company She Keeps* down to her latest collection of essays, *On the Contrary: Articles of Belief 1946–1961,* is not like that of anyone else and certainly not like that of other women. We might naturally wonder from
what blending of bravura and commonsense this tart effervescence has
come.

In America we have had the quiet, isolated genius of Emily Dickinson, on the one hand, and that of Edith Wharton, dignified, worldly, astute, on the other, each holding a prime spiritual location in the national landscape. In the background we might imagine the highly usual romantic glamor of Edna St. Vincent Millay, the romance of lyrics and lovers and tragic endings. Mary McCarthy, because of the radical turn of her mind, has little connection with any of these figures even if there are occasional correspondences to Edith Wharton and Edna Millay. And yet how difficult it is to define the image of this writer. If it is popular fame to figure somehow in the scheme of persons who have not had the time to examine the actual claims of the famous person, then she has popular fame as well as genuine literary distinction. Perhaps to the world her image is composed of the clear eyes of the Cecil Beaton photographs, the strong profile, the steady gaze; and it is certainly made of the candor about Sex in her novels and stories and the "attacks" on gods like Tennessee Williams. This is all very unexpected. There is charm and vigor and an almost violent holding of special opinions. She is, as someone said of Thackeray, "an uncomfortable writer."

Not so long ago, Brooks Atkinson, the retired dean of American drama critics, had the sobering occasion to report that Mary McCarthy had been very hard, in a review in an English newspaper, on the bright young English drama critic, Kenneth Tynan, whom she found neither very bright nor very young in his literary spirit and style. The event was dismaying. Where are you if Walter Kerr lights into Howard Taubman, an unimaginable act of disloyalty for either of those members of the Establishment?

If there were any real ancestor among American women for Mary McCarthy it might be Margaret Fuller. How easy it is to imagine the living writer as a visitor at Brook Farm, a friend of Mazzini's, a journalist in Rome during the 1840's. Both women have will power, confidence and a subversive soul sustained by exceptional energy. A career of candor and dissent is not an easy one for a woman; the license is jarring and the dare often forbidding. Such a person needs more than confidence and indignation. A great measure of personal attractiveness and a high degree of romantic singularity are necessary to step free of the mundane, the governessy, the threat of earnestness and dryness. Moderating influences are essential. Madame de Staël, vexing and far-out as she was, needed her rather embarrassing love affairs to smooth over, like a cosmetic cream, the shrewd image. With Mary

McCarthy the purity of style and the liniment of her wit, her gay summoning of the funny facts of everyday life, soften the scandal of the action or the courage of the opinion.

In the novels and stories, the "shocking" frankness of the sexual scenes is very different from the hot prose of male writers. These love scenes are profoundly feminine, even though other women writers do not seem to want to take advantage of this same possibility. In her fiction, shame and curiosity are nearly always found together and in the same strange union we find self-condemnation and the determined pursuit of experience; introspective irony and flat, daring action. In the paperback edition of *The Company She Keeps* we see on the cover a pretty girl posed for the seduction scene on the train—bare shoulders, whisky bottle, and a reflecting pout on her lips. But the picture cannot give any idea of the unexpected contents of the mind of the actual fictional heroine. The psychological fastidiousness and above all the belligerent mood of the surrendering girl are the essence of the story. The sexual affair with the second-rate "man in the Brooks Brothers shirt" is for the heroine both humbling and enthralling; and so, also in the same way, is the outrageous coupling on the couch in *A Charmed Life* of the remarried young wife and her former husband. The heroine, in these encounters, feels a sense of piercing degradation, but it does not destroy her mind's freedom to speculate; her rather baffling surrenders do not vanquish her sense of her conqueror's weaknesses and absurdities. Of course, these works are comedies; and it is part of Mary McCarthy's originality to have written, from the woman's point of view, the comedy of Sex. The coarse actions are described with an elaborate *verismo* of detail. (The safety pin holding up the underwear in the train scene; in *A Charmed Life* "A string of beads she was wearing broke and clattered to the floor. 'Sorry,' he muttered as he dove for her left breast." The "left" notation is a curiosity, a kind of stage direction, inviting us to project ourselves dramatically into an actual scene.)

Plot and dramatic sense are weak in Mary McCarthy's fiction. Taste and accuracy are sometimes substitutions. What people eat, wear, and read are of enormous importance. The reader follows the parade of tastes and preferences with a good deal of honest excitement and suspense, wondering if he can guess the morals of the kind of person who would cover a meat loaf with Campbell's tomato soup. He participates in a mysterious drama of consumption, in which goods are the keys to salvation. Taste is also used as the surest indication of character.

"There were pieces of sculpture by Archipenko and Harold Cash, and the head of a beautiful Egyptian Queen, Neferteete." Accuracy, unusual situations documented with extreme care, mean for the reader a special sort of recognition. The story "Dottie Makes an Honest Woman of Herself" is about contraception in the way, for instance, Frank Norris's *The Octopus* is about wheat. "Dottie did not mind the pelvic examination or the fitting. Her bad moment came when she was learning how to insert the pessary herself. Though she was usually good with her hands and well-coordinated ... As she was trying to fold the pessary, the slippery thing, all covered with jelly, jumped out of her grasp and shot across the room and hit the sterilizer. Dottie could have died." This story, *memorable* to put it mildly, could not have been written by anyone except Mary McCarthy. Reading it over again, the suggestion came involuntarily to mind that perhaps it was meant as a parody of the excesses of naturalistic fiction, a parody, too, of the brute, prosaic sexual details in, for instance, a writer like John O'Hara. There is an air of imparting information—like whaling in Melville or, more accurately, the examination of dope addiction in Gelber's play, *The Connection*. This aspect of *information* brings to memory the later story by Philip Roth in which a college girl suggests she knows all about contraception because she has read Mary McCarthy.

In a writer of this kind there is an urgent sense of the uses to which a vivid personal nature may be put by a writer's literary talent. There is very often an easily recognized element of autobiography and it is in autobiography that Mary McCarthy excels—that is, of course, if one uses the word in its loosest and largest sense. *The Company She Keeps* and *Memories of a Catholic Girlhood* are richer, more beautiful, and aesthetically more satisfying than, say, *A Charmed Life* or *The Groves of Academe*. The condition that made *The Oasis* somewhat stillborn was that it was more biography than autobiography. In autobiography, self-exposure and self-justification are the same thing. It is this contradiction that gives the form its dramatic tension. To take a very extreme case, it is only natural that critics who find importance in the writings of the Marquis de Sade will feel that the man himself is not without certain claims on our sympathy and acceptance. In Mary McCarthy's case, the daring of the self-assertion, the brashness of the correcting tendency (think of the titles *Cast a Cold Eye* and *On the Contrary*) fill us with a nervous admiration and even with the thrill of the exploit. Literature, in her practice, has the elation of an adventure—and of course that elation mitigates and makes aesthetically acceptable to our senses the strictness of her judgments.

She is not moved by reputation. Indeed her congenital skepticism bears down hardest on the most flattered. Only occasionally, as in her essay on the fashion magazines, does she write about what is known as "popular culture." She does not bother to discuss television, but she might discuss the imperfections of, for instance, J. D. Salinger. In her dramatic criticism, collected in *Sights and Spectacles,* there are times—I think of her remarks on Shaw and Ibsen—when she seems in an uneasy relationship with the great men. Shaw's mad reasonableness is put to the test of her own reasonableness; the toils of Ibsen appear to come off less prosperously than her own toils to define them. One sometimes has the feeling of a mistake in tone, rather than a perversity of judgment, as if the meeting of the author and the subject that everyone expected to go so well had unaccountably gotten off to a bad start.

In her new book, *On the Contrary,* she has written her two best essays: "Characters in Fiction" and "Fact in Fiction." In their manner and feeling these essays suggest a new gravity and sympathy, a subtle change in the air, a change already felt in her large books on Florence and Venice. As for the ideas in the two essays: they are the only new things said about the art of the novel in many years. Paraphrase is difficult because the examples are very fresh and the insights rather angular.

On "Fact in Fiction": fact, "this love of truth, ordinary, common truth recognizable to everyone, is the ruling passion of the novel. Putting two and two together, then, it would seem that the novel, with its common sense, is of all forms the least adapted to encompass the modern world, whose leading characteristic is irreality."

As for "Character in Fiction," the decline in the ability to create character comes, in this view, from the modern tendency to try to reach character from the inside. The author has become a sort of ventriloquist; he is not content to describe but must try to impersonate the very soul of someone quite different from himself. The reader is perplexed; he feels the strain, the insecurity. Water has been put into the whisky; the dilution is the poor author himself, struggling to blend in.

(1961)

Nabokov: Master Class

When Vladimir Nabokov died in Switzerland in 1977, a life chronically challenged by history ended in the felicity of a large, intrepid, creative achievement. Nabokov left Russia with his family in 1919, took a degree at Cambridge University and in 1922 settled among the Russian colony in Berlin, where he began his work as a poet and novelist in the Russian language. In 1937, after fifteen or so un-Teutonic years "among strangers, spectral Germans," he pushed on to France for three years, to those "more or less illusory cities" that form the émigré's past. In 1940, with his wife and son, he arrived in the United States, "a new and beloved world," as he calls it in his autobiography *Speak, Memory* where, among other adaptations, he patriotically stopped "barring my sevens."

To America, Nabokov brought his supreme literary gifts and wide learning and a great accumulation of losses: childhood landscape devastated, gravestones blurred, armies in the wrong countries, and his father murdered, hit by a bullet intended for another on the stage of one of those intense political debates among the Russian exiles in Berlin.

From 1940 to 1960, here he is among us, cheerful it seems, and unpredictable in opinion. Not a bohemian, not at all, and not a White Russian dinner partner, but always dramatic and incorruptible. On the present occasion he is standing before his classes at Cornell University in Ithaca, New York, delivering the now published first volume of *Lec-*

tures on Literature. He is forty-nine years old, an outstanding modern novelist in the Russian language, and still in need of money. During the next ten years, the Ithacan afternoons and evenings will be spent writing in English: *Pnin,* the memoir *Speak, Memory,* and his uncompromised masterpiece, *Lolita,* a financial success that released him from one of the cares of the literary life. When he goes back to Europe, to settle with his wife in an old, interesting hotel in Montreux, Switzerland, he will be one of the great twentieth-century novelists in English.

Not much happened during the American years that escaped transformation to the mosaic of the Nabokov page, with its undaunted English words glittering in their classical, rather imperial plentitude, a plentitude that is never a superfluity. Although Nabokov himself was unassimilable, his imagination is astonishingly porous. It is rather in the mood of Marco Polo in China that he meets the (to us) exhausted artifacts of the American scene. Motels, advertisements, chewing-gum smiles, academics with their projects like pillows stuffed under an actor's tunic, turns of speech advancing like a train on his amplifying ear—for Nabokov it is all a dawn, alpine freshness. His is a romantic, prodigal imagination, with inexhaustible ores of memory buried in the ground of an unprovincial history. "And one day we shall recall all this—the lindens, and the shadows on the wall, and a poodle's unclipped claws tapping over the flagstones of the night. And the star, the star."

As a teacher, Nabokov had, before Cornell, spent a good deal of time at Wellesley College, and not much time at Harvard. His misadventures with the Comparative Literature Department at Harvard, told in Andrew Field's biography, *Nabokov: His Life in Part,* have the comic "Russianness" of some old head-scratching tale of serf and master. Nabokov lectured at Harvard in 1952. There the exile's brightly confident dimming of a long list of classic authors and works shed its blackening attention upon Cervantes. Professor Harry Levin, on behalf of the old Spaniard, said: Harvard thinks otherwise. The remark, put into Professor Levin's pocket like a handkerchief, has the scent of Nabokov's own wicked perfume on it . . . but no matter. And all to the good indeed. Cambridge, Massachusetts, was not the proper setting for the touching derangements of Nabokov's created Professor Pnin and Dr. Kinbote—and not the right New England village in which Humbert Humbert would marry Lolita's mother. So, it was to be Cornell.

The published lectures are, apart from everything else, dutiful, even professorial. They are concrete, efficient, not the wanderings of an imported star who takes off early by way of discussion periods. We are told by Andrew Field that Nabokov's scientific work on butterflies was "painstaking" and marked by a "scale by scale meticulousness." There is something of this also in the approach to the performance before as many as 400 students and the acceptance of certain ever-returning weekends with 150 examination papers to read.

The young audience is there to hear him, even if he does not know what they may have brought with them. Nabokov stands aside in the beginning, perturbed, it may be imagined, not only by the rarity of literature, but by the rarity of reading, true reading. He solicits rather poignantly from the students the ineffable "tingling spine" and "shiver" of the aesthetic response, all that cannot be written down in notebooks and which is as hopeless of definition as the act of composition itself.

The first of Nabokov's Cornell lectures, as printed here, was given to Jane Austen's *Mansfield Park.* This author and this particular novel had been urged upon Nabokov by Edmund Wilson. Wilson was dismayed by Nabokov's cast-offs, those universally admired works that seemed to be resting in overflowing boxes in the Nabokov vestibule, as if waiting to be picked up by the Salvation Army. A lot of it appears to be mischievous teasing by Nabokov, good-humored, even *winking,* if such a word may be used. ("Henry James is a pale porpoise.") Satire is one of Nabokov's gifts, and nearly all of his novels are appliquéd with little rosette-asides of impertinent literary opinion.

In any case, *Mansfield Park* finds Nabokov laying out the plot with a draftsman's care, patiently showing that one parson must die so that another can, so to speak, wear the dead man's shoes. And Sir Bertram must be sent off to the West Indies so that his household can relax into the "mild orgy" of the theatrical presentation of a sentimental play called "Lovers' Vows."

Here there is a curious intermission in which Nabokov tells the class about the old play, summarizing it from the original text. And again when Fanny cries out against a plan to cut down an avenue of trees, "What a pity! Does it not make you think of Cowper? 'Ye fallen avenues, once more I mourn your fate unmerited,' " Nabokov takes time out for a reading of the long, dull poem "The Sofa" by William Cowper. It is true that Nabokov liked to remember the charm of vanished popular works of the sort that slowly made their way over land and sea to the Russian household of his youth. Still, the diversion to these texts is strikingly unlike the microscopic adhesion to the matters at hand in other lectures. There are brushings of condescension in the Jane Austen chapter, delicate little streakings, like a marbleizing effect. She is "dimpled" and "pert," a master of this dimpled pertness.

"Style is not a tool, it is not a method, it is not a choice of words alone. Being much more than all this, style constitutes an intrinsic component or characteristic of the author's personality." Nabokov's method in these carefully prepared lectures is somewhat less impressionistic and darting than one might have expected from his irreplaceable book on Gogol and the fantastical commentaries to *Eugene Onegin*. Words and phrases, even the words of Joyce, Proust, or Dickens, are not themselves often the direct object of inquiry. Plots, with their subterranean themes, are the objects, plots to be dug up tenderly so as not to injure the intention of the author by too gleeful an excavation.

Nabokov goes along the plot, step by step, telling us where we are now and what is happening there; and the steps are not mere excavations but attended by readings aloud from the texts. About Joyce's *Ulysses:* "Demented Farrell now walks westward on Clare Street, where the blind youth is walking eastward on the same street, still unaware that he has left his tuning fork in the Ormond Hotel. Opposite number 8, the office of the dentist . . ."

Flaubert's punctuation and syntax most interestingly command Nabokov's attention. "I want to draw attention first of all to Flaubert's use of the word *and* preceded by a semicolon." And the use of the imperfect form of the past tense in *Madame Bovary*. Translators are rebuked for not seeing, in Emma's musings about the dreariness of her life, the difference between "She would find [correct translation] again in the same places the foxgloves and wallflowers," as against the simple "she found." These moments are the grandeur of Nabokov in the act of reading a novel. And when he speaks in the voice we know from his own novels, "Notice the elaboration of the moonlight in Proust, the shadows that come out of the light like the drawers of a chest. . . ."

Madame Bovary, Mansfield Park, Swann's Way, Bleak House, Ulysses, The Metamorphosis—two in French, one from the German, two from English—and to these a third from English, *Dr. Jekyll and Mr. Hyde*, a Nabokov surprise, so as not to confound expectations. The mad pseudo-science of "Dr. Jekyll" appeals to Nabokov, who in his discussion of *Bleak House* lingered lovingly on the "spontaneous combustion" of the gin-soaked Mr. Krook. He likes the "winey taste" of Stevenson's novel, and "the appetizing tang of the chill morning in London." "Appetizing" is the word most often used about the fable. The plan of Dr. Jekyll's house is the back and front of the man himself. Not too little and not too much is made of the work, "a minor masterpiece on its own conventional terms" and far from "The Metamorphosis," with its "five or six" tragic dimensions.

Kafka is "the greatest German writer of our times." Yes, yes—pause—"such poets as Rilke or such novelists as Thomas Mann are dwarfs and plaster saints in comparison to him." So, proceed. "The Metamorphosis," an exceedingly painful tale about Gregor Samsa waking up one morning to find that he has turned into an insect, arouses in Nabokov the most passionate and emotional moments in the lecture series. As an entomologist, he pronounces Gregor a large beetle, the lowly cockroach being just that, too lowly, for the largeness of Kafka's descriptive inventions. The doors, the poor beetle's legs or teeth or whatever finally turning the lock, the family theme, the "Greek chorus" of the visit of the clerk from Gregor's office, the "coleopteran's" food slipped under the door, the appalling suffering: all of this is tragically affecting once more as the lecturer puts it before us.

Nabokov judges Gregor's world with great feeling, even with indignation. The Samsa relatives are "parasites" exploiting Gregor, eating him "out from the inside." His beetle carapace is the "pathetic urge to find some protection from betrayal, cruelty." But it is no protection and he remains as a beetle as vulnerable as his "sick human flesh and spirit had been." Gregor's sister, in the beginning the only one to acknowledge the metamorphosis and to act with kindness, becomes his worst enemy at last. Gregor is extinguished so that the family can go out in the sunlight once again. "The parasites have fattened themselves on Gregor," Nabokov wrote in the margins of his copy.

If it were not the trade name of a commercial series, Nabokov's lectures might be called "Monarch Notes," in honor of their stately, unfatigued progress through the crowd of words, styles, and plots. What is most unexpected is the patience. *Bleak House:* "Now let us go back to the very first paragraph in the book." *Madame Bovary:* "Let us go back to the time when Charles was still married to Héloïse Dubuc." *Ulysses:*

"Bloom's breakfast that she is to make for him that morning continues to fill her thoughts. . . ."

Following these lectures with their determined clinging to detail, and with the insistent foot on each rung of the scaffolding of the plot, is to be asked to experience the novel itself in a kind of thoughtfully assisted rereading, without interpretation. There is very little ripe, plump appreciative language. "Beautiful" turns are acknowledged by "note" and "mark." In *Madame Bovary* "note the long fine sunrays through the chinks in the closed shutters" and "mark the insidious daylight that made velvet of the soot at the back of the fireplace and touched with livid blue the cold cinders." A novel is a rare object. Look at it with a magnifying glass and the earphones turned off. And curiously each work is alone, not milling about among its siblings, *Emma, Our Mutual Friend, Portrait of an Artist,* and so on and so on.

Novels are fairy tales; *Madame Bovary* yet another fairy tale. Of course, with Nabokov a thing is asserted to counter a repellent, philistine opposition. A novel becomes a fairy tale so that it will not be thought to be a sociological study or a bit of the author's psychohistory, two ideas he may rightly have believed to be running like a low fever among the student body.

Nabokov's own novels very often end, and no matter what the plot, in a rhapsodic call to literature itself. "I am thinking of aurochs and angels, the secret of durable pigments, prophetic sonnets, the refuge of art. And this is the only immortality you and I may share, my Lolita." Also in his novels there are books within books and literature is almost a character. About *The Gift,* Nabokov said, "Its hero is not Zina, but Russian literature." The brilliant *Pale Fire* is entirely a deranged annotation of a dreadful poem.

Perhaps in the end it is not surprising that this writer who has walked every step of the way in two languages should look upon style as the self in all its being and the novel as a slow, patient construction of a gleaming fairy tale. "Let us look at the web and not the spider," he writes about Dickens. The web, the inimitable web, is what these lectures are about.

(1980)

ELIZABETH BISHOP

Over the years, Elizabeth Bishop, the poet, wrote a number of short stories, several portraits (one of Marianne Moore and another of a primitive painter living in Key West), several descriptive pieces set in Brazil, and an introduction to her translation from the Portuguese of *The Diary of Helena Morley.* All are now in *The Collected Prose,* edited and introduced by her publisher, Robert Giroux. Herein one will find Elizabeth Bishop's mastery of a moderate tone, even in the most searing fictions based upon painful recollections of her early life. One will note the characteristic curiosity, in her case often a curiosity about the curious, and it will be muted, as in her poems, by a respect and tolerance for what the curiosity discovers. There is also, here and there, the unusual visual sharpness that prompts her to challenge, as in a duel, the expected adjectives of description. She finds the words to make her victory convincing.

I remember when "In Prison" appeared in *Partisan Review* in 1938. This story, or prose reflection, was immediately famous, if such a claim is possible for a single short work appearing in a small magazine. But those were smaller times, the skyline was not so tall, and fame did not demand the most intensive exploitation of available space. So you were not likely to forget "In Prison" and the chain-gang men sometimes at home for the weekend and *their striped trousers hanging on the wash line.*

Poets can, of course, write prose. They can write it as well as or ill as they write verse, although I think certain slothful and not very intelligent poets are more daring in mediocrity when they write prose, the prose of a review for instance. Sometimes these items on the passing scene show a distraction about word and idea more suitable to the shooing away of the family dog than to a compositional task. Still, when the habit of poetry exists, it will usually invade the poet's prose with a natural suffusion of its peculiar ways. Some have the two talents in a sort of separation. D. H. Lawrence and Thomas Hardy write novels, it seems to me, as novelists—that is, not as poets. Their great production, their themes and ideas, their stories chosen to dramatize a particular history and at the same time to speak of the general fate of human beings: All of this attests to a primary gift for fiction, a conquest of the form so abundant as to seem predestined. They could not refuse to be fiction writers any more than they could refuse to be poets. In their novels we will notice that the thorn of a rose will draw blood at the moment of first love, that the howl of a vicious, virile rabbit will ignite the emotions of a man and woman hesitating in the field. The metaphorical concentrations of poetry quietly seep into the rush and flow of the narration. And yet, neither Hardy nor Lawrence lingered long enough to summon the vast "poetic effects" of Joyce and Proust.

Nothing is more striking to me than the casual prose of poets, with its quick and dashing informality, its mastery of the sudden and offhand, the free and thrown away. "The wretched, fishing jealousies of Leontes." *Fishing?* Yes. That is Coleridge. Corbière's "mild waterfront sensuality"—the words are Laforgue's. Thinking about Mayakovsky's working-class dress, Pasternak saw it not as an affront to the respectable but as a warning to the "black velvet" of Mayakovsky's talent. Protesting the Russian Symbolist's use of images and sets of images as if they were so many handy kitchen utensils, Mandelstam cried out (or so it seems on the page) that an image was inappropriate for everyday use, "just as an icon lamp would be inappropriate for lighting a cigarette."

Elizabeth Bishop's prose, as we read it collected and whole, gives me the idea that she set about the writing as an enterprise, something she would do from time to time with the prose part of her mind. It was the same mind that wrote the poems, but that does not alter the fact that certain of her stories were composed in the generally acceptable manner of the time. I think particularly of "The Baptism," "The Farmer's Children," "Gwendolyn," and "The Housekeeper." I notice that each appeared in due course in such places as *Harper's Bazaar* and *The New Yorker*, and were reprinted in the "Best" collections of the year.

These stories are a skillful blending of the parts; they know how to give information, how to dramatize a scene, and how to reach the popular drift of "epiphany" at the end. (Perhaps only a poet could have loved Gwendolyn for her beautiful name: "Its dactyl trisyllables could have gone on forever so far as I was concerned.") The stories are genuine. You learn from them, and your emotions are solicited by the fate of the characters and the construction of the scene. They are fine examples of the kind of fiction still offered weekly and monthly by the more thoughtful magazines and indicate to me that Elizabeth Bishop certainly could have been a fiction writer had she wished it.

Little in that to amaze. What is startling, on the other hand, is that her best prose fictions ("The Sea and Its Shore," "In Prison," "In the Village") are aesthetically radical, rich, and new in conception and tone. They are "experimental," as we used to say. In the late 1930s, the fiction in the little magazines often struggled with the challenge of Kafka. It was possible to come up with an abstract and fixed situation of interest, but to uncover the mobility of the abstract is a rare gift. The static must move the mind, the invention, in a swirl of significance both intellectual and emotional. Much must happen from the point of stasis, otherwise there is a nullity, and with so much stripped away there is boredom.

"The Sea and Its Shore" is a magical instance of creative invention. A man, with no biography, is hired to keep the beach free of paper. For this purpose, he is given a stick with a nail set in the end, a wire basket in which to burn the day's trash, and a little house, a primitive beach shelter. Gradually, he begins to read the scraps of paper, to be knowledgeable about what the different kinds look like, the quality of the sheets wet and dry and, of course, the garbled messages on the crumpled sheets. He watches the paper blown about by the wind: "The papers had no discernible goal, no brain, no feeling of race or group. They soared up, fell down, could not decide, hesitated, subsided." As he read the "insect armies of type," everything seemed to become print, the whole world. A sandpiper, rushing here and there, looked like a "point of punctuation." Finally, everything must be burned since "burning paper was his occupation." This little treatise and speculation on floating print, wind-tossed paper, fragments of literature, printed letters, nonsense, mysterious truncations, arrives from the wonderfully resonant center of the given idea. The contemplation of the prodigality and expendability of print by way of the man on the beach and his stick with the nail in it is a pure and serene fiction exemplifying what we mean by inspiration.

Two stories are of great autobiographical interest and one, "In the Village," is a brilliant modern short story. The first, "The Country Mouse," was left unpublished, although it is a finished work. It is not more revealing and heartbreaking than the other; one might wonder why it was withheld.

Elizabeth Bishop was born in 1911 in Worcester, Massachusetts. Her father died less than a year after her birth. Her mother, from Nova Scotia, suffered a mental collapse, which finally became permanent when the child was only five years old. From the death of her father up until the age of seven, Elizabeth Bishop lived with her mother's family in Nova Scotia. At the age of seven, she was suddenly removed to Worcester, to the father's family, taken from a simple farm and small maritime village to the well-to-do manufacturing Bishops of Massachusetts.

"The Country Mouse" tells of this removal. "I had been brought back unconsulted and against my wishes to the house my father had been born in, to be saved from a life of poverty and provincialism, bare feet, suet puddings, unsanitary school slates." In her new home, she was miserable and felt much like the nervous, troublesome family dog, Beppo. The last paragraph of the story underlines the year 1918, the recognition that she at seven years was doomed to her identity, to her "I, I, I," as a poem has it. The story ends: "Why was I a human being?"

"In the Village" tells of the mother's return from the mental hospital when the girl is five years old. A seamstress is brought in to make a new dress that will signify the end of the black-and-white mourning clothes. In the midst of the fitting, the mother screams, the scream of a new collapse and the destruction of hope. "A scream, the echo of a scream, hangs over that Nova Scotian village. No one hears it; it hangs there forever, a slight stain in those pure blue skies."

The story then becomes something else, a brilliant rendering and ordering of certain fresh fictional possibilities. It becomes a sort of sonata of sounds filled with emotions for the child. The scream is bal-anced by the sound of Nate, the blacksmith, at his anvil. "*Clang.* The pure note: pure and angelic." Another sound enters like a patch of color on a canvas. *Whack.* The little girl is taking the family cow through the village to a grazing space. *Whack* goes the child's directing stick when the cow meanders about and must be gently brought into line.

The child passes by the village houses, one of them the house of Mr. McLean. (I note that is the name of the Boston hospital where the mother of "the scream" is confined until her death, but no significance attaches since Mr. McLean is a wholesome figure in the village scene.) His old dog, Jock, is, in italics, *deaf as a post.* The sweet sounds of a pas-toral life and the sound of lost hope in the scream are elements smoothly woven into an original fictional tapestry. The degree of com-position is great—the pauses, the contrasts, the simplicity of it so very complicated. The story is true, but it cannot be accurate because of the artfulness.

"The Country Mouse" is finely written but written in a spirit much closer to the documentary, to the statement. "My mother was not dead. She was in a sanitorium, in another prolonged 'nervous breakdown.'" And "I had been brought back unconsulted." For a sensitive and re-served nature, autobiographical accuracy is a greater deterrent to publication than the deeper and more disturbing transformations of experience by art. So "The Country Mouse" lay in the drawer, and "In the Village" was published.

The portrait of Marianne Moore was also found unpublished and somewhat unsettled among the poet's papers. As we have it now, it is one of the best of its kind in our literature, a literature more barren than most in significant memoirs. It is kindly, even adoring. The Moore household in Brooklyn, the cadence of the speech, the remembered odd scene, the visit to the circus are treasures of eccentricity and au-thenticity. Above all, the portrait is illuminated by the equity that pre-vails between the remembered Marianne Moore and the remembering Elizabeth Bishop. Still, I think perhaps it was withheld not from dissat-isfaction but because of a squeamishness about the process of docu-mentation, a hesitation about imposition, about *using.*

Reading over the portrait of Marianne Moore, it occurs to me that Elizabeth Bishop appears to us to have been more like the older poet than she was in life. The friendship leaves things somewhat askew. Both were discreet, brilliant, original, unmarried, quirky, and refined in taste and manners. But Elizabeth Bishop's life was far more complicated— or showed more stress and volatility, since we never know about the inner life. She was less spectacular in wholeness of being, more contemporary indeed as a soul living out the years.

Many things—her orphanage only one of them—weighed on her spirit. She knew also the weight of drinking and the weight of the years of not drinking. She had asthma attacks, allergies, and love affairs that did not always end happily, far from it. She was as open to experience in space as Marianne Moore was pleased to be confined. She went far out to sea in both the literal and metaphorical sense. Like some figure in Thomas Mann, the cold north and the treacherous passions of the south met in her nature. She loved houses and objects, and she had an eye for them, for shells and feathered necklaces made by the Indians of Brazil, for treasures carefully chosen and looked after. And for larger acquisitions also: handsome pieces of furniture, chests and bureaus made from Brazilian woods in various shades and decorated with the diamond patterns of Minas. There was the modern house in Petrópolis, in the hills where the emperor used to have his summer palace. The house was thoughtful and careful, set near a waterfall, and everything in it was standing in its place, arranged just so. There was the ancient house in hard-to-get-to, historic, beautiful Ouro Prêto, a folly perhaps, but who could travel to Ouro Prêto and not put a hand to a fine, falling-down treasure of bygone days in a Brazil nearly out of its mind with love for modernity?

As I remember, there was very little money. What had passed on to Elizabeth came from one of those faded family businesses and from investments that seemed to wither in the box. To go here and there, to have the things and the houses, required an awful prudence and watchfulness, and yet the span was daring and profligate. She *would* go up the Amazon, even if she was quite uncomfortable doing so. Strange things happened in her presence, emanations, a sudden efflorescence that might have come from the rubbing of a lamp. Once, we were in a museum in Rio where there were many Indian artifacts, when Elizabeth suddenly stopped and said, "Look." We turned around, and there was a group of naked Indians looking at Indian artifacts.

And then she left Brazil after so many years and returned home to take up the life of our kind in order to make a living. That is, she began to teach, even though for such a long time she had been afraid or shy of it, even shy about giving readings. Her last post was at Harvard. There she found an apartment, not in Cambridge or on Beacon Hill but down on the waterfront, as a sort of pioneer in the development of that part of the city, a modern and very handsome development but a bit out of the way.

Many look forward to the publication of Elizabeth Bishop's letters, look forward to knowing in full the incomparable glow, the luster of the thoughts and sights written in her small, curling, rather crooked script. Someone is weeding the garden, another has just come up the road in the inconvenient tropics.

Elizabeth Bishop was indeed a perfectionist. She was also a natural writer with an unusual patience; nothing appears to have been excavated with visible sweat and aching muscle. And yet perhaps it was that the great natural gifts seemed too easy, and she must wait to make everything absolutely right in tone and rhythm, without insistence. She didn't want to leave too much paper on the beach.

(1984)

THE SENSE OF THE
PRESENT

GUILT, CHARACTER, POSSIBILITIES

GUILT

Do you know a brooding Bulstrode? Guilt, central to classical fiction, was the secret of dramatic natures who found themselves greedy for something and, when seizing it or annihilating obstruction, were nevertheless conscious of their usurpation and its violation of others. This "type"—greedy, impatient, violent and as the saying goes, "filled with guilt"—lives in a condition beyond irony, the attitude that sweetens guilt and alters it to absurdity or, most frequently, rotten luck.

The private and serious drama of guilt is not often a useful one for fiction today and its disappearance, following perhaps the disappearance from life, appears as a natural, almost unnoticed relief, like some of the challenging illnesses wiped out by drugs or vaccines. The figures who look out at us on the evening news—embezzlers, crooks, liars, murderers—are indeed furiously inconvenienced by the trap that has sprung on the free expression of will. It seems unfair, their chagrined countenance indicates, that they should be menaced by arithmetical lapses, by their natural, self-protecting gun shots from the window of the getaway car, by insurance policies cashed with impugning haste, by the follies of accomplices. And how rapidly does the startled glance of the accused shift to the suspicious, outraged grimace of the wronged.

The ruin of one's own life as the result of transgression is punishment, but it is not guilt, not even remorse. What sustains the ego in its unhappy meeting with consequence, the meeting that was so felicitous for drama and fiction? The "popular" response to error, crime, bad faith in which our own actions are involved, is paranoia. Bad luck, betrayal, enemies, the shifting sands of the self-interest of accusers, briberies, lies: these indeed enter the mind with blinding rapidity. The culprit is carrying a thousand mitigations in his pocket, whether his delinquency be legal or merely having to do with offenses in personal relations. When he is being judged, he is judging, and not himself, but the tangle of obstructions oppressing him. He rages about in a crowd of others, saying that he is not alone; individuals and abstract society are whoring about, shooting, thieving, and going scot-free. You can't go to heaven on other people's sins, we used to say. Well, why not?

CHARACTER

The literature of paranoia is naturally different from the literature of guilt. A wild state of litigious anxiety slides, as if on ice, into the spot held by the ethical. Free-floating, drifting in his absorption and displacement, the paranoid is not a character at all. Most of all he comes to resemble a person with a cerebral stroke and shows peculiar, one-sided losses, selective blocks and impairments, unpredictable gaps.

Nathalie Sarraute said in a lecture that she could not imagine writing a novel about, for instance, a miser, because there is no such thing as a miser. Human beings with their little bundle of traits and their possession of themselves as a synthesis. Yes, they have vanished because they are not what they seemed to be and least of all to themselves, which confuses and undermines the confidence of the observer.

The coquette, the spendthrift, the seducer, the sensitive were points of being, monarchies of self, ruled over by passions and conditions. How smoothly the traits led those who possessed them, led them trotting along the path of their lives, to the end of cause and effect, to transgressions that did not fade but were still there at the last stop. This was known as plot.

When the young man in *The Mayor of Casterbridge* comes into town and decides in his misery to sell his wife and daughter we *know* what is ahead. He will succeed, he will be mayor, and the wife and daughter will return, borne on the wheels of plot, the engine of destiny, and he will be ruined. As he says, in the midst of gathering consequences, "I am to suffer, I perceive."

For us the family could very well vanish into its fate, which is expressed in the phrase, "making a new life." Still, mayors fall, the past is discovered by the opposition and we have our plots—in the conspiratorial sense. Ruin is another matter. It becomes harder and harder to be ruined; for that one must be a dedicated fool. For the well-placed there are always sympathizers. Through support, flattery, and the wonderful plasticity of self-analysis, paranoia enters the wrongdoer's soul and convinces him of his own innocence as if it had been confirmed by the accounting of St. Peter at the gates of Heaven.

Fiction, taking this in, shrugs, and while a shrug is not as satisfactory as ruin in the aesthetic sense, it will have to do. Aesthetics, Kierkegaard said, "is a courteous and sentimental science, which knows of more expedients than a pawnbroker."

POSSIBILITIES

Contrivance is offensive to the contemporary novelist and it bears the further strain of being impossible to make use of without full awareness. Awareness turns contrivance into a self-conscious jest. But without it the novelist is hard put to produce what everyone insists on—a novel. It is easy to imagine that all possibilities are open, that it is only the medium and not life itself that destroys the branches one by one. Caprice, fashion, exhaustion, indulgence: these are what the novelist who has not produced a circular action of motive and resolution is accused of. Meanwhile he looks about, squinting, and he sees the self-parodying mirror and this is his present, now, in its clothes, make-up, with its dialogue, library of books read, his words, his memories of old spy stories, films, baseball scores, murders, revolutionaries, of *Don Quixote* to be rewritten, Snow White, and "all of this happened, more or less."

The newspapers are alive with inexplicable follies. Men, safe in important positions, earning huge salaries, *forget* to file income tax forms. What a block-headed, unrealistic contrivance, *out of character*. We see, particularly in persons high in public and political life, the recurrent, bold dissolutions of the very core of themselves as it has been supposedly observed in endless printed repetitions, in biography, in assertion of principle. The puritan drinks too much it turns out, the Christian is a heathen. Even if a number of opinions and habits have attached themselves like moles to the skin of personality, it is not unnatural that our favorite word for character is *image*—"a reproduction of appearances." Since the image is impalpable, one is not obliged to keep faith either with the details or with the gross accumulation of what one is supposed to be.

Spiro Agnew, an almost forgotten, verbose Vice President, with his long donkey face, his arresting alliterations, his tall, broad-shouldered ease in the pulpit, was, in his reign, old fiction. He might have been Mr. Bounderby. "I was born in a ditch, and my mother ran away from me. Do I excuse her for it? Have I ever excused her for it? Not I." Yet, in collapse, Agnew became an unaccountable post-modernist who ceased suddenly to be a character, his own character, and became a man who roams the world without a memory of alliterative abuse, without a voice, born again in middle age as a baby, alien to the "role" that had brought him to our attention in the first place. So there he is somewhere, freely "mutating" like V.—Veronica, Victoria, Venus, VD, "the incursion of inanimate matter into twentieth century life."

TIME

The three-act play is no longer in fashion, having given way to the long one-act, occasionally punctuated by an intermission, an intermission that is a convenience for the audience rather than the signal of a diversion in the flow. Impatience plays its part as one of the powers of our existence and no doubt it has much to do with dramatic structure. The celestial arithmetic of three acts turned out to be authoritarian and oppressive to the shooting-star conceptions. More importantly— a three-act play implied a three-act life.

Curtain lines ending the first act with a question, a riddle leading to unexpected turns in act two, act three resolving and returning in some way the call of act one. In the realistic American theater it was the habit to have, in the end, flashes of "understanding" which arose like a perfume out of the soil of the past. Yes, these characters would say, I discover that I have been a selfish dolt and just where I had been most convinced of my nobility and rectitude. The curtain fell.

In life, in domestic conflicts, in matters of wounded feelings, it is so often those who have been acted against who are required to uphold a pretense of form. (I don't mind what you do to me, but it is so awful for the children.) The pedantry, the conservatism, the intransigence of the hurt and the inconvenienced are scarcely to be separated, we feel, from bitterness and frustrated will. Suspicion of motive afflicts the decent as well as the dishonorable.

Resolutions, recognitions, the strands at last tied in a knot? Whose experience can that be faithful to? In contemporary theater, it is usually the popular and commercial work, manipulating the assumed moral and aesthetic traditionalism of the audience, that insists the gun hanging on the wall in act one must indeed go off before the final curtain falls.

The tyranny of the nineteenth-century three-volume novel leaves its wreckage in Gissing's *New Grub Street*. A chapter entitled "The Author and his Wife": the wife anxiously inquires about a work in progress, where are you? what have you done?

Reardon, the burdened novelist, cries out, "Two short chapters of a story I can't go on with. The three volumes lie before me like an interminable desert. Impossible to get through them. The idea is stupidly artificial, and I haven't a living character in it."

THE NOVEL

Perhaps we cannot demand a "novel." The most practical solution seems to be an acceptance of whatever designation the publisher has put into his catalogue. The object in hand, its length not defining beyond a hundred pages, is not an essay, not a short story, not autobiography since we are told so much of it is "made up" and altered from the truth; it is then a novel of some kind. In the reviews of Renata Adler's *Speedboat*, a work of unusual interest, many critics asked whether they should consider the fiction *truly, really* a novel. The book is, in its parts, fastidiously lucid, neatly and openly composed. Its structure is linear and episodic as opposed to a circular development and while this is more and more the rule in fictional practice, traditional readers sometimes question the nature of what they are reading.

In *Speedboat*, the narrator—a word not entirely apt—is a young woman, a sensibility formed in the 1950s and '60s, a lucky eye gazing out from a center of a complicated privilege, looking about with a coolness that transforms itself into style and also into meaning. Space is biography and conflict finally, and going from one place to another is the thread of experience.

The girl takes flying lessons; she lives in a brownstone in New York among others little connected to her except as voices, scenery; she visits the starving Biafrans as a journalist ("We had been told to bring cans of food, jerry cans of gasoline, and a lot of Scotch"); she examines her generation ("Some of us are gray. We all do situps or something to keep fit"); she teaches at City College and worries about language (" 'Literally,' in every single case, meant figuratively; that is, not literally").

For the girl, the past has not set limits and the future is one of wide, restless, interesting "leaps." Not the leaps of lovers (she has lovers, but this is a chaste book), not leaps of divorces, employment liberations, but a sense of the way experience seizes and lets go, leaving incongruities, gaps that remain alive and are valuable as conversation—conversation the end result of experience. She writes that, "the camel, I had noticed, was passing, with great difficulty, through the eye of the needle . . . First, the velvety nose, then the rest." And how right she is. If the rich can't get into heaven, who can?

———

To be *interesting*, each page, each paragraph—that is the burden of fiction composed of random events and happenings in a more or less plotless sequence. *Speedboat* is very clear about the measure of events and anecdotes and indeed it does meet the demand for the interesting in a nervous, rapid, remarkably gifted manner. A precocious alertness to incongruity: this one would have to say is the dominating trait of the character of the narrator, the only *character* in the book. Perception, then, does the work of feeling and is also the main action. It stands there alone, displacing even temperament.

For the reader of *Speedboat*, certain things may be lacking, especially a suggestion of turbulence and of disorder more savage than incongruity can accommodate. But even if feeling is not solicited, randomness itself is a carrier of disturbing emotions. In the end perhaps a flow is more painful than a circle, which at least encloses the self in its resolutions, retributions, and decisions.

AMERICAN PRACTICALITIES

Our novelists, sensing the shape of lives around them that do not conform to the finalities of the novelistic, nevertheless are reluctant to alienate, to leave so much of life morally unaccounted for. Novels that are profoundly about illicit fornication have a way of ending on accidents, illness, or death.

In John Updike's *Rabbit, Run,* the young husband is in a restless mood of flight and infidelity; the wife is confused, sore, exhausted, and not sober. The new baby dies in the bath in a powerful scene very near the end of the novel. This is meant as a judgment on poor Harry and Janice. It says that Harry is not supposed to run around and Janice is not supposed to be sitting, drunk, before the television set in the afternoon. In Joseph Heller's *Something Happened,* the hero pays for his disgruntlement, acrimony, and self-absorption by the death of his damaged son. In Francine Gray's *Lovers and Tyrants,* the heroine has a hysterectomy, in what may be thought of as a rebuke to her promiscuity. In *Speedboat,* the girl, perhaps worried that her autonomy is out of line, like an overdrawn expense account, announces that she is going to bear a child. In this way she chooses the impediments of nature to act as a brake on the rushing, restless ego.

Deaths, accidents, illnesses, and babies are a late resurgence of normality or morality (late in the books, that is.) They seem to say that a distraction in the order of things will not go unpunished. It appears that free as we are, determined upon experience as we are, there is a lingering puritanism somewhere, a mechanical accountability that links transgression with loss and grief.

The resolutions are not always convincing, being as they are an afterthought of moral contrivance. The drowning of the baby in *Rabbit, Run* is the most truly prepared for and has the least hinting of an unnecessary, retroactive moral assertion. The unconvincingness of most resolutions is a measure of the practicality, the businesslike accounting at the end of a spree, the drawing back from observed life. The telegram about your mother's death after you have been in bed with your secretary, the automobile accident as you come home from an infidelity: how far all of this is from the indulgent grip on experience that preceded it. The willingness to accept, or to offer for the public, a bleak vision without palliative intrusions is not in the end congenial to the American writer. Perhaps it is that the author steps aside from the scene he has created in such zestful detail to punish not on his own behalf but on behalf of his audience, whom he judges, somewhat patronizingly, as more vindictive than himself.

BANALITIES

A strict and accurate ear for banalities provides much of the subject matter in the work of Barthelme, Vonnegut, Philip Roth, Renata Adler, and many others. Blood, sex, and banality, as Malraux recently described the "terrible world in which we are living."

Vonnegut:
Toward the end of maneuvers, Billy was given an emergency furlough home because his father was shot dead by a friend while they were out hunting deer. So it goes.

Speedboat:
The girl was blond, shy, and laconic. After two hours of silence, in that sun, she spoke. "When you have a tan," she said, "what have you got?"

From a California newspaper:
The pastor of the New Life Center Church in Bakersfield and a woman member of his congregation were arrested on suspicion of plotting to murder the pastor's invalid wife.

Banalities are not meant as a narrowing of intention. They are quite the opposite. Banalities connect the author with the world around him. They connect the extreme and the whimsical with the common life, with America, with the decade, with the type. They serve, in a sense, as a form of history.

BOREDOM

Emma Bovary, struggling along with her last lover, Léon—a man whom even romantic love and adventure cannot sever from the anxious calculations of a bourgeois—finds "in adultery all of the banality of marriage." The most moving instance of such boredom in literature is Vronsky's exhaustion with Anna Karenina's love and with his own. It is not so much that he falls out of love as that the conditions of the great passion are a weariness: isolation, anxiety, idleness, the criticism of society. Boredom with love is as powerful as love itself and, psychologically, much more confusing to the spirit. Anna herself falls into one of the masks of boredom with love, obsessive, random jealousy.

Both of the women, Emma and Anna, try to modernize, to politicize the illicit. Anna and Vronsky live in a corrupt, self-indulgent world that retains its pieties about the details of indulgence. At one point Anna pathetically cries out that in living with Vronsky she is at least being "honest." Emma, a naïve provincial, nevertheless understands that her nature inclines her toward the bohemian, the sophistications of the demimonde. She appears with a cigarette in her mouth and can be seen in town "wearing a masculine-styled, tight-fitting waistcoat." Anna's passion is inseparable from her position in society and Emma's passions soon cannot be severed from her debts. Still, in their different ways, they are "new women," and their husbands represent to them an intolerable boredom they do not see themselves destined to endure. They are to be trapped in a further boredom, but of course that lies ahead.

Sex, without society as its landscape, has never been of much interest to fiction. The limitations of the human body are nowhere more clear than in the fantasies of Sade. Nearly all of his "imaginative tableaux" involving more than two persons are physically impossible. In current American fiction, the novels that are most concerned with sex are becoming more traditional in form and imagination each year, and especially those that attempt solemn scenes of gasping and thrusting, the hopeless pursuit of the descriptive language of sensation, without the comic spirit of, for instance, Henry Miller. The body is indeed a poor vehicle for novelty. In many women writers on the current scene, the union of license and literary conventionality is quite noticeable. More and more they suffer from what Colette called the great defect in male voluptuaries: a passion for statistics.

CONSERVATIVES

The enclosed, static, oppressive nature of Soviet society makes it possible for Solzhenitsyn to write books that are formally conservative and yet profound and far-reaching in their significance. His fictions concern nothing less than the soul of Soviet Russia itself. The cancer ward is more than itself; it is the diseased state; the prison, the concentration camps are the setting in which history acts upon imagined characters realistically. The resonance of these great works from the cage is greater than we can produce in the openness and freedom of our lives; and altogether different. Totalitarianism is nothing if not a structure.

In *Mr. Sammler's Planet*, a novel that is very American and yet conservative in both form and matter, Bellow needs the voice of one who has not shared the experience of the American last thirty years, one who has not come under the free-wheeling economic conditions here after the War, who in his own life has felt no strain from the sexual revolution, the draft, divorce, television—anything. He has chosen rightly. Mr. Sammler, over seventy, a European, profoundly formed and sure in character and values, another planet. Mr. Sammler is a suitable instrument of refusal: he says, I will not accommodate the New Left students or the nihilism of New York. I will not find the Negro pickpocket in his camel's hair coat, his Dior dark glasses, his French perfume, *merely interesting*.

A novel like Pynchon's *V.* is unthinkable except as the composition of an American saturated in the 1950s and '60s. It is a work that, in its brilliant decomposition, explodes in a time of seemingly endless expanding capitalism. It comes out of our world of glut, reckless consumption, enviable garbage, and disorienting possibility. Life is not a prison. It is an airplane journey and on this journey the self is always disappearing, changing its name, idly landing and departing, spanning the world in hours. Geography is a character and town names have as much meaning as the names on the passenger lists. The novel does not end. It journeys on in a floating coda: "Draw a line from Malta to Lampedusa. Call it a radius. . . ."

———

In a recent article on the new fiction, Tony Tanner looks upon much of the work as a game, "games trying to break the games which contemporary culture imposes on us at all levels." Entropy, carnival, randomness—the language of the critics of "post-modernist fiction"—seem to bring the novel too close to a poem, to put it under the anxiety of influence and to find it more subject to refinements and tinkerings of craft than a prose work of some length can actually be.

What is honorable in "so it goes" and in the mournful brilliance of Barthelme's stories (" 'Sylvia, do you think this is a good life?' The table held apples, books, long-playing records. She looked up. 'No.' "), in *Speedboat*, in the conundrums of *V.* is the intelligence that questions the shape of life at every point. It is important to concede the honor, the nerve, the ambition—important even if it is hard to believe anyone in the world could be happier reading *Gravity's Rainbow* than reading *Dead Souls*.

FICTIONS OF AMERICA

CHEEVER;

OR,

THE AMBIGUITIES

In his last years, John Cheever, a man more disorderly than his proud art and his courteous, somewhat remote, manners revealed, tried to set his house in order. After a heart attack nearly fatal, he gave up a fervent addiction to alcohol, quit smoking—and all the while was preparing to die of cancer.

Cheever's was a lyrical talent quite mysterious in its movements. It was always plain that the writer was a New Englander. His stories of New York City and the surrounding prosperous suburbs are filled with men and women who seem, like himself, cast up on the shores of Manhattan's East Side and his suburban Shady Hill and Bullet Park as exiles from values less fretful and uncertain than they now know. Their expectations from life are high and yet reasonable, or so it seems to them. The poisoned dwellings they make for themselves take them by surprise.

The shadowy and troubled undergrowth of Cheever's stories brings to mind something of the temper of Melville and Hawthorne—and Cheever himself is a sort of *Pierre,* a study in ambiguity. His special tone is nostalgic, tender about memories of natural illuminations, the fine day, a sunset, the wind on the sea, and the first years of married love. The nostalgia is curiously, and with great originality, combined with a contemporary and rootless compulsion to destroy, even to crash by repetition, the essence of nostalgia, as when the remembered victories of the college track star become a drunken, fatal vaulting over the sofas in the living room ("O Youth and Beauty!").

In the beautiful early story, "Goodbye, My Brother," there is a characteristic balance or imbalance between the most destructive of family hatreds and the final melodies of celebration:

> The sea that morning was iridescent and dark. My wife and my sister were swimming—Diana and Helen—and I saw their uncovered heads, black and gold in the dark water. I saw them come out and I saw that they were naked, unshy, beautiful, and full of grace, and I watched the naked women walk out of the sea.

Beautiful, full of grace, black and gold in the water. The rapturous cadence seems to come from a vision of hope uncorrupted by the traumas this imagination so swiftly and deftly uncovers beneath the glistening of good taste, privilege, and hereditary goodwill.

"The Housebreaker of Shady Hill," about a man stealing from the houses of his neighbors, has the sweat of financial need and moral collapse lying on the pages. The atmosphere is overcast, clammy with the literal bankruptcy and the criminal solution of Johnny Hake, "conceived in the Hotel St. Regis, born in Presbyterian Hospital, raised on Sutton Place." The execution of the dark thefts is more brilliantly accomplished than Hake's atonement and return to the light world "become so sweet." Violence is to be contained by the memory of "summer nights, loving the children, and looking down the front of Christina's dress." The sentiments, the sacraments, secular and otherwise, are called upon again and again as a protection against self-destruction. It is by language, precise, original in its shaping, almost effortlessly evocative, that Cheever rescues the sentiments from sentimentality, from a mere consoling assertion.

In "The Swimmer," the suburban pools of house after house, backyard after backyard, are imagined to be a continuous river, a "quasi-subterranean stream that curved across the country." A disintegrating man passes through one after another, some surrounded by people eating peanuts and drinking cocktails, and some deserted. He is making his way home to what turns out to be an empty house, the gutters loose, the handles on the garage door rusty, the family gone, the swimming-pool river merely a deranged dream of reconciliation. This modern story is as resonant as an ancient tale. The suburban pools are elevated to a symbolical challenge like that faced by the wanderers in old forests.

Another homely object, "The Enormous Radio," is lifted beyond the anonymity of mere usefulness. On the radio, the nice wife, hoping for proper music, begins to hear the quarrels and distasteful dispositions of her apartment-house neighbors coming through the speaker. The radio gradually becomes a monstrous instrument of exposure, and there is something of the inscrutability of "The Turn of the Screw" about the story. Is it themselves the young couple is listening to?

Just who is the man, John Cheever, the Episcopalian anarch? Susan Cheever, his daughter, has written a memoir, *Home Before Dark*, about the writer as a son, a brother, and a father. She has chosen a tone of elegiac candor. The commemorative aspect is suitable to the 1982 death of this extraordinary man and to the pain of family grief. The candor is suitable perhaps to where the culture is now in matters of lapidary inscription. Candor has come to be the sum of the duties attending the documentation of lives by biography or by the reflection of autobiography. Weakness, temptation, indiscretion, infirmity—it must be said these are interesting. Revelations give "life" to the dead authors known previously to most only through their works and the shape of the head on book jackets. "O quiet form upon the dust, I cannot look and yet I must."

Susan Cheever has written novels, but none is as confidently composed as *Home Before Dark*. Here, she has had the assistance of the thirty volumes of the journals kept by her father. These are not mere jottings. Each excerpt she has called upon, and it is to be hoped the culling does not undermine the publication of this valuable testimony, shines with a limpid fluency and eloquence. The journals are passionately confessional, somehow a defiance of the other side of the coin, the appropriate John Cheever. Confession is the last resort, or even the first, of the captive, and what we learn in this memoir is that Cheever existed lifelong in captivities imposed by the complications of his nature, his masks, his loyalties, and the protection of his talent.

He had an unsettling sense of a lost or ambiguous heritage. New England, and especially the villages and towns around Boston, likes to greet each new dawn with the word "old": old families, old names, old money. This, by entail, becomes the right schools and occupations, "antique" woods in the parlors, Canton china, and so on. Genealogical support for the blue eye, fair face, and Anglo-Saxon name; affirming portraiture is a sort of kitchen scholarship.

Thus, Cheever liked to say that his family came to the new world by way of the passage of Ezekiel Cheever on the *Arbella* in 1630; "The roughnecks had come on the *Mayflower.*" Susan Cheever puts the esteemed Ezekiel on the *Hector* in 1637. But no matter, the Cheevers were by the nineteenth century an "established Brahmin family," most of them engaged in seafaring. The ambiguous circumstances came in the branch; that is, the name endured among prosperous, greatly respected parts of the family, one of whom Susan Cheever rather apologetically calls upon, but status did not endure for all of the Cheevers, not quite.

As so often happens to a sensitive, insecure descendant, the real trouble, the downward slide, happened right at home. Cheever's father sold his interests in a shoe factory that bore his name, invested in stocks, and went broke: ruin at home. His mother set herself up in the genteel but socially déclassé gift-shop business, a move very galling to the men of the family. The father began to drink, and the parents separated amid the usual unrestrained household warfare. In the journals, some four decades later, we have Cheever's memories—written under the transformation of style, that proper affront to the crassness of reality. "An afternoon when he returned home from school and found the furnace dead, some unwashed dishes on the table in the dining room and at the center of the table a pot of tulips that the cold had killed and blackened."

There was trouble at Thayer Academy, and Cheever left school in his junior year. Just what brought about the expulsion is not quite clear: smoking, bad grades, fractious behavior—the accounts given by the delinquent student varied. An older brother, Fred, was a consolation and support, he being, or seeming in youth to be, a plausible and successful New England product. "His love for his older brother, who nurtured and supported him—and whom he was later called on to nurture and support—became the most complicated attachment in his life," Susan Cheever writes. Cheever himself remarked, "When it became apparent that it was an ungainly closeness, I packed my bag and shook his hand and left." Later, he told his daughter that he had wanted to murder his brother and at the same time to live with him after the family collapsed. "Much of the conflict in my father's heart, and many of the themes in his work, grew out of his love for Fred."

The brother's success did not last; indeed, his losses were great—job, money, marriage, and the decline, due in some degree to drink, into an embarrassing, empty heartiness. Thus, the common tendency of families to mistake who will make it to the finish line. The central role of the brother does not truly take shape in the memoir, and one has to accept it, unfleshed by dramatic characterization, as the repeated assertion of Cheever himself. Of the brothers in the fiction, one, Moses Wapshot, is a romantic projection of fulfilled hopes, quite unbelievable; two, the sullen, complaining intruder in "Goodbye, My Brother" and the murdered sibling in *Falconer*, are outstandingly vicious.

Cheever did not live with his brother. Instead, he came to New York. It was 1930, and he was eighteen, and that same year he published his first story, in *The New Republic*. In a few years, 1935, he had his first story in *The New Yorker*. The foundations of this precocity are not examined in the memoir, and we do not know what was read, studied, or the level of aspiration. That his literary hopes were not commonplace we can judge by the act of the submission to *The New Republic* and early publication in *Hound and Horn, Story* magazine, and others, and his fling with lowercase letters in the manner of Cummings. The reader we hear about is the reading of a father to his family, not the solitary reading of the writer. Throughout the daughter's memoir, Cheever's life as a writer is seen by the listing of publication of books, some successful, some less so, by his struggles with the opaque paternalism of *The New Yorker*, by the years of poverty and the years of spending, by late honors and prizes. Certain correspondences between the "candor" of the daughter's memoir, striking revelations, quite detailed, of pitiful bouts of drunkenness and homosexual inclination and flight from marriage, loyalty to marriage, and the use in fiction of these "themes" are offered in a perfunctory way. That certain masks might be required for the act of writing are overwhelmed by the masks of a social being, that is, the son and the father.

Cheever met his wife in 1938 when he was twenty-six years old, and they married three years later. That it was a profound attachment for forty years and that the knowledge of a strained and, inevitably, tormented union influenced his life greatly can be seen in his best stories about the married people they hoped to be or feared to be. Somewhat curtly, the daughter sums it up. "This pattern—my father as the alternately pursuing and rebuffed, resentful male, and my mother as the passive, coerced, resentful female—was held to as long as they were together." There were children, moves from here to there around Manhattan and the suburbs, and the final settling into the house in Ossining and the dogs, the neighbors, the garden.

> In many ways my father's life can be divided into two distinct parts. The first forty-five years or so were devoted to a struggle for stability: the establishment of a professional reputation, the creation of a family, earning enough money to survive, and most of all the search for some kind of home—some place of his own that might confirm his credentials as a gentleman and soothe his insecurities.

And his last twenty years a struggle to escape the trap and "most of all to escape the pressure to continually surpass himself as a writer." But this cannot be true. Writing is not "the establishment of a professional reputation" as if one were a doctor or lawyer; it is not properly in the sentence with creation of a family and the purchase of a home.

Cheever came to New York in the 1930s, the Depression years. He was scarcely more than a boy, and his making his way as a writer of stories is quite astonishing. It was altogether saving that he came to New York. The North Shore or the South Shore around Boston would not have served. His own pretensions are to the point here. "His aristocratic New England background was partly sham, and his patrician airs were mostly his own invention." Displacement is at the center of his view, and, indeed, he was displaced, first from New England and then again in the literary landscape of his time. As a writer, he lived in a scene dominated at first by southerners and later by the arrival of brilliant Jewish fiction writers, neither congenial to his creative sources. He did not have at hand the small-town and rural grotesques of the southern sort, nor were his style and preoccupation similar to the intellectual aspirations and skepticism of the Jewish immigrant experience as seen by Saul Bellow, for instance.

He was poor in New York and, of course, given his own attraction to the pits and to risk, he was liberal in spirit. But he was not radical, not stung by the bees (or wasps) of the political battles of the period, although he knows the country and the minds in it. By the direction of the sentences, the ease of the meters in prose, by names, by floating images attached to stuffs and dishes and furniture, we are aware of a self-education as frenzied as that of any scarecrow in the public library.

The American bourgeois world and its pains are his quarry. Summers on the islands in Massachusetts, skiing weekends, going with your child to catch the private-school bus and meeting a mother and having an affair, spending too much in the memory of what one was supposed to have to spend. His was an Anglican New York and its suburbs a hungover Barchester. But because it was New York, it had the rocking unsteadiness of a metropolis quite different from the Edinburgh staunchness of Boston. The husbands had to catch the 8:10 into Manhattan and come home on the five o'clock quite uneasy, not knowing what they were bringing with them and not knowing either what they would find when they arrived.

The landscape of Cheever's fictions in the 1930s and 1940s did not pause at driveways where the dogs with names like Jupiter were family members. His branch of the family might have fallen back, but the mask of a well-bred patrician remained; he looked like one and spoke like one. Where no one knows your parents and your grandparents, inner being and surface at last unite against the provincial domination by fact. "There seemed to be money everywhere, and the Whittemores, who slept in their worn overcoats in the winter to keep themselves warm, seemed separated from their enjoyment of this prosperity by only a little patience, resourcefulness, and luck" ("The Pot of Gold"). This was the reality that produced the stories, and there was a certain price to be paid since the artfully out-of-place man was also dislocated for a time in the prevailing hierarchy of literature.

The New Yorker printed his stories, and this was fortunate, no doubt. At the same time, he was undervalued, not neglected but also not elevated by the attention of the best critics of the day such as Edmund Wilson and Alfred Kazin. It was felt that he was a minor John O'Hara, a talent much coarser than Cheever's.

The Way Some People Live (1942) and *The Enormous Radio* (1953), collections of brilliant short stories, appeared without causing a racket. We are not told how Cheever felt in these matters, but a dispiriting tension would be fitting to the bland reception to one's best work. It was not until his first novel, *The Wapshot Chronicle* (1957), that the general public and the prize committees took notice. This circumstance brings to mind the dismal delay in Faulkner's stock until after *Intruder in the Dust,* a near parody of his previous work.

There is something parodic in *The Wapshot Chronicle*, although not of the previous work but of the writer, the seafaring Yankee. Writing the novel, or trying to write a novel, took more than twenty years. The first pages are heavy with ancestral adornments, with the treacherous attractions of New England pedantry. The portrait of a not-long-dead founder of the Wapshot (Cheever?) family:

> He appeared in a yellow velvet cap, trimmed with fur, and a loose green velvet gown or bathrobe as if he, bred on that shinbone coast and weaned on beans and codfish, had translated himself into some mandarin or hawk-nosed Renaissance prince, tossing bones to the mastiffs, jewels to the whores, and swilling wine out of golden goblets with his codpiece busting its velvet bows.

Eccentric, rich aunts; eccentric, lovable father, Leander, who keeps a very mannered journal; the rather glamorized journey through occupations and love of the sons, Moses and Coverly.

Cheever is a disappointing novelist. The mellifluous style is always at hand, the courtesy and wistfulness of his way with dramatic encounters remain; and yet the novels fly apart, shred and shed as if some wind of inattention had overtaken them. High-flown backgrounds appear for characters who had otherwise seemed quite recognizable. Like the ancestor, they wear fur and velvet.

Bullet Park (1969) was a commercial failure, despite the success of *The Wapshot Chronicle*. In between, he did the stories in *The Housebreaker of Shady Hill* (1959), and these, like the earlier collections, are what he could so wisely compose in the pure and confident manner of his genius for the short form. *Bullet Park* is not quite serious, that is the trouble. Hammer and Nailles are the names of the two families; such is the beginning folly. Hammer, a suburbanite but actually the bastard son of outlandish, bejeweled parents, tries to immolate Tony, the beloved son of Nailles, in the chancel of Christ's Church and would have done so without the intervention of a kindly guru from the Temple of Light. A certain aspect of Halloween on the streets of Bullet Park.

The Wapshot Chronicle has a biographical interest. Here is the first of Cheever's confessions to homosexual inclinations and the first of what might be called his "gentrification" of the homosexual pass and of the homosexual affair in the later novels. Homosexuality and alcoholism return the thoughts to Susan Cheever's memoir, *Home Before Dark*. These two afflictions or profound wishes shoot out of the memoir with a marked propulsive force.

"It became clearer and clearer that my father was the worst kind of alcoholic. He seemed intent on destroying himself. I suppose he had always been an alcoholic." An invitation to teach at Boston University was accepted, with devastating results. "He narrowly missed being hit by a car as he crossed Commonwealth Avenue in a haze. The police threatened to pick him up for public intoxication—he had lain down on the grass in the Public Garden to share a bottle of hooch in a paper bag with a bum." At last, broken in health, he was sent to an alcohol-rehabilitation center in New York and on from there to AA and abstinence, no doubt painful. In the stories and novels, there is an unusual amount of drinking. Some of it is more or less unconscious stage business such as, "she said, fixing herself another drink"—that sort of line again and again. (A like stage business can be found in the fiction of many alcoholic writers.) But in the stories, drunkenness was often central to the action—cocktail parties, dinners with their insults, shameful outbursts, tears in the bedroom. In the period and the setting there was a naturalness to being drunk, and the plots it occasioned flowed into remorse and ruin and aroused, tenderhearted, forgiving emotions: "Oh, those suburban Sunday nights, those Sunday-night blues! Those departing weekend guests, those stale cocktails, those half-dead flowers, those trips to Harmon to catch the Century, those post-mortems and pickup suppers!" ("O Youth and Beauty!").

That was one thing, drinking. "My father's sexual appetites were one of his major preoccupations, and his lust for men was as distressing to him as desire for women was self-affirming and ecstatic." In the course of writing the memoir, Susan Cheever was telephoned by a young man who had "letters" and perhaps wanted to sell them; she interviewed another who had an unhappy story to tell. On one of his visits to a university, Cheever met Rip, "who would be his close friend, lover, confidant for the rest of his life." The writer's journals of 1978 tell it all:

Absolute candor does not suit me, but I will come as close as possible to describing the chain of events. Lonely and with my loneliness exac-

erbated by travel, motel rooms, bad food, public readings and the su-
perficiality of standing in reception lines I fell in love with Rip in a
motel room of unusual squalor. His air of seriousness and responsibility, the bridged glasses he wore for his nearsightedness and his composed manner all excited my deepest love.

In his last years, John Cheever was much honored. His complete
stories were collected, and the reception and sales were at last an acknowledgment of their fineness. He also wrote two novels, very curious both of them, and one of them, the bizarre *Falconer,* the best of his
work in the long form.

Oh What a Paradise It Seems (1982) is the last of his novels. The confessional mode here is most charmingly engaged, and the torments of
conscience and doubt poor Coverly Wapshot endured over a discreet
homosexual pass have been swept away with a sunny air of innocence
quite perverse. This short book is rich with the love of nature and
memories of skating on ponds now being used as dump sites—and rich
with embarrassments.

Lemuel Sears, "an old man but not yet infirm," stands next to a
handsome young woman in the line at a bank. He is captivated and
soon, after dinners and careful attentions on his part, it is a rainy night,
people jogging on the street, and the girl, Renée, invites him to dine in
her apartment. She meets him at the door wearing a wrapper, and as for
him he is out of his clothes in a minute. "You were hardpacked," she
says. A phrase from the army? It does somehow express the rather
chirpy dash and potency of this distinguished personage with two
wives in the grave. The affair goes on for some weeks, and he arrives at
the apartment one night to find her dressed, ready to go out. He nevertheless "unbuckled his trousers and let them fall to his knees." Her
answer is, "I'm sorry, but I cannot help you." Thinking flowers might
be "a seductive force," Sears goes out to buy them and comes back to
find her gone.

> The elevator door opened. It was not she. It was the elevator operator.
> He was wearing street clothes and a hat. He went directly to where
> Sears stood and embraced him.... The stranger, whose name he hadn't
> learned, took him downstairs to a small room off the lobby, where he
> undressed Sears and undressed himself.

O wishes and fantasies. The little idyll proceeds in a stately way. "We've got to find something else we can do together," Sears says, and so they go on a fishing trip. They sleep together quite peacefully and Eduardo, his name, tells about his wife and sons and says that he will spend the rest of his vacation with his wife in Key West, a union package tour. Sears's last line when they part back in the city is, "Get a great tan."

Cheever is the straightest of homosexual lovers, and thus his last novels are not exactly a contribution to gay lit. The pastoral and nostalgic mood does not desert him, even at the cost of common experience. One might notice the absence of class tension or perhaps imagine that it exists in the passivity of Sears and also of *Falconer's* Farragut, who are so sweetly taken, so accommodated without making a signal. Even the girl Renée appears in her wrapper to begin the seduction. In this winsome dream of Lemuel Sears's—too many autumn leaves.

Falconer is a perturbation. The Cheever artifice, the fall to the dust, and a precipitous act it is, rash and brilliant in the fall. Of course, there is a well-educated gentleman with one of those signifying, protective names, this one Farragut. (Falconer is the name of an old, brutal prison, based on Sing Sing in Ossining, where Cheever went to teach the inmates.) Farragut has been brought to "this old iron place on a late summer's day." Before we know his crime, we see him busy in his cell writing to "his wife, his lawyer, his governor and his bishop." *His bishop,* yes, writing to his bishop while longing for his methadone, since Farragut (his family came to America in 1672 on the *Nanuet*) is a heroin addict, but a fine fellow for all that. He has killed his gross, self-satisfied brother with a poker when the brother screamed that his father didn't want Farragut. "He had an abortionist come to the house. Your own father wanted you killed."

So Farragut is in prison for life. It is all to be inside, and Cheever has, without any previous indication of such powers, created a large cast from the underside of society, created guards and routines, obscene dialogues and mumbled, self-serving prison monologues, all with great imaginative force. There is a "radiant and aching" love affair with Jody. Jody is an ignorant, cunning, petty hustler in jail, or so he says, for burglary, pistol-whipping, and kidnapping of a candy-store operator in order to steal some pari-mutuel tickets. Their meeting, as we would expect, comes through Jody's initiative. He wants Farragut because "you ain't homosexual." No cash, no reward? "From what Farragut had read he had expected this to happen, but what he had not expected was that this grotesque bonding of their relationship would provoke in him so profound a love."

Jody escapes, dressed in drag as an acolyte of the cardinal who has made a ceremonial visit to the prison. Back in town, out of the vestments, the cardinal recognizes Jody for what he is, an escaped convict. And then a Theater of the Ridiculous scene follows. The cardinal and Jody prance about Madison Avenue, and all the while TV actresses and assorted others kneel to kiss the ring and be blown the sign of the cross. He takes Jody to a private room at a tailor's and orders him a suit of clothes for his new life. A miracle.

In Cheever's fiction there are, now and then, moments close to profanation of his insistent churchiness, just as he is compelled to deviation from his insistent passion for women. In prison, having left Jody's private brothel, Farragut writes "Oh, my darling" letters to a mistress, just as Lemuel Sears passes back and forth without mishap from his ecstasy with the girl, Renée, to the love of the elevator man, Eduardo. Whether this is naïveté, a startling unworldliness, willed illusion, or unguarded egotism is hard to say.

Cheever covers his tracks, but the writing dares his own horrors. And he will not give up the pastoral accent. Farragut, a heroin addict and a murderer, escapes prison by posing as a dead body on its way to the morgue. "He held his head high, his back straight, and walked along nicely. Rejoice, he thought, rejoice." And there you have it.

(1984)

Citizen Updike

John Updike, the dazzling author, appeared, and still appears, to be one of Augustine's "fair and fit"—and never more so than when viewed among his male literary colleagues who often tend to show the lump and bump of gene, bad habits, the spread and paste of a lifetime spent taking one's own dictation. For this tall, one wants to say still young, man, despite certain dwindling days, September-song modulations in the composition of his memoir, *Self-Consciousness*, everything seemed to fall into place. An only child, treasured by nice intelligent parents who, if not particularly well-to-do, were prosperous in respect and plausibility; born in a pleasant Pennsylvania village, Shillington, with its "idle alleys and darkened four-square houses," its high school, movie house, stores, avenues, and streets whose names will have on his pages the curved beauty of Havana and Caracas, even if they are Pennwyn and Lynoak.

Updike went on to Harvard and, as a young writer, came under the benevolent paternalism of *The New Yorker,* married early, had children, moved to Massachusetts, and with an uncommon creative energy wrote stories, novels, poems, essays, and still writes on and on with great success about suburban landscapes or small-town ones efflorescent in observed detail, prodigal in image, and brashly knowing and accomplished in the rhythms of current dialogue and steaming with the orifices and bodily fluids of many fluent copulations.

And then, with an admirable and defiant gallantry, he designed in *The Coup* his African country, Kush, whose

> peanut oil travels westward the same distance as eastward our ancestors plodded, their neck-shackles chafing down to the jugular, in the care of Arab traders, to find in the flesh-markets of Zanzibar eventual lodgings in the harems and palace guards of Persia and Chinese Turkestan.

And then again, he, as productive of print as a Victorian, transmogrifies himself into a sluggish, anxious Jewish novelist, *Bech,* mooning on Riverside Drive with an exact ironical accent before taking off for a government-sponsored tour of the Soviet Union and various satellite capitals in Eastern Europe where he treads the ancient, war-worn stones and confers with the resident writers, one of whom says he plans to "defect as soon as he gets his laundry back."

A promiscuous, astonishing span, a labyrinthine talent through which the author makes a smooth, experienced, dashing, even dandyish passage. A bit of a parson, too, something icy inside the melting flesh of concupiscence.

Updike's memoirs bear the title *Self-Consciousness,* to indicate the natural authorial awareness and, more unexpected, to reveal a distress arising from the envelope of the self, the flesh and bones and organs that have been the source of pain and of the "self-consciousness" of hidden damage. He has lived with torments devastating, if not life-threatening, and it is a hard heart that could turn from these ills with a shrug. The greatest suffering has been a long battle with a virulent psoriasis. His account of the scabs, blisters, eruptions, and treatments is of such fullness and wounded feeling one would not want, in description, to substitute a version other than his own. The disease was not only hurtful and exhausting but also humiliating, as when he was required to learn to swim at Harvard. On a somewhat descending scale, he has endured bouts of stuttering, asthma, tooth and gum problems. So there it is, a host of imperfections and acute discomforts, woes rendered with an eloquent and almost sunny confidence.

My sufferings are purely physical, the aged, dying Santayana is supposed to have said in order to fend off the redemptive efforts of nuns and priests who might wish, at the end, to seduce him from the teasing ambiguity of "There is no God and Mary is His mother." Updike, far from the end and friendly to redemption, if it should come, has a way of translating the threat of moral ravage into symptoms. "I tried to break out of my marriage, on behalf of another, and failed, and began to have trouble breathing." Succeeding in the breakup, as determined people will, he writes: "My face broke out, my shoulders and neck became so encrusted I couldn't turn my head without pain."

He will go further, twirling, you might say, on a steel toe like a skater in the crisp New England air: "So wrapped in my skin, so watchful of its day-to-day permutations, I have little concern to spare for the homeless, the disenfranchised, the unfortunate who figure so largely in the inner passion of smooth-pelted liberals like my first wife." "A man's foes will be those in his own household," the Redeemer Himself opined. "Smooth-pelted liberal," sardonic locution, is attached to the sufferer's first wife, mother of four Updikes, daughter of a Unitarian clergyman. No doubt Updike regrets the homeless and the unfortunate as much as another. His distance here is atmospheric, a distaste for the fair, blue-eyed Unitarians in Cambridge, Massachusetts, the attachment to "causes" shown by the rosy-cheeked, trust-fund descendants of the balmy vapors coming from Concord and thereabouts. For Updike, the Over-soul Unitarians, brushing away the Trinity like dust in a dark corner, will not do, although he had a try with the placid church before settling down more or less as a Congregationalist and their "sweet bare rites descended from the Puritans."

Congregationalists are a mild enough church of choice for the census taker, not exacting or likely to be interfering or reforming in matters of conduct. It would not have been fitting to take a leap into the Roman Catholic Church where confession and forgiveness are followed by the intention to go and sin no more, a source of plot dilemma for Graham Greene and for the almost-forgotten Christian novelist François Mauriac. (Sartre: "God is not a novelist and neither is M. Mauriac.") The awesome basilicas, rituals, and elaboration of Christian duties in the Roman Church, appealing to the faith hunger of many converts, would be too richly aesthetic for Updike, too denying of Middle America, the other creed embraced in these confessions.

So it was the Congregational Church and its pleasant meetings—or was it? Updike was born a Lutheran, and there lives in him still a degree of the social conservatism of the great reformer who opposed the Peasants' War of the sixteenth century because it destabilized the state and the power of the Protestant nobles. So Updike shifts in the manner of the creative, leaves the Church and the site of his youth for self-definition and also, as his memoirs seem to say, to discover and to reclaim for his contribution to literature the meaning of who he was and where he was placed in the American scene.

Settling for the beauties of Massachusetts was not only a flight from Shillington but also from New York. Updike was happy, he tells us, in Ipswich, an old village on the North Shore of Boston with a number of quite dominating old families, a place notable for the charms of wooden saltbox houses, the wide shores and cold water of Crane's Beach, and, a formidable barrier to assimilation, the Myopia Hunt Club. And perhaps Ipswich is now notable for its transformation into Tarbox, the name of the town in Updike's novel *Couples*. Tar, an odorous viscous liquid, and box—well, guess. Of course, *Couples* is a work of fiction, and Tarbox need only be a convenient address of some status, the sort of town young-professional couples with children might feel a certain pride in attaching themselves to. In any case, Tarbox acts in a peculiar manner upon the pulsing libidos gathered there as if for some pagan festival of nymphs and satyrs and maenads or, perhaps, closer to the bone, a remembrance of Merry Mount, carnal and gun traffic with the Indians, frontier revels around the maypole before the English Puritans shipped Mr. Morton back to where he came from. Anyway, Updike was happy in the actual Ipswich—happy except for the period, the middle 1960s, coming like some loud neighbor's quarrel over the fence.

"On Not Being a Dove," the most striking section of the memoirs, is a sort of regimental assault, bayonets preceding, on the peace movement occasioned by America's fierce assault on Vietnam. It is meant to roil and rile the deracinated louts at their homefront barricades, the treasonable clerks in the literary establishment, the fashionable metropolis and its feathered dissent, the barefoot, braless flag-burners, the pious army deserters fleeing the hallowed shores for Sweden and Canada. Certainly, the inanities of the expressive side of the peace movement, the flower children, make love not war, the pouring of blood on this and that—on these antics anyone free from permanent brain shock might look back in embarrassment.

The protest movement, which had begun in the solemn Fiftyish pronouncements of the Port Huron Statement and the orderly civil-rights strategies, by the time of the '67 Washington march and the '68 convention of mischievous voodoo and street theatre and, finally, a nightmare of anarchy, of window-smashing and cop-bopping and drug-tripping and shouting down.

That's one thing and not the whole of the peace movement, as the Dance of the Seven Veils is not the whole of the *Herodiade*. Updike's positions are not merely a shudder for the misdemeanors of broken windows and the heretical processions of candlelight blowing in the wind; he proposes a tangled support for the actual war in Vietnam, an implied, or rather insisted upon, duty that once in combat there is something cheap and hollow about agitating against the elected government, taking upon oneself matters of state that because of the horrible circumstances of war require patriotism, standing together, a national, if troubled, acquiescence. That's the way he sees it, altogether too much carrying on by the motley and mottled mob and worse by the scriveners, their wrists swollen from signing a thousand petitions. What do *they* know, who are they, poets and screen stars, to demand out-of-Vietnam or, for that matter, to change the scene to earlier foreign manifestations that toppled and diverted governments, to demand out-of-Suez, out-of-Algeria?

There are a number of points in his indictment, some about the nature of citizenship and others concerning the particularities of the Vietnam War.

> One source of my sense of grievance against the peace movement when it came was that I hadn't voted for any of its figures—not for Abbie Hoffman or Father Daniel Berrigan or Reverend William Sloane Coffin or Jonathan Schell or Lillian Hellman or Joan Baez or Jane Fonda or Eugene McCarthy. I had voted for Lyndon Johnson, and thus had earned my American right not to make a political decision for another four years.

A peculiar idea of the franchise, considering the porousness of the mandate on this and that, the frenzied concentration in Washington at the end of the day on how "it played" on the evening news and in the polls, representing after all the raw opinion of the unqualified, on what came to the telephone operators computing the yeses and nos, what arrived in the legislative mail bag then, as always, casting a shadow over the morning D.C. sunlight.

Updike believes that Johnson was repudiated because he was not chic, altogether too down-home and as unmanicured as a coyote. "Cambridge professors and Manhattan lawyers and their guitar-strumming children thought they could run the country and the world better than this lugubrious bohunk from Texas." Henceforth, California began to run the country. And, true, not one of the successors could bring a tear to the eye like the memory of the unbuckled Johnson paddling nude in the White House pool or conferring on the toilet.

The war—Updike seems to come to rest on the dubious doctrine of "credibility," meaning the credibility of American power to sustain noncommunist allies wherever and whenever they were attacked. "Credibility must be maintained; power is a dirty business, but whoever said it wasn't?" Whether it was *prudent*, given the loss of lives, the waste and vast expense, still to be paid for, to send airplane after airplane each day with bombs, napalm, Agent Orange, soldiers, condoms, whiskey, cornflakes, and chewing gum—that's something else, the basis for dissent even among some skeptical, cautious men around Washington, along with the perception that the war was "unwinnable." And for the conscientious patriot Updike, should this war be morally allowable, considering the gross inequity of destructive means between ourselves and the enemy?

Such, such were the days, and a little power struggle took place at *The New Yorker*, a filtering down or pushing up of conflict on West Forty-third Street, and Updike, an occasional political commentator, was made to give way in "Notes and Comments" to Jonathan Schell and "more leftish hands."

"The world is fallen, and in a fallen world animals, men, and nations make space for themselves through a willingness to fight. Christ beat up the money-changers in the temple, and came not to bring peace, He distinctly said, but a sword." When Christ, who famously blessed the peacemaker, spoke of not peace but a sword, He had no thought of wars between nations but induced instead the household declarations of war that would supply the troops for his crusade. (Matthew 10:34–35: "Think not that I am come to send peace on earth: I come not to send peace, but a sword. For I come to set a man at variance against his father, and the daughter against her mother, and the daughter in law against her mother in law.") Certainly, most of us would join the army rather than embrace the poverty and repudiation of family and earthly concerns these troublesome early Christians were to accept as their lot.

Neither Jahweh nor Christ can be, after the biblical period, slipped into war alliances even if it is natural, in the midst of wholesale death, that the suffering should seek divine sanction for their cause. Bavarian Christian leaders in the last war seemed to have no trouble piling up sanctions with or without the aid of divinity. Updike goes far afield to find advice, even from the Bhagavad-Gita: "Therefore you must fight. ... Freedom from activity is never attained by abstaining from action." And in another obscure reference, obscure in intention at least, he thinks of men at war and of our national honor and writes: "In Sunday School, I had been much impressed by the passage where Peter denies Christ three times before the cock crows." The disciple Peter, with his noticeable Galilean accent, divesting himself of the beleaguered Christ, saying "I know not the man" thrice—this betrayal by propinquity or rhetorical extension seems to be attached to the milling throngs of the peace movement denying Johnson and Kissinger and Nixon. Perhaps the hippies should, like Judas in some accounts, hang themselves, as in an awful pop sense many of them did. ... A slippery journey all this was. In a brilliant recent book about, among other matters, God and national policy in Victorian England up to the First World War, a young man recruited in 1914 is quoted as saying, "I've been a Christian all my life, but this war is a bit too serious."[*]

Updike's moral complexion is revealed with passion in his memoir and with a high degree of almost lapidary affection for the values of his youth, the war stamps and nickels in the church collection plate, the mainstream in its decency, allegiance, and sacrifice. Along the way, he scolds the "anti-establishment militants" gathered for a summer on Martha's Vineyard, scolds Mailer and Philip Roth and even the long dead holdouts, New England with its "haughty disavowal of the Mexican-American War"—that skirmish, or those skirmishes, in which Mexico ceded two-fifths of its territory, which, being long accustomed to Texas and California, we were pleased to have.

Updike votes for the Democrats and is one of those Americans who retain from their parents a memory of the Depression and of the in-

---

[*] Derek Jarrett, *The Sleep of Reason: Fantasy and Reality from the Victorian Age to the First World War* (New York: Harper and Row, 1989).

spiration of Franklin Roosevelt. The upper-middle classes, he observed, voted Democratic out of "humanitarian largesses," because they saw it as the party of the left-out and needy. For himself, "I was simply poor and voted Democratic out of crude self-interest." He notes that his childhood contained the bicycles and so on beyond necessity and "when, many years later, I was recalling some of these happy circumstances in the company of my father, he interrupted me with an exclamation almost anguished, 'Oh, no, Johnny—we were *poor*.' "

The young man from Shillington is interesting indeed, and his autobiographical composition, the work of a master writer, is a document of some uniqueness in our contemporary literature, something like a desk full of stunningly local photographs preserved by accidents; or it would be so if photographs had opinions. And yet, there is something droll about the picture of himself as déclassé while he wandered about Harvard, carrying with him his "humble beginnings" and his relative deprivation. With his Christianity and out-of-line distrust of the antiwar movement, he places himself as an object of aesthetic distaste like Johnson in politics, and in religion a lonely swimmer "sworn to seek / If any golden harbour be for me / In seas of death and sunless gulf of Doubt." Of course, he is the true and sweetly acceptable celebrity of art, that world of the self-made where attitude and pose have a license as plain as that of a mosquito.

A sort of citizen self-consciousness seems to accompany him as he goes into the Sunday-morning church service, there perhaps to sing the popular hymn, pleasantly negotiable for tenor and soprano, "Once to every man and nation comes the moment to decide," words actually taken from a Civil War poem by J. R. Lowell. Or to return home to the town meeting, home from the cynical caverns of New York.

> I walked with my suitcase, on a winter night, up to the high school, where the town meeting was in progress. I gave my name, was checked off and admitted, and stood there in the gymnasium-auditorium in my city suit, looking into the brightly illuminated faces of my fellow citizens.

"Among the repulsions of atheism for me has been its drastic uninterestingness as an intellectual position." Dear spotted atheism, the homely, wrinkled queen of heaven for the Big Bang, mother of the depressing claims of the prehistoric upright ape and the joke of the Piltdown Man—uninteresting? For this multiplex American talent, so various, as studious as a monk and as sly as a defense attorney with certain flashing difficulties in his case, here is the equation: "Down-dirty sex and the bloody mess of war and the strenuous act of faith all belonged to a dark necessary underside of reality that I felt should not be merely ignored, or risen above, or disdained."

"Down-dirty sex"—here the novelist can be seen to slip out the door of the prayer meeting and the vote on the zoning law, saying as he leaves to attend to business, "In Adam's fall, we sinned all." Updike began with *The Poorhouse Fair*, a charming fable about some old men in a country home. "It'll make a f.ing black mark in Connor's book," the dialogue goes, chaste typography of the year 1959, before the libertinism of the detestable sixties brought in the newfangledness of typewriter fucking. Updike embraced the wide exemptions with a curious fervor, and his genius began to show a concubine's patience in the diversification of descriptions of the sexual act, not to mention the largest circus of performers. "Whoso list to hunt I know where is an hind."

To risk the opprobium of being against sex and candor in fiction, of withholding appreciation for the wearisome struggle with adjective, verb, and noun, the difficult rhythms of the alexandrines of copulation, brings on as much social uneasiness as not being a dove. Perhaps *Couples* and the cocky antics of *The Witches of Eastwick* are best thought of as Restoration comedies, fantasies of cuckolds, loose-girdled ladies, toffs, lecherous squires, theatrics free at last from the Roundheads. But then the triad: down-dirty sex, God, and country?

Updike himself worries the scab of the union of these three, one original with him perhaps. God knows all, and so cannot be shocked, he says. No, God is not easily shocked, but He is not one to forgo wrath about the evil and adulterous generations—a problem, yes, of Updike's own making, there's that to be said for it. We note in the crowd of characters those most sympathetically imagined, Piet Hanema in *Couples*, and Rabbit Angstrom in the trilogy devoted to him, are given a sort of club handshake: They go to church.

Roger's Version, a later novel, is prodigiously learned in theology ancient and modern, in physics, computers, whatever is necessary. There are four main characters: Roger Lambert, a professor of theology, rather cynical, tweedy, as he goes about giving lectures on Tertullian in a place like the divinity school at Harvard; his second wife, Esther, mother of their one child; Dale, a student, nerdish master of the computer who wishes to use its arcane possibilities to prove the existence of God; and Verna, Roger's niece, a foul-mouthed flower child, with a child of her own, half black, whom she bangs about and injures sufficiently to be rightly accused of child abuse at the hospital.

In the novel, Dale, with his waxy pallor and acne, will have an affair with the professor's wife, Esther; the professor will sleep with his dreadful niece, Verna. Some justification, religious, is needed for this willful "cage of unclean beasts," as the Puritans were thought of in Holland. Remember, the text Updike quotes tells us, that Tertullian allowed: "There's nothing to blush for in nature. Nature should be revered."

Nature—Esther with Dale:

He is coming. She stares at the little dark eye, the *meatus uranarius*, and with a stern helpfulness gives a downward tug at his engorged phallus ... and when the first gob comes, as if in slow motion on a pornographic film, she has to have it herself ... all that startling pure whiteness, ravenously nimble ... and holding him firm with that hand at his kicking root, centers her cunt above his prick quickly and impales herself.

And, etc.

Roger meanwhile at his desk, weary of translating Tertullian's difficult Latin, nods off to imagine, in quite pretty Kodachrome, his wife and Dale together:

I pictured a white shaft: tense, pure, with dim blue broad veins and darker thinner ones and a pink-mauve head like the head of a mushroom set by the Creator upon a swollen stem nearly as thick as itself, just the merest little lip or rounded eaves ... overhanging the bluish stretched semi-epiderm where pagan foreskin once was, and a drop of transparent nectar in the little wide-awake slit of an eye at its velvety suffused tip.

Verna, in confrontation, with Uncle Roger: "Because you want to fuck me. You want to lick my cunt." At every point in this curious, yellow novel there are asides to make way for religious imagery and longer disquisitions about the Fall and meaning of flesh, all bringing to mind those philosophical longueurs in the Marquis de Sade that interrupt the tableaux and stagy criminality. Of course, Sade despises God, and Updike's is a domestic, harmless imagination. What seems to make a remote connection between the two is the felt need for justification. When Verna and Roger are in conversation at the kitchen table and Roger instructs her in the Christian belief that "even little babies are bad," he elaborates from the unlikely pulpit: "Augustine did. Calvin did. All the best Christian thinkers did. You have to [believe in the badness of babies], otherwise the world isn't truly fallen, and there's no need for Redemption, there's no Christian story." (Pelagius thought Adam's sin was his alone and we must commit our own sins. But no matter.) There is much that is dismaying and unpleasant and tiresomely perfunctory in this violent congress between the pornographic impulse and Christian doctrine (e.g., the plastic cross that Dale, the callow Spinoza at his computer, wears and to which Esther, the divinity wife, gives whatever attention she has to spare).

If the novels, the hotter ones, need a vindication the need is not theological but aesthetic, a matter of fiction, and also a grounding in social credibility, the treadmill of fictional truth. The actors in the drama will be a biochemist, a Radcliffe graduate, a Congregationalist minister, an amateur violinist, all turned into colliding bodies, objects, to whom inhibition, anxiety, debts, the eye of the neighbors, the practical world, the overhanging aura of the divinity school, time itself, the bother, the bother, the boredom ("Fulfillment's desolate attic"—Philip Larkin) are completely absent. The matings of these married, switching couples do not take place in some 1920s demimonde or in Haight-Ashbury but are consummated in a wondrously laid-out realistic world, heightened by Updike's intense visual imagination. *Witches:*

The night was moonless. The crickets stridulated their everlasting monotonous meaningful note. Car headlights swept by on Cocumscussoc Way, and the bushes by the church door, nearly stripped of leaves, sprang up sharp in the illumination like complicated mandibles and jointed feelers and legs of insects magnified. The air smelt faintly of apples making cider by themselves.

And *Couples:* "The blue fire, layer on layer, of swallowed starlight, was halved by a dissolving jet tail."

In the early pages of *The Great Gatsby*, the lower-class mistress makes a telephone call to the Buchanan estate at the dinner hour. This small event foretells the *tristesse* of the entire novel, sets the compositional tone for the eye and the special sensibility of the narrator. "Among the broken fragments of the last five minutes at table I remember the candles being lit again, pointlessly, and I was conscious of wanting to look squarely at every one, and yet to avoid all eyes." Saddest of all is the distant picture of the mistress at the telephone, she who literally doesn't know where she is with Tom Buchanan and his golden Daisy, she who can have no idea.

Updike's shimmering knowledge of the way things look, how they deface or illuminate the towns, the roads; his almost effortless command of the tradesman's shops, the houses, cars, sports, and the speech of America, his dialogue's wit, swiftness, and deftness in placement— in all this he is unsurpassed. But the greatly pleasurable gifts hang like white, puffy clouds around the humbly repetitive pandemonium of the relentless f.ings that do not advance the plot. On and on they go, fore and aft, signifying description itself, interspersed with the voyeur's homely and infidel conversation. "Neff allowed to Alexandra that Greta [his wife] was ardent but strenuous, very slow to come but determined to do so." In *Witches*, one of the women has a leaking pipe in the kitchen; the plumber is called ... and so on. At a point in their lovemaking, she suggests an unappetizing way of getting off, and the man of the people, the licensed journeyman with perhaps another leak on the intercom, says, "How about I give you a rain check on that?"

> *In the beauty of the lillies, Christ was born across the sea*—this odd and uplifting line from many of the odd lines in "The Battle Hymn of the Republic" seemed to me, as I set out, to summarize what I had to say about America, to offer itself as the title of a continental *magnum opus* of which all my books, no matter how many, would be mere installments, mere starts at singing of this great roughly rectangular country severed from Christ by the breadth of the sea.

An extraordinary statement, beautiful in the quotation and in the lilt of the flow of aspiration. If Updike has done as he wished, he has done so in the Rabbit trilogy—*Rabbit Run, Rabbit Redux,* and *Rabbit Is Rich:* "I, who seemed to be full of things to say, who had all of Shillington to say, Shillington and Pennsylvania and the whole immense mass of middling, hidden, troubled America to say." True—the novelist's glory here is *saturation,* the jungle density of memory, experience, and imagination. The volumes span twenty years or so and they take place in a thick vegetation, crabgrass, and rotten dandelions pushing up over the lost basketball tournaments, the car lots, the aging elders, the songs and creaking beds, bad jobs, the growing and failing business of the lower-class and petit-bourgeois landscape. In these novels, it is the lived years of Harry—Rabbit as he is called—Angstrom and Janice, née Springer, that grow and grow with their mess, their cars, their flights, their domestic vagrancy, their inchoate sense of things, the spendthrift poverty and the TV dinners and hot dogs scrounged up on an evening.

Rabbit Angstrom is created out of recalcitrant materials, the high-school basketball court and finally the Toyota distributorship in Brewer—the facts, you remember, much like those of the truckstop minimalism in favor just now. But in Updike there are no staccato notations; it unwinds and unwinds, scene after scene, a long flow of attention and feeling. It is difficult to describe just who this young man from Brewer might be because of the subtlety of his claim on our sympathy, the peculiarities of his unease, his "running," this is, running away in the first volume.

In earlier American fiction, the custom was to give a character like Rabbit, Middle Western, feeling cramped in spirit, to give him a touch of the poet, some little closet of Jude-like hesitant bookishness. But Rabbit is not leaving town, nor would he wish to exactly. He runs to get away, runs by car, and sometimes walks out of his too-early marriage to Janice because, well, as he puts it, "she's such a mutt." He has an inchoate sense of things "invisible" and goes to church where "the pressed suits of portly men give substance and respectability to his furtive sense of the invisible." He feels the need to ask forgiveness for his days at the used-car lot. "You see these clunkers come in with 80,000 miles on them and the pistons so loose the oil just pours through and they get a washing and the speedometer turned back and you hear yourself saying this represents a real bargain."

Rabbit is not a rebel against small-town hypocrisy and narrowness, the so-familiar plight. He's got a flag decal on his car, and he's a patriot in the barroom: "Poor old LBJ, Jesus, with tears in his eyes on television, you must have heard him, he just about offered to make North

Vietnam the fifty-first fucking state of the Goddam Union if they'd just stop throwing bombs." If he has a spiritual quest it is to his old coach, Tothero, where he takes up with Ruth, a tired and realistic woman, available but not exactly a whore, just hanging on. He flees while Janice is back home experiencing their second child, and he leaves Ruth to return, leaving her pregnant after convincing her not to use the "flying saucer."

The years of Janice and Rabbit go on and lots of coitus, sometimes amid the residue of too much Gallo and too many bologna sandwiches. The Springers, the cabin in the Poconos, a couple-swapping trip to the Caribbean, very heavy, Rabbit's days as chief sales representative of the Toyota franchise in Brewer. "This is a Corolla. . . . This particular car has four-speed synchromesh transmission, fully transistorized ignition system, power-assisted front disc brakes, vinyl reclining bucket seats, a locking gas cap." *Saturation*, its reward. At the end, Rabbit is a grandfather. "Through all this she has pushed to be here, in his lap, his hands, a real presence, hardly weighing anything but alive. Fortune's hostage, heart's desire, a granddaughter. His. Another nail in his coffin. His."

These wonderful novels are acts of conservation, a gathering of plant specimens north of the Delaware River, a rare and lasting collection of the fertilities of Updike's genius. Along the way, his diversions, vacations perhaps, have been a sort of brilliant excess, as if thrown away; but the novels *Bech* and *Bech Is Back* are magical travel books, the best since Evelyn Waugh. His literary criticism, *Hugging the Shore* and pieces following, does not hug the shore but instead sails out in an open boat where his curiosity and great intelligence seem to sail on and on, wherever.

(1989)

Paradise Lost: Philip Roth

American Pastoral is Philip Roth's twentieth work of fiction—an accretion of creative energy, a yearly, or almost, place at the starting line of a marathon. But his is a one-man sprint with the signatures, the gestures, the deep breathing, and the repetitiveness, sometimes, of an obsessive talent. Roth has his themes, spurs to his virtuoso variations and star turns in triple time. His themes are Jews in the world, especially in Israel, Jews in the family, Jews in Newark, New Jersey; fame, vivid enough to occasion impostors *(Operation Shylock)*; literature, since his narrators or performers are writers, actually one writer, Philip Roth. And sex, anywhere in every manner, a penitential workout on the page with no thought of backaches, chafings, or phallic fatigue. Indeed the novels are prickled like a sea urchin with the spines and fuzz of many indecencies.

In *American Pastoral,* we are, on the first page, once more in Newark; and on page sixteen we are told "I'm Zuckerman the author." Nathan Zuckerman is the author of *Carnovsky (Zuckerman Unbound),* an alternative title like those sometimes used in foreign translations. In English, the novel is, of course, *Portnoy's Complaint,* which provoked among many other responses an eruption of scandal. The author of the book that brought about a fame and a "recognition factor" equal to that of Mick Jagger is Philip Roth. Or so it is in *Zuckerman Unbound,* where even a young funeral director, attending the remains of a Prince Seratelli, pauses to ask for the author's autograph—all part of this wild, very engaging minstrel show in which the writing of a book, not just *any* book, may serve as the lively plot for a subsequent book. Of course, we cannot attach Zuckerman or David Kepesh or Peter Tarnopol or Alexander Portnoy to Philip Roth like a fingernail. Not always.

However, if he follows Zuckerman to *The Anatomy Lesson,* the reader will gain or lose a shiver of interest if he knows that the late critic Irving Howe published in *Commentary* some forthright reservations about Roth's work and that Howe is the "source" of the character Milton Appel. Howe had written—among other thoughts, some favorable— that "what seems really to be bothering Portnoy is a wish to sever his sexuality from his moral sensibilities, to cut it away from his self as a historical creature. It's as if he really supposed the super-ego, or *post coitum triste,* were a Jewish invention."

Zuckerman or Roth cries out some years later in *The Anatomy Lesson:* "Milton Appel had unleashed an attack upon Zuckerman's career that made Macduff's assault on Macbeth look almost lackadaisical. Zuckerman should have been so lucky as to come away with decapitation. A head wasn't enough for Appel; he tore you limb from limb." If he is indeed torn limb from limb, this ferocious paraplegic author pursues Appel/Howe in a motorized wheelchair for almost forty pages.

The structure of Roth's fiction is based often upon identifying tirades rather than actions and counteractions, tirades of perfervid brilliance, and this is what he can do standing on his head or hanging out the window if need be. The tirades are not to be thought of as mere angry outbursts in the kitchen after a beer or two, although they are usually angry enough since most of the characters are soreheads of outstanding volubility. The monologues are a presentation of self, often as if on the stage of some grungy Comédie Française, if such an illicit stretch may be allowed. Here is Monkey, the trailerpark Phèdre of *Portnoy's Complaint,* in a cameo appearance:

Picking on me all the time—in just the way you *look* at me you pick on me, Alex! I open the door at night, I'm so *dying* to see you, thinking all day long about nothing but you, and there are those fucking orbs already picking out every single thing that's *wrong* with me! As if I'm not insecure enough, as if insecurity isn't my whole hang-up, you get that expression all over your face the minute I open my mouth . . . oh, shit, here comes another dumb and stupid remark out of that brainless twat . . . Well, I'm not brainless, and I'm not a twat either, just because I didn't go to fucking Harvard! And don't give me any more of your shit about behaving in front of *The Lindsays.* Just who the fuck are *The Lindsays?* A God damn mayor, and his wife! A fucking *mayor!* In case you forget, I was married to one of the richest men in France *when I was still eighteen years old*—I was a guest at Aly Khan's for dinner, when you were still back in Newark, New Jersey, finger-fucking your little Jewish girl friends!

There you have Monkey and her expressive grievance.

For tirades and diatribes of a more demanding content, nothing Roth has written equals the bizarre explosions of *Operation Shylock,* a rich, original work composed with an unforgiving complexity if one is trying to unravel the design. It is about the double, the impersonator, the true self, one's own estimation, and the false self known to the public, the latter brilliantly examined in an account of the trial in Jerusalem of Ivan the Terrible, the allegedly murderous Ukrainian at Treblinka, who is also John Demjanjuk, "good old Johnny, the gardener from Cleveland, Ohio." And standing at not too great a distance from the actual ground of the novel we are reminded of the bad Philip Roth, creator for laughs of American Jewish life in its underwear; and, on the other hand, Philip Roth, artist, observer, inspired comedian, "the litanist of the fleas, the knave, the thane, the ribboned stick, the bellowing breeches"—comedian of the folkloric Portnoys and others of their kind.

In *Operation Shylock,* Philip Roth is in New York, recovering from depression and suicidal impulses brought on by the drug Halcion. (The doubling mystery of pharmaceutical messages—may cause insomnia or drowsiness. Remember President George Bush, reportedly on Halcion, ever windblown and smiling as he relentlessly raced up and down in his "cigarette" boat on the waters outside the summer White House in Kennebunkport, Maine.) Roth, from Halcion, down as a bottom-dwelling flatfish, is planning to go to Israel to interview the novelist Aharon Appelfeld. He learns, as if he had already departed and landed, that someone is giving interviews and lectures under his name, speaking on the radio and announcing an appearance in the King David Hotel on the subject of "Diasporism: The Only Solution to the Jewish

Problem. A lecture by Philip Roth." The double, the impostor, given the fairy-tale name of Pipik, is one of the disputatious inhabitants of the mind of the actual Roth, who creates at interesting length the faux, but not altogether faux, debate on the present position of Israel in the world.

Diasporism: "The time has come to return to the Europe that was for centuries, and remains to this day, the most authentic Jewish homeland there has ever been, the birthplace of rabbinic Judaism, Hasidic Judaism, Jewish secularism, socialism—on and on. The time has come to renew in the European Diaspora our preeminent spiritual and cultural role." In questions and counterarguments between the true and false Philip Roth, the horror of the Holocaust is remembered but is now claimed to be a "bulwark against European anti-Semitism." The mad Pipik is arguing in effect: Europe's had that, it's over. "No such bulwark exists in Islam. Exterminating a Jewish nation would cause Islam to lose not a single night's sleep, except for the great night of celebration. I think you would agree that a Jew is safer today walking aimlessly around Berlin than going unarmed into the streets of Ramallah."

Pipik has in the name of Roth not only proposed his program of diasporism, he has also organized A.S.A., Anti-Semites Anonymous, which leads to the appearance in the plot of a nurse who is valiantly and with commendable self-discipline in "recovery," *she* having taken the twelve steps. In this Israel, "the pasturalization of the ghetto," prophets and pundits roam the streets, all the while giving off the noise and fumes of opinion. Here, Philip Roth encounters an acquaintance from the past, a Harvard-educated Egyptian enrolled at Roth's time as a graduate student at the University of Chicago and now a famous professor. His name is George Ziad *(sic)*. Zee, as he is called, is also a diasporist but for his own reason. His program is to get the Jews out of Israel and thereby return the land to his ancestors, the Palestinians.

Believing that the old Philip Roth of his acquaintance has been transmogrified into the passionate diasporist of Pipik's caper, Zee holds forth with feeling about the sufferings of the Palestinians and the inferiority and provincialism of Israeli culture by comparison with that of the Jews in their true homeland, Manhattan. "There is more Jewish spirit and Jewish laughter and Jewish intelligence on the Upper West Side of Manhattan than in this entire country. . . . There's more Jewish heart at the knish counter at Zabar's than in the whole of the Knesset!"

Then the true Philip Roth, taking on the garments of the impostor Pipik, performs in his fluent rhythms about the greatest diasporist of all, Irving Berlin.

> The radio was playing "Easter Parade" and I thought, But this is Jewish genius on a par with the Ten Commandments. God gave Moses the Ten Commandments and then He gave to Irving Berlin "Easter Parade" and "White Christmas." . . . Easter he turns into a fashion show and Christmas into a holiday about snow. Gone is the gore and the murder of Christ—down with the crucifix and up with the bonnet! . . . If supplanting Jesus Christ with snow can enable my people to cozy up to Christmas, then let it snow, let it snow, let it snow!

So goes this curious, hilarious work of a profligate imagination unbound.

Along the way, it dashes into subplots of many befuddlements and allocations of adventures offered with the pedantic assurance of a mock court indictment. It is suggested, or more or less sworn to, that Philip Roth, the living author, acted as an agent for the Mossad, the CIA of Israel, by spying upon "Jewish anti-Zionist elements threatening the security of Israel." Serving counterintelligence by impersonating the impersonator? The novel is subtitled: *A Confession.* The preface claims that "the book is as accurate an account as I am able to give of actual occurrences that I lived through during my middle fifties and that culminated, early in 1988, in my agreeing to undertake an intelligence-gathering operation for Israel's foreign intelligence service, the Mossad." A solemn affidavit? Not quite. A note to the reader at the end of the book reads, "This confession is false." An operatic divertissement? Aida, the Ethiopian princess stealing war plans from her Egyptian lover for the benefit of her country. Or the false Dimitri and at last old Boris Godunov, Philip Roth, saving the state from the diasporists and in a cloud of redemption expiring.

The talent of Philip Roth floats freely in this rampaging novel with a plot thick as starlings winging to a tree and then flying off again. It is meant perhaps as a sort of restitution offered in payment of the claim that if the author has not betrayed the Jews, he has too often found them to be whacking clowns or whacking-off clowns. He bleeds like the old progenitor he has named in the title. Since he is, as a contemporary writer, always quick to insert the latest item of the news into his running comments, perhaps we can imagine him today as poor Richard Jewell, falsely accused in the 1996 Olympic bombing in Atlanta because, in police language, he fit the profile but was at last found to be just himself: a nice fellow good to his mother.

And yet, the impostor, the devil's advocate for the diaspora, has, with dazzling invention, composed not an ode for the hardy settlers of Israel but an Ode to the Wandering Jew as a beggar and prince in Western culture, speaking and writing in all its languages.

After fame and mischief on the streets of Jerusalem, Roth in a sort of recidivism returns to the passions of his youth with a "hero," Mickey Sabbath, certainly not in his first youth, but shall we say, still trying. *Sabbath's Theater*, a much admired book, is seriously filthy. *Portnoy's Complaint*, by comparison and to put the best face on it, is lads and lassies a-Maying. *Sabbath's Theater* is mud, a slough of obscenity with some lustrous pearls of antic writing embedded in it. The first line: "Either forswear fucking others or the affair is over." That is Drenka, a fifty-two-year-old Croatian voluptuary with ovarian cancer of which she dies, but not before thirteen years of insatiable carnality with Sabbath and more years than that with others.

Sabbath, now sixty-four, refuses to forswear, saying it would be repugnant to him to break the "sacrament of infidelity." And that is, perhaps, why he is given the name Sabbath, the day of worship, to suggest a sort of Black Mass of fucking. The world is out to crucify the master puppeteer of his Indecent Theater, but the aging, arthritic, disheveled puppeteer is irresistible to all except his wife Roseanna, who spends her days in an alcoholic stupor and when at last belligerently sober, by way of AA, takes off with a lesbian and often turns her thoughts to the penis clipper, the well-named Lorena Bobbitt.

Among the breathlessly accommodating are a Barnard girl; Christa, a runaway German au pair; and Rosa, a Spanish-speaking maid, "four childs," another in her belly; and a student at a liberal-arts college from which Sabbath is fired as an adjunct professor of puppet theater, owing to the discovery of a taped telephone conversation of outstanding lasciviousness, published in full at the bottom of the pages, a priapic academic footnote. This leads to an apologia, attributed to Sabbath, which can be attributed to the author, Philip Roth.

Not even Sabbath understood how he could lose his job at a liberal arts college for teaching a twenty-year-old to talk dirty twenty-five years

after Pauline Réage, fifty-five years after Henry Miller, sixty years after
D. H. Lawrence, eighty years after James Joyce, two hundred years after
John Cleland, three hundred years after John Wilmot, a second earl of
Rochester—not to mention four hundred after Rabelais, two thousand
after Ovid, and twenty-two hundred after Aristophanes.

To the challenge of white satin, spring flower epithalamia, the "realist" offers the rude, raging insistence of Nature. In Roth's novels, the
erotic pushes and thrusts where it will, even in imagination to the
iconic Anne Frank and Franz Kafka. In *The Ghost Writer*, a young female
student, a refugee from Europe at the time of the Holocaust, turns up
as an assistant to the esteemed writer Lonoff, living in Massachusetts,
the snowscape Yankeeland. Zuckerman, young and only on the first arc
of the happy curve of his talent, enters the shrine of literature as a
guest in Lonoff's house. He soon imagines the attractive assistant to be
a living Anne Frank, rescued from death only to be sent in the still of
the night to the bed of Lonoff, or he to her bed.

In *The Professor of Desire*, David Kepesh this time, rather than
Nathan Zuckerman, goes on a journey to Prague, the holy city of the
painfully reserved, tubercular genius, Franz Kafka. In a dream, a jeu
d'esprit, Kepesh is taken to see "Kafka's whore," a hideous old fraudulent tourist attraction, and a foul scene follows.

Sabbath's journey into the underworld is sex and death, the classical Manichaean union. He is haunted by his mother, who was haunted
by the death of his brother, Morty, shot down in the Philippines during World War II. Sabbath, at the end of his tether, or so you might put
it, masturbates and pisses on the grave of the exuberant Drenka of the
"uberous breasts." He is found there by her son, a cop, whose outrage
is so great he will not arrest or shoot him to death, as Sabbath wishes.
Let him lie in the muck. "You desecrate my mother's grave. You desecrate the American flag. You desecrate your own people. With your
stupid fucking prick out, wearing the skullcap of your own religion!"
So Sabbath is doomed to life. "He could not fucking die. How could he
leave? How could he go? Everything he hated was here." Here is
Drenka's cemetery, in America, in the spurious romanticism of lovemaking, marriage, fidelity? Sabbath and his theater of indecent pup-
pets like Drenka, Christa, and so on are not a happy band of buskers.
There is illness, prostate affliction, ovarian cancer, madness, drunkenness, the scars of his brother's death and his mother's annihilating grief.

Perhaps he is saying he cannot bring himself to suicide because of the life-giving force of hatred—an idea indeed. But it is not always useful to seek abstractions in fiction. When you turn to the last pages of *Sabbath's Theater* not much is clear beyond the anarchic brilliance of the swarm of characters, the rush of language, the willful chaos of the inspiration.

American Pastoral: Paradise remembered: The Fall; Paradise Lost in New Jersey, Philip Roth's singular turf, Newark "before the negroes," its raucous, fetid airs memorialized by his art as if they were the zephyrs in a sportsman's sketches. Zuckerman is called to tell the story of the fate of Seymour Levov, a supreme high-school athlete, called "the Swede." His is a life that began in gladness and came to an end in a conflagration of appalling desolation. The Levov family, the marriages, the children, the business, the houses are the landscape of toil and success, an ever-upward curve horribly deflected by the America of the 1960s. The elder Levov has through his unceasing labor and shrewdness, his toughness, built a business in the manufacture of ladies' gloves, the firm going by the name of Newark Maid Leatherwear.

Newark Maid at the time of the novel's action has moved to Puerto Rico, but the roots of the family go back to the old Levov grandfather, who arrived in America in the 1890s and "found work fleshing sheepskins fresh from the lime vat." The slow, punishing development of Newark Maid by Lou Levov, the father of Swede and his brother Jerry, is the ancestral cord of blood and sweat that will be broken in subtle ways by the agreeable Swede and in violent ways by the bomb-throwing murders committed by Swede's daughter, Merry, a child of the 1960s.

The elder Levov was "one of those slum-reared Jewish fathers whose roughhewn, undereducated perspective goaded a whole generation of striving, college-educated Jewish sons." Lou Levov went to work at the tannery at fourteen: "the tannery that stank of both the slaughterhouse and the chemical plant from the soaking of flesh and the cooking of flesh and the dehairing and pickling and degreasing of hides." At the workhouse, "the temperature [rises] to a hundred and twenty degrees... with hunks of skin all over the floor, everywhere pits of grease, hills of salt, barrels of solvent—this was Lou Levov's high school and college." The labor, powerfully imagined and researched here, brings to mind the Lower East Side tenements and the brutal hours at the sewing machines that led in time to the garment district on Seventh Avenue.

On the domestic scene, the increasing prosperity of Newark Maid gloves sends the Levov family from the streets of the lower- and middle-class Jews to "Keer Avenue . . . where the rich Jews lived." They become Keer Avenue Jews, "with their finished basements, their screened-in porches, their flagstone front steps, . . . laying claim like audacious pioneers to the normalizing American amenities." Swede, the athletic, tall, blond Levov, "as close to a goy as we were going to get," survives the Marine Corps, plays baseball at Upsala College in East Orange, New Jersey, turns down a club contract offer, and joins his father's business. And in a sort of sleepwalking way, out of natural inclination, he crossed a line—or what would seem to be a line to the old inbred Levovs: he married Miss New Jersey. "Before competing at Atlantic City for the 1949 Miss America title, she had been Miss Union County, and before that Spring Queen at Upsala. . . . A shiksa. Dawn Dwyer. He'd done it."

As the novel opens, the Swede is almost seventy, and he has sent a letter to the author, Zuckerman, asking for a dinner meeting. The old Levov had died at age ninety-six, and the son is struggling to write a memoir about him to be distributed to family and friends. He wants to discuss his father with Zuckerman, who is a friend from high-school days. In the note, he says about his father that he suffered "because of the shocks that befell his loved ones." Indeed, the shock that caused the old man to keel over dead was the discovery that Seymour's daughter, Merry, had, after a somewhat fortuitous connection with young radicals in New York City, fallen under the spell of violent resistance to society, the Vietnam War, rejection of family, the whole package. One early morning, she planted a bomb at the post office of her town and blew up the popular town doctor who was picking up his mail. She went into hiding at the home of her speech therapist, for little Merry suffered from a stutter; in time, she "connected" again and after robbery and rape and gross ill treatment took part in an "action" that killed three people in Oregon.

This is the fall, paradise lost, the dramatic center of the novel. Yes, it could have happened; young men and women better educated than Merry Levov blew up a house in Greenwich Village, killing some of their own, went underground, and later some of them, low on funds, held up a Brinks money truck, killed the black driver, and subsequently went off to jail. There are other bombings and deaths listed in the book. So poor Seymour, the Swede, still well meaning and now a suburbanite, must wake up one morning like the Mayor of Casterbridge and say: I am to suffer, I perceive.

The bomb-throwing plot is not altogether convincing on this particular stage. Merry must make a passage from her Audrey Hepburn scrapbook days to a loquacious, sneering radical life that has to be accepted as given. The most provocative shift in the portrait of Merry as a death-dealing 1960s revolutionary is that she later passes from radicalism to the old Indian religion of Jain, which sought to release the spirit from the bonds of the flesh. Merry adds her own self-destructive interpretations of Jain, with its passivity and pacifism. She eats almost nothing out of regard for the integrity of animals and also that of plants. When found by her father, she is shrunken, living in filth, wandering alone in dangerous spots of Newark with the serenity of the abandonment of selfhood. This reminds us of the cultist aspect of the American revolutionaries of the sixties, sometimes a small band bound together by their rants, paranoia, and above all the exaggeration of their power and the foolish underestimation of the power of society. Even the militia groups of the nineties with their guns and explosives are swollen with a cultish sense of empowerment, a poisonous edema of stockpiling, camaraderie on the rifle range—until the transition of indictment for murder turns them into whimpering, plea-bargaining, helpless victims of consequence. Little Merry Levov takes instead the spiritual life in a drastic extension, but Roth, if he must have her as a bomber, has shown imagination about the loss of revolutionary enthusiasm when the aftermath must be faced alone.

That the Levov family is to suffer, by way of Merry, a catastrophe remote in a statistical sense, undermines the interesting close calls on the road of the Swede's American journey. The Swede has made a right turn into the highway of assimilation and this, it appears, is the true direction of the novel's intellectual and fictional energy. First, the Swede has married the beauty queen, Dawn Dwyer, a Roman Catholic. Even though Dawn surreptitiously had Merry baptized in the faith, they are, in the words of Seymour's brother Jerry, a bullying, big-time coronary surgeon in Florida, a "knockout couple. The two of them all smiles in their outward trip into the USA. She's post-Catholic, he's post-Jewish, together they're going to go out there to Old Rimrock to raise little post-toasties."

Old Rimrock is a posh bit of the New Jersey countryside to which Seymour takes himself and Dawn in a sort of paroxysm of enthusiasm for open fields and great old trees. Old Rimrock in WASP, Republican Morris County. His father had wanted him to settle in a modern house in the "rock-ribbed, Democrat" Newstead Development, where he could live with his family among young Jewish couples. No, for the Swede it is to be a hundred acres of land, "a barn, a millpond, a mill-stream, the foundation remains of a gristmill that had supplied grain for Washington's troops." And an old stone house and a fireplace "large enough for roasting an ox, fitted out with an oven door and a crane to swing an iron kettle around over the fire." Why shouldn't it be his? Why shouldn't he own it? "Out in Old Rimrock, all of America lay at their door. That was an idea he loved. Jewish resentment, Irish resentment—the hell with it." Dawn is somewhat concerned with Protestant ill feeling about Catholics, but for the Swede, "the Protestants are just another denomination. Maybe they were rare where she grew up—they were rare where he grew up too—but they happen not to be rare in America. Let's face it, they *are* America."

In the 1940s, Jews might have felt some anxiety about their reception in a rich enclave of old-family inhabitants viewing them with condescension if not rudeness. Such would not be true today, when a Jewish media billionaire would, if such an opportunity arose in a period of regal retrenchment, be urged to buy an ancient bit of land in the woods of Windsor, where he could, on an occasional weekend, tramp about over the bones of Queen Victoria. In Old Rimrock, the Levovs make the acquaintance of an architect, Bill Orcutt, from a Morris County family that has filled the local cemetery with worthies for two hundred years.

The Swede, by the time he meets Zuckerman in a New York restaurant, has been divorced from Dawn and has a new wife and children; and Dawn, brought near to suicide by the cruel biography of her daughter, has returned to life with a Swiss face-lift and, in a thunderous rush of plot, made an alliance with the tombstone genealogist, Orcutt. It didn't work out, as the saying goes, the idyll of the young couple. Jerry, the angry sawbones brother, turns Merry in to the FBI, and along the way, driven by his fraternal jealousy of his paragon brother, denounces the life Swede and Dawn shaped for Merry. "Out there with Miss America, dumbing down and dulling out. Out there playing at being Wasps, a little Mick girl from the Elizabeth docks and a Jewboy from Weequahic High. The cows. Cow Society. Colonial old America. And you thought all that façade was going to come without a cost. Genteel and innocent. *But that costs, too, Seymour.* I would have thrown a bomb. I would become a Jain and live in Newark. That Wasp bullshit!" But Seymour in his love and grief for his daughter knows better. "It is chaos. It is chaos from start to finish." America gone berserk.

Among the ruins of time is the city of Newark, where Roth reared the author, Zuckerman, with his elegiac memories of interiors, "the microscopic surface of things close at hand ... the minutest gradations of social position conveyed by linoleum and oilcloth, by yahrzeit candles and cooking smells, by Ronson table lighters and venetian blinds." And outside, autumn afternoons on the football field; down the main drag to movies on a Saturday afternoon; record shops offering Glenn Miller; and at the high-school reunion, damaged faces that still carry the trace of teenage beauty.

When the Swede and Zuckerman meet so many years later, Newark has been the scene of devastating riots in 1967. It is now the "car theft capital of the world"; shops are boarded up; houses, once the shrines of relentless homemakers, are now smashed and splintered orphans; gunshots split the air, causing no more wonder than the screech of big trucks backing into parking spaces: Newark, long ago the little Jewish Eden of Roth's youth.

American Pastoral is a sort of Dreiserian chronicle of the Levov family. Their painfully built fortune, even without the disgrace, might have declined owing to obsolescence. Maids have not for some decades been in need of the finely stitched, soft leather gloves in matching colors. Gloves, except on the coldest winter days, have gone the way of the ribbon shops in the West Thirties of Manhattan, ribbon for hats that were to go on the heads of proper women whenever they left the house.

Still, the saga of the Levov family is a touching creative act and in the long line of Philip Roth fiction can be rated PG, suitable for family viewing—more or less.

(1997)

IN THE WASTELAND: JOAN DIDION

Joan Didion's novels are a carefully designed frieze of the fracture and splinter in her characters' comprehension of the world. To design a structure for the fadings and erasures of experience is an aesthetic challenge she tries to meet in a striking manner: the placement of sentences on the page, abrupt closures rather like hanging up the phone without notice, and an ear for the rhythms and tags of current speech that is altogether remarkable. Perhaps it is prudent that the central characters, women, are not seeking clarity since the world described herein, the America of the last thirty years or so, is blurred by a creeping inexactitude about many things, among them bureaucratic and official language, the jargon of the press, the incoherence of politics, the disastrous surprises in the mother-father-child tableau.

The method of narration, always conscious and sometimes discussed in an aside, will express a peculiar restlessness and unease in order to accommodate the extreme fluidity of the fictional landscape. You read that something did or did not happen; something was or was not thought; this indicates the ambiguity of the flow, but there is also in "did or did not" the author's strong sense of willful obfuscation, a purposeful blackout of what was promised or not promised—a blackout in the interest of personal comfort and also in the interest of greed, deals, political disguises of intention.

Joan Didion's novels are not consoling, nor are they notably attuned to the reader's expectations, even though they are fast paced, witty, inventive, and interesting in plot. Still, they twist and turn, shift focus and point of view, deviations that are perhaps the price or the reward that comes from an obsessive attraction to the disjunctive and paradoxical in American national policy and to the somnolent, careless decisions made in private life.

I have the dream, recurrent, in which my entire field of vision fills with rainbow, in which I open a door onto a growth of tropical green (I believe this to be a banana grove, the big glossy fronds heavy with rain, but since no bananas are seen on the palms symbolists may relax) and watch the spectrum separate into pure color. Consider any of these things long enough and you will see that they tend to deny the relevance not only of personality but of narrative, which makes them less than ideal images with which to begin a novel, but we go with what we have.

Cards on the table. (*Democracy*)

This writer is the poet, if you like, of the airplane and the airport. Offhand journeys to Malaysia or to troubled spots in Central America are undertaken as if one were boarding the New York–Washington shuttle. For the busy men, we learn somewhere in the pages that any flight under eight hours is called a "hop." So, we head out for the blue yonder by air as earlier novelists wrote of signing up for a term on ship. "Sailors are the only class of men who now-a-days see anything like stirring adventures; and many things which to the fire-side people appear strange and romantic, to them seem as common-place as a jacket out at elbows" (Melville, preface to *Typee*). Flying round the world every day is for her characters just a "jacket out at elbows." Nothing unusual. Trying to keep pace with an ethereal mobility now become as mundane as a dog trot is a mark of this writer's original sensibility: "She had been going from one airport to another for some months; one could see it, looking at the visas on her passport. . . . People who go to the airport first invent some business to conduct there. . . . Then they convince themselves that the airport is cooler than the hotel, or has superior chicken salad" (*A Book of Common Prayer*, 1977).

And from her most recent novel: *The Last Thing He Wanted*.

I see her standing in the wet grass off the runway, her arms bare, her sunglasses pushed up into her loose hair, her black silk shift wrinkled from the flight, and wonder what made her think a black silk shift bought off a sale rack at Bergdorf Goodman during the New York primary was the appropriate thing to wear on an unscheduled flight at one-thirty in the morning out of Fort Lauderdale–Hollywood International Airport, destination San Jose, Costa Rica but not quite.

Her first novel, *Run River,* appeared in 1963. It is rich in talent and also rich in the virtues of traditional fiction: families, generations, births and deaths, changes of fortune, betrayals. Set in the Sacramento Valley between 1938 and 1959, it begins with a gunshot: "Lily heard the shot at seventeen minutes to one." ("Seventeen minutes to one" brings to mind the surgical precision of the information that will be offered in the later fiction.) The intervening pages and chapters explain what went before the opening shot. In the final pages of the last chapter, we read, "She sat on the needlepoint chair until she heard it, the second shot." The first shot was the husband killing the wife's lover, and the second shot was the husband killing himself. Some families in *Run River* are descendants of the pioneers who made the trip of hardship and promise across the Great Plains. There are hardship passages in the subsequent fictions, although not in a covered wagon but in an airplane carrying your uncertain identity in a six-hundred-dollar handbag.

Her nerves are bad tonight in the wasteland of Haight-Ashbury; she has migraines, generalized and particular afflictions that bring on tears in "elevators and in taxis and in Chinese laundries." Joan Didion's revelation of incapacity, doubt, irresolution, and inattention is brought into question by the extraordinary energy and perseverance found in *Slouching Towards Bethlehem, The White Album,* and the later collection, *After Henry.* If she has "nerves," she also has "nerve" in the sense of boldness and fortitude. She will do the lowest work of a reporter; make the call, try again when the promised callback is not forthcoming. She scouts the neighborhood, finds the houses, and once inside notes the condition of the sink, the baby lying on a pallet and sucking its thumb, and the five-year-old on acid—"High Kindergarten." She spends time with Otto and Deadeye, among other stoned hippies; visits that need the self-denial of a Sister of Charity, although what she brings is a presence, free of strategies of redemption.

At three-thirty that afternoon Max, Tom and Sharon placed tabs under their tongue and sat down together in the living room to wait for the flash. Barbara stayed in the bedroom, smoking hash. During the next four hours a window banged once in Barbara's room.... A curtain billowed in the afternoon wind. Except for the sitar music on the stereo there was no other sound or movement until seven-thirty, when Max said, "Wow!" (*Slouching Towards Bethlehem*)

Moving down the coast from the numb deprivation of Haight-Ashbury to the alert consumerism of Ronald and Nancy Reagan in the governor's mansion in Sacramento and then in the White House, Didion finds them apart from the usual politicians who cherish, or so pretend, their early beginnings in Hyde Park, Kansas, or Plains, Georgia. The Reagans' habits, or perhaps their modes of operation, do not spring from marks left by their placement on the national map. The Reagans come from the welfare state of Dreamland; their roots are Hollywood.

This expectation on the part of the Reagans that other people would take care of their needs struck many people, right away, as remarkable and was usually characterized as a habit of the rich.... The Reagans were not rich; they and this expectation were the product of studio Hollywood, a system in which performers performed, and in return were cared for.... She [Nancy Reagan] was surprised to learn ("Nobody had told us") that she and her husband were expected to pay for their own food, dry cleaning, and toothpaste while in the White House. She seemed never to understand why it was imprudent of her to have accepted clothes from their makers when so many of them had encouraged her to do so.... The clothes were, as Mrs. Reagan seemed to construe it, "wardrobe"—a production expense, like the housing and catering and first-class travel and the furniture and paintings and cars that get taken home after the set is struck—and should rightly have gone to the studio budget. (*After Henry*)

Play It as It Lays (1970) is the first of the digressive, elusive novels, typical in style and organization of the challenging signature of a Joan Didion work. Shadowy motivation, disruptive or absent context in a paragraph or pages here and there are not properly to be read as indecision or compositional falterings. They display instead a sort of muscular assurance and confidence, or so one is led to believe in the face of a dominant, idiosyncratic style that if nothing else scorns the vexation of indolent or even sophisticated readers who prefer matters and manners otherwise expressed. But, as she says, we go with what we have. The author is in control of the invention, and if the machine is a little like an electric automobile or one running on pressed grapes instead of gasoline in a field of Chevrolets, the autonomy—it does run—puts the critic in an uneasy situation.

The opening sentence of *Play It as It Lays* is: "What makes Iago evil? Some people ask. I never ask."

"I never ask" is a useful introduction to Maria Wyeth: the sound of the extreme negativism, withdrawal, depression, or terminal disgust of this still young woman, a marginal figure in the movie business, brought up in Silver Wells, Nevada, by her drifting parents, divorced, finally in the book from her husband, a director. One might, however, question that the unanswerable evil of Iago would be on her mind, an evil that led even the great Coleridge to fall back upon "motiveless malignity." But who's to say she has not at a bar heard a discussion of the ecstatic treachery of Iago that makes its tragic progress to the suffering and death of Desdemona and Othello? It's just that the inclination to pedantry in instances of piddling, measly inconsequence are sometimes the only protection one has against the witchery of this uncompromising imagination, the settings so various and the sometimes sleepwalking players who blindly walk through windows and fall into traps of great consequence such as the Vietnam War or the world of the Contras.

The women in the novels suffer losses, serious blows from fate that enshroud them like the black dress European peasant women wear lifelong for bereavement; but they are not wearing a black dress except for stylish definition, like the black dress of Anna Karenina in her first appearance at the ball. Maria Wyeth in *Play It as It Lays* has a damaged daughter off somewhere in a hospital; she loves the girl obsessively, but there is no reciprocation from the screaming, indifferent child. Maria has had a cruel abortion. At the end of the book, a lover or sometime lover dies in her bed from an overdose of Valium, saying "because we've been out there where nothing is."

In *A Book of Common Prayer*, the daughter of Charlotte Douglas has disappeared and is wanted by the police for a political bombing. In

Democracy (1984), Inez Victor's daughter is a heroin addict and Inez's father, in an onset of lunacy, has killed her sister and another person. Inez has also had cancer. In *The Last Thing He Wanted,* Elena McMahon has lost her mother and in walking out on her rich husband has lost the affection of her daughter. The interior in which the women live is a sort of cocoon of melancholy, but their restlessness is modern and cannot be expressed like that of a country wife sighing at the moonlight as it hits the silence on the front porch. Maria Wyeth sleeps by her pool when she is not driving the L.A. freeways all night, stopping only for a Coke at a filling station. But she is driving a Corvette. The women have credit cards, bank drafts, an Hermès handbag, or a large emerald ring. In the heart of darkness, men fall in love with them, bereft and downhearted as they are. The sheen of glamour is useful to give entrance to the melancholy adulteries and to the plot of costly wild travels and also, in some cases, to politics that come out of the Oval Office or some room in the White House basement and turn up on the runway in Saigon or Costa Rica.

A Book of Common Prayer is a daring title, a risk, even, some would name a presumption. Perhaps the title is meant to bring to mind: "Have mercy on us in the hour of our death . . . *Prega per noi.*" Charlotte Douglas is wandering the earth by air, aimlessly hoping to run into her daughter, Marin, "who at eighteen had been observed with her four best friends detonating a crude pipe bomb in the lobby of the Transamerica Building at 6:30 AM, highjacking a P.S.A.L. 1011 at the San Francisco Airport and landing in Wendover, Utah, where they burned it in time for the story to interrupt the network news and disappeared." Charlotte Douglas goes to a miserable, corrupt little place called Boca Grande, an ungoverned and ungovernable country near Caracas. Her plane took her there with the blinkered idea that her daughter must be somewhere—and why not Boca Grande? Charlotte is killed by some machine-gun-toting activist in the almost weekly coups and countercoups. And meanwhile, Marin, the Berkeley Tupamaro, is actually in Buffalo. *A Book of Common Prayer* is an odd and most unusual study of secular violence and, in the case of the wandering mother, a sort of heathen inanition. Unable to think on the appalling plight of her daughter, Charlotte fills her mind with memories of her happy at the Tivoli Gardens in Copenhagen, devouring coconut ice under "the thousand trunks of Great Banyan at the Calcutta Botanical Garden."

Democracy: Washington, Honolulu, Hong Kong, Kuala Lumpur, Saigon, and Jakarta appear along the road in this novel of outlandish ambition, justified and honored by the scope, the subtlety, the agenda, as they call it. The time is 1975, the aftermath of Vietnam still in the air, and we go back to the way of setting the scene, a sort of computer lyricism:

> I would skim the stories on policy and fix instead on details: the cost of a visa to leave Cambodia in the weeks before Phnom Penh closed was five hundred dollars American. The colors of the landing lights for the helicopters on the roof of the American embassy in Saigon were red, white, and blue. The code names for the American evacuations of Cambodia and Vietnam respectively were EAGLE PULL and FREQUENT WIND. The amount of cash burned in the courtyard of the DAO in Saigon before the last helicopter left was three-and-a-half million dollars American and eighty-five million piastres. The code name for this operation was MONEY BURN. The number of Vietnamese soldiers who managed to get aboard the last American 727 to leave Da Nang was three hundred and thirty. The number of Vietnamese soldiers to drop from the wheel wells of the 727 was one. The 727 was operated by World Airways. The name of the pilot was Ken Healy.

One of the leading characters in the novel, Jack Lovett, is in love with Inez Victor, who is married to Harry Victor, a member of the United States Senate and a onetime candidate for president; easy to believe since it is the dream of everyone who has ever had a term in the state legislature of whatever state. Lovett is perhaps CIA but not a villain, instead a realist who can say, "A Laotian village indicated on one map and omitted on another suggested not a reconnaissance oversight but a population annihilated. Asia was ten thousand tanks here, three hundred Phantoms there. The heart of Africa was an enrichment facility." In these novels, you do not just take an airplane from Florida to Costa Rica, you board a Lockheed L-100; and in another aside, if such it is, you learn how to lay down the AM-2 aluminum matting for a runway and whether "an eight-thousand foot runway requires sixty thousand square yards of operational apron or only forty thousand."

This author is a martyr of facticity, and indeed such has its place in the fearless architecture of her fictions. You have a dogged concreteness of detail in an often capricious mode of presentation. The detail works upon the mind of the reader, gives an assurance, or at least a feeling, that somewhere, somehow all of this is true, fictional truth, or possibility. It could have happened, and Inez Victor did in fact go off to Kuala Lumpur to work in the refugee camps. And that is where we leave her after her love for Jack Lovett and after her escape from a somnambulistic time as a politician's wife who must say over and over, "Marvelous to be here," and be "smiling at a lunch counter in Manchester, New Hampshire, her fork poised over a plate of scrambled eggs and toast." That is, you may accept or allow for the aesthetically doubtful because of the interesting force of the factual in which it is dressed.

In any case, every page of the books is hers in its peculiarities and particulars: All is handmade, or should we say, hand cut, as by the knife of a lathe. Some unfriendly reviewers, knowing Didion has written screenplays, will call the frame or action cinematic. But the fictions, as she has composed them, are the opposite of the communal cathedrals, or little brown churches in the vale, built by so many willing slaves in Hollywood. The first cry of exasperation from the producers, script doctors, watchful money crunchers with memories of hits and flops would be, What's going on here? What's it about?

If you can believe that Robert "Bud" McFarlane, Reagan's national-security adviser, could fly off to Iran, carrying with him a cake and a Bible in order to make a deal for the shipment of arms to the Contras, you can believe the less bizarre happenings in *The Last Thing He Wanted*. In this novel, Joan Didion has placed a woman, Elena McMahon, on a plane filled with illegal arms bound for Costa Rica, or the off-the-map border installations set up by the Americans, the Freedom Fighters. At the end of the flight, she is to collect the million dollars owed her dying father, a man who does "deals." Collect the money and fly back, or so she has been led to imagine. In the usual percussive Didion dialogue, Elena says, "Actually I'm going right back. . . . I left my car at the airport." The pilot says, "Long time parking I hope." She doesn't return and at the end of an elaborate plot is assassinated by "the man on the bluff with the pony tail"—the same sinister man who had met her at the landing strip in Costa Rica.

And there is Treat Morrison, the romantic lead you might say, who first sees Elena McMahon in the coffee shop of the Intercontinental Hotel, where she was "eating, very slowly and methodically, first a bite of one then a bite of the other, a chocolate parfait and bacon." The odd menu is mentioned several times but does not give up its meaning beyond the fact that the parfait and bacon had bothered him, Treat Morrison. Morrison is an "ambassador at large" for the Department of State, a troubleshooter, a fixer. Like Jack Lovett in *Democracy*, this is another love-at-first-sight matter, and, odd as it might be, not necessarily as hard to imagine as some of the more portentous occasions. The attractions are ballads: I saw her standing there and my heart stood still—something like that. Treat Morrison and Jack Lovett are attractive men of the world, at work, as the collision of romance leads them to the forlorn, needy women standing there, waiting.

In *The Last Thing He Wanted*, Joan Didion appears on the page directing, filling in, being, often, a friend from the past or a journalist on the case. "For the record this is me talking. You know me, or think you do." Here she is a moralist, a student of the Contra hearings. "There are documents, more than you might think. Depositions, testimony, cable traffic, some of it not yet declassified, but much in the public record." Of course, Elena McMahon is a fiction, but we are to remember the actual people "all swimming together in the glare off the C-123 that fell from the sky into Nicaragua." Among those caught in the glare was "the blond, the shredder, the one who transposed the numbers of the account at the Credit Suisse (the account at the Credit Suisse into which the Sultan of Brunei was to transfer the ten million dollars, in case you have forgotten the minor plays)."

The Last Thing He Wanted is a creation of high seriousness, a thriller composed with all the resources of a unique gift for imaginative literature, American literature. There remains in Didion's far-flung landscapes a mind still rooted in the American West from which she comes. When in *Slouching Towards Bethlehem* she visits the venerable piles in Newport, Rhode Island, she remembers the men who built the railroad, dug the Comstock Lode for gold and silver in Virginia City, Nevada, and made a fortune in copper.

More than anyone else in the society, these men had apparently dreamed the dream and made it work. And what they did then was to build a place which . . . led step by step to unhappiness, to restrictiveness, to entrapment in the mechanics of living. In that way the lesson of Bellevue Avenue is more seriously radical than the idea of Brook

Farm. . . . Who could think that the building of a railroad could guarantee salvation, when there on the lawns of the men who built the railroad nothing is left but the shadow of the migrainous women, and the pony carts waiting for the long-dead children?

She is saying that Bellevue Avenue in Newport is not what the West was won for.

(1997)

Reckless People: Richard Ford

From the stories in Richard Ford's collection *Rock Springs* (1987): "This was not going to be a good day in Bobby's life, that was clear, because he was headed to jail. He had written several bad checks, and before he could be sentenced for that he had robbed a convenience store with a pistol—completely gone off his mind." Bobby's ex-wife is giving him his last breakfast, and the man she is now living with is telling the story, with some disgruntlement ("Sweethearts").

In the title story, the narrator, Earl, with his daughter, Cheryl, her dog, Little Duke, and Earl's girlfriend, Edna, are driving through Wyoming in a stolen car.

> I'd gotten us a good car, a cranberry Mercedes I'd stolen out of an opthalmologist's lot in Whitefish, Montana. I stole it because I thought it would be comfortable over a long haul, because I thought it got good mileage, which it didn't, and because I'd never had a good car in my life.

The car develops trouble in the oil line, and they have to abandon it in the woods. Somehow, the little group gets to a Ramada Inn, and after a bit of food and lovemaking Edna accepts Earl's offer of a bus ticket and takes off.

There he is, Earl, with Cheryl, the dog, and no car. They might as well be a stone urn of wilting geraniums outside the inn. In the dark of night in the parking lot: "I walked over to a car, a Pontiac with Ohio tags, one of the ones with bundles and suitcases strapped to the top and a lot more in the trunk, by the way it was riding." Standing beside the car, Earl's inner soliloquy runs:

> What would you think a man was doing if you saw him in the middle of the night looking in the windows of cars in the parking lot of the Ramada Inn? Would you think he was trying to get his head cleared? Would you think he was trying to get ready for a day when trouble would come down on him? Would you think his girlfriend was leaving him? Would you think he had a daughter? Would you think he was anybody like you?

Another story, "Optimists," begins: "All of this I am about to tell you happened when I was only fifteen years old, in 1959, the year my parents were divorced, the year when my father killed a man and went to prison for it, the year I left home and school, told a lie about my age to fool the Army, and then did not come back." The father was working in the railroad yards when a hobo tried to jump off a train and was cut into three pieces. The father comes home ashen and trembling from the horrible accident he has seen. At home some recent acquaintances of his wife are playing cards. The visitor, more or less a stranger to the father, turns out to work for the Red Cross. He interrupts with a pedantic interrogation about tourniquets, resuscitation, all the while insisting that technically, as it were, the hobo didn't have to die had the father acted properly.

In a rage of grief and at the presumption of the lecture, the father hits the man, who is killed by the blow. The father goes to prison, comes out in a state of deterioration, begins drinking and brawling, and disappears off somewhere. The years pass, and one day the son sees his mother with a strange man shopping for groceries at a mall. The son and mother talk briefly, but with a good deal of inchoate affection. And that is more or less it. "And she bent down and kissed my cheek through the open window and touched my face with both her hands, held me for a moment that seemed like a long time before she turned away, finally, and left me there alone."

The smooth and confident use of the first-person narration in these brilliant stories is especially remarkable when they are told by petty thieves, the stranded and delinquent. Here the "I" is not remembering or recasting but living in the pure present, in the misbegotten events of the day. The focus is of such directness, the glare of reality so bright, that the shadow of the manipulating author does not fall inadvertently on the deputed "I"—who is in no way a creature of literary sensibility. The tone and the rhythm of the composition, the feat of being inside the minds or the heads as they make their deplorable decisions infuse the pages with a kind of tolerance for false hope and felony and rotten luck.

The Montana landscape in *Rock Springs* is empty and beautiful and lonely. The men do whatever kind of work turns up and are always being laid off. There is nothing but hunting and fishing, sex, and drinking and fighting. Wives go off to Seattle or Spokane, just for a change. Young girls and not-so-young men turn up in the taverns and get into a lot of trouble for themselves and others. So your wife has taken off with a groom from the dog track, and a couple of huge, rough women turn up at your door with a deer gruesomely slain lying in their pickup; and you will be glad for their knock, for the company, which will be a mistake. Recklessness is the mode of life, but what the stories seem to be saying is that people are not always as bad as what they do, something like that. No judgment is solicited, and yet the desperation and folly arouse pity, the pity that everywhere sends girlfriends, mothers and children, grandparents and old pals trundling out to the prisons for visiting hours.

In the novel *Wildlife* (1990), a son is the observer of the sudden defections and panics of his parents. "In the fall of 1960, when I was sixteen and my father was for a time not working, my mother met a man named Warren Miller and fell in love with him." The tactful, muted eloquence of the tone is a sort of balance for the unstable inner and natural landscape. It is Great Falls, Montana, and the forest fires of summer are still smoking and glowing in the autumn sky. The parents have lived and been to college in Washington State and have come to Montana from Idaho, thinking money could be made from the oil boom. But prosperity does not extend itself to them, and so the father works at the air base two days a week and otherwise as a golf pro at the local country club. He is rudely laid off at the club because of a false accusation. In Ford's fiction, the West, with its fabled openness under the big sky and all that, is a place of emotional collapse from forced or glumly accepted idleness, an invitation to dangerous brooding over the whiskey bottle. After such an acute brooding and character upheaval the father somehow gets a chance to save his soul, or self-image, by being allowed to take a place with the knowledgeable firefighters in the forest, although he had no experience beyond the flaming egos on the golf course.

The mother is alone for three days. She and the son visit the voracious Warren Miller, a man with a limp and soon to die of a "lengthy illness," a man with lots of money, grain elevators, and other assets, and a wife who has gone off somewhere—a man with a house. In the house, the mother and son spend the night after the older folks have been drinking and dancing. The unresisting mother is seduced on the spot, decides to leave her husband and set herself up in a rented flat, there to accommodate what she foolishly believes will be a better life with Warren Miller. Shifts in direction, improvisations, sleepwalking into calamitous consequence seem to be in the fiction part of the effect the Western states have upon the mind. The characters are still pulling the wagon across the frontier, looking for a place to settle.

The father comes down from the burning hills to meet his domestic surprise. In a fury ignited by betrayal and alcohol, he picks up a can of gasoline at a local pump and, thinking his wife is inside, sets fire to Miller's house; the fire is not serious and no charges are filed. Indeed, Miller fled the scene with another woman in tow, not the wife. After some years of wandering, the mother returns to Great Falls, and the son reflects that something has died between them but something remained. "We survived it." A benign accent in the style of narration covers *Wildlife* in a forgiving mist. The quiet pacing through the threat of the landscape and the predatory challenge of experience is a compromise, the rain falling on the blackened trees.

Before he went West, so to speak, in his stories and in *Wildlife*, Richard Ford had published three books of fiction: *A Piece of My Heart* (1976), *The Ultimate Good Luck* (1981), and *The Sportswriter* (1986). *A Piece of My Heart* is an elaborate, stylistically ambitious, and complex novel, somewhat in the Southern Gothic vein. The setting is Mississippi, and there are two old people in their decayed mansion, the man a relentlessly loquacious, cursing, shrewd old fellow. The estate is connected by boat to an island where people from town pay to hunt duck and for the turkey shoot in season. Two young men, each of whom has an alternating section of the book, come to the spread. One is a Columbia graduate student enrolled in the University of Chicago Law School; he's in a slump, and his girlfriend thinks that, since he is a native Mississippian, he might pull himself together by a spell at the estate owned by a relation of hers. This character, perhaps an echo of Faulkner's Quentin Compson, is not entirely successful, owing to the mingled yarn in the knit of his rather far-flung situation.

The other young man, named Robard, could be a character in one of the stories in *Rock Springs*. His fate is powerfully and alarmingly conceived in the intense thicket of the action. Robard wakes up in the dark of early morning, looks at his wife peacefully sleeping, and, although he has gentle feelings for her, takes off without leaving a word. His journey, his hardscrabble trek to the swamp of sex, has come about from a curious, oblique feeling of obligation to experience. Some years before, Robard had picked up a young woman on the road when her car broke down. They ended up in a motor court for a raw, lascivious night or two, and for Robard that was the end of it, but not for her, Beuna by name. Beuna is a seriously dreadful encounter, a sex fiend, a sort of barnyard creature of befoulment.

Time has passed, and Beuna is married to W.W., a broken-down bush-league ballplayer and deputy sheriff. Beuna does not find much satisfaction in W.W., and since she knows where Robard lives, she begins to send messages to him and to make disturbing phone calls, delivered with a panting absolute demand for a reunion. Robard finally takes off to meet her. His emotions are murky and guarded, and he means to return. Beuna's insistence over the weeks and months gives Robard the sense that something has entered his life he can't altogether deny. He is broke, and to complete his destiny he takes a job at the estate, acting as a guard on the island to keep poachers away.

His true "business," as he calls it, is to go into town in the evening to find Beuna. They meet and bed down in a scabby rent-a-cabin place, where she says the proprietor wouldn't care if you took a "goddamn sheep in here." For the tryst, Beuna has brought a plastic bag of excrement. There is a merciful blackout of the subsequent congress, but at last it is the cue for Robard to climb out of the pit of eros, find his truck, and get back to the island. W.W. is nosing after him in his Plymouth, shotgun at the ready. Almost free of the pursuing furies, Robard meets his death, his release, when he is thought to be a poacher and shot by a boy who is taking his place as guard on the island.

The backcountry landscape, the waters of the river at night, the woods, the sullen towns are rendered with a tireless fluency. As a principal in a sordid tangle of compulsion, Robard, nevertheless, is conceived in tragic terms and is the most touching of Richard Ford's doom-stricken young men, rushing to certain destruction, to Beuna, who, by the unfortunate meeting on the road, has become "a piece of my heart."

Ford's second novel, *The Ultimate Good Luck,* is another trip altogether, this time to Mexico, around Oaxaca. It is a steamy ride through the south-of-the-border labyrinth, with characters who are defined by situation, plot, intrigue, and dénouement. They have a certain brittleness as they act out their roles; and there is a cinemanoir aspect to the landscape of drug smuggling, prisons, bribery, disappearances, threats of murder, and actual murder. Quinn, a Vietnam vet, and his mistress or whatever, Rae, are engaged in an effort to get Rae's brother, Sonny, out of the hell of a Mexican prison. Sonny has been picked up for drug smuggling, and his escape or release is to be accomplished by bribery, mysterious connections, and enigmatic maneuvers under the direction of a shadowy lawyer named Bernhardt, who, along the way, is murdered for his efforts in the matter or perhaps for some other malfeasance.

The language of the novel is rich; there is, or so it seems, a haunting absorption of the countryside, the bars, the alleys, the prison, the midnight world. No one is sympathetic; there's not much to be said for Quinn, and Rae, embarked on her act of charitable rescue, is stoned most of the time. Sonny is not an object of moral concern since he is stupid, greedy, and a natural loser. *The Ultimate Good Luck* has a curious sheen of high glamour as a genuinely imaginative example of a genre, if that is the proper word for this visit to the underworld.

The Sportswriter followed the first two novels and preceded the Western stories and *Wildlife.* Frank Bascombe is a sportswriter, living by choice in Haddam, New Jersey, a pleasant suburban town of moderate physical and social dimensions, suitable to Bascombe's moderate expectations from life. He has published a book of stories that did moderately well, started and abandoned a novel, and is moderately content to be something of an oddity in the arts, where an early kiss from the Muse is likely to leave a lifelong discoloration on the cheek. He is not a failed writer but one who fails to write another fiction or poem. What is to prevent your writing, dear? the forlorn wife in George Gissing's *New Grub Street* asks of her miserable husband trapped in the period of the three-decker novel. Bascombe's answer would have been a cheer-ful I prefer not to.

But even Bascombe's cheerfulness is moderated by the dark wings of melancholy after the death of his son Ralph and the divorce from his wife, here called X. The most remarkable aspect of this engaging character is his remove from paranoia, the national and literary mode of the time. Bascombe is offered a job on a well-known sports magazine, published in New York, to which he chooses to commute. Needless to say, he does not take sports or sportswriting with undue seriousness.

> I make my other calls snappy—one is to an athlete shoe designer in Denver for a "Sports Chek" round-up box I'm pulling together on foot injuries.... Another call is to a Carmelite nun in Fayetteville, West Vir-ginia, who is trying to run in the Boston Marathon. Once a polio vic-tim, she is facing an uphill credentials fight in her quest to compete, and I'm glad to put a plug in for her in our "Achievers" column.

The scene shifts, as it often does in this work crowded with incidents and people met along the way, this time to a trip to Detroit to interview Herb Wallagher, an ex-lineman who lost his legs in a ski-boat accident and is now in a wheelchair. The interview is not profitable, even though the sportswriter tires to rouse Herb about the game of football: "But I'd still think it had some lessons to teach to the people who played it. Perseverance. Team work. Comradeship. That kind of thing." To which, Herb replies: "Forget all that crap, Frank."

The trip to Detroit is made with Vicki, cute and with far greater common sense than Bascombe, she being a nurse. She talks about a "C-liver terminal, already way into uremia when he was admitted, which is not *that* bad cause it usually starts 'em dreamin about their pasts and off their current problem." Scenes and characters flow into this suburban novel on the wide stream of Bascombe's obstinate re-ceptiveness. The Divorced Men's Club, which Bascombe attends, brings him into an encounter with poor Walter Luckett, whose wife has taken off to Bimini with a man named Eddie Pitcock. Walter has a se-cret he wants to share. After a few drinks with a Wall Street colleague, he finds himself going to bed with him in the fellow's New York apart-ment, not once but again and again. Walter is troubled and as naive as a country-boy sailor on his first shore leave in Naples. In what could be called a sentimental confusion, for that is his nature, he commits suicide one night.

One of the most brilliant scenes is Bascombe's Easter Sunday visit with Vicki's family. Her father, a turnpike toll-taker, has somehow gotten an old Chrysler into his small, wet basement and is restoring it fin by fin, with full attention to broken and rusted chrome. Her brother, Cade, a boat mechanic, is on the waiting list at the Police Academy. Cade has already "developed a flat-eyed officer's uninterest for the peculiarities of his fellow man." Lynette, the father's second wife, is working on the crisis line at the Catholic church. She has "transformed her dining room into a hot little jewel box, crystal-candle chandelier, best silver and linens laid" for "the pallid lamb congealed and hard as a wood chip and the . . . peas and broccoli flower alongside it cold as Christmas." In the midst of all this, Bascombe's thought is: "What strange good luck to be reckoned among these people like a relative welcome from Peoria."

The Sportswriter is a sophisticated book that celebrates life as it comes and speaks in its voice, often with devastating humor. Easter Sunday: "the optimist's holiday, the holiday with the suburbs in mind." The sermon about the Resurrection: "Well now, let's us just hunker down to a *real* miracle, while we're putting two and two together. . . . Let's just let plasma physics and bubble chambers and quarks try to explain *this* one." The vitality of the novel lies in the freedom and expressiveness of this first-person excursion through New Jersey, Detroit, the Berkshires, and the bearable shambles of Bascombe's life.

Independence Day, Richard Ford's most recent novel, returns to Frank Bascombe. *Rabbit Redux?*—not quite. Bascombe is an upscale ruminant, now in his forties, with opinions about everything, and Emerson's "Self-Reliance" in the glove compartment. There is no outstanding typicality in him; instead, he has the mysteriousness of the agreeable, nice person, harder to describe than the rake, the miser, or the snob. As a professional, or as a working man, his résumé is unsteady: short-story writer, sportswriter, and now a "realtor." The wobbly nature of Bascombe's status makes him a creditable collector; nothing need be rejected, not the trash of the road signs, clichés produced with a ring of discovery, the program on TV, the decor of the Sleepy Hollow Motel on Route 1, or the "fanlights, columned entries and Romany-fluting" of the houses on the better streets.

Selling real estate is a good way to get about town but a poor way to reach "closure." The business is a serial plot of indignities—tune in tomorrow. Joe and Phyllis Markham have decided to get out of their hand-built house in Vermont, "with cantilevered cathedral ceilings and a hand-laid hearth and chimney, using stones off the place," to try a suburban New Jersey lifestyle and better schools for their daughter. They "have looked at forty-five houses—dragging more and more grimly down from . . . Vermont." The fearsome negotiations, or lack of them, provide a miserably comic underpinning to Bascombe's days and nights.

The other block of the story is a hazardous trip, a Fourth of July journey with his son, Paul, to the Basketball Hall of Fame in Springfield, Massachusetts, and the Baseball Hall of Fame in Cooperstown, New York, where they stay in The Deerslayer Lodge. Paul is a thoroughly complicated and unpredictable young man of fifteen. He has stolen boxes of condoms, for which he had no use, from a pharmacy; he barks like a dog in memory of his dead dog and probably in memory of his dead brother, Ralph. Underneath his basket of misdemeanors and off-tone noises, he is a gentle teenager and will probably come to resemble his father's more acceptable waywardness. At the Baseball Hall of Fame, Paul seriously damages an eye in the batter's cage, a tourist attraction that allows one to seem to swat a ball like Babe Ruth. His mother, now remarried to a rich architect, comes up in a helicopter and takes him to New Haven for surgery.

There are many other diversions: Sally, Bascombe's girlfriend, the renters of a house he owns, old friends, or a new passerby. And as always with Richard Ford, the sense of place, towns, houses, highways is luminous in lavish, observed detail.

I drive windingly out Montmorency Road into Haddam horse country—our little Lexington—where fences are long, white and orthogonal, pastures wide and sloping, and roads . . . slip across shaded, rocky rills via wooden bridges and through the quaking aspens back to rich men's domiciles snugged deep in summer foliage. . . . And here, wedges of old-growth hardwoods still loom, trees that saw Revolutionary armies rumble past, heard the bugles, shouts and defiance cries of earlier Americans in their freedom swivet, and beneath which now tawny-haired heiresses in jodhpurs stroll to the paddock with a mind for a noon ride alone.

In passing, it might be remarked that Ford is the first, if memory serves, to give full recognition to the totemic power in American life of the telephone and the message service. At one point, he pauses at the Vince Lombardi Rest Area, across from Giants Stadium, to check his messages. There are ten of them, listed with content, among them obscenities from Joe Markham, client. Often, Bascombe will interrupt the plot to make a dreamy call to a former lover, who might not immediately place him or might be cooking dinner. In *The Sportswriter*, the call is to Selma, a friend from his spell as a teacher at Berkshire College. In *Independence Day*, he gets on the line to Cathy, a medical student he spent time with in France a few years back. He's hoping for "a few moments out of context, ad hominem, pro bono phone treatment." Ring, ring, ring, click, click, click, and the machine answers: "Hi. This is Cathy and Steve's answering mechanism. We're not home now. Really. I promise." In Frank Bascombe's world, a good deal of the information necessary to move forward is given over the phone.

(Recently, in the O. J. Simpson criminal trial, the prosecution, following week after wearying week, month after month building its beaver dam of circumstantial particulars, spent quite a lot of time with the record of Simpson's car phone around the time projected for the murders. The record keeper for the phone company dutifully went down the list, the purpose seeming to be that the number of busy signals and no answers might slip into the minds of the jurors as yet another twig in a rage that led to double homicide.)

Independence Day, if you're taking measurements like the nurse in a doctor's office, might be judged longer than it need be. But longer for whom? Every rumination, each flash of magical dialogue or unexpected mile on the road with a stop at the pay phone, is a wild surprise tossed off by Richard Ford's profligate imagination as if it were just a bit of cigarette ash. *The Sportswriter* and *Independence Day* are comedies—not farces, but realistic, good-natured adventures, sunny, yes, except when the rain it raineth every day. The new work, *Independence Day*, is the confirmation of a talent as strong and varied as American fiction has to offer.

(1995)

LIVES

KATHERINE ANNE PORTER

Katherine Anne Porter died at the age of ninety. She had one of those very long lives the sickly, with their bronchial troubles and early threats of tuberculosis, achieve as a surprise to us and perhaps to themselves. It was just two years ago, in September 1980, that she died and now we have a biography devoted to this long life.

Biographers, the quick in pursuit of the dead, research, organize, fill in, contradict, and make in this way a sort of completed picture puzzle with all the scramble turned into a blue eye and the parts of the right leg fitted together. They also make a consistent fiction, the fiction being the arrangement, artful or clumsy, of the documents. Biography casts a chill over the late years of some writers and, perhaps from their reading the lives of those they had known in the too solid flesh, has often provoked the insistent wish that no life be written. Among those who wished for no life after life were W. H. Auden, George Orwell and T. S. Eliot. The result has been two lives already of Auden and Orwell, and Eliot's life is in the making, waiting to be lived again by way of the flowing bloodstream of documentation.

Sometimes very fine writers and scholars undertake biographies, and their productions have at least some claim to equity between the subject and the person putting on the shoes. Others hope to establish credentials previously lacking by hard work on the abounding materials left by a creative life. In any case, a biography appears to be thought of as a good project, one that can at the very least be accomplished by industry. And if there is a lot of busywork in it—many visits to the libraries, a store of taped interviews, and, of course, the "evidence" of the writer's work itself (the last rather a difficulty since it is not precisely to be understood by research)—the book gets written, and the "life of" is, so to speak, born.

In her eighty-sixth year, Katherine Anne Porter appointed Joan Givner to undertake the re-creation of her many decades. The biographer might be thought to be in luck since Miss Porter advised her to "get at the truth," an always murky command when ordered on one's own behalf. The real luck about the truth turned out to be that the distinguished writer was unusually inclined to fabrication about her past. These fabrications, dashing often and scarcely news and only mildly discrediting, seem to be the driving engine behind Joan Givner's accumulation of the facts of life.

How certain human beings are able to create works of art is a mystery, and why they should wish to do so, at a great cost to themselves usually, is another mystery. Works are not created by one's life; every life is rich in *material*. By the nature of the enterprise, the contemporary biographer with his surf of Xerox papers is doing something smaller and yet strikingly more detailed than the great Victorian laborers in the form. Our power of documentation has a monstrous life of its own, a greater vivacity than any lived existence. It makes form out of particles and finds attitude in a remembered drunken remark as easily as in a long contemplation of experience—more easily in fact. It creates out of paper a heavy, obdurate permanency. Threats to its permanency will come only by way of other bits of paper, a footnote coup d'état. No matter—a territory once colonized in this way has had its indigenous landscape and culture put to the heel.

In Joan Givner's book, the root biographical facts have the effect of a crushing army. Everything is underfoot. Each character and each scene of Miss Porter's fiction is looked upon as factuality honored by its provenance as autobiography. And separate fictions are mashed together as bits of the life recur or are suggested in different works. Miss Porter, in a manner impertinently thought of as dilatory, did not often translate experience in a sequential fashion. So she is writing *Hacienda* while she is "living" *The Leaning Tower*. She is boarding the ship of fools before the Mexican stories have been accomplished. It is something of a tangle to get this particular life and its laggard production into time slots, and the result is an incoherence in regard to the work. Information about when each story was actually completed, when published and where, is lost in the anecdote of days and nights. No doubt the information is somewhere among the pages, but it is a slogging task to dig it out.

The life—some scandal and a considerable amount of folly: Katherine Anne Porter was born in a log cabin in Texas and grew up in hardship without a really good education. She knew a genuine struggle to provide for herself and slowly to define herself. Gradually, along the way, after her stories became known, she slipped into being a Southern belle and into being to some extent a Southern writer after *Flowering Judas*. The role was there for the choosing since to be a belle and to be a Southern writer is a decision, not a fate. (Poe, for instance, was a Southerner but not a Southern writer.) Perhaps under the influence of the very talented Southern Agrarians—Allen Tate, Caroline Gordon, and others—she began to appropriate a rather frantic genealogy of Daniel Boone and certain Southern statesmen; in addition, she developed some soothing memories of plantation dining rooms, "several Negro servants, among them two aged former slaves," and so on. In this way, she filled in the gap between what she was and what she felt like.

She was handy, too, in disposing of the traces of her various mismatings, the first a marriage at sixteen. "I have no hidden husbands," she once said. "They just slipped my mind." She was beautiful, a spendthrift, an alert coquette, and, since she lived long, a good many of her lovers and three of her husbands were younger than she was. She lopped off a few years here and there. The book goes into a determined sorting out, and the husbands are lined up, the years restored.

Her serious work was slow in coming about because of a scratchy, hard life after she literally ran away from her first husband—just ran off, as they say. She tried acting, did very provincial newspaper work and finally got a job on the *Denver Post*. Everything was hard, poorly paid, hand-to-mouth. During this period, she seems quite Western or Middle Western, like someone in a Willa Cather story trying to find the way out. Her story "Maria Concepción" was published when she was thirty-four, and her first book, *Flowering Judas*, appeared when she was forty. Fortunately for her future work, she went to Mexico as a reporter; she was in and out of Greenwich Village, where she met writers and no doubt increased her sophistication about literature and the act of writing.

At this point, the shape of her life falls into a sort of twenties pattern. She went to France and to Germany with her third husband, Eugene Pressly—her second husband, a person named Ernest Stock, "deadly Ernest," as she called him, having been run away from while he was sleeping. In Mexico, she met the Russian film director Eisenstein; in Germany in 1932 she met Göring; in Paris, she met Hemingway. Eisenstein became Uspensky in *Hacienda*, the ship upon which she traveled from Mexico to Germany became the *Vera* in *Ship of Fools*. In Berlin, she stayed on alone, having encouraged Pressly to return to America for a holiday without her. She never liked the constant presence of her husbands or lovers and did not like, she soon found out, to be alone—a dilemma in one shape or another common to most of mankind. The pension where she stayed in Germany went, with little need for renovation, into *The Leaning Tower*.

Research finds that in Germany, Katherine Anne Porter did not always conduct herself with generosity or moral refinement. She had a young friend, Herb Klein, a newspaper reporter, who tells years later of her leaving a seamstress without paying for a dress she had ordered—leaving the dress, too—and in this way embarrassing Klein's mother, who had brought the two together. He also discredits her claim to have met Hitler and feels strongly that she did not move widely or knowledgeably about the Germany of the time. So, a little more unstitching of the embroidery here.

Also, and again many decades later, she made in an interview slanderous, nasty remarks about Sigrid Schultz, a reporter in Berlin in the thirties for the *Chicago Tribune*. All of this, no doubt rightly, brings on a fit of temper by the biographer, who finds that the German experience, as the chapter is called, "forms a dismal record of cheating, lying, slander and malice." She sees ruthlessness, alienation (?), and brutality at the "beginning of her fifth decade." Garrulousness and a certain untidiness in 1932 are excavated and rebuked in 1982, showing at least one of the dangers of living. The celebrated do not understand that they are chatting away in a bugged universe.

The few times in the biography that a particular work comes under Joan Givner's critical scrutiny—divorced for the moment from her main concern, which is the presumed umbilical attachment of life and fiction—the same inclination to outrage flares up. She finds Braggioni, the revolutionary in *Flowering Judas,* to be a "complete caricature." She adds that he "looms in the story like a grotesque Easter egg in shades of purple and yellow."

Katherine Anne Porter wrote:

He bulges marvelously in his expensive garments. Over his lavender collar, crushed under a purple necktie, held by a diamond hoop; over his ammunition belt of tooled leather worked in silver, buckled crudely around his gasping middle; over the tops of glossy yellow shoes Braggioni swells with ominous ripeness.

So, the animadversion of the biographer is not quite to the descriptive point. And to be a revolutionary is in some sense to assume a pose. Costume, gesture, personal style, slogan, poster become personification of idea, especially in Latin America.

Perhaps in this remarkable early story, the pure, tasteful, puritan elegance of the American girl, Laura, is somewhat extended beyond credibility. Yet this girl, who has been born a Catholic and is now living among the Mexican revolutionaries, provides an outstanding instance of the magical detail that gives the stories their preeminence.

Laura sometimes slips into church, but no suitable emotions come to her. "It is no good and she ends by examining the altar with its tinsel flowers and ragged brocades, and feels tender about the battered doll-shape of some male saint whose white, lace-trimmed drawers hang limply around his ankles below the hieratic dignity of his velvet robe." It is not always clear that the biographer understands the elegance of the prose. Instead, she knows from her file cabinet that it was Mary Doherty, an interesting radical living in Mexico, who was probably the model for Laura.

On the subject of Adam, the young soldier in *Pale Horse, Pale Rider,* Mrs. Givner is also casually dismissive: "An insubstantial figure, completely lacking in vivid details and turns of phrase that usually animate the characters based on people whom Porter knew." "Completely" implies the self-evident in what is a sketchy opinion. The young soldier who is to die of influenza after looking after and being enchanted by the infected Miranda—who does not die but recovers—is necessary to the structure of the story. He serves it well by the charm of his dialogue; the irony of the romantic, accommodating American gives a tragic force to this thoughtful creation about a moment in history, the devastating influenza epidemic of 1918.

The influenza epidemic, Mexico in the days of the Revolution and after, the feeling of World War I, Berlin in the thirties, the Irish in America: The situations in Katherine Anne Porter's stories show the unexpected felicities of "homelessness." Afterward, she came to disown the log cabin that sent her out to the highway, and she fell back, still with her stylistic gracefulness, on nostalgia and memory, or the aura of it, of a more traditional kind.

In what are called the "Miranda" stories, Miranda seems to stand for the author's sensibility, if not for the actual author. These stories often combine scenes contemporary with Miranda's (Porter's) life mixed with family anecdotes about dead relations—the "old order." The old order is a cavalier landscape of powerful grandmothers; a former slave, Old Nannie; the scandalous, bewitching Aunt Amy; the little girls, Miranda and her sister; their attractive father who reads from Spenser, Shakespeare, and Dante and brightens their childhood with prints from Dürer and Holbein—all the pleasant baggage, supposedly, of the old Southern aristocracy. It does not seem to the point that this was not the author's life, that it is a burial of the detested log cabin in which she was born. The eye that looks across the track might be dangerous to Southern presumption, but what we have so often in the "old order" work is an eye that is too readily assimilating. Miranda's present is nearly always more vivid and original than her past. The present is harder, more shaded with sadness and uneasy defiance, and in the long run more genuinely dramatic. "Old Mortality" is elevated as a conception by the bitter alcoholic collapse of Uncle Gabriel, his decline into a brilliantly observed social seediness by way of his hysterical, misplaced hopes at the racetrack.

"Noon Wine" is a success indeed, a story of plot, a sort of realistic tale, tightly composed in the manner of *Ethan Frome*. In this story, felt to be odd because of the backwoods setting, there is no doubt that Porter knows where she is. She knows in transfiguring detail what a dairy farm is like. "The churn rumbled and swished like a belly of a trotting horse." And hens "dying of croup and wryneck and getting plagues of chicken lice; laying eggs all over God's creation so that half of them were spoiled before a man could find them, in spite of a rack of nests." If this knowledge came from the time she lived on a relative's farm outside Buda, Texas, and from certain characteristics in the dairy farmer, Mr. Thompson, that can be traced to her own father—"ambivalence" toward whom figures gravely in the biographer's grave quilt of patches—that is only the beginning. The story has its roots in pioneer and rural American fiction and even in Faulkner. The ancestry of literature is, of course, another story of kinfolk.

Katherine Anne Porter, from the first appearance of her stories, made her mark and impressed other writers by the way she wrote. It is not easy to define her purity of style. The writing is not plain, and yet it is not especially decorative either; instead, it is clear, fluent, almost untroubled. Everything necessary seems at hand: language and scenery, psychology and memory, and a bright aesthetic intelligence that shapes the whole. Sometimes she claimed to have written certain stories at one sitting, but it is known that many were started and abandoned, taken up again and made into something new. She was dilatory perhaps, but the completed work as we now have it does not reveal any deformation of character, and indeed is expansive enough in theme and achievement to satisfy the claims of her high reputation. She was very vain as a beauty and just as vain as a writer, and this latter vanity perhaps accounted for a good deal of the waiting and stalling, a stalling filled with romantic diversions.

Joan Givner, throughout, sees what are often creative problems as problems of life, usually linked to an unsteady childhood that weeps its lacks and resentments right up to the age of ninety. In the case of a complicated egoist like Katherine Anne Porter, the biographer is altogether too insistent upon the writer's "longing for love." A typical passage reads: "It should be remembered, however, that Porter's need for love was far beyond the ordinary, a desperate, compulsive need inspired by the nagging, ever present sense of her deficiencies." The biographer's rather smug provincialism distorts the worldly and amusing mishaps of a woman who was not made for marriage and thus married four times. It is agreeable to come upon the writer's sniffs in the midst of the biographer's rampaging "longings" and doubts of "self-worth." When she happened to remember the fiftieth anniversary of her first marriage, Miss Porter observed that the fiftieth was a lot more pleasant than the first.

Ship of Fools was a long novel and long in the making: from 1941 to

1961. The book made over a million dollars and, of course, for poor Miranda that made a difference. Its reception was very favorable at the beginning, but thereafter followed some fierce reservations. The setting of the book is 1931, a ship going from Vera Cruz to Bremen with a passenger list very long and outlandishly challenging. A fixed arena in which persons who would not ordinarily meet can be realistically gathered together would seem to be a gift of structure, in the manner of large hotels or prison camps or hospitals. But the gift of this natural and ordained diversity is claustrophobic, like a sea journey itself. Characters are given their traits, their tics of manner, their past histories. But then they are trapped in them in the dining room, on the deck, in the bar. Diversions of distress or comedy are offered with great skill, but the sea rolls on and the characters roll on, clutching their gestures.

The significant promise of the novel lies in the date and destination: It is 1931, and the boat is on the way to Germany, carrying with it Germans who must somehow prefigure what is to come by way of German arrogance and moral limitation, what is to come for the poorly conceived solitary Jew—an unattractive man who makes his living selling Christian religious objects—and what is to come for the German whose wife is Jewish but scarcely knows it, an assimilated person answering to the name of Mary. The historical promise is too pressing for the imagination in the novel. All is too static, and the implied parable is never quite achieved. There is something a little musty, like old yellowing notes. The flawless execution of the single scenes impresses, and yet the novel remains too snug and shipshape for the waters of history.

With the publication of *Ship of Fools,* Katherine Anne Porter was past seventy, but since she was to live twenty more years, there was time for a daunting accretion of foolishness. She can fight with faithful friends and relatives, she can spend, she can fall in love, she can drink too much, she can buy a large emerald ring, a "longing" from which she did not run away. She also has time for her increasing anti-Semitism: "Everybody except the Jews knows the Jews are not chosen but are a lot of noisy, arrogant, stupid, pretentious people and then what?" She pronounced on desegregation, leading her close friend Glenway Wescott to declare that "her poor brain is just simply one seething smoking mass of molten lava."

Biographies inevitably record the demeaning moments of malice and decline and have the effect of imprinting them upon the ninety years. In the biographies of today, all things are equal except that the ill winds tend in interest to be—well, more interesting.

Katherine Anne Porter did not have a happy life. She was better at sloughing off love than retaining it. She was often lonely in between her rushes to attachments. Her egotism was disabling. Throughout her life, the most useful condition for her work and for her sense of things came from the part of her that was an audacious, immensely gifted, independent Sister Carrie who knew about poverty and rooming houses and bad marriages and standing alone. The folly of the claim to represent somehow an aristocratic example of taste and moral excellence was not wisdom but just the downward path.

The ending of the biography, a flourish, is an unhappy image of the limitations of the method of composition. It reads: "At the very end she lay, like La Condesa on the *Vera*, drugged and demented, bereft of her home and jewels, but defiant until the last moment when on September 18, 1980, the little point of light flickered and failed." The truth is that Katherine Anne Porter was drugged and demented from strokes and the ghastly illnesses of extreme old age. It is not a useful summarizing sentiment to think of her as a fiction, just as it has not been altogether wise to think of her fiction as her life, or for that matter "the life of" as precisely her life.

(1982)

EDMUND WILSON

Edmund Wilson, one of our country's supreme men of letters, is sometimes remembered as being autocratic and intimidating. My own
memory, not the most intimate, is of a cheerful, corpulent, chuckling
gentleman, well-dressed in brown suits and double martinis. As a literary and cultural critic, Wilson produced many volumes on an astonishing range of subjects. And beyond that, every scrap of his diaries, his
letters, and his autobiographical writings appear to have been collected and published. He liked to write about himself, his friends, his
wives, his love affairs, his days and nights, sometimes formally composed in an essay, sometimes transformed, more or less, into fiction or
preserved in his voluminous daily jottings. With the author having left
so few gaps, it is not surprising that the present biography by Jeffrey
Meyers can be said to be the first devoted to Wilson.

A "first" is something of a rarity for the very productive Meyers,
who has practiced his craft in the prevailing scene of biography, in
which the lives of writers and the remains of certain flamboyant artists
and musicians are examined in one large volume after another. A new
letter here or there, an untapped acquaintance, a passing stranger
remembering a misdemeanor, might offer what is called in court "a
window of opportunity." In any case, Jeffrey Meyers has produced biographies of Fitzgerald, Hemingway, Robert Lowell, Joseph Conrad,
and others. In this field study, each new digger will need to explore the

previously looted pharaonic tombs in search of an overlooked jewel in the stone eyes prepared for eternity.

If Jeffrey Meyers has broken the tape in the matter of Wilson's biography, he might not hold the title for long. The scholar Lewis Dabney has been "working on Wilson" for some years, and his labor is known as "authorized." What that distinction means is not always clear. Is it to be thought of as similar to the Queen of England's stamp on Pear's Soap? For a biographer, authorization seems to indicate the choice and support of family or heirs by providing access to papers, letters, drafts, mementos, photographs not available to all and sundry. In fact, almost everything or its equivalent—another photograph, for instance—is available to all and sundry, leaving the family members or others interested in restriction with not much beyond the power of refusing a personal interview.

Papers are sold, deposited, given as gifts or charitable deductions to libraries and other institutions suitable for preservation, cataloging, and reproduction, and they are for the most part open to academics and others with useful credentials. Collections are not meant usually as an honor to the collector but as a source of cultural history. If a biographer sets about his task, writes letters and receives replies about the subject, goes here and there for interviews, visits birth and burial sites perhaps, reads the work and the critical response to it, offers or stresses a few preferences, then with reasonable experience in doctoral programs or independent critical work, a biography can be produced. They are far from being, in most cases, a rich source of income; a lot of time is consumed, and if one is led to wonder just to whom the works are addressed, there is always one answer—the subsequent biographer.

Auden, George Orwell, and T. S. Eliot come to mind as distinguished writers who pleaded that there be no biography. They were like old wanderers on the road in Russian fiction, crying, "Have mercy on me, good folk!" The prayer seemed to have been heard as an impertinence and certainly an alert. Each got his biography and not one but several, the "interpretation" of Eliot's life flowing down to *Tom and Viv* on the stage. Scandal, or merely selfish and imprudent behavior, can be found in most lives as surely as the dates and ancestral records. It happened, didn't it? The unguarded moment or lifelong indiscretions, yes, or most likely, and so the biographer proceeds, as if under oath "to the best of my knowledge."

In the Victorian period, great figures often shared some of the majesty of the monarch, but even there the authorized memorialist could turn out to be somewhat less awed by the connection than the great one had imagined. Carlyle asked his friend and more or less disciple, the historian James A. Froude, to edit his memorial to Jane and to tell the tale, as it were. Froude wrote: "Carlyle never should have married." A curious emendation or explosion about the celebrated couple who lived together for forty years and famously reigned at 5 Cheyne Row. This assertion later led the unreliable Frank Harris to report that a doctor had examined Jane in her forties and found her to be "virgo intacta."

The poet Philip Larkin may have believed he was out of the literary scene by spending a good part of his life acting as a librarian in the provincial city of Hull. But he spoke and complained and wrote letters that achieved his own damnation by way of deeply unpleasant opinions promiscuously expressed. These utterances of ideas and prejudices appear in the recent biography by his sincere admirer, Andrew Motion. Larkin's contemptuous disapproval of blacks, wogs, foreigners, and so on bleakly enshroud the dour melancholy of his witty, beautiful poems—for the moment.

There have been outstanding biographies in our time, works of unremitting scholarly labor that add to our knowledge, elucidate the texts, and are composed with a refinement of style and judgment that honor the subject and give pleasure to the reader. Although these large undertakings are admirable in documentation and many other qualities, English literature is also enriched by odd, personal, less than definitive, glories—De Quincey's exhilarating memories of the Lake Poets, Henry James on Hawthorne, and a forgotten book, a quirky biography of Stephen Crane by the poet John Berryman.

"But they are wrong!" biographers in the stacks complain about so many irreplaceable documents of the past. Even Wilson is condescending to the miracle of Boswell's life of Johnson. Wilson promotes, with reservations, a newer work by Joseph Wood Krutch, itself, of course, superseded. To speak of Dr. Johnson: the heartrending, brilliant *Life of Mr. Richard Savage* is etched in falsehoods offered by Savage himself. Johnson's "life" is a sort of unwitting forgery written with genius, alive after the original, the true Richard Savage, has fallen into dust.

Edmund Wilson, were he living now, would be over one hundred years old. Jeffrey Meyers begins his biography with the chapter heading: "Red Bank, 1895–1907." Red Bank, New Jersey, was the scene of Wilson's birth, and for those of a literary inclination he may be said to have put the town on the map. His great-great-grandfather Kimball, on the mother's side, had married a Mather of New England. Meyers's first paragraph opens with this fact or stress:

> Edmund Wilson's ancestors served the altars of learning and committed murders in the name of God. He was descended from Cotton Mather, seventeenth century puritan divine and zealous witch hunter during the Salem trials, and shared many characteristics—intellect, bookishness, linguistic ability, temperament, energy, productivity and multiple marriages—with his eminent forefather. The prodigiously learned Mather, more widely read than any other American of his time, had entered Harvard at the age of twelve and spoke seven languages. Known for his arrogant manner and aggressiveness in controversy, he overtaxed his nerves by indefatigable industry, poured out more than 450 works on an enormous range of subjects and still managed to acquire three wives.

Except for the demonism that captured the extraordinary mind of Cotton Mather with abominable results, Wilson does share the learning and immense productivity of his ancestor and managed to exceed him in the matter of wives by having four. Perhaps the opening of Meyers's book is not so much to indicate the intellectual brilliance of the two as to alert the reader to a consanguineous "arrogant manner and aggressiveness in controversy."

> During his formative years Wilson grew up with a secure place in upper-middle-class society (a position he was unable to maintain for most of his writing career) and became attached to his ancestral home. He was shy and sensitive, interested in flowers and in drama, fantasy and magic, and always absorbed in books. He felt alienated from his parents, developed a difficult, demanding character, and inherited from his father an irritable disposition and a peremptory mode of discourse.

Wilson was not a New Englander of the seventeenth century in temperament or attraction to religion. When the poet Allen Tate became a Roman Catholic, or a sort of Catholic since he subsequently took advantage of the civil law and obtained two divorces, Wilson wrote him in a letter: "I hope that becoming a Catholic will give you peace of mind; though swallowing the New Testament as factual and moral truth seems to me an awful price to pay for it. You are wrong, and have always been wrong, in thinking I am in any sense a Christian. Christianity seems to me the worst imposture of any of the religions I know of. Even aside from the question of faith, the morality of the Gospel seems to me absurd."

Jeffrey Meyers's *Edmund Wilson* is organized in the conventional chronological manner, which serves well here and follows more or less the organization Wilson employs in his autobiographical volume, *A Prelude,* which takes him up to 1919, the date of his release from service in World War I. Wilson was not much like other young men. He was clumsy and bulky, short, five feet six inches, immune to the attraction of competitive sports. And yet, at the Hill School in Pottstown, Pennsylvania, he made interesting friendships, learned to admire certain of his teachers, studied among other subjects Latin, Greek, and French without, as Meyers tells us, making especially good grades but nevertheless building the foundation of his interest in languages. He went on to Princeton, an important part of his life, and there wrote and studied, made friends, notably Scott Fitzgerald and the scholar Christian Gauss.

Princeton social life lay in the eating clubs: "These clubs are remarkably uninteresting," he wrote, and added: "Since I did not play billiards or bridge, there was nothing to occupy me except to sit, as I sometimes did in winter, in front of our big open fireplace and read the papers and magazines." Odd as Wilson might have been, it does not appear that he felt himself so or in any way suffered from shame or anxiety about his nature or how he might appear to others.

Wilson grew up an only child, but he had a very well-populated family of connections. On his first trip to Europe when he was thirteen years old, the party was large: his parents, uncles, aunts, and cousins, each of whose character and fate he describes. The diary of this thirteen-year-old is printed in *A Prelude*. "I do not recommend for its interest the 1908 diary of my first trip to Europe, but I am printing it for the sake of completeness, and because it provides me with a pretext for explaining certain family matters."

The existence of the diary is the interesting consideration here. The keeping of diaries and, in Wilson's case, a lifelong journal are marks of confidence and self-esteem, an early sense of vocation. What one experiences is important to record, even when events are trivial, because the diarist is present. Still, the confidence, the being comfortable with his body and mind, are perhaps clues to the daunting and, in a way, unexpected inclusion in later years of precise, he believed, details of sexual adventures. Wilson's diaries were not published until after his death, and then they were edited and arranged by decades such as *The Twenties, The Thirties,* and so on up to *The Sixties.* They are a remarkable exercise of creative, intellectual, and physical energy produced as if under some self-appointed duty by one who was forever publishing reviews, extended essays, complex books, and undertaking exhausting journeys all over the world. The diaries are casual, perhaps, but they show a workman's sense of care, craft, and also thrift. Some of the recordings therein, such as those on Scott Fitzgerald and Edna Millay appear intact or, expanded, in book collections.

Throughout his life, here and abroad, Wilson was acquainted with a great number of distinguished and interesting people, and many became attached to him for his charm, his knowledge, his vivid conversation—indeed, the specially high quality of his work and of himself. But there is a latitudinarianism in Wilson, an open spirit, not disclaimed by a certain gruffness at times. As he writes about his daily life, he will give many pages to, for instance, an old farming family, the Munns, to their daily affairs, the various members of the family. The diaries, as we have them, are not different in style from his professional work. The collections of literary articles, written for *The New Yorker* and other magazines, found in *Classics and Commercials* and in *The Shores of Light* and *The Bit Between My Teeth,* are not diminished by thinking of them as the diaries of a professional man at his desk, with the texts to be examined, the author's life to be wondered about, in much the same way as he approaches the vast army of real persons who have passed his way.

In Meyers's biography of Wilson, wives and other ladies, "mistresses" and fumbles, have their place and their more than considerable number of pages. The publications of books are mingled with the calendar of life events and critical judgment is supplied by the reviews lying about in the attic of magazines and newspapers. The "fight" with the IRS over unpaid taxes owes its details to Wilson's book on the subject. More interesting for literary history and personal display is the "quarrel" with Vladimir Nabokov. The combats with the IRS and Nabokov were comedies, however painful each might have been for the participants.

About the IRS: There was Wilson, a gentleman always broke and with expenses not unwarranted, if often uncovered. He worked more diligently and with more conspicuous concentration than a president in the Oval Office. Wilson must have felt that as an independent, self-employed producer of strange small-business goods he was somehow not a wage earner required to give his deputed allotment with a burdensome regularity. The use of the nation's taxes for the Cold War and other misappropriations, as he viewed them, probably entered his mind later, although his distaste for militarism, weapons, and so on was sincere and marked by vehemence. The fact probably was that he simply didn't want to pay his taxes and this led to a pleasing amnesia as the time rolled around and led in the end to grimly calculated penalties and much harassment. Still, the affair was a comedy in the operatic sense, with the distracted, tousled hero and the rogues looking for gold under the bed.

Nabokov's translation with commentaries of Pushkin's *Eugene Onegin* was a folly of such earnest magnitude that it might have been conceived in *Bouvard and Pécuchet.* It was attacked by Slavicists for its wild, peculiar vocabulary in English and for its "original" dissertations on matters of prosody. Wilson was critically dismayed and moved without hesitation to say as much. He felt himself competent in the Russian language and certainly knowledgeable about Pushkin, to whom he had devoted an essay in *The Triple Thinkers.* Indeed, in that volume he translated "The Bronze Horseman" into "prose with an iambic base." The translation is a gift to those who wish to receive it. It is instructive and agreeable to read, much in the helpful spirit of the prose translation at the bottom of the page in the Penguin series of poetry in German, Spanish, and other languages. Wilson had embarked on a formidable accomplishment in his study of Russian, which he followed with his astounding assault on Hebrew. In his mid-sixties, we find him in a state of excitation about Hungarian. About this late effort, he was heard to say that he felt like "an old character in Balzac, huffing and puffing to his last liaison."

Wilson did not show any special modesty or hesitation in his contentious review of Nabokov's *Eugene Onegin*; however, the scholar Clarence Brown found Wilson guilty of the "unbelievable *hubris* of reading Nabokov's petulant little lessons about Russian grammar and vocabulary, himself blundering all the while." The pages of literary magazines were stuffed to grogginess with Wilson and Nabokov eloquently engaged about the properties of Russian and English pronunciation, metrical traditions in both languages, personal and literary qualities. John Updike's review of *The Nabokov-Wilson Letters* takes its title, "The Cuckoo and the Rooster," from an Ivan Krylov fable. In the midst of the battle, Nabokov wrote with his characteristic left-handedness, "I have always been grateful to him [Wilson] for the tact he has showed in not reviewing any of my novels while constantly saying flattering things about me in the so-called literary circles where I seldom revolve."

Wilson reviewed Nabokov's book on Gogol with a generous degree of plus and a scattering of minus. His reservations are the clue to an irreconcilable difference in the practice of the two writers: the style of composition. Nabokov's Gogol book is one of the most exhilarating, engaging, and original works ever written by one writer about another. Wilson acknowledges its uniqueness, but he finds himself annoyed by Nabokov's "poses, perversities and vanities." These "perversities" are the glory of Nabokov's writing, and they are the grandiloquent, imaginative cascade of images and diversions Wilson could not normally accept. He dismissed *Lolita:* "I like it less than anything of yours I have read." After *The Real Life of Sebastian Knight*, Nabokov's first novel in English, Wilson was more or less "disappointed."

In *Patriotic Gore*, a dazzling monument in the national literature, Wilson has a chapter on "American Prose." It is his idea that American writing abandoned the cultivated standards of the eighteenth century and in the first half of the nineteenth century fell into deplorable exaggeration, rhetorical display, fanciful diversions more or less arising out of the models of the sermon and public addresses. Therein, he writes a shocking appraisal that suggests the impossibility of his finding pleasure and beauty in Nabokov:

> There is nothing in the fiction of Hawthorne to carry the reader along: in the narrative proper of *The Scarlet Letter*, the paragraphs and the sentences, so deliberately and fastidiously written, are as sluggish as the introduction with its description of the old custom house. The voyage of

the *Pequod* in *Moby-Dick,* for all its variety of incident and its progression to a dramatic end, is a construction of close-knit blocks which have to be surmounted one by one; the huge units of *Billy Budd,* even more clottedly dense, make it one of the most inappropriate works for reading in bed at night, since it is easy to lose consciousness in the middle of one.

The chapter on Charles Dickens in *The Wound and the Bow* is one of Wilson's glowing achievements. It is rich in complexity, original in ideas, moves around the challenge of the novels and of the life of Dickens with a speculative and interrogating ease that is altogether remarkable. The essay is also a perfect example of Wilson's method as a critic. The title of the collection is suggested by Sophocles' play *Philoctetes,* and the theme is that the sufferings and traumas in the lives of artists have a deep connection with the release of creativity.

In the case of Dickens, the "wound" is well known: The family fell on hard times, and the boy was taken out of school and sent to work in a blacking factory, a cruel, degrading, and forever damaging fate. At the end of the day, the boy would visit his family, now residing in Marshalsea Prison due to the father's debts. Even when the elder Dickens received a legacy, the family did not immediately take the boy out of the factory and return him to school, a lapse he could never forgive. This wound in his youth has naturally been seen as the base for Dickens's hatred of cruelty to children, his exposure of hypocrisy throughout society, his contempt for knavery, social and intellectual pretense, money grubbing, lying—all embodied in a host of characters, an army invading London. These smarmy characters have their opposites in good, long-suffering, generous little people and sometimes good big people.

It is Wilson's idea that the bad people/good people duality arose from Dickens's inability to create characters of mixed motives and believably warring inclinations. He feels the author was approaching this in the unfinished novel, *Edwin Drood,* which is examined in great detail. Scholarship, recounted by Wilson, has shown that there were other humiliations in Dickens's past: His grandparents had worked as domestic servants in the household of Lord Crewe; the father of Dickens's mother was found guilty of embezzlement and fled. The facts about Dickens's past were hidden by Dickens himself. One of the most interesting stories is told by his son; not long before the author's death, the family was playing a word game and Dickens came up with: Warren's Blacking, 30 Strand. No one present understood what he was talking about. So there is a feeling, as the essay maintains, in Dickens himself of a kind of inauthenticity. By an argument too dense and detailed to examine here, the number of murders in the novels, the obsession with the murders indicate in the end that Dickens had murdered himself, a psychological element in Wilson's study.

So there is the "wound," but what about the "bow"—Dickens's style? The breathless flow of adjectives, metaphors, and similes, the description of clothes, houses, streets, alleys, and occupations, the skewered visual genius of one who describes the knobs on an impostor's head as "looking like the crust of a plum pie." The perpetual motion of Dickens's outrageous imagination seems wearisome for Wilson.

Nabokov's lectures at Cornell on *Bleak House* seize the novel when it is flying off the page, seize it with delight. The listeners are invited to note the lamplighter as he goes about his rounds, "like an executioner to a despotic king, strikes off the little heads of fire" or the Jellyby children "tumbled about, and notched memoranda of their accidents on their legs, which were perfect little calendars of distress." On and on the lecturer goes, remarking on names, alliteration, and assonance.

In his essay on American prose, Wilson explains his own preference in literary style. He sees the tragedy of the Civil War as breaking the fabric of romantic exaggeration, embroidery, false eloquence. His models are the stories of Ambrose Bierce and Lincoln's Gettysburg Address, among other examples. Sobriety, terseness, lucidity, and precision—and, indeed, his own compositions are wonderful in clarity, balance, movement, language, always at hand to express the large capacity of his mind and experience, whether current fiction, the Russian Revolution, or the Dead Sea Scrolls.

And yet Wilson, for all the practicality of his method, could be unpredictable and never more so than in his embrace of Joyce's *Finnegans Wake*, another language to learn, as it were. "In conception as well as in execution, one of the boldest books ever written," he remarks in the essay devoted to the novel in *The Wound and the Bow*. The essay is somewhat parental in approach as he guides the reader through whatever factual information might be useful, such as the age, occupation, marriage, and children of Earwicker. There are some rebukes, typical of Wilson's household rules: "And the more daring Joyce's subjects become, the more he tends to swathe them about with the fancywork of his literary virtuosity." Still, he brings to *Finnegans Wake* a beaming affection and solicitude.

Sex, Mary McCarthy, *Memoirs of Hecate County,* and so on. Mary McCarthy has written in her memoirs of her detestation of Wilson's body and soul, information provided by her decision to become his wife. She has disguised him in satirical portraits in her fiction, a disguise on the order of sunglasses. They were divorced after a span of seven years during which she bore a son by Wilson and after which she lived, wrote, and added two more husbands. A marriage, however successfully escaped, rankles more in the memory than an old, ferocious bout of the flu, but no matter, her preoccupation is extreme. She had much in common with Wilson, especially in the need to instruct. Some persons are not content to have a deep aversion to another but feel the command to have others share the documented distaste. This is different from jealousy of, for instance, Wilson's subsequent marriage to the attractive, cosmopolitan, domestically gifted, and loyal Elena Mumm Thornton. It would appear that McCarthy wanted to instruct Elena in the true nature of her husband, instruct Elena and everyone else. Otherwise consider the oddity of the amount of repetitive energy put into denunciation of the past by one so pleasantly situated in life, so rich in experience, friendships, new loves, handsome surroundings—all of that.

What was Wilson thinking of in descriptions in his diaries of his swaying home after an "encounter," only to awaken the next day and put it all down? He was, of course, thinking of himself, the principal actor in the drama, the "I." The "I" in a partnership on the bed or couch, or whatever, will, if he is in a mood to leave a record, need to move into the sensations of the "she." About Marie, a pickup, "Her cunt, however, seemed small. She would not, the first time, respond very heartily, but, the second, would wet herself and bite my tongue, and when I had finished, I could feel her vagina throbbing powerfully."

Memoirs of Hecate County, a fiction, more or less, with the real-life persons serving in the short and the longer story run down by the biographer, like a policeman tracking suspects. The book was banned, but it has survived and is probably still read because of its interesting reputation for salaciousness and the genuine interest of the book. It was a bizarre composition to add to the stately list of literary and cultural studies already long and commanding when it was published in 1946. "The Princess with the Golden Hair," the principal, most arresting tale, became the occasion for a good number of amusing, unfavorable reviews. The "princess," a remote and withholding beauty of the pre-Raphaelite sort for whom the narrator longs, did not arouse a like yearning in many readers. Interest, if not quite yearning, arrives when the princess-frustrated, first-person narrator, an art critic, takes a diversionary spin down to Fourteenth Street and a dance hall called the Tango Casino. There he meets Anna, a "hostess." She is poor, has spent time in an orphanage, has a brutal husband and a little girl and much misery and deprivation in her life. This background is finely done by Wilson as it flows in and out of the "couplings." Anna is a "relief"— not much more, if a lot of relief. Her lower-class "hard protruding little thigh bones" seem inadequate when at last the "luxurious" princess is brought to bed. "Her little bud was so deeply imbedded that it was hardly involved in the play, and she made me arrest my movement while she did something special and gentle that did not, however, press on this point, rubbing herself somehow against me—and then came, with a self-excited tremor."

"Clinical" was applied to the sex writing in the diaries and in the fiction. Cyril Connolly thought the fornications had "a kind of monotony," and John Updike found the writing "leaden and saturnine"; Raymond Chandler said Wilson managed to make "fornication as dull as a railroad timetable."

Jeffrey Meyers has produced a long book, 483 pages. There is a lot of Wilson to be sifted, and so there is a lot of Meyers. We might think the biographer has brought together the immense flow of Wilson's life and work, both of which are scattered in the many publications and collections. Meyers has certainly not made of the object of his labors the worst one could imagine—drinking, vanity, and so on—nor has he been able to create the brilliant, irreplaceable mind and spirit. Too many facts, of whatever laudatory or dismissive nature, destroy the shape of all lives as they are experienced by even the most unreflective in a flashing, quick, and unstable form. But that cannot be the way of biographers. And so we bid farewell to the unlikely presence in our literature of a great thinker, writer, and unusual being. Farewell, until the next time, the Wilson biography Professor Dabney has been working on for lo, these many years.

(1997)

TRUMAN CAPOTE:
TRU CONFESSIONS

Chatty, gossipy remembrances of the deplorable history of Truman Capote's last years may be read, in some instances, as revenge or payment-due for the dead author's assaultive portraits of friends and enemies, although few of the interlocutors can command Capote's talent for the vicious, villainous, vituperative adjective. George Plimpton has spent some years tracking down and taking down the remarks of those who crossed Truman's journey to literary fame and to his unique crocodilian celebrity. The remarks are deftly arranged to avoid lumps of monologue piling up one after another like wood stacked for the winter. Instead the voices having their say about the charms and deficits of the absent one find Plimpton at the console professionally mixing the sound, as it were. His phrase for the effect is the unrehearsed, companionable exchange at a cocktail party. This is a large accommodation to raw opinion, to mincing literary judgments of hapless inappropriateness, to character analysis sweet as peaches or impugning as a jailhouse witness for the prosecution. It must be said that method and result have a suitability to the subject, since Capote himself, when not writing, was party-going, forever receiving and producing banter about feckless stumblings and torrid indiscretions.

He was born in 1924 in New Orleans and spent his early years in Monroeville, Alabama. His mother, Lillie Mae Faulk, married at seventeen a man named Arch Persons by whom she had the child, Truman. He was left in the care of relatives, maiden ladies of an eccentric turn useful to the Southern literature of Capote's period. After a time his mother divorced and the son was brought to New York and to Connecticut, where Lillie Mae, name now changed to Nina, married Joseph Capote, who adopted the child under the name of Truman Garcia Capote. *Other Voices, Other Rooms* was published when Truman was twenty-four years old, and this happy beginning of his creative life was in pitiable contrast to his family life. His mother committed suicide five years later, and two years after that Mr. Capote was sent to Sing Sing prison for forgery and grand larceny.

So Truman was on his own and on his way. He was an early master of camp flamboyance and defiance. He was short, effeminate, with a very noticeable, high-pitched, whining voice. And pretty enough, if never quite as fetching as the photograph that enhanced the cover of *Other Voices, Other Rooms*. It appears that with his curious voice, his ways, he decided to brazen it out, to be himself with an ornamental courage and an impressive conceit. He was a figure, what old ladies used to call a "sketch," and smart and amusing, ambitious as a writer and as a society darling, a coquette of wit at the great tables, on the yachts, in the splendid houses in Italy, France and Mexico. Southern accent, cascades of anecdote, boy genius, as all including himself conceded, and productive in the hours of the afternoon when the hostess was napping.

Other Voices, Other Rooms: the best of his down-home fictions, confidently written, picturing a small-town world in the South. Moth-eaten grandeur, garrulous ne'er-do-wells, colored-folk exchanges in the kitchen with the only souls who lift a hand and here named Missouri, called Zoo, and her Papadaddy, Jesus Fever, and others who enter the action with drag-queen names like Miss Wisteria and the hermit, Little Sunshine. It is a coming-of-age story for young Joel Knox, as the fictions of his closest Southern contemporaries are likely to be: Carson McCullers's *The Heart Is a Lonely Hunter* and *The Member of the Wedding;* Harper Lee's *To Kill a Mockingbird*. We might note that in these books the girls are as tomboyish as Capote's Joel is girlish. Reading over these writers brings to mind the triumph of their contemporary Flannery O'Connor, painting a similar landscape and filling it not with cute hunchbacks and dwarfs but with predatory swamp rats, literally God-forsaken Bible salesmen intoning their handy lies in magical speech rhythms, all transcending the fictional clichés in the dramaturgy of the generation after Faulkner.

In Capote's novel, Joel Knox, age twelve, has been left in the care of his relations after the death of his mother and the flight of his father. At last he is summoned by the father, now married to Miss Amy, to join him at Skully's Landing, a run-down estate that will have no modern plumbing facilities or electricity, but the boy will discover that once in the parlor there were gold draperies, a gilded sofa of lilac velvet, and so on—all now covered with dust. Both the present decay and the parlor trumpery of a more glamorous past are not unexpected when the domestic scenery is to be assembled for a place called Skully's Landing and in a Southern state.

The father does not appear, nor is information given about him until later in the novel, and then we learn that he is upstairs, paralyzed, and communicating his needs by throwing tennis balls down the stairs. The plot is complicated by ghostly appearances, crazy down-South ways of passing the time, but we can find it held together by the sweetness of the boy's nature and a lyrical generosity about the follies of grown-ups. And by the kindness of the black cook, Zoo, a sort of kissing cousin to Ethel Waters in the staging of *The Member of the Wedding*.

The most interesting of the "characters" living in Skully's Landing is Cousin Randolph, a connection of the stepmother, Miss Amy. Randolph, a painter and sherry-drinking idler, has a history; he's been around, studied abroad, and while in Madrid copying the old masters in the Prado he meets Dolores, a cold but somehow overwhelming beauty, and they become lovers. The two of them abandon Europe and land in Florida, where Dolores takes up with Pepe, an impressively muscled boxer, mean, handsome, potent and violent. Randolph, in a ferocious epiphany, discovers himself in love with Pepe and filled with a devastating longing.

> I could not endure to see him suffer; it was agony to watch him fight ... I gave him money, brought him cream-colored hats, gold bracelets (which he adored, and wore like a woman), shoes in bright Negro colors, candy silk shirts ...

The end of it was Pepe, drunk, destroying Randolph's paintings, calling him "terrible names" and breaking his nose. And then Pepe is off with Dolores, off no one knows where, but Randolph sends letters to random post offices here and there. "Oh, I know that I shall never have an answer. But it gives me something to believe in. And that is peace."

Randolph is a nice, rather lachrymose fellow, a well-born "queer" of some cultivation and too many afternoon sips from the bottle, altogether a configuration at home in the little towns, and no doubt still there. Joel, the boy, is moved by Randolph's confession and also moved to an awakening of his own nature. In a final scene they go to an old abandoned hotel, once a brothel, and in a somewhat murky rendering spend the night together.

Plimpton has printed a review of *Other Voices, Other Rooms* by the majorful Diana Trilling, which was published in *The Nation,* January 31, 1948. Despite the "claptrap" she praises the compositional virtuosity of the novel and finds that such skill in one so young "represents a kind of genius." However, she is morally distressed about Cousin Randolph, "a middle-aged degenerate aesthete," and more dismayed by what she reads as the *lesson* of the plot.

> At the end of the book the young Joel turns to homosexual love offered him by Randolph, and we realize that in his slow piling up of nightmare details Mr. Capote has been attempting to recreate the emotional background to sexual inversion. What his book is saying is that a boy becomes a homosexual when the circumstances of his life deny him the other, more normal gratifications of his need for affection.

The devil made me do it. A shirking of moral responsibility, as she sees it, and in no way faithful to the text and to Joel's relation with Randolph. One thing you can say about Capote is that the "closet" was never, never anything to him except a place to find bits of silver cloth, old faded snapshots, love letters and trinkets.

The Grass Harp is blown about by the winds of whimsy, here, rocking the cradle in the treetop. The narrator, again a young boy once more sent to live with relations, two unmarried ladies who are sisters. They and others spend a good deal of time picnicking and chatting in a house high up in a chinaberry tree. The tree house was fifteen or twenty years old, "spacious, sturdy, a model of a tree house, it was like a raft floating in a sea of leaves . . . to sail along the cloudy coastline of every dream." Up in the tree you can hear the grass harp "always telling a story—it knows the stories of all the people on the hill, of all the people who have ever lived, and when we are dead it will tell ours, too." The novel was composed while Capote was living in an "absolutely marvelous" villa in Sicily, named La Fontana Vecchia. It was, astonishingly, turned into a grandiose Broadway production, music by Virgil Thomson and sets by Cecil Beaton. Thomson describes the debacle:

> The set which Cecil designed, particularly the one with the big tree, was so large and heavy that nobody ever saw it until the opening in Boston. There was no point in setting it up in New York for rehearsals ... On the Sunday afternoon before we left for Boston, there was a professional matinee ... Everybody wept buckets. Then we moved up to Boston, and once we got into the set, nobody out there in the seats ever wept anymore. The set was too large and complicated—very grand, something for the Metropolitan Opera.

Well, no matter. Such was Capote's celebrity that "House of Flowers," a scrawny short story set in Haiti, was mounted as a Broadway musical with music by Harold Arlen, set by Oliver Messel, choreography by George Balanchine and direction by Peter Brook. The A list for little Tru.

The South, the days of youth gone by, the downtown with its shops and taverns and their funny names, the collection of harmlessly deranged kinfolk, were there to be called on by the writer as a sort of *spécialité*, like Key lime pie and conch fritters, to be exploited again and again in holiday postcards such as *A Christmas Memory, One Christmas*, and *The Thanksgiving Visitor*.

Cousin Randolph, the tree house, and the rest of it will serve the muse for a time, and then Capote will bring his fiction to New York City, that place Marianne Moore, in a poem, found "starred with tepees of ermine and peopled with foxes." In his portmanteau, Capote will be carrying, like some revivifying patent medicine, a very useful stimulant in the composition of the successful *Breakfast at Tiffany's*, that is, Christopher Isherwood's *Goodbye to Berlin*.

Into Plimpton's time capsule we have the wish of several young, or once young, ladies to be the inspiration for the beguiling Holly Golightly, the center of *Breakfast at Tiffany's*. Doris Lilly, identified as a gossip columnist and author, is as insistent as if she were the claimant in an inheritance battle.

> There is an awful lot of me in Holly Golightly. There's much more of me than there is of Carol Marcus (who is now Carol Marcus Matthau) and a girl called Bee Dabney, a painter. More of me than either of these two ladies. I know.

Primogeniture does not adhere to any of the pals circling around the house in New York. Fortunately for the attractiveness of *Breakfast at Tiffany's* (1958), the model is the "Sally Bowles" section in Isherwood's book of 1938. In both novellas, the first-person narrator is a young writer who finds himself living next door to an interesting young woman, Sally Bowles in a Berlin pension and Holly Golightly in a shabby New York town house broken up into small apartments.

Both girls are beautiful, each afloat and searching for a place to land with a man if not rich at least giving evidence of being in touch with money. They attach themselves to one after another, only to find themselves abruptly dropped, an annoyance from which they bounce back in a way that reminds one of professional boxers, on the mat one minute and up the next, a little unsteady, but with fist in a salute. Among the many correspondences between Isherwood and Capote we have the fleeing man's tendency to leave a letter.

Klaus to Sally Bowles:

> My dear little girl, you have adored me too much. . . . You must be brave, Sally, my poor darling child. . . . I was invited a few nights ago to a party at the house of Lady Klein, a leader of the British aristocracy. I met there a beautiful and intelligent young English girl named Miss Gore-Eckersley. . . .

And so it goes.

José, a Brazilian diplomat making his escape from Holly Golightly's radar:

> My dearest little girl, I have loved you knowing that you were not as others. But conceive of my despair upon discovering . . . how very dif-

ferent you are from the manner of woman a man of my faith and career could hope to make his wife . . . I am gone home.

Sally Bowles gives herself a *faux* "county" background in a very amusing imitation:

Daddy's a terrible snob, although he pretends not to be. . . . He's the most marvellous business man. And about once a month he gets absolutely dead tight and horrifies all Mummy's smart friends.

Holly Golightly, from Tulip, Texas, real name Lulamae Barnes, was a runaway starving orphan picked up by a country horse doctor whom she married at age fourteen, and ran away from to New York. The horse doctor turns up in New York hoping to reclaim his wife and providing one of Capote's most inventive comic interludes. However, Tulip, Texas, does not always inhabit Holly Golightly's conversational style—the rhythms of Sally Bowles perhaps overwhelming national boundaries. (There is a mention of French lessons given to smother Holly's Texas defect in preparation for a film career.) Nevertheless here she is in a typical locution: "But, after all, he *knows* I'm preggers. Well, I am, darling. Six weeks gone. I don't see why that should surprise you. It didn't me. Not *un peu* bit." At times her diction crosses to the Rhine. "I suppose I'll sleep until Saturday, really get a good *schluffen*."

The two stories come to an end on a postcard. Sally Bowles, off on her amorous journey, sends a card from Paris, another from Rome with no address.

That was six years ago. So now I am writing her. When you read this, Sally, if you ever do—please accept it as a tribute, the sincerest I can pay, to yourself, and to our friendship. And send me another postcard.

Holly in a postcard goodbye from South America: "*Brazil was beastly but Buenos Aires the best. Not Tiffany's, but almost . . . Will let you know address when I know it myself.*" And the narrator reflects: "But the address, if it ever existed, never was sent, which made me sad, there was so much I wanted to write her."

Breakfast at Tiffany's has its own charms, and if the astute Capote has done a transatlantic rearrangement perhaps we can think of it in musical terms: Variations on a Theme by Haydn. Something like that.

Christopher Isherwood, resident of Los Angeles, was present at Capote's funeral, and Plimpton publishes what the novelist John Gregory Dunne remembered about the moment. "And Chris did the most graceful thing of all. He said, 'There was one wonderful thing about Truman. He always made me laugh.' He started to laugh, turned around, and sat down. Perfectly graceful and gracious." And then Carol Marcus Matthau, who in Doris Lilly's deposition is definitely *not* the model for Holly Golightly, has some unpleasant things to say about Isherwood. (Unpleasantness about persons not the object of the enterprise in "oral biography" is a treacherous fallout of the indiscriminate form.) Truman Capote in his fiction never achieved anything as rich and beautiful as the stories in *Goodbye to Berlin,* of which "Sally Bowles" is only one, or as brilliant as *Mr. Norris Changes Trains* and *Prater Violet.* Not to the point here, since with a few exceptions, it appears that the only "brilliant writer" and "genius" the assembly is aware of is Truman Capote. No, mournful as it is to remember, there is another writer mentioned again and again in Plimpton's pages, a writer who, like Capote, knew a lot of rich people and who wrote something herein called "Proustian."

In November 1966 Capote gave in the Plaza Hotel in New York what you might call his "in-cold-blood party" for five hundred guests. As a sort of provenance for the fête, the calendar moves backward. The murder of the Clutter family, husband and wife and two teenage children, occurred in November 1959, in the town of Holcomb, Kansas. After reading an account in the press, Capote soon took off for the site of the crime. Two young men were arrested a month later and in March 1960 convicted of the crime and sentenced to death. On April 14, 1965, Perry Smith and Dick Hickock, the convicted murderers of the Clutter family, were hanged in the Kansas State Penitentiary for Men in Lansing, Kansas. Six years had passed after the conviction, by way of legal appeals and stays of execution, before the author, Truman Capote, could write *finis* to *In Cold Blood,* his account of the killers, the detectives, the town, the trial. Six months after the hanging, the serialization in *The New Yorker* began, and publication in book form soon followed.

At last it was Carnival time, with beads, masks, spikes of feathers in voodoo headdresses, bunny fur, witch wigs and a band playing show tunes. The party at the Plaza acquired the fame of a coronation for the very successful book, still a work of riveting interest for its portrait of the misshapen bodies, language, highway felonies and idiotic plans and dreams of two savage, talkative, rawhide murderers, Perry Smith and Dick Hickock.

After the publication of the book, Capote spends a good deal of his time and thought on nomenclature, that is, his naming of the work a "nonfiction novel" and claiming to be the only begetter of the form. Sometimes in the discussion one might be reading about an eagle-eyed blind man, but that would have a greater philosophical interest. In most works of any length about crimes there is much that is not mere documentation; there is the setting of the scene: the neat little trailer before the blood-splattered walls, the dog at the garbage can with an arm in it, the handsome house, usually called a mansion, where the deceased was just putting night cream on her face when . . . There are scenes in Capote that appear to be "fiction"; one early chapter has Nancy Clutter, the daughter, at home on the day of her death, chatting on the phone about a lesson in pie-baking or about her boyfriend, Bobby. This is followed by Mrs. Clutter in a conversation with Jolene, the thirteen-year-old for whom Nancy was to give the lesson in pie-baking. The Clutters are dead, and the reader supposes the quite banal chapter to be what the author would imagine to be the actions of a "normal" family living out their last hours in Kansas farm country. Not easy to enliven since the family is denied the bizarrerie of Alabama homesteads. However, in an interview, Capote seems to disclaim imagination and to place the origin of everything in the testimony of the living who overheard or took part in the conversations.

Perry Smith, thirty-one years old, and Dick Hickock, twenty-eight years old, are on parole from prison and, at the beginning of the composition, are making their journey to commit a robbery and kill whoever will frustrate their plan. They made their way to the house in Kansas and in the interest of "leaving no witnesses" slaughtered the four family members. The case was solved when the police were told by a cellmate who had once worked for Mr. Clutter that he had given information about a safe in the house containing ten thousand dollars—given the information to Smith and Hickock as they gathered their meager belongings and abilities and were set free. There was no safe in the house, and the cons came away with forty dollars, a radio and a pair of binoculars.

On the way from birth to death, as it were, there is an appallingly rich lode of archival gold for Capote to shape and polish and send to market, all of which he does with a skillful hand. The detectives on their way to pawnshops and motels and the very striking confession of the killers about their wanderings before and after, their description of their gruesome destruction of each single Clutter; accounts of the early life of the killers by their relatives and their own summations given at the request of a court psychiatrist; Capote's interviews, his visit to the holding cells where the two awaited execution, his claim of having corresponded with each twice a week for the five years between conviction and execution.

While both the condemned and the author were waiting out the stays, Capote made no secret of his *qué sera, sera* impatience to get it over with. Quite a few remembered this curious bit of literary oral history. When the book was published, it did occasion jokes and some serious memories which the pugnacious and vindictive Capote did not find amusing. On a TV show, William Buckley, Jr., said, "Well, we've only had a certain number of executions in the last few years— whatever it was—and two of them were for the personal convenience of Truman Capote." The composer Ned Rorem at a party heard Truman say about his book, "But it can't be published until they're executed, so I can hardly wait." Rorem, when the book came out, sent a letter to be published in a magazine, which said, among other things: "Capote got two million and his heroes got the rope." (Needless to say, Rorem got *his* in Capote's later book *Answered Prayers*.)

Party-going with its temptation to social misdemeanors was also the ground of a confrontation between Capote and the English critic Kenneth Tynan. After hearing that the execution date had been irrevocably set, Capote, according to Tynan's wife's interview with Plimpton, said: "I'm beside myself! Beside myself! Beside myself with joy!" Tynan reviewed *In Cold Blood* for *The Observer* in London:

> For the first time, an influential writer of the front rank has been placed in a position of privileged intimacy with criminals about to die and, in my view, done less than he might have to save them . . . No piece of prose, however deathless, is worth a human life.

Truman, in his reply to the paper, wrote that Tynan had "the morals of a baboon and the guts of a butterfly."

Capote never showed an interest in political or moral debate, and perhaps that was prudent since ideas, to some degree, may define one's social life and could just be excess baggage he didn't need to bring aboard; and, worse, boring, like the ruins and works of art he declined to get off the yacht to see. In any case, he could not have "saved" Smith and Hickock, who had confessed; the appeals rested upon legal matters such as the competence of the state-appointed defense attorneys, whose summation took only ninety minutes—the jury before returning the death sentence "deliberated" only forty minutes.

Still, one might reflect about the book and wonder what a sentence of life without possibility of parole might have been for the execution of the nonfiction novel. Two alive central characters with plenty of time to become jailhouse lawyers would not have been useful to the author, publisher or movie-maker. These are troublesome men. And then there is the actual hanging in the dreadful Kansas shed, "a cavernous storage room, where on the warmest day the air is moist and chilly"; and: "The hangman coughed—impatiently lifted his cowboy hat and settled it again, a gesture somehow reminiscent of a turkey buzzard huffing, then smoothing its neck feathers—and Hickock, nudged by an attendant, mounted the scaffold steps." Wouldn't that have been missed?

There is a moment in *In Cold Blood* when Perry Smith says to his partner in the murders: "I just don't believe anyone could get away with a thing like that." In *Answered Prayers,* the unfinished nonfiction novel, using the actual names of a transcontinental cast of mostly well-known persons or, if disguised by a fictitious name, carefully designed to be identifiable, Capote made his own shackled step to the social gallows. The first of the scatalogical offenses to be published was "La Côte Basque," a story or something, taking place in the fashionable restaurant of the same name. It is lunchtime and the proprietor is seating or not seating according to the heraldic rankings of the metropolitan scene. Capote, under his *nom de plume* of P. B. Jones, or "Jonesy," is lunching with "Lady Coolbirth" in the absence of the Duchess of Windsor, she having canceled because of a bout of hives.

Champagne is ordered, which somehow promotes a scurrilous bit of anecdote about the composer Cole Porter. On and on to the supposedly overheard conversation of two identified nymphs about town. Across the way in the restaurant, dining with a priest, is the wife who in a *famous* court case was acquitted of having shot her well-born, rich husband. But she is not to escape the dossier proposed by Jonesy and Lady Coolbirth detailing her rise from a "country-slum" in West Virginia, real trash with a pretty face, who went on to a whirl on the continental carousel where she was known as "Madame Marmalade—her favorite *petit déjeuner* being hot cock butter with Dundee's best." The woman in fact committed suicide a few days before "La Côte" appeared in *Esquire* magazine. Whether she knew the unveiling in store for her is not certain, but at least she was out of the way.

Others were still around to meet themselves in degrading tableaux, sometimes performing under an alias which was a pasted-on Woolworth's mustache that failed to fool any tots in the playground. The chitchat proceeds: "Why would an educated, dynamic, very rich and well-hung Jew go bonkers for a cretinous Protestant size forty who wears low-heeled shoes and lavender water?" It seems the "porcine sow" was the governor's wife, and in a grotesque seduction on the Pierre Hotel sheets the gentleman was proving something, avenging the old days when even the most established Jews weren't welcome in WASP country clubs, boarding schools, and so on. The gentleman in this unaccountably destructive and self-destructive portrait was everywhere quickly identified as the husband of the most elegant woman in the city. From what we read she had been for some years a true friend, the most valuable and perhaps most surprising trophy, solid silver, Truman had won, scored in the field.

Capote had, like a leper with a bell announcing his presence, horrified those he most treasured, and with many he was marked with the leper's visible deformities, a creature arousing fear of infection. There is much ado about this in Plimpton: calls unanswered, intervention by friends unavailing. "Unspoiled Monsters," another section of *Answered Prayers,* concerns itself with the chic homosexual world and what used to be called the stars of stage, screen, and radio. P. B. Jones is again the narrator, about thirty-five, a writer, sponger, and wit: "Starting at an early age, seven or eight or thereabouts, I'd run the gamut with many an older boy and several priests and also a handsome Negro gardener. In fact, I was a kind of Hershey Bar whore—"

Jonesy gets around, to a room in the YMCA, "work" as a prostitute masseur, and off to every grand spot in Europe. It's not quite clear just how a back rub could get the little charmer from the Y to the Ritz in Paris, Harry's Bar in Venice, everywhere. But he must move about in order to reveal all the habits, hang-ups, perversions, fears, unpaid bills of the slit-savoring bitches, muff-divers, whining masochists, drug addicts, patrons of Father Flanagan's Nigger Queen Kosher Cafe. Woe to all who passed his way, with Capote toting their names, occupations, contorted faces, the passports of their public identities, material that makes *Answered Prayers* resemble the files of J. Edgar Hoover.

What was Capote thinking of? At times one is led to imagine him afflicted with Tourette's syndrome, a disease described in recent years with much sympathy by Oliver Sacks. It brings on facial tics, not unusual in other physical misfortunes; the true peculiarity of the symptoms is echolalia, endless talking characterized by an uncontrollable flow of obscenities. Still, Capote knew all there was to know about gossip and understood that in a gifted form it will not be about imagined persons but about real people, not about John Doe but about Cecil Beaton, to name one of his many punitive divertissements.

In his own love life, about which he never wrote, the record seems to ally Truman with Cousin Randolph and his sudden devasting passion for the boxer Pepe. First, the man who came to fix the air conditioner and was snatched away from his wife and children, spiffed up with new clothes, dental rehabilitation, and taken along to the great palazzos in Venice, to the yachts sailing in blue summer waters. The poor fellow gets very bad reviews at every port and perhaps to his credit returned them by taking off, leaving Truman "devastated," in a "big collapse."

And there was John O'Shea, a sort of financial adviser, with wife and four children, and ready to abandon all for a luxe life with Truman. Vodka, gunplay, theft and the disappearance of O'Shea; heartbreak and atonement by Truman, who helped the O'Shea family and brought the attractive, honest daughter to stay in the flat in New York.

Capote himself wasn't a pleasant vision in his last years of drugs and drink, but he collected new friends who cared for him up until his death in Los Angeles, out West where new life, if you can hang on, begins. An unexpected fact from his last will and testament: In honor of Newton Arvin, a critic and professor of literature and an early friend of Truman and his writing, Capote endowed two handsome yearly prizes, one for fifty thousand dollars and the other for one hundred thousand dollars. They were to be given to writers of imaginative criticism.

(1998)

NORMAN MAILER:

THE TELLER AND THE TAPE

The "oral tradition," if that is a suitable slot in which to deposit the large number of books arising from the taped interview, is a labor-saving curiosity in which our country leads the world. We have here a "literature" of remarks, a fast-moving confounding of Gertrude Stein's confident assertion that "remarks are not literature." The exuberant exploitation of the possibilities of this "vampire capital" are just beginning and, indeed, the whole enterprise has about it a limitlessness in all its aspects.

"The transcript totaled twenty thousand pages" (*Mailer: His Life and Times*, by Peter Manso). "A major biography."

"For the third time, Cathy Zmuda transcribed hundreds of thousands of spoken words—perhaps millions in this instance" (*Working*, by Studs Terkel).

"It is safe to say that the collected transcript of every last recorded bit of talk would approach fifteen thousand pages" (*The Executioner's Song*, by Norman Mailer, a novel).

Quite a lot taken down, but why not more? What is to deter? The spoken "pages" each of us produces in a lifetime would outpace all the libraries of the ancient and modern world. First-person narration, this stratospheric memory bank floating freely in the universe, idling there, waiting for the button and the circling tape, is of a simplicity quite beautiful in shape. Like a bank account under a prescription, it can be "attached" by the collector, in print known as the author, and drawn upon in circumstances of great variety and for purposes strange or banal or merely useful. To ponder the field, scan the prospect of effortless remembering and remarking, opens up a prodigiousness on the loose, a monumentality of retailed playback.

Give voice to the voiceless, remember the neglected and the isolated. Sometimes the starting point is an awareness of the impending ending; we are always at a point where time is running out for those who have lived through this or that, significant or insignificant. Slave narratives, old soldiers, superannuated craftsmen, Indians, Appalachian folk, immigrants, blacksmiths—a bond of mutuality arises between the instrument and the voice, the sophisticated person's research plan and the honoring of the survivor by the very gesture of seeking out, taking down. What is said, details, turns of speech, life rhythms, bygone social patterns might be interesting in themselves and useful for the historian down the way. Of course, the historian's scrutiny will have a somewhat diminishing effect upon the unexamined flow because of the limits of spoken memories as documentation and the limits of each of us as a representation of historical events.

The modesty of the philanthropic intention commends it to us. The tapes and transcripts resting in the eternal peace of the libraries are a sort of gravestone for vanished persons who lived their days among a group not fully articulated. If nothing much is done with it, there is a charitable satisfaction in knowing that it exists. Liberalism, egalitarianism, a form of reverence, sent the WPA researchers to the Okies and tenant farmers, to field hands and prisoners with their songs and stories.

As documents, the innocent tapes bear a resemblance to the letters and diaries of obscure persons who happened to live in a time of upheaval or who by mere placement in the scheme of things were led to thoughts beyond the weather and family greetings. But these solitary compositors worked under the conventions of literacy, of writing, and the restraining self-consciousness of their written documents is different from the restraints, selections, and omissions of speech. It is often the task of the historian and the imaginative writer to discover the silences behind speech, the silences that produced the romantic text of James Agee's *Let Us Now Praise Famous Men*.

LISTENING IN.

The tape-recorded books of today are not a gift to the cemetery of history. Instead, what we have here is a sort of decomposed creativity, a recycling similar to that of the obsolete ragman who turned old clothes into paper. Propagation is the intention, and storage is failure. Thus, confrontation enters between the asker and the asked, and the relation is more insinuating, less sentimental, more modern, you might say, and certainly more efficient.

The books are various indeed. Appeal is to the point, appeal of the subjects, the root idea. Except in a few cases, appeal can be said to be the only measure of quality. Taped books are roughly to be divided into the active solicitation of the words of the unknown and the active solicitation of the remarks of the known, or remarks about the known, the celebrated—or if not celebrated, notorious.

MONO.

The simplest method is to give each person his time and move on to the next. The sequential interviewer is likely to reign over the text in the benevolent and more or less disinterested manner of the anthropologist or social worker. The "composition" is fluid, open, carefree. Exploitation is circumvented by the general air of affirmation. The worth of the recorded person is what is being affirmed rather than the singularity of the voice, the words.

Studs Terkel, for instance, appears in a manner surely much like that of the scouts in the WPA days. He is updated by the large extent of his own packaged and distributed tapes, but still old-fashioned, the sympathetic, thoughtful leftist, true to the proletariat and the dispossessed and ignored. His task is clever and concrete, even if he must travel hither and yon and come back burdened with a trunk full of *oh* and *well, you know* and *I mean* and *let's see here.*

Working: People Talk About What They Do All Day and How They Feel About What They Do* is almost six hundred pages of small, crowded type, some 135 occupations, among them doorman, airline stewardess, farmer, miner, model, cabdriver, spot welder, hooker, and a few names

---

*New York: Pantheon, 1984.

such as Pauline Kael, Eddie Arroyo, Bud Freeman—that is, critic, jockey, jazz musician. About all this Terkel briefly sets the scene or briefly interrupts here and there. ("He's the doorman at a huge apartment building on Manhattan's Upper West Side. . . . The walls could stand a paint job. . . . He wears his uniform.")

The pages turn, the workers flow by as if coming out of the mill at the end of the day shift. Not one makes an impression, can be remembered—many they are and many another they might be. Just who is the hairstylist or the cabdriver? Or, rather, what are they? They do not have clothes, tics, parents, houses, fantasies. These persons are not metaphors, not a composite, and none has the weight of a line of statistics on position, social status, religion, training, whatever. The most striking thing is that few have vocal particularity. There is seldom an ear in the talking pages, hardly an echo of the fractured expressiveness heard around us.

> *Cabdriver:* "I hate to admit that driving a cab is no longer the novelty to me that it once was. It has its moments, but it's not the most ideal job in the world as far as determining one's attitude is concerned."

> *Sanitation worker:* "You get just like the milkman's horse, you get used to it. If you remember the milkman's horse, all he had to do was whistle and whooshhh!"

The sanitized diction brings to mind *60 Minutes,* and this is not necessarily a prudent pruning for publication. The current stranger and his tape recorder, whether wishing it or not, find the subjects living in the atmosphere of television with its neat dispersal of the claims of the individual person, its condensations and programmings, its inattention and formalized forgetting, its dehydrated vocables ready for the freezer.

Tape recording without an interpretive intelligence is a primitive technology for history. It offers a moment of publicity in an undermining void. The protocol of the meeting and the docile instrument steadily transmitting pages are an orthodoxy, promoting a cheerful but rigid disengagement. The spuriousness of the encounter is ordained by the one-sidedness of advantage, all of it accruing to the "author."

To understand the meaning of attention to the unknown and unrecorded, one can go back to the great Victorian masterpiece, Henry

Mayhew's *London Labour and the London Poor.* Or in our own time to Ronald Blythe's *Akenfield: Portrait of an English Village* (1969). Here the old bell ringer talks and is "taken down" by some method. But his presence moves the listener, Blythe, to reflections: "Lost in an art-pastime-worship based on blocks of circulating figures which look like one of those numismatic keys to the Great Pyramid secret, the ringing men are out on their own in a crashing sphere of golden decibels."

POLYPHONIC.

Taped books about persons of established interest are now designed to make a more sophisticated use of the gathered material. A person, or rather a personality, is the center, replacing an abstraction of theme or place. Slabs of recollection, one after another, would dilute the attention to the central subject; the "authors" of interview books are now allowed to slice up the interviews and disperse the remarks throughout the pages, to bring them in at appropriate points, to create something like a conversation in a crowded room. There is no intention to reproduce dialogue; each recollector is on his own, but his or her holding forth is subject to judicious interruption in the interest of narrative. The speakers are witnesses, coins in a box, offerings, gratuities. They are the base metals to be transmuted into gold—that is, into pages.

In *Mailer: His Life and Times*, by Peter Manso, "more than two hundred people were interviewed over a period of forty months, some interviews filling more than ten hours." Transcript close to 20,000 pages, offered as a "major biography" of Mailer, and itself a "major literary event"; gigantism is something of a phenomenon in written books and on the fairgrounds, but for the taper the world is a hippodrome of garrulity.

All contemporary biographers rely upon the interview as one of many sources, including the biographer's vision, necessary for the construction of a life. In Manso's biography, the interview is the only source, except for a few snippets from reviews and letters, and thus it seems to offer a fresh aesthetic of sorts: You, and in this case your times, are what people have to say about you. The high interest of the unfolding of this proposition, the assertiveness of the speakers, has to do with the large proportions of Mailer himself, his confidence and intrepidity, his florid pattern of experience, his disasters met with an almost erotic energy of adaptation. This promiscuity, the volume of pre-cipitous encounters from which he has emerged like a knight from the forest, seems to have encouraged an elevation of indiscretion among the contributing friends, a situation much in the interest of the pages. Manso tells us the right of review was sometimes requested but "in most, not."

The drastic distances between gossip, the libertine loquacity of the dinner table, and print dissolves, as we would expect since the enter-prise is committed to print only as a vessel of the waters of orality. Wives are snubbed, well-known people are maliciously hooked by a phrase and flounder about like so many fish trapped in a net. Mailer himself enters briefly here and there, but of course his presence, his invulnerable presence, is in every line.

The absence of an author, the lack of a signature of responsibility, the conception of ideas as shadows of comment, vague and unde-fended, in a like way absorbs the activity of the commentator, the critic. What can be said about more than six hundred pages of anecdote? De-scription is possible and recapitulation of lively asides, but that in-volves a measure of culpability, the passing on of gossip. Yet any reader will think some of these books are more appealing than others, and *Mailer: His Life and Times* might be judged to score—to score more or less, since an equation of judgment rests merely on the availability of consenting voices.

Perhaps one can judge Mailer to be a "good" idea. He is a spectacu-lar mound of images and, like such self-creations, mystifying and im-personal, and thereby a structure of anecdote corresponds in some way to his own accumulated articulations. His writings, the frame of the structure, are to be incorporated only glancingly or studied in the anecdotal pile, but then the work, the sharp intrusion, is the knife in the heart of most biographers.

We see that the writer had a youth, a formidable, adoring mother somewhat along the lines Freud thought friendly to a son's success. The family is smart—cousin, sister, and Mailer himself making their way from Brooklyn to Harvard. Constant writing from the beginning, *The Naked and the Dead,* a splendid success, the army, marriage, politi-cal complexity increased by friendship and "reality," second wife, "vi-olent and orgiastic period" (his words), self-advertisement, stabbing of wife, antiwar activity, prisoner of sex, children, more marriages, Marilyn Monroe, Jack Abbott, Gary Gilmore, further marriages and children, impressive alimony, and with a new wife and child a mellow middle age. And, of course, books at every point.

Total recall adds much to the outline, even if Mailer's public has its own storehouse of dramatic recollection. Since little has been hidden along the way, Mailer is then a subject to be discussed rather than discovered. Revelation is scarcely to be wished about the living, but this premature interment is something of a finale. What we have here is a tomb of pharaonic memorabilia, brick upon brick in the sand.

The compositional blur of Mailer's *The Executioner's Song* is once more engaged by the frenzied entrance of the promoter Lawrence Schiller into the life and time of N.M. Schiller claimed his space in the "real-life novel" and received the recognition of the results of his relentless encroachments in the formation of that spectacular publication. Schiller's memory is composed of dollars, deals, contracts, and every kind of worry in the motel room and on the telephone. Crisis is his overcoat, and he sweats from one threatened crash to another, crashes such as Gilmore's "cop-out" suicide attempt or, worse, his refusing to, as they say, die with dignity rather than accept, if it came, a reprieve to a life sentence.

Schiller is a most interesting gladiator in combat with reluctant witnesses, negotiations, speed, and deadlines. In the canniness of his inquisitions he often exceeds himself, but he is a professional and brings to mind the shock of method. (Solzhenitsyn experienced the shock of the West in an encounter with two hopeful biographers. Withdrawing, he said, "The collection of 'information' in this way is not different from police spying.")

Preparation for *The Executioner's Song* is detailed once more in Manso's compilation. Schiller: "By then [May 1977] I'd given him about 9,000 pages of what eventually was over 16,000 pages of interview transcript." The interviews are put together and come out quite un-Mailerish, as was noted. We find the author in a bit of staging such as, "In the mountains, the snow was iron gray and purple in the hollows, and glowed like gold on every slope that faced the sun." Just a bit of that here and there, nothing much when compared with Truman Capote's *In Cold Blood,* another killer book of great interest and of another kind.

Capote's research, acquaintance with the cast of characters, the reputed dialogue and landscape are presented in the authorial manner throughout, incorporated into a text. About one of the killers, we read that he had a face "halved like an apple, then put together a fraction off center.... The left eye being truly serpentine, with a venomous, sickly-blue squint that although it was involuntarily acquired, seemed nevertheless to warn of bitter sediment at the bottom of his nature." This could not be *said* by anyone.

Mailer had his tapes in abundance; having them, he came forth, to the astonishment of a few, with a text remarkable for its plainness, its anonymity. He *shaped,* as it were, *The Executioner's Song.*

Arthur Kretchmer, editor of *Playboy:* "You've got the fucking plains in your text. It's right there." Earlier Mailer said: "I picked it up from Norris. If the book has any feeling of small-town life, I guess I picked it up from Norris." Norris Church, his wife, grew up in Atkins, Oklahoma, population 1,391.

Schiller, about *The Executioner's Song* and the possibility of its winning the Pulitzer Prize (it did, for fiction): "Because the detailing is there, the flatness, and Mailer doesn't exist in the book. They have to give him the award." This bit of literary criticism is engaging. Schiller seems to fear that *The Executioner's Song* would be written—like Mailer's *Marilyn,* perhaps. At the worst in the thick, resonant diction, the demonic, original clutter of Mailer's high style, which would impugn the gray-hide, elephantine mass of the record and its extraordinary, deathly appeal.

It's true that Mailer "doesn't exist in the book"—or largely true. And has he created the voice, the plains, the flatness, the Westness of it? Aren't the voices and landscape those of Vern and Brenda, Nicole and Garry and Bessie, accurately taped, recounting the scenery of their life with Gilmore, filling in for Schiller or whoever, appearing on every page against the dental drill of the pursuit?

THE INVISIBLE HAND.

A bit of neatening, of course, and punctuation, the period, the comma. The taped text is always a great, gluey blob, and what is needed are sentences dry and separate as kernels of corn. A close reading of taped books suggests that the invisible hand is less busy than might be imagined. Punctuation, laying it out, pasting it up. The real labor of the books returns to the source, the wretched bulk of the testimony, the horror of its vast, stuttering scale. The collector is much impressed, and perhaps depressed, by the challenging magnitude. He has lifted it, sorted it, had secretaries hard at work to contain the monstrousness of what his machine has brought into being.

We notice the invariable publicity given to numbers: the thousands of pages, the millions of words, the long, long hours of interviewing, the large cast tracked down. The insistence upon number indicates that it is a validation. But a validation of what, of whom?

Tapes are what they are, no more and no less than themselves. They are the property of the speaker, even if he has freely surrendered his rights; surrendered or not, nothing belongs to the author. Excision, deletion, yes, and placement, the packaging of the property. It is accepted that the gibberish must be shaped up and, thereby, allowed to become itself, the speaker's words made legible.

Additions are a moral problem. The author can receive his book as a liberal, in all senses, gift, but he cannot reciprocate, cannot in good faith add decorative phrasing and color as an advancement of the verbal interest and appeal of his given text. For the imaginative writer, wit and a pleasing intervention of adjective and image might be a natural temptation. But here the prohibition seems clear. The author's own words in the mouth of an interviewed subject are artificial, illicit, a reverse and most peculiar form of plagiarism. There is little evidence that the compiler of talk feels this as a constraint. What is needed from time to time is the practical matter of emphasis, keeping the attention of the reader.

The Executioner's Song is the apotheosis of our flourishing "oral literature" thus far. (To see it as Mailer's best book, as many have done, is much too fast. Mailer is a river of words, ornamental, evocative words, and cascading notions and designs. There is no plainness, flatness in him, but there is, was, a lot, in the tapes.)

He—and Capote also in his different construction—had a plot and, through none of their devising, an adjunct in the death penalty. This publicly ordained ending from which there was no escape might have prompted Mailer to his most genuine contribution to the tale of Gary Gilmore. Mailer's mark on the book is an accentual one. By accent, placement, and distribution, and finally insistence, no matter what a contrary cynicism about reality might have suggested, he created a romance. From Schiller's pit, we can say that Mailer has excavated a *Liebestod*, possibly proposing it as a redemption of the squalor of this long, long death trip so arresting to the voyeur in most of us.

We can imagine a fraudulent tape-recorded production offered by a shy recluse as his own thousand pages of unheard sound. No, that would mean writing—and the tape recorder is first and last a labor-saving instrument.

(1985)

INDEX

Permissions Acknowledgments

Grateful acknowledgment is made to the following for permission to reprint previously published material:

Farrar, Straus & Giroux, LLC.: Seven lines from "The Fish," from *The Complete Poems 1927–1979,* by Elizabeth Bishop. Copyright © 1979, 1983 by Alice Helen Methfessel. Four essays from *A View of My Own: Essays on Literature and Society,* by Elizabeth Hardwick: "Disgust and Disenchantment: Some British and American Plays," "Eugene O'Neill: A Sketch," "Mary McCarthy," and "Anderson, Millay, and Crane in Their Letters." Copyright © 1962 by Elizabeth Hardwick. Reprinted by permission of Farrar, Straus & Giroux, LLC.

Grove/Atlantic, Inc.: Excerpt from "Rock Springs," from *Rock Springs,* by Richard Ford. Copyright © 1987 by Richard Ford. Reprinted by permission of Grove/Atlantic, Inc.

HarperCollinsPublishers, Inc.: Excerpts from "Daddy," "Death and Co.," "Edge," "Cut," "Contusion," and "Lady Lazarus," from *Ariel,* by Sylvia Plath. Copyright © 1963 by Ted Hughes. Excerpts from "Lesbos," from *Ariel,* by Sylvia Plath. Copyright © 1965 by Ted Hughes. Excerpt from "For a Fatherless Son," from *Winter Trees,* by Sylvia Plath. Copyright © 1971 by Ted Hughes. Excerpt from "Last Words," from *Crossing the Water,* by Sylvia Plath. Copyright © 1971 by Ted Hughes. Excerpt from "Wodwo," from *Wodwo,* by Ted Hughes. Copyright © 1962 by Ted Hughes. All excerpts reprinted by permission of HarperCollins*Publishers,* Inc.

Houghton Mifflin Co.: Excerpts from *American Pastoral,* by Philip Roth. Copyright © 1997 by Philip Roth. All rights reserved. Reprinted by permission of Houghton Mifflin Company.

Alfred A. Knopf, a division of Random House, Inc.: Excerpt from *self-consciousness,* by John Updike. Copyright © 1989 by John Updike. Reprinted by permission of Alfred A. Knopf, a division of Random House, Inc.

Hilary Masters: Selected lines from *Spoon River Anthology,* by Edgar Lee Masters. Reprinted by permission of Hilary Masters.

ABOUT THE AUTHOR

ELIZABETH HARDWICK is the author of four previous collections of literary essays, *Bartleby in Manhattan, A View of My Own, Seduction and Betrayal,* a National Book Award finalist, and *Sight-Readings,* a *New York Times* Notable Book of the Year. Her novels are *The Ghostly Lover, The Simple Truth,* and *Sleepless Nights,* which was nominated for the National Book Critics Circle Award. Among her honors are the Gold Medal for Belles-Lettres and Criticism awarded by the American Academy of Arts and Letters and a Citation for Lifetime Achievement awarded by the National Book Critics Circle.

A NOTE ON THE TYPE

The principal text of this Modern Library edition
was set in a digitized version of Janson,
a typeface that dates from about 1690 and was cut by Nicholas Kis,
a Hungarian working in Amsterdam. The original matrices have
survived and are held by the Stempel foundry in Germany.
Hermann Zapf redesigned some of the weights and sizes for Stempel,
basing his revisions on the original design.